S-87 S-161 Sp88
M-442   Sp 92

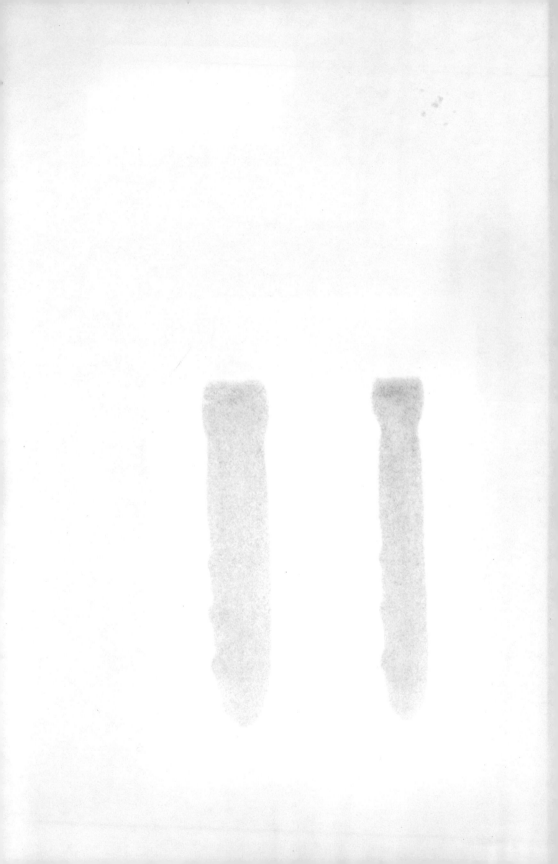

THE
REAGAN
RECORD

THE REAGAN RECORD

An Assessment of America's Changing Domestic Priorities

John L. Palmer and Isabel V. Sawhill, editors

WITHDRAWN

An Urban Institute Study

BALLINGER PUBLISHING COMPANY
Cambridge, Massachusetts
A Subsidiary of Harper & Row, Publishers, Inc.

7414

Copyright © 1984
THE URBAN INSTITUTE
2100 M Street, N.W.
Washington, D.C. 20037

Library of Congress Cataloging in Publication Data
Main entry under title:

The Reagan Record.

(An Urban Institute Study)
Updated ed. of: The Reagan experiment. ©1982.
Includes index.
1. United States—Economic Policy—1981– .
2. United States—Social policy—1980– . 3. Intergovernmental fiscal rela-
tions—United States. I. Palmer, John Logan II. Sawhill, Isabel
V. II. Reagan experiment IV. Series.
HC106.8.R422 1984   338.973   84-11001
ISBN 0-88730-000-6
ISBN 0-88730-001-4 (pbk.)

Printed in the United States of America

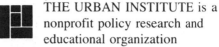 THE URBAN INSTITUTE is a nonprofit policy research and educational organization established in Washington, D.C. in 1968. Its staff investigates the social and economic problems confronting the nation and government policies and programs designed to alleviate such problems. The Institute disseminates significant findings of its research through the publications program of its Press. The Institute has two goals for work in each of its research areas: to help shape thinking about societal problems and efforts to solve them, and to improve government decisions and performance by providing better information and analytic tools.

Through work that ranges from broad conceptual studies to administrative and technical assistance, Institute researchers contribute to the stock of knowledge available to public officials and to private individuals and groups concerned with formulating and implementing more efficient and effective government policy.

Conclusions or opinions expressed in Institute publications are those of the authors and do not necessarily reflect the views of other staff members, officers or trustees of the Institute, advisory groups, or any organizations which provide financial support to the Institute.

Advisory Board of the
Changing Domestic Priorities Project

CONTENTS

TABLES

FIGURES

FOREWORD

With the election of Ronald Reagan in 1980, the United States embarked on an experiment with domestic policies that is perhaps as significant as the New Deal. The Reagan administration has raised fundamental questions about the appropriate role of government in national life, and it has been partially successful in implementing a program—one with distinct premises about economic and social behavior—that substantially alters that role. Because this program and the responses to it have had such far-reaching implications for the character of our public policies and our nation, a rigorous and impartial assessment of the record is clearly needed.

The Urban Institute's Changing Domestic Priorities project was begun in early 1982 to help meet this need. The three-year research effort, made possible by major support from the Ford Foundation and the John D. and Catherine T. MacArthur Foundation, builds on the Institute's long-standing work in assessing the consequences of public actions. The effort has drawn on the accumulated expertise of Institute staff and other researchers, as well as on an established tradition of objective public policy analysis. The scope of the project has been broad, relying heavily on collaborative research across disciplines and areas of study in order to capture the interactions among, and public responses to, both the policy changes and their effects.

The Changing Domestic Priorities project was designed with three objectives:

1. To monitor and interpret significant shifts in domestic policy
2. To determine their actual and likely consequences
3. To explore their implications and possible alternatives for further public actions

The project's first book, *The Reagan Experiment*, was published in late 1982 under the leadership of codirectors John L. Palmer and Isabel V. Sawhill. It focused primarily on the first of these objectives and the inferences that could be drawn about consequences on the basis of events through the spring of 1982. Subsequent more detailed activities have emphasized specific areas of policy concern. These activities have resulted in six volumes of papers and proceedings from conferences of experts from across the country on budget policy, economic policy, governance, natural resources and the environment, regulatory policy, and social policy; and in more than a dozen other volumes by scholars within and outside the Institute on topics such as state and local governments, health, housing, and the deficit.

The Reagan Record addresses all three project objectives with the hindsight of nearly four years of events and three years of study. It is intended to synthesize the project's findings in a form that is accessible to the general public. The authors document the magnitude and character of the shifts in federal domestic policy as well as some of the policies that the president has proposed for consideration. The authors report on the impact of the changes thus far on people, places, and institutions, and they project probable further impacts. Finally, they discuss the implications for future public policy and the possible consequences of the major changes that have already taken place. In doing so, they draw heavily on all the project's output as well as on the work of other scholars and observers.

An important aspect of any assessment of a president's policies is the frame of reference. How does one fairly assess the Reagan record? Should the focus be on the administration's success in achieving its own objectives even though not everyone would endorse those objectives? Should one delineate a broader set of objectives, acknowledging that the task is easily pervaded by one's own values? Or, should the scientific approach be adopted by analyzing just the measurable consequences of specific actions and allowing readers to draw their own interpretations—even though this approach still involves judgment in the selection of material presented and leaves unanswered questions about the significance of various events. Given these dilemmas, the authors of this book, recognizing that no one approach is entirely satisfactory, have used a variety of approaches.

Obviously, a comprehensive and impartial assessment of the domestic record of an administration still in office is a difficult undertaking—one that to my knowledge has never before been undertaken. More time and distance are necessary before a complete accounting can be rendered. Nevertheless, we and the sponsors of this project believe it is critical that a serious attempt be made now, while the country is in the throes of such major policy change and such fundamental reexamination of the purposes of government. Objective analysis and timely feedback on the significant impacts and implications of these shifts in policy are essential to informed consideration by the public and better decisions by policymakers. The Changing Domestic Priorities project has already proven useful in this regard, and I believe this book will substantially further that aim.

I want to express my appreciation for the assistance and support provided by our funding sponsors, our board of advisers, and numerous outside scholars and public officials who have given generously of their time and wisdom. The views expressed herein are the authors' and should not be attributed to The Urban Institute, its trustees, its funding sources, or the members of the advisory board of this project.

William Gorham
President
The Urban Institute

ACKNOWLEDGMENTS

This book is the collective and collaborative effort of numerous people. We are particularly grateful to the authors of the individual chapters. We also thank Stephanie Gould and Felicity Skidmore for their invaluable editorial work.

Shaun Murphy, Francesca Moghari, and Theresa Walker of The Urban Institute Press efficiently shepherded the book through the production process. Cathy Cromer and Mary Kate Smith were able research assistants. Joyce Munns helped with the first chapter, and Lisa Burns and Ann Guillot gave us untiring administrative and secretarial support under extraordinary pressures.

The Reagan Record has benefited from the comments and guidance provided by members of our Changing Domestic Priorities Advisory Board and from the comments and work of many other scholars and practitioners, inside and outside of The Urban Institute, who have participated in the Changing Domestic Priorities project and its various forums. Finally, we are grateful to the Ford Foundation, the John D. and Catherine T. MacArthur Foundation, and the Carnegie Corporation whose grants made the project and this book possible.

CHAPTER 1

OVERVIEW

John L. Palmer
Isabel V. Sawhill

Because America has always been more pragmatic than ideological, its citizens have seldom strayed from the middle of the political road. Neither a George McGovern nor a Barry Goldwater has been able to attract more than a modest degree of popular support. Yet in 1980, the public elected a president from the conservative wing of the minority party. His rejection of the moderate to liberal consensus that had come to dominate both Republican and Democratic administrations over the previous forty years, his vision of a better America based on less government and more individual enterprise, and his efforts to translate this vision into a new agenda for the nation have been both distinctive and controversial. Not since 1932 has there been such a redirection of public purposes.

How extensive is this redirection of domestic policies? What consequences has it produced over the past four years? And will it leave a lasting imprint? These are the questions addressed by the authors of this book. Time, of course, will provide more definitive answers about the Reagan experiment; nevertheless, considerable evidence for an assessment of the Reagan record already exists. This evidence is examined in detail in the succeeding chapters, which focus on the way President Reagan has governed, his economic and budget policies, his stewardship of natural resources and the environment, his reorientation of social welfare policies, and the impact of all of these on states and localities, businesses, nonprofit organizations, and, most important, families and individuals.

In this chapter we provide an overview of the Reagan record and its significance. We begin with a brief discussion of the administration's goals and philosophy. Then drawing on the other chapters, we review the administration's success in implementing its agenda and in achieving its main objectives and go on to summarize the intended as well as unintended consequences of its policies. We conclude with an overall assessment of the administration's domestic policies.

Goals and Philosophy

The Reagan administration, more than most others, has had a clear vision of what it was trying to accomplish. Its continuing objectives have been to reduce the size and influence of government, to restore economic prosperity, and to improve national security. Strengthening the traditional values of work, family, neighborhood, and church has also been an element in the Reagan agenda, and one that was given increased prominence in his 1984 State of the Union address. But during the president's first three years in office, the so-called social issues were not given nearly the same level of attention as the administration's economic and national security objectives.

All presidents are for peace and prosperity and for God and family. What is distinctive about Ronald Reagan is his conviction that prosperity requires a much more limited role for government, while the preservation of peace and of traditional values, requires, in many cases, an expanded role. He thus combines the libertarian's distrust of government in the economic sphere with a more traditionally conservative belief in moral absolutes and in the need for a strong defense against external threats. It is a consistent philosophy, given its premises: that economic growth will flow from the inherent entrepreneurial spirit and enterprise of the American people; that social problems can be largely solved by church, family, and neighborhood; that freedom is our greatest national asset; and that its protection requires, above all, military strength.

Some people have interpreted Reagan's victory at the polls in 1980 as an indication that the electorate was becoming increasingly conservative. But such an interpretation is not borne out by public opinion polls.[1] There were no significant changes in the proportions of self-described liberals or conservatives or in the proportions of the electorate identifying with one party or another during the 1970s. The public had become more liberal on social issues, such as abortion and women's rights; and a large majority believed that current government spending was either too low or about right in most areas (the exceptions being foreign aid and "welfare"). At the same time, there was some disaffection with government, especially with Jimmy Carter's government. For the most part, however, the 1980 election was less a mandate for a conservative agenda than it was a rejection of an unpopular president and a signal that the American people wanted a change.

Although the administration's philosophy was more conservative than the general public's, the problems it promised to address, and the general direction in which it promised to move the country struck a responsive chord. Inflation, slow growth, high taxes, excessive regulation, a loss of confidence in big government, and a perception that national security and prestige were eroding were all high on the public's list of concerns in 1980. Candidate Reagan promised to deal with these problems, but President Reagan would need a specific program, and the more specific it became, the more it would be open to criticism. Although there could be broad agreement about such goals as reducing inflation, reviving the economy, reducing tax and regulatory burdens, and improving national security, the best ways of achieving these objectives and of making trade-offs among them would be controversial. The Reagan administration initially dealt with this problem in the time-honored way: by promising some of everything. Taxes would be reduced, defense spending accelerated, and the federal budget balanced. Inflation would be curbed without a rise in unemployment, and the solutions to the nation's economic ills would be "equitable with no one group singled out to pay a higher price."[2]

Of course, it is not possible to achieve all good things simultaneously. Tough choices are required, and as the events of the past few years have unfolded, the administration's priorities have become clearer.

First, the tax cuts and the defense buildup took precedence over balancing the budget. Second, reducing inflation took precedence over moderating the recession.

Third, it turned out that there was not enough fat in the domestic side of the federal budget to avoid reducing benefits and services. The deepest cuts were proposed for grants to state and local governments and for programs serving the poor. Little was done to reduce rapidly rising expenditures for Social Security, Medicare, government employee pensions, and other predominantly middle-class programs that have been the chief source of growth in the federal budget since the 1950s.

Fourth, the tax cuts were designed with economic growth not equity in mind. The fraction of each extra dollar of income earned that went to taxes had risen sharply since the mid-1960s and the administration was determined to reduce the disincentives these high marginal rates implied for saving, investment, and work. Consequently, rates were cut across the board, providing the greatest benefits to higher-income families.

Fifth, the administration's regulatory policies emphasized productivity over the protection of health, safety, civil rights, and the environment. Productivity growth had slowed during the 1970s, in part because of some of the actions taken to deal with these problems, and the administration's intent was to swing the pendulum back in a progrowth direction. A similar pattern prevailed in its natural resource policies. Production of energy resources took precedence over conservation—whether in the Department of Energy's budget or in the Department of Interior's management of public lands and wilderness areas.

Implementing the Agenda: Governance in the Reagan Era

In making the trade-offs just outlined, the administration often found itself at odds with Congress and the rest of the country. Specifically, after an initial year of overwhelming legislative victories and reasonably successful regulatory initiatives, the administration increasingly had to compromise with Congress or deal with judicial restraints and a public backlash against many of its proposals.* By 1983, in part because of Democratic gains in the midterm elections and shifting attention to the 1984 elections, stalemate had largely set in, and the administration had little additional success in advancing its agenda.

This pattern was quite predictable from the experience of previous administrations. Indeed, the conventional wisdom in recent years has been that presidents are greatly handicapped by certain features of our governmental and political institutions: the proliferation of organized interest groups, the decline of political parties, a more assertive and less disciplined Congress, expanded judicial activism, a less controllable budget, and the need to share authority with local officials.

In view of these developments, the administration was more successful—particularly initially—in implementing its agenda, both legislatively and administratively, than most people would have predicted. As detailed in chapter 2, this success was related to many factors: the president's own leadership and communications skills, the perception that he had received a mandate in 1980, the philosophical coherence of his agenda, the clarity of presidential priorities, the effectiveness of the administration's political liaison with Congress, and a willingness to compromise when necessary to maintain the president's reputation as a winner.

---

*The material in this section is drawn from chapter 2 by Lester M. Salamon and Alan J. Abramson.

Facing a Democratic majority in the House and potential splits in the ranks of Senate Republicans, the administration chose to move quickly before the opposition could organize. Its strategies included drawing on the president's personal powers of persuasion, making administrative changes (overseen by carefully selected political appointees) in preference to legislative ones, centralizing the policy management process in the White House, implementing "top-down" budgeting at the Office of Management and Budget (OMB), and using the reconciliation provisions of the congressional budget process in an unorthodox way.*

As the last example suggests, the administration's immediate success in implementing its policy agenda would sometimes mean sacrificing an opportunity to nurture the institutions and processes through which political decisions are reached and carried out. Indeed, there is often tension between what is required for short-run political success and what is required for longer-run improvement in these basic institutions and processes.

Based on early indications, however, the impact of the Reagan administration on some political institutions and processes has been positive. For example, the administration has done much to restore public confidence in the efficacy of the presidency and to focus more political attention on the broad issues and trade-offs that must be faced in the formulation of public policy. It has also strengthened the operations of both major political parties and has demonstrated the potential effectiveness of the "bipartisan commission approach" to developing consensus in areas of great political sensitivity. At the same time, the administration's unwillingness to forge broad coalitions with congressional conservatives and moderates on important issues—such as the deficit—has left it more dependent on a political realignment to achieve its purposes.

The impact of the administration on the central management processes and institutions of government (the civil service, the Executive Office of the President, the budget process, and the like) is also worth noting. In many respects, the Reagan administration has been creative in adapting this infrastructure to its own purposes. For example, it has increased presidential control of the budget process and facilitated more effective budgetary interaction with

---

*Reconciliation is a complicated feature of the 1974 Congressional Budget Act originally intended to enable the congressional Budget Committees to enforce spending targets at the final stages of the appropriations process. The administration succeeded in moving a binding reconciliation measure to the beginning of the process, thereby wrapping the entire administration budget and program reform package into one massive piece of legislation. Otherwise, its proposals would have had to be dealt with in thirteen separate appropriation bills and numerous authorizing committees as usual.

Congress, developed methods for more effectively translating the administration's policy objectives into practice at the agency level, and strengthened OMB regulatory review procedures. These achievements, however, were sometimes gained at the expense of the longer-term ability of these institutions to function effectively. The administration's initial heavy-handed use of the congressional budget process has already been mentioned as one example. Another example is its use of OMB staff and its treatment of the civil service, which are widely viewed as having weakened the ability of career staff to provide professional input into the policy process.

Whatever the impact of the Reagan administration on political and governmental processes, it will ultimately be judged more on the basis of its substantive agenda—the specific policies proposed, their implementation, and their consequences. These are examined in chapters 3 through 10, the highlights of which we now review.

Reviving the Economy, Shrinking the Government, and Reordering National Priorities

Because its overriding objectives have been to restore prosperity, reduce the size of government, and increase national security, the administration has focused most of its attention—and the attention of Congress and the country—on the economy and the budget. The administration has had some, but not complete, success in achieving its objectives in these areas, and there have been some important unintended consequences. The record on these fronts is analyzed in chapter 3 (on the economy) and chapter 4 (on the budget).

The Economy

The economic goals of any administration are price stability, high employment, and long-term economic growth.* The hope of the Reagan administration was that a restrictive monetary policy would lower inflation and that supply-side tax, spending, and regulatory policies would lead to greater economic growth and lower unemployment.† So far the administration has

---

*The material in this section is drawn from chapter 3 by Isabel V. Sawhill and Charles F. Stone.

†Supply-side policies are those that increase the economy's capacity to produce goods and services through more capital formation, work effort, or productivity. Demand-side policies, in contrast, encourage greater utilization of existing capacity.

successfully reduced inflation and, although the economy is recovering from recession, unemployment was no lower in mid-1984 than it had been when the administration took office. The prospects for long-term growth remain uncertain.

Consumer price inflation dropped from more than 12 percent in 1980 to under 4 percent in 1983 and has subsequently increased only a little. About half of the drop was the result of the 1981–1982 recession brought about by the Federal Reserve's restricting the growth in the money supply. Much of the remainder would have occurred without so severe a recession as a result of favorable movements in food, energy, and import prices and the over-statement of housing inflation by the Consumer Price Index in the early 1980s—a flaw which has subsequently been corrected. In short, the administration's success on the inflation front was considerable, but both good luck and the cooperation of the independent Federal Reserve were critical ingredients.

The long-term economic and psychological benefits of living in a non-inflationary world may be substantial, but the costs of the recession have been high and unequally shared. The unemployment rate rose to a postdepression high of 10.7 percent in 1982. The recession and the continuing economic slack that was its aftermath led to a cumulative reduction in the average person's real (inflation-adjusted) after-tax income of about $1,000 between 1981 and the end of 1983. Because the incidence of unemployment is very uneven, the heaviest burden was borne by lower-income families.

Some degree of recession was needed to bring inflation under control. However, an alternative, less restrictive economic policy combining a tighter fiscal policy (a balanced high-employment budget) with a looser monetary policy (faster growth in the money supply) starting in 1981 might have lowered the costs of the recession substantially while still bringing consumer price inflation down considerably. Such a policy would have had a number of additional advantages. It would not now require further wrenching changes in taxes and spending to bring future deficits under control; it would have lowered interest rates and the value of the dollar, making it easier for American industry to compete in world markets; and it would have put the economy on a higher long-term growth path.

As things stand, the prospects for achieving the supply-siders' goal of higher long-term growth are clouded by the prospect of budget deficits that would remain large even in a high-employment economy. A strong recovery, fueled primarily by government purchases and consumer spending, is under way in 1983–1984. Investment has also been higher in these years than it would have been without the Reagan tax cuts for business. But, as the economy approaches high employment, the positive effects of the tax cuts on investment are likely to be more than offset by high interest rates if the private sector has to compete with the Treasury for available savings. By themselves, deficits would adversely affect long-term growth, lowering real gross national product (GNP) as much as 2 percent by the end of the decade.

Of course, action to reduce future deficits may well be taken before these adverse consequences materialize, and such action, in combination with the administration's supply-side regulatory and tax policies could put the economy on a higher, long-run growth path. In fact, in the absence of the deficits, saving and investment (and, therefore, capital formation) are likely to be greater, and the labor force and productivity are likely to grow more rapidly, as a result of Reagan policies. However, the effects on growth are likely to be small, eventually adding about 5 percent to the level of real GNP under the most optimistic assumptions about the magnitude of these effects.

The Budget

Besides wishing to revitalize the economy, the administration wanted to reduce the size of the federal government and to greatly expand the nation's defense capabilities.* The administration proposed to lower spending and taxes in relation to the size of the economy and to balance the budget by 1984.

Although the growth of domestic spending has slowed, federal spending as a share of GNP is now higher than when the president took office (an estimated 24.1 percent for FY (fiscal year) 1985 versus 23.5 percent in FY 1981) and is projected to be higher in the late 1980s than it would have been had pre-Reagan policies been continued.

The administration was much more successful in achieving its tax objectives. Between FY 1981 and FY 1985, the federal tax burden will have fallen from 20.8 to 18.7 percent of GNP. At the same time, the federal tax structure has become less progressive because it relies more on payroll taxes and because the personal income tax cuts favored people with higher incomes.

The administration has also successfully reordered federal budget priorities. Real defense outlays have increased by 7 percent a year since the president assumed office, raising their share of total program outlays from 26 percent in FY 1981 to 32 percent in FY 1985. A substantially larger portion of this enhanced defense budget is now being allocated to weapons purchases relative to current operations and maintenance.

Because the defense expansion has been almost as large as the domestic budget cuts, because the tax cuts substantially reduced revenues, and because

---

*The material in this section is drawn from chapter 4 by Gregory B. Mills.

the deep recession contributed greatly to rising debt and interest outlays, federal policies under the Reagan administration have led to huge deficits. Nearly as much national debt will have accumulated in the past four years as in the entire history of the country prior to this administration. (The debt will rise from less than $800 billion in FY 1981 to more than $1.5 trillion in FY 1985.) As a result, one out of every seven dollars of federal spending in FY 1985 will be for interest on the debt, in contrast to one out of every ten in FY 1981. If no further measures were taken to reduce the deficit, structural deficits would exceed an unprecedented 5 percent of GNP (almost $300 billion) by FY 1989. The national debt would then exceed $2.6 trillion, and one out of every six dollars of federal spending would be for interest.

The president has placed most of the blame for the large deficits on Congress for failing to cut domestic programs sufficiently. Such spending will have been reduced by about 10 percent, or $56 billion, by FY 1985 (compared with what it would have been under pre-Reagan policies). Although this restraint is substantial, it is only half of what the president proposed and far less than what he needed to control the deficit. (Had Congress granted the president all he requested, the deficit would now be one-third less.)

In the past, deficits could be controlled by appropriating less money or allowing revenues to increase as inflation automatically pushed people into higher tax brackets. In the future, more explicit and more difficult actions will be necessary. Beginning in 1985, personal income taxes will be indexed for inflation, ending their automatic rise with inflation. Furthermore, an increasing proportion (32 percent in FY 1985) of total budget outlays reflects commitments for interest and past spending obligations that the government has little choice but to honor, and a smaller fraction (9 percent in FY 1985) represents nondefense programs for which appropriations are reviewed annually. Thus, if spending growth is to be curtailed, it will require restraints in the defense budget and in legislatively mandated ("entitlement") programs—the largest of which are Social Security and Medicare.

Most economists argue that the structural deficit should be no higher than 2 percent of GNP. Achieving this goal over five years would require deficit reduction measures with an *annual* impact of about $200 billion by FY 1989. To accomplish this, further nondefense spending restraint concentrated in the so-called middle-class entitlement programs, substantial tax increases, and a considerable slowdown in the president's planned defense buildup are necessary. In his FY 1983–FY 1985 budgets, the president showed unwillingness to consider substantial action on any of these fronts and, as a consequence, a willingness to tolerate large and growing deficits. Congress has demonstrated greater political courage but has yet to face the truly difficult choices.

If and when the deficit genie is bottled, much of the current imprint of Reagan's policies on the level and composition of spending and taxes could well be eliminated, but it is hard to imagine a scenario under which there will not be continued pressures to keep a tight rein on domestic spending.

Implications for Domestic Policy: Natural Resource and Social Policies

With or without deficits, the reordering of federal budget priorities to achieve the administration's national security objectives meant that domestic program responsibilities had to be curtailed. Similarly, the regulatory relief program that was one of the cornerstones of the administration's Program for Economic Recovery had implications for the environment, health and safety, and civil rights. Although this budgetary and regulatory retrenchment was justified partly on the basis of its presumed benefits for the economy and for defense, it was also consistent with the administration's general philosophy of more limited government. The ramifications of this retrenchment for natural resources, the environment, and social welfare are examined in chapters 5 and 6.

Natural Resources and the Environment

The Reagan administration's policies dealing with natural resources and the environment have been largely consistent with its free-market orientation and its desire to shift the balance between economic growth and resource development, on the one hand, and protection of the environment and conservation of land, water, and energy resources on the other.* The administration's activities in these areas have also been very controversial. But this controversy stemmed as much from the initial appointments to the Environmental Protection Agency (EPA) and the Interior Department, and the approach of these appointees to their jobs, as from the substantive content of their policies. Indeed, the administration has accomplished much less than it proposed or is believed to have occurred. It remains to be seen whether new and more widely respected leadership at EPA and at the Departments of Interior and Energy will change the outlook significantly.

---

*The material in this section is drawn from chapter 5 by Paul R. Portney.

In view of its philosophical bent and the problems it inherited, the administration might have been expected to review carefully the effectiveness of existing environmental regulations; to propose changes in the Clean Air, Clean Water, and other acts that would permit costs and benefits to be better balanced in setting standards; and to expand the use of flexible, incentivelike approaches to environmental regulation. None of this happened. Instead, Administrator Burford and her top subordinates at EPA became involved in one controversy after another resulting from inexperience, poor judgment, and conflicts of interest.

The administration did significantly reduce EPA's budget and staff: real spending declined more than 50 percent and full-time staff was reduced almost 30 percent between 1981 and 1984, with all important components of EPA's program—research, monitoring, and enforcement—affected. During these years EPA took fewer enforcement actions against violators and made little use of the Superfund to clean up areas endangered by hazardous wastes. EPA gave the states more responsibilities for monitoring activities and enforcing standards but greatly reduced financial aid to the states for carrying out these responsibilities. If allowed to continue, such a curtailment of EPA research, monitoring, and enforcement activities would be harmful: standards would be based on even poorer data than is now the case, less would be known about actual environmental conditions and their effects, environmental scofflaws would be less likely to be detected and punished, and human health would be affected.

There have been more policy changes at the Department of the Interior than at EPA but still less than all the controversy would suggest. Secretary Watt initially attempted to greatly expand the leasing of public lands and the Outer Continental Shelf for energy and mineral development, to open up wilderness areas for this purpose, and to sell off public lands. But because of adverse congressional and public reactions, leasing activities—although substantially greater than previously—have temporarily slowed; and the sale of public lands and the expansion of commercial activity in wilderness areas have not been significantly greater than in previous administrations.

With new and more moderate leadership at both the EPA and the Interior Department, the indications are that a more reasoned approach to policy-making is being pursued.* Nevertheless, it will take time to rebuild the public trust and political consensus needed if the basic laws and regulations developed

---

*William Ruckelshaus replaced Anne Burford in April 1983, and William Clark replaced James Watt in October 1983.

over the past decade are to be reformed in ways that are generally acknowledged to be desirable.

The Department of Energy, originally slated for extinction, now has its second secretary and has taken several significant and commendable actions. The timetable for oil price decontrol was accelerated, a sensible plan to deregulate natural gas prices has been proposed (but not enacted), the nation's ability to withstand another oil supply disruption has been increased by additions to the Strategic Petroleum Reserve (done with congressional prodding), and priority has been given to dealing with the problem of nuclear waste disposal. At the same time, apart from adding to the government's petroleum stockpile, there has been no real planning for a possible oil supply disruption, and expenditures for energy conservation and renewable energy sources have been reduced without adequate review of what these programs were accomplishing.

In sharp contrast to its free-market orientation in dealing with the environment, public lands, and energy, the Reagan administration's agriculture policies, whether intentionally or not, have been the most interventionist in history. In an attempt to reduce burgeoning budget costs for agricultural support payments, the administration introduced a new Payment-in-Kind (PIK) program in January 1983 that paid farmers in crops rather than in cash for idling their land. Its terms were so generous that far more acres were taken out of production than the administration expected, with the result that agricultural price supports ballooned to $19 billion in FY 1983, only a little less than cumulative expenditures for this purpose during all four years of the Carter administration. This increased federal assistance, together with the higher market prices expected to result from reduced production, is good for farmers but bad for consumers and taxpayers. Apart from this unfortunate experiment, largely terminated in 1984, the administration has generally worked to restore more competition to agricultural markets—although the next major opportunity for an overdue restructuring of U.S. agricultural policy will not occur until 1985, when the farm bill expires.

Social Policy

President Reagan challenged many of the principles governing social policy in this country over the past half-century of growing federal responsibilities for social welfare.* He has attempted to change the scope of social programs, their goals, and the means used to achieve these goals.

---

*The material in this section is drawn from chapter 6 by D. Lee Bawden and John L. Palmer.

To limit their scope, the president proposed to reduce annual spending on social programs by nearly $75 billion, about 17 percent, below prior policy levels by FY 1985. The deepest cuts (nearly 60 percent) were proposed for the smallest component of social spending—the myriad of fixed-dollar grant programs that primarily fund the delivery of education, health, employment, and social services by state and local governments. Substantial cuts (28 percent) were also proposed for the somewhat larger category of benefit programs targeted on the low-income population, such as Food Stamps, Aid to Families with Dependent Children (AFDC), child nutrition, housing assistance, and Medicaid, while more modest reductions (11 percent) were slated for the social insurance programs, such as Social Security, Medicare, and Unemployment Insurance, which account for about two-thirds of all social program spending. These social insurance programs are the first line of defense against misfortune, and as such, constitute the upper tier of the social safety net. However, many people are not caught in this net and must rely on the lower tier of means-tested benefit programs.

Congress acceded to most of the president's proposed cuts in FY 1982 but to far less in the succeeding years. As a consequence the budget savings have been approximately half what the president sought, and federal spending for social programs will be about 9 percent—$38 billion—less in FY 1985 than under prior policies. The pattern of reductions, however, is generally consistent with what the president sought.

The administration changed not only the scope of these social programs but also their goals by reducing or eliminating benefits for those groups it believed ought to rely upon work and other means of private rather than public support. Thus, the recipients of upper-tier safety net programs whose benefits were most drastically curtailed are those on the margins of the work force— the "questionably" disabled, the long-term unemployed, and early retirees. The administration found Congress a willing ally in reducing upper-tier benefits for high-income recipients, who are now less likely to qualify for student aid and whose Social Security and Unemployment Insurance benefits are subject to greater taxation.

Lower-tier safety net programs were generally cut by imposing tighter income eligibility limits and offsetting benefits more fully for earnings and other sources of income. The result has been to exclude many of the working poor and near-poor from government programs (e.g., an estimated 400,000 to 500,000 AFDC families and nearly a million potential Food Stamp beneficiaries), to greatly reduce benefits for others, and to target a higher percentage of the reduced funds on the poor. For people who have no private source of income, program coverage and benefit levels have remained largely intact, in part because of Congress's unwillingness to cut the programs as much as the president proposed. In fact, real benefit levels for some types of low-income households (nonworking AFDC and Supplementary Security Income recipients) have declined at a slower rate over the past two years than during the latter 1970s largely because of the drop in inflation.

Nevertheless, the safety net is less effective than it was. Government programs do less now than in the past to protect people from poverty. These programs lifted less than 38 percent of those who otherwise would have been poor above the poverty line in 1982 compared with nearly 44 percent in 1976. Moreover, the proportion of the population officially defined as poor increased from 11.7 percent in 1979 to 15.0 percent in 1982, its highest level since 1965. Recession and recent cuts in social programs contributed about equally to the increase.

To replace social program assistance for the poor, the administration has advocated a two-pronged approach: economic growth and more work effort. Greater economic growth would certainly be helpful. However, even if the current economic recovery is sustained, the poverty rate will probably not decline within this decade to its lows of the 1970s, because the poverty population is increasingly made up of individuals and families—particularly female-headed families—to whom the benefits of economic growth do not generally "trickle down."

The second prong of the administration's strategy to reduce poverty— increased work incentives and work requirements—also may produce disappointing results. Few states have implemented "workfare" programs that cover much of the eligible welfare population, and there are indications that even these programs are of questionable effectiveness.* And although there is no evidence that working welfare mothers who have been eliminated from the rolls are quitting their jobs in order to requalify for benefits (as critics of the administration feared), neither is there any evidence that the overall reduction in social program benefits will have more than a very minor positive effect on work effort, increasing overall labor supply by perhaps .5 percent.

Because of the president's emphasis on self-sufficiency and productivity, the administration might have been expected to give some emphasis to human resource programs (education and training, public service employment, nutrition programs, Medicaid, and social services) as a means of addressing poverty and welfare dependency. Instead, these were the very programs in which the administration generally proposed the deepest cuts. Some of these

---

*Workfare is the term generally applied to programs that require welfare recipients to work in specially created public jobs for no pay in order to retain eligibility for cash assistance. The administration proposed making them mandatory, but Congress only granted states the option to have them.

were ripe for a pruning; however, the administration appeared to distinguish little among more or less effective ones. That job was left to Congress, which proved more selective.

The expansion of human resource programs under the Great Society was, in part, an effort to provide greater equality of opportunity. The growing prominence of civil rights and affirmative action on the legislative and regulatory agenda in the 1960s and 1970s was similarly motivated. Toward the end of the 1970s, however, various commentators, politicians, and private citizens had begun to seriously question whether the government had gone too far, too fast, especially regarding affirmative action measures. The Reagan administration clearly believed it had. Thus, it proposed the following: to reduce federal involvement in regulating the behavior of individuals and organizations, encouraging instead voluntary compliance; to require proof of intent to discriminate rather than relying on a pattern of effects before taking remedial action; and to reject the use of quotas, numerical goals, and time-tables as a means of redressing the present consequences of past discrimination. Actions taken to implement this new philosophy included a 9 percent reduction in real outlays for all civil rights and equal opportunity enforcement throughout the federal government, reduced litigation and enforcement activity, administration attempts to amend—weaken, in the eyes of its critics—the Voting Rights Act, the Justice Department's position in a number of controversial cases, and the administration's own appointments record. Many of these actions reversed policies that had proven somewhat effective in promoting opportunities for women and minorities.

Turning to the administration's preferred means for achieving social program objectives, we see that there has been substantial devolution of responsibility to lower levels of government (discussed in the next section) and somewhat more reliance on the private sector (such as in the redesign of housing assistance and employment and training programs). But the administration's plans to substitute vouchers for more direct public provision of benefits or services in a number of areas (housing, education, and health care) have made little headway. Finally, more efficient management and closer regulation of programs have produced some modest cost savings but far less than the administration's early expectations.

In sum, given his way, the president would have eradicated most of the hallmarks of the Great Society and would have shrunk social insurance programs to a scope approximating their New Deal origins. As things have turned out, Congress and the courts have moderated the president's intentions. Congress acted to protect many of the more effective programs and to hold together the bottom tier of the safety net. Congress and the courts rejected several of the administration's more ambitious efforts to narrow or reinterpret civil rights laws. Nevertheless, President Reagan has successfully shifted the nation's social policy agenda from problem solving to budget cutting, and as long as the federal deficit remains a problem, there is little room for the agenda to shift back.

Impacts on State and Local Governments, Nonprofit Organizations, and Businesses

A more limited federal role in managing the economy and in promoting social welfare meant, as a corollary, an expanded role for other institutions. Governments closer to the people would decide what services to provide, private charity would substitute for the federal dole, and the positive response of businesses to the administration's supply-side tax and regulatory policies would restore the health and competitiveness of the industrial sector. At least, this was what the administration hoped. To what extent were its expectations borne out? The impacts of administration policies on local governments, voluntary organizations, and businesses are examined in chapters 7, 8, and 9.

Federalism and the States

In 1982, as part of its New Federalism initiative, the administration proposed to turn major income support responsibilities (AFDC and Food Stamps) over to state governments in return for federal assumption of the costs of health care for the poor (Medicaid).* The administration also sought to gradually eliminate federal responsibility in many other areas of domestic policy, such as elementary and secondary education and social services. Unlike previous Republican administrations that had also advocated greater flexibility for state governments in the spending of federal aid, the Reagan administration proposed to greatly reduce the amount of this grant aid, which it believed had undesirably stimulated local spending (because of matching requirements). Thus, it had two goals: to return decision-making authority to lower levels of government and to restrain domestic spending at all levels of government.

The extreme program devolution envisioned in the administration's New Federalism proposals has been subjected to public debate and found to lack a sufficient constituency. In this respect, the Reagan years have constituted a political experiment in federalism with a clear outcome. Nevertheless, the administration has succeeded in reducing federal aid to state and local governments

---

*The material in this section is drawn from chapter 7 by George E. Peterson.

as a proportion of their revenues to the levels of the mid-1970s. And the administration's policies have had an important influence on intergovernmental relations and states' behavior in a number of areas.

First, recent federal initiatives have encouraged greater spending restraint in the large entitlement programs, such as AFDC, Medicaid, and Unemployment Insurance, in which expenditures vary with the number of people seeking assistance and costs per person and financing is shared by different levels of government. For example, the federal government is now providing greater incentives for Medicaid cost control and allowing states the flexibility to decide how to control costs. In 1982 these changes, in combination with the recession, resulted in a rate of growth for Medicaid spending about one-third that of immediately prior years. States have used their new discretion to arrange fixed-rate payments to hospitals rather than reimbursing them for costs.

Second, the administration (by its own count) has reduced the number of separate grant programs from 361 in FY 1981 to 259 in FY 1983 by eliminating some and consolidating other categorical (special purpose) grants into block (general purpose) grants. States have used their own funds to replace a considerable proportion of the losses in federal funds that accompanied this consolidation.* In addition, they have used the flexibility of the block grants to change funding priorities. For example, under the Social Services Block Grant, a greater share of spending now goes to protective services (e.g., child abuse programs) and adoption or foster care and a smaller share to family planning and day care. School desegregation assistance was also a big loser in the budget reallocations.

One of the rationales for devolution was that it would improve administrative efficiency and reduce the cost of services. Although there is little evidence of such cost savings, states have sometimes substituted less expensive types of services for the more expensive ones previously mandated under federal standards. For example, one state has put more children into day care but has spent less per child by relaxing training requirements for staff and staff-pupil ratios.

Overall, although some of the reductions in federal aid have been offset by greater local spending, the net effect has been to reduce benefits and services. These declines would have been steeper if most states and localities had not raised taxes to compensate for the loss of federal aid and the revenue effects of the 1981–1982 recession. Between 1980 and 1983 state and local

---

*Earlier studies showed very little such replacement because many of these decisions were deferred until FY 1983, but recently state and local governments, private organizations, and individuals have all shared in partially filling the gap left by the federal cutbacks.

tax burdens increased for the average family in twenty-two out of twenty-seven major cities. Now that an economic recovery is under way, higher tax rates are yielding sizable budget surpluses for these governments, and they must decide how to use these surpluses. A backlog of deferred spending obligations, particularly for capital facilities and wage increases for public employees, ensures some increase in their spending rates. But, it also appears that much of these state-local budget surpluses will be used to grant tax relief.

In sum, the administration has reversed the trend of growing financial dependence of lower levels of government on the national government, put in place a grant structure that is less restrictive and provides less encouragement to local spending, challenged the assumption that there should be uniform national standards for public services, and more fully engaged the states as partners in the effort to contain domestic program costs.

Nonprofit Organizations

States and localities are not the federal government's only partners in delivering, and paying for, a variety of social services.* President Reagan hoped to involve the nonprofit sector as much as the state-local sector in taking on greater responsibility for meeting human needs.

The voluntary sector is much larger than commonly assumed. There are about 375,000 nonprofit, charitable organizations in this country. In 1980 they spent $114 billion and employed more than 4.6 million persons. Of their total revenues, 35 percent came from the federal government, 20 percent from private contributions, 5 to 10 percent from other levels of government, and the rest from fees or charges and earned income.

President Reagan hoped that reductions in taxes and domestic expenditures would restore the vitality of the voluntary sector. However, these reductions have adversely affected the finances of nonprofit organizations and thus their ability to provide services for two reasons. To begin with, lower tax rates raise the cost of charitable donations because the deductions permitted for this purpose are then worth less to the taxpayer. Over the period 1981–1984, the Reagan tax changes discouraged donations by an estimated $10 billion. What is more important, reductions in domestic spending have taken a heavy toll on some types of nonprofit organizations. By FY 1984, real federal spending for programs relevant to nonprofit organizations was below FY 1980 levels: 3 percent below if Medicare and Medicaid are included, 15 percent below if these health programs are excluded.

---

*The material in this section is drawn from chapter 8 by Lester M. Salamon.

An Urban Institute survey of nonprofit, charitable service organizations found that between 1981 and 1982 these organizations lost 9.2 percent of their government support. These cuts translate into a 3 percent decline in overall income for the sector as a whole (because 35 percent of their revenues, on average, have come from the federal government). However, the effects have been quite uneven. Agencies established under the aegis of the Great Society and those focusing services on the poor have been hit especially hard by the federal cutbacks. Unable to close the funding gap with sufficient private donations or with charges for services, many agencies have had to reduce their activities, especially those engaged in housing and community development, legal services, social services, and employment and training.

In contrast, other agencies (especially those in health-related fields and in the arts and culture) have been able to maintain, or even increase, their spending by replacing lost government funds with increased private donations or the use of fees or charges for services, or both.

Businesses

Whether the services are delivered by private voluntary or public agencies, the need for many forms of assistance from soup kitchens to training programs depends on the state of the economy and the number of people who have jobs.* Thus, if the administration were to be successful in revitalizing the private, for-profit sector, many of these needs would never arise. For this and other reasons, the president placed rekindling the nation's entrepreneurial instincts and capabilities at the center of his domestic agenda. In particular, regulatory relief and tax cuts for businesses were intended to replace the heavy hand of government with the invisible hand of the market, enabling productivity and private incomes to rise.

For at least the first two years of the administration, supply-side measures to increase investment and productivity had to swim against the tide of demand-side measures (mainly a restrictive monetary policy) that depressed business sales and capacity utilization while keeping real interest rates and the value of the dollar high. The effects of these demand-side policies have been mixed. On the positive side, the recession has induced wage concessions, changes in work rules, and management efficiencies that should reduce unit costs and contribute to making U.S. goods relatively cheaper and more competitive in world markets. However, there is considerable uncertainty about how permanent these changes will be and the extent to which any benefits from them will erode as the economy expands. On the negative side, the

---

*The material in this section is drawn from chapter 9 by Perry D. Quick.

recession, high interest rates, and the rise in the dollar have (at least temporarily) slowed productivity growth, dampened investment, encouraged U.S. companies to locate more of their capacity overseas, and allowed foreign competitors to expand their market shares at the expense of U.S. companies. This latter phenomenon could have serious long-term implications for U.S. companies by placing them at a competitive disadvantage in industries where early gains in market share create cumulative benefits that are difficult to reverse later.

The substantial business tax cuts resulting from legislation passed in 1981 and 1982 should encourage greater business investment and productivity in the long run. Overall corporate tax burdens have been reduced by 15 to 20 percent, and the effective cost of new plant and equipment investments has been reduced by about 8 percent. These tax incentives can be expected to raise net business investment by perhaps 10 percent above what it would otherwise have been over the next several years. (However, their effects may be offset by the high interest rates and excess industrial capacity that could exist if deficits are not greatly reduced and if moderately strong economic growth is not sustained.) On a less positive note, the tax changes did little to correct the preexisting distortions and inefficiencies that flow from the differential tax treatment of various types of assets. Moreover, tax relief was skewed toward encouraging greater investment in capital-intensive enterprises at the expense of high-tech firms and thus may slow the ongoing adjustment of the economy from an industrial to a technological base.

The Reagan administration believed "a dramatic, substantial *rescission* of the regulatory burden" was needed to improve the performance of American business. Although regulatory changes have hardly been dramatic, some relief has been granted.

The administration continued the earlier trend toward freeing business from economic regulations that govern prices and conditions of entry and toward a more flexible antitrust policy that treats corporate size and market share more flexibly, in line with the emerging needs of a complex and increasingly internationalized economy. Much more important and controversial were its plans to rescind a host of social regulations, and here it appears that the actual benefits resulting from the changes made by the administration are not nearly so large as it claimed. The modest reductions in social regulations that did take place can be expected to give a small one-time boost to productivity. However, the administration's controversial handling of these issues and its strong tendency to pursue administrative rather than legislative change has probably set back the cause of long-term regulatory reform.

In trade policy, as in agricultural policy, the administration's free-market ideology and its actions diverged sharply, helping the affected industries (e.g., autos, steel) at the expense of consumers, who are paying higher prices. The political pressures for protectionism were strong, however, and another administration probably would have done no better and could have done far worse.

Has Reagan's "industrial policy" worked? In the long run it may. American industry has been put on notice that it should expect no special help from the government—other than a general reduction in taxes and regulations and some occasional import relief—and that could turn out to be the best policy. Thus far, however, there is no clear evidence of overall favorable effects. By early 1984, productivity had grown no more rapidly than is typical in recoveries from recession, and continuing high interest rates and an overvalued dollar remain obstacles to improving the health and competitiveness of American industry.

Impacts on Family Incomes

The failure of the administration's supply-side initiatives to immediately revive the economy means that standards of living improved little between 1980 and 1984.* Furthermore, even if these policies are successful, the prospects for the remainder of the decade are not very encouraging. These topics are the subject of chapter 10.

Overall, real disposable income per family (i.e., income adjusted for inflation and after taxes) fell in 1981 and 1982 before beginning to rise again in 1983. Its 1984 level ($21,000) will be 3.5 percent higher than its 1980 level, a small gain by historical standards.

Not all of the change in standards of living that occurs during any president's term can be attributed to the policies of his administration. Indeed, the economic and budget measures peculiar to the Reagan administration had little overall net effect on the growth of real disposable family incomes between 1980 and 1984. As noted in the discussion of the economy, the particular mix of a stimulative fiscal policy and tight monetary policy endorsed by the administration led to a deeper recession than otherwise might have occurred—and, thus, a smaller rise in real earnings. However, the Reagan tax cuts boosted *after-tax* incomes enough to offset this. Because these same budget policies have also created deficits that will require future tax increases and benefit cuts, some of this boost will turn out to be temporary. For now,

---

*The material in this section is drawn from chapter 10 by Marilyn Moon and Isabel V. Sawhill.

though, families have lower real earnings but more take-home pay, on average, than they otherwise would have had.

Not all families shared in the income growth that occurred between 1980 and 1984. In fact, since 1980 the real disposable income of the poorest one-fifth (quintile) of all families declined by nearly 8 percent, while that of the top quintile rose by almost 9 percent. The income of the typical middle-class family (the middle quintile) grew by a scant 1 percent. Because of underlying economic and demographic trends, some of this widening of the income distribution would have taken place regardless of who was president. But the particular tax and benefit reductions that President Reagan supported exacerbated the trend. His policies helped the affluent but were detrimental to the poor and the middle class.

How a family fared over this period depended more on its income level than on its other characteristics, but such factors as age, sex, and race also played a role. For example, the incomes of the elderly rose substantially; the elderly were also the major gainers from Reagan's policies. In contrast, female-headed and black families did poorly, and they were the major losers from the administration's policies.

Of course, there was nothing sacrosanct about the distribution of income prevailing in 1980. In fact, rising tax burdens and growing government benefits had reduced the degree of inequality over the previous two decades. Moreover, the initial support President Reagan received for his tax and spending policies may partially reflect a public consensus that the equalizing process had gone too far by 1980, although there have been subsequent indications in the polls that people are concerned about the contrasting treatment of the rich, the poor, and the middle class.

And what of the future? As the recession fades further into the background, will the Reagan administration's policies encourage people to work, save, and invest more, and thus produce a higher rate of economic growth that will make everyone better off?

As was noted earlier, these policies should have a modest positive effect on long-term economic growth if currently projected deficits are greatly reduced. Thus, the future growth of real GNP could be quite strong. Indeed, the administration's own GNP projections assume this will be the case. However, strong GNP growth will not necessarily translate into equivalent gains in standards of living because large deficits will necessitate some tax increases and benefit reductions that will adversely affect disposable incomes. Assuming measures are taken to lower the structural deficit to $100 billion by 1988 and the administration's expectations for the economy are realized, real disposable income per family will grow by about 4 percent from 1984 to 1988—slightly more rapidly than it did from 1980 to 1984.

The way in which the deficit problem is resolved will have major implications for who is better off by the end of the decade. Realistically, any deficit reduction plan must involve both tax increases and spending reductions. If these policy measures and the benefits of economic growth are evenly distributed across income groups, then the poorest quintile of families will still be worse off in 1988 than in 1980, the middle three quintiles will have realized small to modest gains, and the top quintile substantial gains. However, there are many possible deficit reduction plans, which can yield equivalent budgetary savings but have very different effects on the relative fortunes of different families. For example, under a prototypical "conservative" deficit reduction plan, lower-income families would once again experience an actual loss in their real disposable income over the next four years, while the affluent would realize a greater than average gain. Conversely, under a prototypical "liberal" plan, poorer families' incomes would rise sufficiently over the next four years to more or less offset the losses of the last four, while the affluent would realize only small additional gains. In short, the recent trend toward greater income inequality could be accelerated, left unchanged, or reversed depending on the specific nature of future White House and congressional actions on the deficit.

An Overall Assessment

Such are the highlights of the chapters to follow. The remainder of this chapter offers a somewhat more personal and, admittedly, selective assessment of the significance of the Reagan experiment along four dimensions: its success in redirecting the national agenda, some areas in which it failed to act, its contributions to individual welfare, and its legacies for the future.

Revolution or Evolution?

The conservative cast of the Reagan administration's ideology and its proposals have caused some observers (including us) to label this redirection of domestic policy the Reagan revolution (or counterrevolution).[3] What must be understood is that it has been revolutionary in purpose but evolutionary in practice.

The essence of the revolution was President Reagan's belief that government was the problem. Other recent presidents, whether Democratic or Republican, accepted the basic premise that if something were wrong, it was the government's responsibility to fix it. To be sure, there were disagreements about how deeply the government should get involved and the means it should use but not about its ability to contribute positively to the nation's welfare.

And because no one is ever completely satisfied with the status quo, there was almost no end to the set of problems that the government would be asked to address, and its responsibilities grew accordingly.

President Reagan planned a full-scale retreat from this march toward a welfare state. He sought a reduction in domestic spending of more than one-quarter, which would have eliminated the hallmarks of the Great Society. His New Federalism proposals would have largely returned federal-state responsibilities to their status before the New Deal. And his proposed rollback of tax and regulatory burdens—along with the spending reductions—would have substituted market incentives for Keynesian interventions as the key to a healthier economy.

The president's retreat was only partially successful. The economy, Congress, the courts, state officials, and others did not always cooperate. Consequently, it would be a serious mistake to conclude that a revolution has taken place. Even a strong president—as Ronald Reagan has proved to be—must operate within a system of checks and balances, and this president's strongly conservative ideology together with the failure of the economy to perform as he had hoped, the mishandling of some politically sensitive issues (e.g., Social Security, the environment, and civil rights), and his perceived intransigence on the budget made his task more difficult.

The president exercised far less fiscal discipline than economic realities required and got only half of the domestic spending restraint he requested from Congress. As a result he now presides over the largest federal budget and the biggest peacetime deficit in history. He was thwarted by the courts and by a congressional and public backlash in his attempts to undo many existing regulations. He reduced federal income taxes, but personal tax burdens rose because of payroll and local tax increases. And he was rebuffed by the governors and others in his attempt to radically devolve federal responsibilities to the states—in part because they favored cooperative federalism in place of a stricter separation of powers and in part because he failed to overcome their suspicion that such devolution was budget cutting in disguise.

But, if the glass is half empty from the president's perspective, it is also half full. Countercyclical economic policies were not adopted to cut short the recession; instead, Congress and the Federal Reserve "stayed the course" in the face of painfully high unemployment. The domestic agenda is substantially leaner than when the president took office, and the savings have been reinvested in defense. Tax burdens, although still high, are lower than they otherwise would have been. States have become willing partners in controlling the costs of government, and there has been some genuine devolution of responsibilities to lower levels of government and to the voluntary sector, each of which is now exercising its own priorities more freely than before.

Despite deep cuts in means-tested social programs, the safety net is still largely intact for the nonworking poor. Moroever, people removed from the welfare rolls appear to be continuing to work even when they might be better off quitting their jobs and reapplying for government assistance.

Finally, after years of spiraling prices with their debilitating psychological effects, inflation has been reduced to its lowest level in more than a decade. Businesses have been freed from much of the burden of taxes and new regulations (though not from the scourge of high interest rates and an overvalued dollar).

All these achievements were consistent with the president's intentions. Although many had their roots in prior administrations, he greatly slowed a fifty-year trend toward a larger, more intrusive domestic government. All in all, it is a record of substantial, if not revolutionary, change. Its purposes remain controversial.

Missed Opportunities

This period of substantial change might have been expected to produce not only a retrenchment in domestic policy but also an improvement in the effectiveness of federal policies. However, the Reagan administration has done little to reform spending, tax, and regulatory policies.

The need for such reform was overdue. The rapid expansion of social welfare spending under the Great Society and of environmental regulations following the celebration of "Earth Day" in 1970 have been criticized for producing many ineffective and inefficient policies. It was the public's reaction to these perceived inadequacies that helped to send the policy pendulum swinging in the other direction in the late 1970s. Indeed, Reagan was elected on a promise to reduce domestic spending by eliminating waste, fraud, and abuse.

Once in office, however, it quickly became apparent to administration officials that improved program management—which they have pursued with some vigor and success—could not contribute much to shrinking the federal budget. Benefits and services, of varying effectiveness, would have to be cut. In making cuts, the administration wielded its budget knife somewhat indiscriminately. Moreover, the initial and largest round of cuts in 1981 was achieved through "reconciliation" without the benefit of congressional hearings or committee deliberations. When Congress did have an opportunity to review the administration's proposals, it showed more interest than the administration in separating the wheat from the chaff, with the result that the pattern of enacted reductions in social spending is more defensible on cost benefit grounds than were the original proposals.

One would not want to make too much of this point. The budget knife took plenty of bad with the good, and as the administration understood, too much deliberation can provide an opportunity for special interests to distort the process. But then, it is not as if the administration took on the more powerful groups. Business subsidies and "middle-class entitlements" were left virtually untouched. In fact, it was the failure to successfully tackle the latter that is the major reason for the administration's failure to reduce the size of government.*

A similar story, only in reverse, might be told about the defense budget. The share of the budget devoted to defense outlays had declined for some years, leading in the late 1970s to a bipartisan commitment to rebuild the nation's defenses. But defense spending is now growing so rapidly as the result of the administration's policies that one can easily imagine some future administration tackling an "over-grown" defense budget rife with "fraud, waste, and abuse" in much the same way the current one has tackled the nondefense budget. Indeed there are already signs of waning public support for this dramatic shift in priorities and growing concern among experts about the scale and the composition of the buildup—both of which appear to have been chosen with little thoughtful analysis.[4]

In the tax area, there is another kind of inefficiency that has received insufficient attention—and, indeed, has been exacerbated—over the past four years. Known as "tax loopholes" to the general public and "tax expenditures" to the experts, these too had proliferated during the 1960s and 1970s, adding considerable complexity and arbitrariness to the federal tax system. Many of these tax preferences have been justified as achieving one good purpose or another; however, they also distort the efficiency of the market and lead to as much "abuse" as government transfer programs to which they are comparable in size. (The major difference is that transfer programs are tilted toward families in the lower half of the income distribution whereas tax expenditures are tilted toward the upper half.) All these tax preferences cost the average taxpayer as much or more as would direct expenditures for the same purposes because they necessitate higher tax rates to compensate for the revenue losses they entail.

---

*After being pressured by Senate Republicans, the administration did attempt to make an immediate large reduction in Social Security benefits, which was poorly conceived and was unanimously rejected by Congress. Later the president was forced to turn to a bipartisan commission to resolve Social Security's financing problems, leading to one of the most significant and far-reaching changes in domestic policy in the past four years. The solution, however, placed much greater weight on tax increases than on spending reductions in the short run.

Both middle-class entitlements and tax preferences have strong political support. Thus, any attempt to reduce them would have been fiercely resisted and might have jeopardized the Reagan administration's chances of obtaining the tax and spending cuts that were enacted in 1981. The fact that the president did little to advance such reforms is perhaps less surprising than the fact that he has done so little to build the political and popular support needed to take on these controversial issues in the future. Reducing the size of government is painful, and deficits cannot be a permanent solution to the public's desire to pay less taxes while continuing to receive substantial health care and pension benefits, tax breaks for homeownership, and other expensive subsidies.

With respect to regulatory reform, the administration appears to have "poisoned the well" (literally, in the case of the improprieties surrounding hazardous waste cleanups at EPA) by its poor initial choice of leadership at several key agencies and its inept handling of a number of regulatory issues. The result was that few regulatory statutes were amended, and the cause of regulatory reform was set back as public confidence eroded in the administration's commitment to the basic goals, as opposed to the means, of regulation.

The spending, tax, and regulatory reforms discussed in this section would be tough political challenges for any administration. Nevertheless, given the president's mandate to reduce "fraud, waste, and abuse," his strong leadership and communication abilities, and the political skills of his Executive Office team, the administration did less than one might have hoped to improve the existing structure of programs, taxes, and regulation.

Are We Better Off?

Whatever the accomplishments of the Reagan administration in changing the scope or nature of government policies, it is more likely to be judged by the effects these changes have on people's lives than by the nature of the policy changes themselves.

The problem lies in determining what these effects are. No one can evaluate them completely. Some will become evident only in the very long term. And some, such as whether people are safer, freer, or happier, are intangible. Nevertheless, on the dimension which we can measure—and which the president himself has chosen to emphasize (material standards of living)—the answer is reasonably clear.

First, the notion that supply-side policies would quickly reduce both inflation and unemployment and make everyone better off has been largely discredited. Although the administration's tax cuts provided a dose of Keynesian medicine that helped to fuel the recovery in 1983, they did not immediately lead to more work, saving, investment, and productivity as supply-siders had predicted.

The longer-term effects of the administration's economic policies could be more positive. Under optimistic assumptions, their cumulative effect (over many years) would be to raise real standards of living about 5 percent above what they would have been in the absence of these policies and to produce an extra $1,000 in income for every family. Under more pessimistic assumptions, their cumulative effects would be negative.

Even under optimistic assumptions, standards of living for most people will rise less in the 1980s than they did in the 1970s and far less than they did in the 1960s. The typical middle-class family experienced a negligible increase in real after-tax income between 1980 and 1984 and has at best only a modest increase to look forward to over the rest of the decade. Lower-income families have lost substantial ground and are unlikely to regain it in the remainder of this decade. Only the most affluent families are likely to realize major income gains.

Legacies

In addition to these consequences for standards of living, what are the other major legacies of the policies pursued over the past four years?

Foremost are deficits. Their significance for the future of the country lies along a number of dimensions. First, their very existence undermines confidence in government and crowds other important matters off the public agenda. Second, if not brought quickly under control, they will slow economic growth—not immediately, but by the end of the decade and beyond—and negate any positive effects the president's supply-side policies might otherwise have had. (The uncertainty about whether and how they will be reduced also promotes exactly the kind of instability in the business environment that the president attributed to past economic policies and wished to undo.) Third, deficits result in a rapidly growing share of the taxpayer's dollar going to pay for interest on the debt rather than for current benefits and services. Fourth, they have created the temporary illusion that people are better off when the reality is that bringing them under control will mean smaller than normal gains in standards of living over the next several years. Finally, whether intentionally, or not, deficits have become a means of advancing the Reagan revolution. Whoever is elected to the White House and Congress in 1984 will feel the pressure to curb federal spending, and budgetary pressures may even break the political logjam inhibiting spending restraint in major entitlement programs.

Deficits will probably not be the only factor restraining domestic spending in the years ahead. The merits of federal solutions to public problems are also being more strongly questioned. In part because of the president's skillful adaptation of an old populist theme, big government has replaced big business and big labor as the new bete noire of a large segment of the American public.[5] Even among people less susceptible to populist rhetoric, one finds harder and more thoughtful questions being asked about the role of government in various areas. The president has, in effect, established tougher standards against which new domestic initiatives will be measured in the future. The burden of proof has shifted subtly but perceptibly from those who would do less to those who would do more.

Set against the continuing downward pressure that deficits will place on spending and a more questioning attitude about the benefits of government solutions to domestic problems are two aspects of Reagan policies that call into question the durability of their imprint. First, the administration has done little to codify and institutionalize its agenda. There have been some significant changes in legislatively mandated programs, but much of the budget cutting has occurred in discretionary programs, and there have been almost no statutory changes in the regulatory area. Thus, many of these actions are easily reversible by subsequent administrations. (For this reason perhaps, the president has indicated his intention, should he be reelected, to amend the Constitution as a means of achieving his objectives of controlling government spending and advancing the New Right's social agenda. In addition, he probably would have an opportunity to make several appointments to the Supreme Court.)

What is more important, the administration's unwillingness to substantially compromise its program in order to develop a broader working coalition has left it more dependent on a major political realignment to accomplish its objectives. Thus far, there is little evidence that such a realignment is occurring. In fact, the administration may have underestimated the extent to which its policies have awakened and strengthened opposition among women, minorities, the poor, and working-class families. These groups perceive that they are not "better off than they were four years ago," at least in part because of Reagan's policies, and the evidence suggests it is an accurate perception.

It is possible to dismiss such opposition as the hue and cry of special interests. But it is also an indicator of how far from the center are the administration's views and priorities. Many people will applaud its actions to date but not its vision for the future. The president appears to have led the country as far to the right as it wants to go in domestic policies. At the same time, deficits and his questioning of the value of "big government" will probably ensure that it does not move leftward for awhile. Another round of New Deal style liberalism does not appear to be on the horizon.

Conclusions

If liberalism has been called into question, one reason may be because it promised more than it could deliver. As Budget Director David Stockman put it, "When you have powerful underlying demographic and economic forces at work, federal intervention efforts designed to reverse the tide turn out to have rather anemic effects."[6] Critics argue, with some merit, that liberalism has been sustained as much by its ability to deliver benefits to its own constituencies and by its deeply ingrained faith in government's ability to improve the general welfare as by any widespread evidence that such improvements were in fact taking place.

But Ronald Reagan's brand of conservatism has similar flaws. His faith, of course, is in unfettered private initiative. Government is the problem and not the solution. However, across-the-board reductions in taxes, domestic spending, and regulations also turn out to have rather anemic effects. If government is not always the solution, neither is it always the problem. Moreover, the process of shrinking government has simply substituted one set of beneficiaries for another. Indeed, changes in social priorities and in the distribution of well-being over the past few years have turned out to be precisely what a constituency-based theory of government would have predicted. Stockman had hoped it would be otherwise. "We are interested in curtailing weak claims rather than weak clients. . . . I think that's critical to our success—both political and economic success."[7]

We agree with Mr. Stockman. What most citizens want is better government. What they have too often gotten is simply more government or less government with one set of favored beneficiaries replacing another. Under these circumstances, public disillusionment about the process may grow. As the chapters to follow demonstrate, the Reagan administration has some significant accomplishments to its credit. It has implemented a substantial shift in national priorities and sparked a fresh debate about the purposes of government. But the administration's policies have often failed to produce the promised results.

CHAPTER 2

GOVERNANCE

THE POLITICS OF RETRENCHMENT

Lester M. Salamon
Alan J. Abramson

Judging from the conventional scholarly and journalistic wisdom as of
the late 1970s, the impressive achievements of the Reagan administration
during its first year in office, could hardly have happened. The almost universal belief on the eve of Reagan's inauguration was that the presidency,
and the rest of the political system that depended on it, were in serious
institutional and political trouble. Far from being "imperial," wrote former
President Gerald Ford in the week of the 1980 election, the American presidency was seriously "imperiled," structurally incapable of meeting the expectations placed on it. Vice President Walter Mondale was even more graphic,
complaining that the American presidency had become "the fire hydrant of
the nation." As political scientist James Sundquist put it, the combination of
built-in structural obstacles and new developments over the past several decades "will make effective government even more difficult to attain in the
1980s than it has been in the decade just ended and those that have gone
before." A panel convened by the National Academy of Public Administration
concurred, concluding in 1980 that "the cumulative effect of many trends
and events is threatening America's capacity for self-government," neces-
sitating steps to strengthen the presidency in its dealings with other centers
of power. So profound was the sense of institutional enfeeblement that one
of the nation's leading constitutional lawyers and Washington insiders seriously proposed that we scrap our existing constitutional arrangements and
move toward a parliamentary system instead.[1]

31

Against this backdrop, the first year of the Reagan administration appears to represent an unusual political triumph that significantly changed the terms of the national policy debate, prompting two important questions: How could it happen? And what is its longer-term significance? This chapter seeks to answer these questions by evaluating the impact and performance of the Reagan administration in the area of "governance." Unlike the other chapters in this book, the focus here is primarily on the institutions and processes of government rather than on the substance or consequences of policies although, in practice, substance and process are too closely interwoven to separate fully.

In particular, we focus here on three dimensions of presidential effectiveness in the domestic arena:

1. The president's immediate success in accomplishing his purposes
2. His administration's longer-term impact on our nation's political processes and institutions
3. The political viability of the substantive policy choices he makes

Effective governance in the first sense means skill in articulating a program, winning support for it, and putting it into effect. Sundquist had this dimension in mind when he defined a government that "works" as one in which a presidential candidate puts forward "a program to address the central problems that concern the people" and then the "winning candidate . . . proceed(s) to accomplish the program."[2] Effective governance in the second sense means acting in ways that strengthen the capabilities of the nation's political institutions to function over the long run. A president is not simply the manager of a particular agenda; he is also the inheritor of a set of institutions and processes which can facilitate or complicate the job of achieving political agreement and which must in turn be handed on, in better or worse shape, to a successor.

Finally, effective governance in the third sense involves achieving a set of policies that are perceived as being programmatically workable over the long run and therefore that win continued voter acceptance. No set of criteria for evaluating presidential effectiveness can wholly ignore the substantive ends of political action. A presidency that advances a program that ultimately proves foolhardy can scarcely be judged an effective presidency. Yet judgments here are inevitably value laden and, in a democracy, must ultimately rest with the voters. Lacking the perspective of time, we can be even less definitive about this dimension of the Reagan presidency than about other dimensions, but there are some useful signposts.

To determine how the Reagan presidency measures up against these three standards of governance, we begin by looking at the conventional wisdom about the relative impotence of the modern presidency, in order to identify the major long-term trends in the political order that might help us interpret Ronald Reagan's early successes and judge their probable durability. Against this backdrop, we turn to the advantages Reagan enjoyed as he entered office and the way he capitalized, or failed to capitalize, on them. We then review the administration's legislative and administrative record through early 1984 before turning, in the final section, to an assessment of the longer-term implications of this record for the ongoing governmental institutions and processes of the country, and for the political viability of the administration's programmatic legacy.

What emerges from this analysis is a picture of an immensely skillful politician and political team which managed to make the most of the advantages they enjoyed and to escape temporarily the prevailing constraints of contemporary American politics. But the long-term impact of this administration on the nation's political institutions and processes, as well as on its substantive policies, is likely to be far more limited and possibly counterproductive.

The Context: Obstacles to Presidential Influence

The defining characteristic of the American political order over the past twenty years has been its tendency to concentrate responsibility for problems at the center while dispersing the power to deal with those problems to an ever-expanding array of increasingly autonomous groups and institutions. The combination has put great strain on our integrative institutions—particularly the presidency—and has raised questions about the governability of the nation.

These questions are, of course, not new. Fragmentation of power is part of the American constitutional design, institutionalized in the sharing of authority among the three branches of the federal government, and between the federal government and the states. It is for this reason that Richard Neustadt termed presidential power merely "the power to persuade" in his classic book on the topic.[3] But recent developments have accentuated these problems while intensifying the need for political action to overcome them.

One reason for this is the growing complexity and interrelatedness of current policy issues, which has tended to focus responsibility on the presidency. Decisions on benefit levels for the Aid to Families with Dependent Children (AFDC) program, for example, affect the cost of the Food Stamp program; the nature of farm price supports influences our foreign relations with the European Economic Community. Each issue turns out not only to be complex on its face, but to wear several faces, affecting policy in a number of different arenas.

As the only elected official with a national constituency, the president has become more and more the one entity in a reasonable position to bring a societywide perspective to bear on the increasing conflicts and trade-offs among policies. But despite the enlarged public expectations of their office, modern presidents have been increasingly hampered in their capacity to bring such a perspective to bear.

In the first place, the ability of the president to build the supporting coalitions needed for him to capitalize on his unique perspective has been made more difficult by the proliferation of interest groups, the weakening of political parties, and the dispersion of power in Congress. Faced with this disaggregation or "atomization," the president's job has been likened to the task of "building coalitions out of sand." The number of interest groups increased sharply in the 1960s and 1970s, as myriad new social, economic, and "issue" groups organized to press their claims through the political system. The Washington, D.C., telephone book tells this particular story well: listings of associations in the Yellow Pages alone now stretch some twenty-seven columns in length and embrace more than 1,500 listings, ranging from cocoa researchers to manufacturers of metal name-plates. These groups supplement their individual lobbying activities with participation in the electoral process through separate political action committees (PACs), which have themselves skyrocketed in number to at least 2,000 by 1980 and 3,525 by 1984.[4]

As citizens have found themselves able to express their preferences more precisely through narrow interest groups, their allegiance to political parties has fallen off; in consequence, the number of independents has come to rival the number of Democrats and Republicans, split-ticket voting has increased, and the party apparatus has been displaced by primaries in the selection of candidates for elected office. Not surprisingly, once in office, candidates who have run personal campaigns with the aid of media consultants and citizen volunteers feel little obligation to support fellow partisans when such support conflicts with election concerns. The upshot has been a substantial weakening of the political parties, one of the most important sets of integrating institutions in the political system, and a potential unifying instrument for the president.[5]

The diffusion of political power among an escalating number of narrow interest groups and the corresponding dilution in the power of political parties have in turn generated strong forces for diffusion of power within Congress. Turnover in both the House and Senate has been high. By 1980 nearly half of the members of the House had been first elected since 1974, and 48 of the 100 senators were in their first terms. In addition, new members have not shown themselves particularly respectful of some of the most cherished institutions of the Congress—seniority and the committee system. Subcommittees have proliferated and committee chairmen have lost much of their ability to hold them in check. Equipped with franking privileges and increased staff, and with access to PACs to finance member campaigns, Congress, in the view of one observer, came to resemble the Polish Diet, "where hundreds of independent members, bound by no ties of party and each as proud as a sovereign, jealously guarded the power to block anything the king might attempt, without ever organizing any means of putting forward alternative policies of their own."[6]

Besides having to operate in the midst of widespread political fragmentation, the president also had to deal with institutions and processes which were increasingly hostile to him or otherwise resistant to his lead. Chastened by the experiences of Vietnam and Watergate, and emboldened by the influx of new blood and the successful challenge to existing power arrangements internally, Congress moved in the 1970s to exercise increased independence through a series of "presidency-curbing" measures, such as the War Powers Act and the Congressional Budget Act. Concomitantly, presidential success in Congress declined steadily under both Democratic and Republican administrations, at least according to the blunt measures of Congressional Quarterly's presidential success ratings: Carter (76.4 percent average success rate) did worse than Johnson (82.8 percent) and Kennedy (84.5 percent); Ford (57.7 percent) did not fare as well as Nixon (67.0 percent) or Eisenhower (72.2 percent).[7]

Compounding the problems of a hostile Congress were several other major trends that further constrained the president's capacity to manage the government. These included the growth in judicial activism;[8] the rise in uncontrollable spending and the emergence of a "hidden budget" comprised of such devices as loan guarantees and tax expenditures;[9] and the rise of "third-party government," the use of nonfederal actors—such as state and local governments, nonprofit institutions, and banks—to carry out federal programs.[10]

In short, while increasingly called on to do more, the American presidency increasingly found itself in a position to do less. What is more, the other potential centers of integrative power that might share with the presidency the task of reconciling competing interests and setting priorities—such as parties and the leadership in Congress—were in either disarray or decline. None of this made the exercise of political leadership impossible. To be sure, although fragmentation has been a chronic feature of the American political system from the beginning, significant policy breakthroughs have occurred, most recently during the mid- to late 1960s and early 1970s, when an extraordinary series of social welfare, consumer, and environmental measures was enacted. But this breakthrough was not possible until the political system had been buffeted by an incredible set of shocks—the assassination of a president, the most lopsided presidential election victory since Roosevelt defeated Landon in 1936, a destructive wave of urban riots, an increasingly militant antiwar movement, and the emergence of mass-based civil rights and consumer movements. Thus, the prospects for a bold redirection of national policy in "normal" times appeared doubtful at best, particularly in light of the further fragmentation since the mid-1960s.

Reagan's Advantages and Strategy of Governance

A conservative president might be expected to applaud the obstacles to presidential activism outlined. After all, through much of our modern political history active presidencies have been associated with liberal political agendas and with the expansion of federal responsibilities, while conservatives have utilized their positions in Congress and their influence at the state and local level to resist governmental growth. By 1980, however, this situation had changed dramatically. Thanks to the policy changes of the 1960s and 1970s, the liberal-consumer-civil rights-environmental agenda that had been stymied for decades by what one political scientist termed "the deadlock of democracy"[11] had become institutionalized in a host of new governmental programs, in a variety of governmental agencies, in counterpart bureaucracies at the state and local level, in the courts and the legal system, and in the dispersed centers of power in Congress. Under these circumstances, the activist presidency, once the nemesis of conservatives, came to be seen as the best hope for restraining the liberal state. As one observer has put it, "Today, an administration cannot be conservative by doing little, it can only be conservative by doing a great deal."[12]

The Reagan administration, from all indications, understood this point all too well. But given the obstacles to presidential influence that it faced, how did it make the headway that it did?

One possible answer is that the political developments of the past several decades may not have been as corrosive of presidential influence as the conventional wisdom seemed to suggest. Diffusion of political power can, after all, be a two-way street; the president may have less coherent forces working for him, but he also has less coherent ones arrayed against him. Second, and more interesting in the context of our present concerns, President Reagan brought major advantages to the office and his administration made effective use of them. Finally, there is the possibility that the Reagan administration has not in fact disproved the conventional wisdom as much as many people have assumed, that its accomplishments have been overstated and its capacity to implement and sustain its program exaggerated. This section examines the president's advantages and strategy, reserving the last issue for our discussion of his accomplishments and his legacy later in the chapter.

The Reagan Advantages

Any discussion of the advantages that the Reagan administration brought to the presidency must start with the president himself. His disarming manner and unusual communication skills have earned him a popularity that has helped his administration survive even major gaffes. Beyond this advantage, two others stand out: the results of the 1980 election and the presence of a simple and straightforward ideology and program to guide the administration and its allies.

The 1980 Election. Perhaps the single most important advantage that the Reagan administration enjoyed going into its first year was the widespread impression that it had won a substantial mandate from the voters for a bold departure in national policy. "Reagan Buoyed by National Swing to the Right" is how a *New York Times* headline interpreted the election results, and the Reagan team was happy to accept that interpretation. In fact, of course, the results of the 1980 election were far more ambiguous than the headline snapshots. Ronald Reagan's 9.7 percent margin of victory in the popular vote, though substantial, was actually below the 11.4 percent average for elections since 1932 (table 2.1). Also, ample evidence suggests that the election was as much a rejection of Jimmy Carter as an embrace of Ronald Reagan; in 1980, nearly 60 percent of the public disapproved of the way Carter was handling his job, as contrasted with the more than 60 percent who approved of Gerald Ford, even as he was losing his presidential bid in 1976.[13]

Underlying the dissatisfaction with Carter was discontent with the state of the economy—notably the high rate of inflation. In 1980, 60 to 70 percent of the public named the economy as the biggest problem facing the country, and Reagan consistently outpolled Carter as someone who would do a better job handling the economy. Furthermore, economic dissatisfaction apparently outweighed the impact of party and ideology. As one analyst commented, "Despite their philosophy, those liberals who felt worse off financially opposed Carter. Despite their partisanship, those Democrats suffering economically defected to Reagan and Anderson." In fact, compared with 1976, there was no increase in the number of people who identified themselves as conservatives (table 2.2).[14]

TABLE 2.1

MARGIN OF PRESIDENTIAL POPULAR VICTORIES, 1932–1980

Year	Winner	Loser	Margin of Popular Vote Victory (Percentage)
1936	Roosevelt	Landon	24.3
1972	Nixon	McGovern	23.2
1964	Johnson	Goldwater	22.6
1932	Roosevelt	Hoover	17.7
1956	Eisenhower	Stevenson	15.4
1952	Eisenhower	Stevenson	10.7
1940	Roosevelt	Willkie	9.9
1980	Reagan	Carter	9.7
1944	Roosevelt	Dewey	7.5
1948	Truman	Dewey	4.5
1976	Carter	Ford	2.1
1968	Nixon	Humphrey	0.7
1960	Kennedy	Nixon	0.2
Average			11.4

SOURCE: U.S. Department of Commerce, Bureau of the Census, *Statistical Abstract of the United States, 1982–83* (Washington, D.C.: Government Printing Office, 1982), p. 472.

TABLE 2.2

IDEOLOGICAL PREFERENCES OF VOTERS, 1976–1980

Ideology	November 1976 (Percentage)	November 1980 (Percentage)
Liberal	20	18
Moderate	48	51
Conservative	32	31

SOURCE: Kathleen A. Frankovic, "Public Opinion Trends," in Gerald M. Pomper et al., eds., *The Elections of 1980* (Chatham, N.J.: Chatham House, 1981), p. 114.

The question of whether the 1980 vote was more a rejection of Carter than an endorsement of Reagan and his program was put directly to the public. "Sixty-three percent said the Reagan victory was mostly a rejection of the Carter administration, whereas only 24 percent felt it was a mandate for conservatism. Even Republicans (54 to 34 percent) and self-described conservatives (57 to 30 percent) felt that the election was more a rejection of Carter than a conservative mandate." This interpretation finds support, moreover, in the 1980 congressional elections. The members of Congress who were defeated lost more as a result of their seniority and visibility than their support for liberal policies. Junior incumbents, both Democrats and Republicans, did better than their senior colleagues in many cases regardless of ideology.[15]

Even though most voters supported Reagan's stands only slightly more than they supported Carter's, the election was widely interpreted as a decisive mandate. The major reason probably was the electoral vote margin—489 to 49 (81.8 percent)—the third highest of the thirteen elections since 1932. Even casual observers of the election-night results could hardly avoid an overwhelming sense of a major sweep, thanks to the television image of the states going to Reagan. The margin of victory also was unexpected; as late as election day, the *New York Times* was reporting that predictions of Reagan's victory were still within the "margins of error" of various surveys. Further strengthening the impression of a Reagan mandate were the congressional races, which produced the largest presidential-election-year increase of House Republicans since 1920 and of Senate Republicans since 1868. Perhaps most important, the election gave Republicans control of the Senate for the first time since 1954, providing Reagan with an immensely helpful base of power in Congress and accentuating the sense of fundamental change. Finally, though voters did not support the specifics of the Reagan program, they did seem to be calling for something new. This is evident in the fact that traditional Democratic voters abandoned a Democratic presidential candidate *because* of economic issues—which usually work for the Democrats—suggesting the possibility of a more wholesale retreat from "liberalism." In short, although polling results suggest that the 1980 election represented merely what one expert has termed "a strong call for moderate change," administration officials had grounds to interpret it instead as a strong call for radical change, especially because the press and many members of Congress seemed prepared to go along with the administration view.[16]

An Uncomplicated Program. In addition to a conviction of its mandate, the Reagan administration had the advantage of a relatively simple and straightforward set of ideas about government that seemed to accord reasonably well with certain popular sentiments:

- That governmental—especially federal—involvement in domestic affairs, including economic affairs, had grown much too large and needed to be pared back extensively

- That American foreign policy had grown far too timid and that a more activist American presence geared to promoting American national interests and backed by a military force equal to or greater than that of the Soviet Union was urgently needed

- That "supply-side economics" (in particular large tax cuts) would
  limit the further growth of the federal government and simultaneously
  stimulate private-sector investment and economic growth

- That the government should strive to restore more traditional moral
  and religious values to American society, or at least to eliminate those
  government policies that impede the operation of those values[17]

These ideas conveniently tied together two principal concerns that pollsters had been detecting in the American population for more than a decade:
(1) dissatisfaction with the performance of the economy and (2) frustration
at the cost and apparent ineffectiveness of government. What Ronald Reagan
did was to convert these two concerns into a program of action by identifying
the growth of government as the cause of the poor performance of the economy. As a result, the administration was able to claim broad popular support
for the substance of its program despite the ambiguities of the electoral result.[18] Also, the simplicity and clarity of the ideas made executive branch
management a lot easier. Complex agonizing over policy could be dispensed
with in favor of clear-cut marching orders to shun increases in domestic
spending and favor defense outlays as far as possible.

Finally, the administration's political ideology fit well with the prevailing
constraints of the political system, which made it difficult to make progress
on a wide variety of goals at once. As such, it enabled the Reagan administration to overcome one of the widely perceived shortcomings of the Carter
presidency, its failure to articulate a clear-cut sense of purpose and direction
around which to mobilize public and congressional support. Reagan's Budget
Director, David Stockman, was quite explicit on this point in his "Economic
Dunkirk" memo (which served as the game plan for the administration's early
policy initiatives): "To prevent early dissolution of the incipient Republican
majority, only one remedy is available: an initial administration economic
program that is so bold, sweeping and sustained that it . . . totally dominates
the Washington agenda during 1981. . . ."[19]

The Reagan Strategy: Centralization in the Service of Decentralization

Not content to rest on its advantages, the administration developed an
active strategy for capitalizing on them that consisted of five key features: a
radical narrowing of the policy agenda so far as the president was concerned;
a highly centralized policy management process predicated on top-down budgeting and a tightly knit Executive Office working group to control the agenda;

close attention to political liaison, especially with Congress; an "administrative strategy" including careful personnel selection and use of administrative means to pursue policy goals; and finally, a capacity for pragmatic compromise when necessary to maintain the president's reputation as a winner. Taken together these steps significantly concentrate power in the presidency. In short, confronted by an entrenched liberal establishment, Reagan found it necessary to adopt the approach of Wilson and Roosevelt in order to pursue the objectives of Coolidge and Harding. To appreciate how the activist presidency, long considered the instrument of liberal goals, could function in Reagan's hands as the instrument of conservative purposes, we examine each element of the administration's strategy in more detail.

Restriction of the Central Agenda. At the heart of the Reagan administration's strategy was a concerted effort to limit the range of subjects in which the president was personally and publicly involved. This facet of the Reagan strategy was a direct outgrowth of one of the major criticisms of the Carter presidency—that it went off in too many directions at once—obscuring public priorities and clogging the channels of decision in Congress. It was also consistent with the administration's philosophical position, which stressed the need to reduce the number of issues that came to the federal government for resolution. Nevertheless, success in narrowing the agenda was by no means assured. A critical part of the Reagan constituency, after all, was more populist than conservative, more interested in the so-called social issues (e.g., abortion, school prayer, busing) than in the subtleties of supply-side economics.* This constituency continued throughout the administration to push hard for a broad assault on the social issues. That no such assault materialized was due partly to advice from the Republican leadership in the Senate, partly to the campaign commitments to bold economic initiatives, and partly to the exigencies of the budget process and the outlook of the new budget director, David Stockman. Stockman developed an economic proposal that was in and of itself so comprehensive and complicated that it would almost necessarily leave no room for any other item on the agenda. "To keep control of the agenda and to maintain Capitol Hill focus on the Stabilization and Recovery Program," Stockman urged that informal agreements be reached with the key Republican committee chairmen in the Senate to defer action on some of the pet projects of the New Right, such as "the labor policy agenda" (e.g., repeal of the

---

*Reagan actually ran behind Ford among business and professional people while chalking up most of his largest gains "among voters with cultural and religious issues on their minds— Northern Catholics, Orthodox Jews, Western Mormons and white Southern fundamentalist Protestants." Kevin Phillips, *Post-Conservative America: People, Politics, and Ideology in a Time of Crisis* (New York: Random House, 1982), p. 15

minimum wage and Davis-Bacon Act†) and the "Moral Majority agenda."
As Stockman successfully argued, "Pursuit of these issues during the 100-
day period would only unleash cross-cutting controversy and political pressures which would undermine the fundamental administration and Congressional GOP economic task."[20]

Centralization of Executive Decision Making. As originally contemplated, the Reagan administration planned to use a modified form of cabinet
government to operate the executive branch, with the cabinet functioning, in
Reagan's words, as an "inner circle of advisers—almost like a board of
directors," and a series of "cabinet councils" or subcommittees of the cabinet
serving to refine options for presidential consideration. Once the decision was
made to focus the agenda on the economic program, however, it became clear
that this vision of collegial decision making was unworkable, given the volume
and speed of the decisions required. Nor could the administration risk allowing
its allies to disrupt its central game plan by floating their own policy priorities.
Accordingly, executive branch decision making, at least for the major economic and budget decisions, was centralized in the Executive Office of the
President and, more specifically, in a relatively small group of key advisers
in the White House. This was achieved through two principal devices: first,
a transformed budget process; and second, a more informal White House
decision process overseen by the "triumvirate" of chief presidential aides
James Baker, Michael Deaver, and Edwin Meese.[21]

The reliance on the budget process was not surprising, given the
administration's emphasis on spending restraint. But the traditional budget
process—involving submissions from the departments and agencies indi-
vidually reviewed by OMB "examiners" and then assembled in the president's budget—was quickly seen as ill-suited to the administration's purposes
and timetable as was the notion of cabinet government. Instead, a radical
centralization of executive-branch decision making occurred in OMB as
an institution, and in David Stockman as an individual. Stockman and his
lieutenants formulated budgetary proposals from the "top down" with only
minimal involvement by agency staff and, frequently, only perfunctory
input from OMB staff. Furthermore, in the drive to maintain control over
the central budgetary agenda, Stockman subsequently took on many of the

---

†The Davis-Bacon law stipulates that contractors on projects supported with federal funds
must pay prevailing (i.e., union) wage rates. Opponents have long argued that this unnecessarily
inflates the costs of federally supported projects and increases unemployment by inducing employers to turn to labor-saving methods since they cannot hire low-skilled, nonunionized labor
at bargain wage rates.

traditional functions of agency heads in lobbying for the administration's budget in the Congress.[22]

Equally important, on the advice of congressional leaders, particularly Senator Pete Domenici (R-N.Mex.), the administration came up with a plan for maintaining the integrity and momentum of its budget as it moved through the Congress. The heart of this plan was the "reconciliation process," a complicated feature of the 1974 Congressional Budget Act intended originally to enable congressional Budget Committees to enforce spending targets in the final stages of the appropriations process. The Reagan administration, however, succeeded in moving a binding reconciliation measure to the beginning of the process, thereby wrapping the entire administration budget and program reform package into one massive piece of legislation—the Omnibus Budget and Reconciliation Act of 1981—that could be moved through the Congress under time deadlines set by the congressional budget process and overseen by the Budget Committees, rather than having it split apart into thirteen separate appropriation bills and scattered authorizing legislation as is commonly done. The administration was thus able to concentrate its political pressure on a few highly publicized congressional votes.[23]

If the budget process was the engine of the administration's reorientation of domestic policy, the driver was an informal working group of top White House aides that monitored congressional developments and fine-tuned the proposals in order to ensure congressional passage. At the heart of this group was the trio of Baker, Meese, and Deaver, who emerged during the administration's early months as a "subcommittee of the presidency." Despite disagreements and stylistic differences, these three managed to develop a working relationship that allowed the administration to present a remarkably solid front to the world. Operating through a "legislative strategy group" involving their own key aides and representatives from the White House legislative liaison operation and OMB, the triumvirate managed to settle the intense disagreements that inevitably arose as the president's program confronted the realities of congressional pressure and—perhaps more important—came up with critical mid-course corrections as elements of the administration program seemed to unravel in the latter part of 1981 and early 1982. The result has been government by floating, informal committee—hardly the arrangement most conducive to effective cabinet input, but one highly conducive to the conduct of an ongoing battle and negotiation with Congress.[24]

Another element of the Reagan White House, less important but still significant, was the network of cabinet councils established under the direction of Edwin Meese. Since these were not established until February 1981, by which time the central elements of the policy agenda had already been set, the councils, with the possible exception of the Cabinet Council on Economic

Affairs, ended up serving more of an information sharing than a decision-making purpose, ensuring a common administration front on sensitive issues. This use of the cabinet council structure as a way to control the cabinet rather than as a way to allow the cabinet to control the administration's agenda has been acknowledged by Meese. "The difference in this presidency," Meese pointed out, "is that Reagan has used his system so that the cabinet members feel closer to him than they do to their departments. And he gives them a lot of opportunity to remember that."[25]

In addition to a highly centralized budget process, a tightly structured White House-dominated policy management team, and a network of cabinet councils to keep cabinet members "on the team," the Reagan administration also made extensive use of a fourth mechanism for policy control: an elaborate procedure for regulatory clearance and review. Established by a presidential executive order in mid-February 1981, the Reagan regulatory review process built on a precedent going back to Richard Nixon and importantly expanded by both Gerald Ford and Jimmy Carter, all of whom sought in various ways to establish a presidential presence in reviewing the regulatory issuances of executive agencies, which previously had been made on the department's own authority following the review and comment requirements stipulated in the Administrative Procedures Act. As the scope of federal regulatory activity and its accompanying costs and confusion mounted, this hands-off presidential approach came to be viewed as inadequate, particularly in the face of congressional threats to take a more direct hand in regulatory oversight itself through imposition of the so-called legislative veto.*[26]

President Ford began, and President Carter elaborated, procedures to review selected agency regulations with an eye to evaluating their benefits against their costs. President Reagan expanded and strengthened these procedures further, establishing a Task Force on Regulatory Relief under the chairmanship of Vice President Bush to develop regulatory policy and adjudicate regulatory disputes, and creating a more formal institutional structure within OMB to review proposed regulatory issuances of the departments and agencies before their publication in the *Federal Register* and determine whether they met more stringent cost-benefit standards. Taken together, these steps significantly expanded central presidential influence over the regulatory process and over the policy process more generally.[27]

---

*A legislative veto typically allows one house of Congress, and occasionally a single committee, to disapprove a regulation issued by an executive branch agency and thereby prevent the agency from promulgating it. Recent court decisions have significantly narrowed the permissible range of such vetoes.

Improved Political Mobilization. The Reagan strategy also involved a comprehensive effort at political mobilization aimed at both Congress and the public at large. This effort was spearheaded by the president himself. Certainly in the period following the attempted assassination, the president managed to use dramatic television appearances and other media events to solidify his hold on the electorate, putting tremendous pressure on Congress to give him what he wanted. But Reagan did not leave it at that. He followed up his effective television appearances with a more old-fashioned type of political hand holding that paid handsome rewards in its own right. The courting of Congress began even before his election. In 1977 Reagan had organized a political action committee, the Citizens for the Republic, to finance Republican candidates; in the 1980 campaign, Reagan supporters in Congress created a network of congressional advisory committees to assist him. In September 1980, candidate Reagan appeared with congressional Republicans on the steps of the Capitol in a "media event," in which they all pledged support for a compact of principles. These efforts continued during the transition with a series of meetings and social gatherings with members of Congress. Although the president was subsequently criticized by some for his apparent lack of substantive knowledge, his personal charm and evident enjoyment of political life earned him real popularity on the Hill despite considerable hostility to his programs.[28]

The president's personal efforts at maintaining legislative good will were augmented by the substantive contributions of the White House legislative strategy group, mentioned earlier, and by the fence tending of the formal legislative liaison operation in the White House. Unlike his predecessor, Reagan took pains to assemble an experienced legislative liaison team to maintain contact with Congress and to improve the general climate of presidential-congressional relations. Although the liaison office does not set the overall bargaining strategy or carry out negotiations, it does supply invaluable intelligence in deciding strategy. As Kenneth Duberstein, who took over the office in 1982 put it, the function of the office is " 'handicapping' Congress: I'm there to say, 'This has a chance of flying if it's done this way.' "[29]

To reach beyond the halls of Congress, the administration also developed an impressive public relations operation, including an in-house pollster, a public liaison office, a political affairs staff, and a separate White House Planning and Evaluation Office to chart broad trends in public attitudes that might have implications for the president down the road. As one long-time president watcher has noted: "Perhaps more than any other administration, the Reagan White House uses polling and public opinion analyses and media and marketing research as contributory elements in the decision-making process and the selling of the presidency. This is probably not surprising considering the high state of the art and the fact that Ronald Reagan, the 'Great Communicator,' is President.''[30]

The Administrative Presidency. A fourth key element in the Reagan administration's strategy of governance has been its reliance, wherever possible, on administrative instead of legislative changes to implement policy. Since the success of this strategy rests on the presence of reliable administration supporters in key bureaucratic positions, the administration paid close attention to the appointment process. As one observer has noted, ''The predominant characteristic of the Reagan approach to personnel selection was its emphasis on centralized, unrelenting White House control of the appointment process.'' The control was achieved through a variety of means: starting the personnel search early; giving the personnel chief access to the president; discouraging independent ''head hunting'' on the part of cabinet secretaries; making a heavy commitment of senior White House staff time to the selection process; and reserving for the White House all final decisions even on subcabinet selections. Also, the Reagan personnel selection process subjected candidates to an unprecedented effort to ''align presidential appointment decisions with presidential policy objectives.'' Appointees were carefully screened for policy and political background, legislative ties, ethics, and general compatibility with the core team—with sign-offs required from key people in each area.[31]

The early appointees at the cabinet level turned out to be more moderate, pragmatic, and politically balanced than might have been expected (David Stockman, James Watt, and Jeane Kirkpatrick constituting the more prominent ideologues). But Reagan's second round of appointments, to subcabinet positions, exhibited ''an uncommon degree of ideological consistency and intensity.'' In addition, the Reagan administration extended the reach of political appointments much further down into the operating staffs of the agencies, filling a higher proportion of allowable noncareer senior executive positions than had been done in the previous administration, so that noncareer appointees as of September 1983 constituted over 10 percent of the executive population for the first time. In addition, by August 1983 the number of Schedule C (political) appointees to lower-level positions was greater than the total number employed under Carter during his four-year term.[32]

While moving ideologically screened appointees in, the administration also moved career federal employees out. From January 1981 to September 1983, the civilian (not including Post Office or Defense) employment of the government dropped by 92,000—7.4 percent—from 1,240,000 to 1,148,000. Twelve thousand employees lost their jobs as a result of reductions in force

(RIFs) in FY 1981 and 1982. In the Labor Department, for example, RIF notices were sent to the entire management staff of the Employment and Training Administration, and after the required notice period elapsed, a large number were terminated. Also, the administration made generous use of the provisions of the Civil Service Reform Act of 1978 to reassign executives from one job or geographic location to another, resulting in some controversial and well-publicized resignations.[33]

The real heart of the administrative strategy, however, was not simply to put ideologically sympathetic personnel into sensitive administrative positions, but to encourage them to use their administrative power to advance the administration's policy objectives. Broadly speaking, this took three forms:

- The administration launched an early assault on pending regulations, killing the numerous regulations that had been issued during the final months of the Carter regime and using the new presidential executive order and OMB procedures to slow the issuance of new ones.

- Enforcement action diminished in many regulatory areas because of severe budget cuts, staff reductions, and a general easing of regulatory vigor. Federal Trade Commission Chairman James Miller, for example, cut personnel in his agency's local offices and its Bureau of Competition from 350 to fewer than 200. Secretary of the Interior James Watt closed regional surface mining offices and eliminated dozens of federal mine inspectors, and enforcement activity slowed as well in the Occupational Safety and Health Administration (OSHA), the National Highway Traffic Safety Administration (NHTSA), the Antitrust division of the Justice Department, and the Environmental Protection Agency (EPA).

- Reagan appointees used their administrative flexibility to reinterpret the conduct of agency business in accord with the administration's philosophy. Thus, for example, the Mine Safety and Health Administration, the EPA, and OSHA began to stress cooperation with business rather than confrontation in achieving regulatory compliance.[34]

In short, while press and public attention focused on the central legislative struggle over the budget and taxes, an ideologically oriented team of subcabinet officials moved into place and began implementing the Reagan agenda by administrative means, particularly in the regulatory arena.*

---

*For additional detail on some of these actions, see chapters 5 and 9 of this volume.

Pragmatism. Finally, in its approach to governance, the Reagan administration has exhibited an important element of pragmatism. Pragmatism has not, to be sure, generally characterized the president himself; by all accounts, he has tended to resist movement from his basic game plan more stubbornly than have many of his close advisers. Rather, pragmatism has been a characteristic of the staff system and decision apparatus the president has created, which balances those staff members whose principal concern is allegiance to a central policy agenda with others whose principal concern is maintaining a modicum of support within the other centers of political power, most notably, Congress.

The resulting tension, of course, has spawned more than its share of internal disputes, some of which occasionally spill over into public forums, and many of which cause delays that alienate potential moderate allies. But it has also led the administration to some important tactical retreats that have served its strategic objectives well. Most notable, perhaps, was the endorsement of a major tax increase in mid-1982, when it began to be apparent that the hoped-for economic recovery had not materialized. Similar was the administration's last-minute endorsement of the FY 1983 budget resolution, which ran counter to the administration's original proposals. In short, the administration has exhibited a political appetite for remaining on the winning side, even at the sacrifice of some ideological purity.

Summary. The Reagan administration thus entered office facing a formidable array of obstacles to the conservative program it was committed to implementing, but also with a number of important advantages. These included the popularity and persuasiveness of the president himself and the perceived mandate of the 1980 election. Facing a Democratic majority in the House and the potential for splits in the ranks of its own party in the Senate, its strategy was essentially opportunistic—to move quickly, before the opposition could organize, to rely heavily on the personal popularity of the president, and to use whatever tactical maneuvers were available, including administrative changes instead of legislative ones, top-down budgeting, tight control of the policy agenda from the center, and unorthodox use of the reconciliation provisions of the congressional budget process.

Against this backdrop, how does the administration measure up against the three standards of presidential effectiveness identified earlier—success in implementing its basic program, improvement in the institutions of government, and long-run programmatic viability? It is to these questions that we turn in the next two sections, looking first at the immediate programmatic success and then moving to an assessment of the longer-run effects of this administration on the country's political institutions and on public support for its policies.

The Record

In terms of the first standard of effectiveness identified above—success in carrying out the basic features of its programmatic goals—the Reagan administration may well be judged one of the most effective presidencies in recent history. Certainly in its first nine months in office, the administration made a significant downpayment on its long-run objective of changing the terms of the national policy debate, putting in place a significant constraint on federal domestic spending, setting in motion a major defense buildup, and restraining the growth of federal regulation. Yet on closer scrutiny it is also clear that the administration hardly suspended the prevailing realities of American politics noted earlier, and that it soon found itself stymied like many of its predecessors. Indeed, there is a sense in which the Reagan administration, while winning many of the early battles, may be in danger of losing the war. To see this, it is useful to review briefly the record the administration compiled in both the legislative and administrative arenas.

Legislative Record

Despite a popular impression of unmitigated success, the Reagan administration's dealings with Congress have followed three more or less distinct phases that resemble all too clearly the course that previous presidencies have taken, with an initial period of achievement followed by periods of congressional dominance and legislative stalemate. As Senator Slade Gorton (R-Wash.) put it, "1981 was the year of the president. 1982 was the year of the Senate Republicans. And 1983 is the year of living dangerously."[35]

The Year of the President. The Reagan administration's reputation as a highly effective David in its battles with an obdurate congressional Goliath was set in its first nine months in office, during which it managed to push through Congress the central features of its Economic Recovery Program: domestic budget and tax cuts, accompanied by a massive defense buildup. Two triumphs in the summer of 1981, the massive Omnibus Budget and Reconciliation Act and the Economic Recovery Tax Act of 1981—symbolized the achievement and cemented for many the president's reputation as an effective leader who could make government work.

Three factors in Congress contributed most significantly to these achievements: Republican solidarity, the support of a key group of conservative southern Democrats in the House (the Boll Weevils), and a spirit of resignation among the House Democratic leaders.

Republican solidarity was particularly evident in the Senate, where the party had acquired majority status for the first time in decades. But the sense of responsibility for advancing the president's programs was strong among House Republicans as well. As Max Friedersdorf, Reagan's legislative liaison chief observed, "The young Republicans are extremely aggressive to make their mark. They want to win and they are fully aware they have power in unity." This sense of "united we conquer" was encouraged by the White House, by the flexible leadership that both Senate and House Republicans chose for themselves—Howard Baker in the Senate, and Robert Michel in the House—and by the common debt Republican congressmen owed to the GOP national fund-raising effort, which was able by 1980 to contribute substantial amounts of money to Republican candidates.[36]

Republican support for the president's program was hardly automatic, however. Early on, for example, the Republican-dominated Senate Budget Committee rejected the president's FY 1982 budget proposal out of hand because of what the committee considered (correctly, as it turned out) to be overly optimistic economic assumptions and insufficient concern for the deficit problem. Also, moderate Republicans from the midwest and northeast (the so-called "Gypsy Moths") threatened to defect from the ranks over some of the proposed cuts in areas of particular concern to their regions, such as mass transit, student loans, and energy conservation aid. To counter the potential defections, the administration struck some strategic bargains, moderating somewhat certain of the proposed cuts. Also, the administration's decision to keep the divisive social issues—school prayer, antiabortion, busing—largely off the legislative agenda, went a long way toward preserving moderate support.[37]

These efforts paid off handsomely. House Republicans were unanimous, 190-0, in their support for the president on the first budget resolution (Gramm-Latta I). On Gramm-Latta II, the endorsement of the president's reconciliation package, House Republicans voted 190-1. In the Senate, on the budget cut instructions, Republicans voted 51-1 in favor of the president's position. Overall, Republican Senators voted with Reagan 80 percent of the time in 1981, the greatest loyalty any president has commanded from members of his own party in the 30-odd years of *Congressional Quarterly* voting studies.[38]

Equally crucial to the administration's early achievements was its success in attracting the support of conservative southern Democrats (the so-called "Boll Weevils"). To be sure, Republicans and conservative southern Democrats have been making common cause in Congress for years, but this "conservative coalition" nevertheless had its most efficacious year ever in 1981, winning 92 percent of the votes in which it was active, and providing the critical margin of 30 to 60 votes Reagan needed to carry his budget and tax proposals in the House.[39]

Who were these Boll Weevils, and what induced them to defy their party and support Ronald Reagan in 1981? As table 2.3 suggests, the Boll Weevil alliance with Reagan does not seem to have resulted from fear of losing to a Reagan Republican in an election since the Boll Weevils generally won in 1980 by more substantial margins than the Democratic opponents of the president in their states. The operative element, rather, seems to have been simple ideological affinity reflecting constituencies that tended to be more rural, pro-Reagan, and generally with lower proportions of blacks in their populations than the districts of southern Democrats who opposed Reagan. Interestingly, the Boll Weevils were also more junior than their southern Democratic colleagues who voted against Reagan and less likely to hold chairmanships—suggesting that they felt less a part of the congressional establishment and more disposed to follow the lead of a popular president who

TABLE 2.3

Comparison of House Democrats from Five Southern States: Reagan Supporters Versus Opponents of Gramm-Latta I

	Reagan Supporters ("Boll Weevils") n = 24	Reagan Opponents n = 20
Average percentage of votes won by representatives in their districts in election of 1980	77	70
Average years in office (as of November 1980)	7	13
Percentage holding committee chair	4	55
Percentage holding subcommittee chair	29	55
Average rating by Americans for Constitutional Action[a]	55	33
Average percentage of vote for Carter in 1980 in district	47	53
Average percentage minority population in district[b]	23	40
Average percentage rural population in district	40	26

Source: Compiled from data in Alan Ehrenhalt, ed., *Politics in America: Members of Congress in Washington and At Home, 1982* (Washington, D.C.: Congressional Quarterly Press, 1982) and U.S. Department of Commerce, Bureau of the Census, *Congressional District Data Book, 93rd Congress* (Washington, D.C.: Government Printing Office, 1973).
Note: The states are Georgia, Mississippi, Missouri, North Carolina, and Texas. Gramm-Latta I was the first budget resolution for FY 1982.
a. The ACA is a conservative lobby group which rates congressmen according to their agreement with ACA positions. "100" indicates perfect agreement with the conservative position.
b. Includes blacks in all states and Hispanics in Texas.

had carried their districts and, not coincidentally, could offer them media coverage and a pivotal seat at the budget table.

The president consciously cultivated this disposition, both by offering not to campaign personally against the Boll Weevils (to the dismay of some House Republicans who hoped for a House majority) and by offering them policy concessions beneficial to their constituents. In his March 10, 1981 budget proposals, for example, Reagan protected funding for big southern public works projects such as the Clinch River, Tennessee, breeder reactor and the Tennessee-Tombigbee waterway; and to his tax bill he added new breaks for oil producers and changes in estate taxes attractive to farmers and small businesses. He also dropped his objections to new sugar price supports and to continuing the highly regulated peanut program.[40]

Finally, the "Year of the President" owes much to the behavior of the House Democrats, who chose a strategy of concession over defiance. Fearing a potential realignment in the electorate toward the Republicans and the more immediate possibility that southern House Democrats would bolt and vote with Republicans in organizing the House, Speaker Tip O'Neill quickly gave up one of his greatest powers—control of the legislative agenda. As one of his advisers explained: "What the Democrats did, in extraordinary fashion, was to recognize the cataclysmic nature of the 1980 election results. The American public wanted this new president to be given a chance to try out his programs. We weren't going to come across as being obstructionists." Even in their own bills, Democrats conceded a lot to Reagan: as a House Democratic whip acknowledged: "We have no game plan. We're just going to get killed. It's really pathetic."[41]

The Year of Congress. The momentum of Reagan's initial congressional victories declined abruptly in the late summer of 1981, however, as the economy refused to meet the administration's expectations and deficits began to mount. The administration's new "fall budget offensive" met with a cool reception in Congress, which approved only half of what the administration wanted. By the time the administration submitted the FY 1983 budget in February 1982, opposition was running high even among Republicans, and the Republican-dominated Senate Budget Committee rejected the administration's budget 21-0 in early April 1982.

When the president refused to compromise with congressional moderates, congressional leaders, particularly in the Republican Senate, decided to take matters into their own hands. The result was a budget proposal essentially drafted in Congress which denied the administration most of its proposed additional domestic budget cuts and provided for a significant tax increase hitherto adamantly opposed by the president. In the end, the administration accepted the package and worked for its passage, though the result was a far cry from what it had proposed. At the same time, the administration was stalled on many of its other legislative initiatives, including the new federalism proposals the president announced in his 1982 State of the Union message, the reauthorization of the clean air and water acts, regulatory process reform, and urban enterprise zones.

The Year of Stalemate. The worsening economic conditions throughout 1982 and the 1982 congressional elections, which yielded 26 additional House seats for the Democrats and eliminated a significant number of the so-called "Reagan robots" (the class of 1980 Republican representatives who had pinned their careers to the Reagan program) intensified the president's difficulties. With the economy and the electoral results spelling trouble for the president, the Republican coalition began to splinter and Democratic unity began to grow. For the first time in the Reagan era, House Democrats managed to pass their own budget plan. Senate Republicans attempted to find some common ground between House Democrats and the administration in order to scale back growing deficits but ultimately failed. Essentially, the political system settled down to a pattern of stalemate. As the deficit swelled, Congress and the president agreed to disagree on whether it was a problem and how to deal with it if it was, and the country drifted into what Senator Robert Dole referred to as an "aimless stupor" on economic policy, relieved only by an incipient recovery in mid-1983.[42]

The Administrative Record

A similar pattern of early success followed by stalemate and reversal characterized President Reagan's administrative record.* Here, as in the budget arena, the administration has altered the terms of debate, slowing the rush toward regulation and strengthening the commitment to the concept of calculating regulatory costs. But there were significant limitations to the achievements. In the first place, at the same time that it was reducing regulation, the administration was also taking some actions that increased it. This was particularly true in the management of federal assistance programs, where the drive to avoid fraud, waste, and abuse generated heavy costs in terms of new regulation. In the second place, the success the administration has had in reducing regulations at the federal level seems to have been partly reversed at the state and local level, raising the danger of significant variations in regulations applying to particular industries or products in different parts of the country. In the third place, the administration's early actions on the regulatory front created a political backlash that may, over the long run,

---

*More details on this subject can be found in chapters 5, 7, and 9.

reinforce the federal government's regulatory role. Perhaps most significantly, congressional hostility to the Reagan team's administrative actions undermined support in Congress for legislative change and contributed further to judicial intervention. David Stockman anticipated this in his Dunkirk memorandum and urged that "a fundamental legislative policy reform package" be developed to insert mandatory cost-benefit analysis into some of the basic enabling acts. "Without statutory changes," Stockman warned, "administrative rule-making revisions in many cases will be subject to successful court challenge."[43]

As predicted by Stockman, the inability of the administration to follow up its administrative actions with legislative change has caused problems for it in the courts. In fact, courts have overturned several of the administration's decisions, including its attempts to suspend the requirement for automatic seat belts or air bags in cars; to allow tax exemptions for private schools that practice racial discrimination; to refuse the participation by certain groups in the federal government's workplace charity drive; to require notification of parents when minors seek contraceptives; and to suspend standards of wear on auto tires.[44]

Faced with this backlash, the administration began to beat a retreat. Signs of retreat could be seen in the replacement of EPA Director Burford by William Ruckelshaus, and the departure of Watt at Interior. In August 1983, the president's task force declared that the regulatory problem had been solved and the task force disbanded. Around the same time the administration began to step up regulatory activity in several areas, including the restriction of the chemical ethylene dibromide (EDB); new guidelines for polluters to share toxic waste cleanup costs; emergency regulations to limit worker exposure to asbestos; the hiring of more air safety inspectors; the doubling of recalls of autos for safety reasons; stricter agreements with oil companies charged with overbilling and price violations; and preemption of state regulations concerning the use of roads by two-trailer trucks.[45]

A Summing Up

Despite a string of early successes, the Reagan administration's record of political achievements strongly resembles that of most other modern American presidents. Like them, Reagan managed to take advantage of a honeymoon period to push through a significant portion of his program. But like them also, he soon confronted some of the enduring obstacles to presidential influence and sometimes acted in ways that intensified them. In Reagan's case the initial victories were significant enough to alter some of the basic terms of the policy debate so that the effect of political stalemate was somewhat less than it might have been. Nevertheless, the frustration over mounting deficits, the backlash against the dismantling of federal regulatory involvement, and the inability to move forward on such widely touted initiatives as the ''new federalism'' proposals all reveal a familiar pattern. In short, evaluated against the standard of its success in implementing key elements of its program, the Reagan administration must be judged above average, but not overwhelmingly so. Although he is an effective political leader, Ronald Reagan has by no means escaped the normal rhythms of American politics.

The Legacy

The inability of the Reagan administration to extend its early successes beyond its first year in office, despite the president's personal popularity and political skill, points up the strength of the obstacles to effective presidential leadership identified earlier in this chapter. But it also raises important questions about the impact of this administration on the long-run operation of the American political system.

Ultimately, as we noted at the beginning of the chapter, the test of a presidency cannot be simply its success in implementing its policy agenda, important though that may be. Effective governance, particularly in a democracy, also requires a strong commitment to preserving the basic ''rules of the game,'' nurturing of the institutions and processes through which political decisions are reached and carried out, and pursuit of policy goals that can win long-run voter acceptance. In view of the infirmities in our institutions and processes discussed above, such commitments appear particularly critical; yet because of these infirmities, such commitment appears very hard indeed for politicians to muster. A tension seems to exist between what is required for short-run political success and what is required for long-run improvement in the basic institutions of government.[46] In the context of extensive fragmentation of power, long-run improvement in the functioning of the political system requires strengthening the central integrative institutions of government—parties, congressional leadership, broad-based interest groups—and reinforcing or building reliable institutional processes. However, to achieve short-run success, this same fragmentation encourages grabbing allies where they can be found; moving quickly, often without the necessary information or the time to build consensus; and disregarding existing institutions and processes when that is convenient.

This situation posed a particular problem for a presidency committed, as Ronald Reagan's was, to a major program of change inspired by a coherent ideology. Confronted by a Congress with split party control,

Reagan faced a choice between moderating his program and developing a working coalition with centrist elements of both parties in Congress, or sticking to the basics of his program in the hopes of achieving enough early success to set in motion political currents strong enough to alter the existing political realities, indeed strong enough to produce a major political realignment. Although the administration has followed both of these courses at different times, the latter course has clearly tended to dominate. Although this may yield significant long-run improvements in the operation of the political system, the evidence to date is hardly persuasive. Indeed, in some respects the administration's strategy seems equally or more likely to complicate the task of governance and possibly to unravel some of the administration's own achievements. To see this, it is necessary to explore two further dimensions of the Reagan administration's record—first, its impact of the nation's governance institutions and processes, both political and administrative; and second, the long-run political viability of its policy choices.

The Impact on Political Institutions and Processes

In his first year in office, President Reagan appeared to make some important contributions to strengthening the integrative mechanisms in the American political system. The administration's initial legislative victories restored a significant degree of confidence in the responsiveness of the system and the efficacy of the presidency. As one journalist noted, "President Reagan has made a mockery of the conventional wisdom that the country was ungovernable." According to a *New York Times*/CBS News poll in January 1984, 72 percent of a survey of registered voters concurred that Reagan had "strong qualities of leadership." This sense of presidential efficacy persisted, moreover, despite the subsequent lack of movement on the president's agenda after 1981.[47]

In addition to restoring an important measure of confidence in the presidency and in the capacity of the political system more generally, the Reagan administration has also bolstered the operations of the political parties. Most obviously, the administration's economic recovery program stimulated an unusually high degree of party voting in Congress, initially among the Republicans, and later, in reaction, among the Democrats. As measured by *Congressional Quarterly*, the extent of "party voting," that is, the share of votes in which a majority of one party votes on a different side of an issue from the majority of the other party, totaled 51 percent of all votes in 1983, up from about 42 percent in the last half of the 1970s.[48] Simultaneously, the administration gave its support to the on-going efforts of the Republican

National Committee to systematize and professionalize its direct mail fund raising—which efforts, in turn, prompted the Democrats to do likewise. As a result, the parties have actually managed to improve slightly their position as funders of political candidates during a period of extraordinary expansion of campaign finance costs. Between 1977–1978 and 1981–1982, party contributions to House and Senate candidates grew by 230 percent, while overall spending increased a somewhat smaller 195 percent (table 2.4). Despite this increase, of course, the parties still accounted for only 8 percent of the reported total expenditures of House and Senate candidates; nevertheless, their systematic attention to fund raising seems to have forestalled further deterioration of their position. What is more, the administration worked with the Republican National Committee to channel PAC money to particular Republican candidates in the 1982 election in what one observer called "an unprecedented White House coordination of political money."[49]

The Reagan administration has also experimented quite effectively with the "commission approach" to governance. The commission approach is not new, of course, but the Reagan team gave it a new twist by using commissions explicitly to "precook" a consensus in areas of great political sensitivity.[50] Most notable here is the Greenspan commission, organized in 1982 to develop

TABLE 2.4

Sources of Campaign Funds Contributed to House and Senate Candidates, 1977–1978 to 1981–1982

Sources	*1977–1978*		*1979–1980*		*1981–1982*	
	In $ million	*Percentage*	*In $ million*	*Percentage*	*In $ million*	*Percentage*
Party[a]	10.4	6	14.8	7	23.9	8
PACs	31.8	20	51.9	25	79.7	25
Individuals and others	120.3	74	144.0	68	213.2	67
TOTAL[b]	162.5	100	210.7	100	316.9	100

Source: U.S. Federal Election Commission, *FEC Reports on Financial Activity, 1977–1978, Interim Report No. 5, U.S. Senate and House Campaigns* (June 1979), pp. 31–32; *FEC Reports on Financial Activity, 1979–1980, Final Report, U.S. Senate and House Campaigns* (January 1982), pp. 49–50; *FEC Reports on Financial Activity, 1981–1982, Final Report, U.S. Senate and House Campaigns* (October 1983), pp. 33–34.

Note: Includes primary and general election financial activity of general election candidates only; some totals may not add because of rounding.

a. Party figures include direct contributions to candidates and expenditures made on behalf of candidates in the general election.

b. Includes party expenditures made in behalf of candidates. Excludes transfers between all committees within a campaign.

a politically viable solution to the intractable and controversial financing problems of the Social Security program. Following a politically disastrous administration initiative in this area in 1981, the president cooperated with congressional leaders in creating a commission that would involve those actors most crucial to the ultimate resolution of the problem. By getting all parties to agree on the basic facts of the situation before moving to potential solutions, and by securing presidential willingness to abide by the consensus solution, the commission was able to defuse significantly one of the great landmines in American politics.

Finally, the administration has made some headway in loosening the grip of narrow interest and advocacy groups on the policy process. It did so in part by shifting the locus of budget and entitlement decisions from the individual appropriations subcommittees and authorizing committees to the budget committees in Congress, where special interest contacts are more limited; in part by keeping attention focused on the budget aggregates rather than on the individual programs that comprise them; and in part just by moving so quickly that there was little opportunity for the mobilization of group responses. Also, the sweeping nature of the administration's proposals, both legislatively and administratively, encouraged the banding together of interest groups—particularly in the environmental area—a reversal, in part, of prior trends toward the proliferation of increasingly narrow groups. Finally, the administration worked effectively with some of the larger business coalitions, such as the U.S. Chamber of Commerce, to stimulate grass-roots support for its tax and budget proposals, buttressing the political credibility of these umbrella groups in the process.[51]

In spite of these useful contributions to strengthening some of the integrative institutions in the political system, however, the administration's overall record in this area looks more negative than positive, raising doubts about the durability of its achievements. The most obvious doubts arise from the hinging of achievement too narrowly on the personality and persuasive powers of Ronald Reagan himself. At each of several crucial points, major policy breakthroughs came to depend on the ability of the "great communicator" to convince the public and Congress to go along. Although effective in the resolution of isolated issues, this "cult of personality" approach leaves the operation of the political system vulnerable to the frailties and preferences of a single individual and to the fickleness of public affections. Ronald Reagan certainly has managed to sustain his personal popularity despite policy setbacks that would have sunk many previous presidents (prompting Representative Patricia Schroeder (D-Colo.) to label his administration the "Tefloncoated presidency"). Yet even Ronald Reagan has been vulnerable to swings in popular opinion. In fact, Reagan's public approval score during the first two years of his term was, on average, actually lower than Carter's during the comparable portion of his term, and lower than Nixon's during the first three years of their respective terms (table 2.5).

Perhaps most importantly, reliance on the president's personal popularity can encourage the misleading impression that efforts to build a broader and more enduring governing coalition are unnecessary. Although, as noted earlier, the administration made some useful contributions to the parties and other integrative institutions, its overall approach did little to foster, and in some respects it undercut, the formation of a durable coalition to sustain its policy achievements and overcome the forces of fragmentation in Congress and elsewhere. The building blocks for such a coalition were available in the senior Republican leadership in the Senate and House, as well as in some of the centrist Democratic leadership in the House, such as Budget Committee chairman Jim Jones and Ways and Means Committee chairman Dan Rostenkowski. While working with these leaders on occasion, the Reagan administration also frequently left them "twisting in the wind." During the first year, for example, the administration tended to bypass the Republican leadership in the House, dealing directly with the Boll Weevils and other Democratic moderates or conservatives on the crucial budget and tax bills. Similarly, in the initial budget battles of 1981 the administration persisted in advancing economic projections deemed indefensible by most of the Republicans on the Senate Budget Committee. As the credibility of these projections began to dissolve in the latter part of 1981 and into 1982, so too did the president's support among congressional moderates and conservatives, the groups most likely to have formed a stable working majority for him. Rather than meeting this moderate block midway, Reagan's style of governance, particularly after the first year, has been marked by ideological intransigence, last minute compromises, and opportunistic maneuvers that frequently alienated potential allies. Thus, the president gave scant encouragement until very late in the process to Republican Senator Robert Dole's 1982 effort to forge a tax bill

TABLE 2.5

PRESIDENTIAL APPROVAL RATINGS (*Percentage*)

	Average for Year			February
	1st Year	*2d Year*	*3d Year*	*4th Year*
Reagan	58	44	44	57
Carter	62	46	38	55
Nixon	61	57	50	52

SOURCE: *Gallup Report* (December 1983), p. 18 and *National Journal*, vol. 16, no. 9 (March 3, 1984), p. 440.

to offset the growing deficit, a pattern that was also evident on the FY 1983 budget and FY 1984 appropriations bills.

In short, faced with a significant opportunity to forge a moderate-conservative coalition in both the House and Senate behind a program of domestic spending constraint and military growth, Ronald Reagan has tended to stake out an extreme position, and hold out for the "whole loaf" when it has seemed clear to most that two-thirds of the loaf is all the political system will accommodate. Although a case can be made that this represents an effective bargaining strategy, the costs are considerable in terms of the staying power of the administration's policies and the consolidation of a workable coalition in Congress. By 1983, in fact, moderate Democrats in the House felt the president had cut the ground out from under them, and even Republican support for the administration had deteriorated considerably: On ten key issues, only four of fifty-four Republican Senators voted with Reagan every time, and the average GOP Senator voted against the party position three times.[52] Many key moderate-conservative leaders were rhetorically abandoning ship, and an unusual number in the House Republican leadership left the fray by retiring. (The retirement of Representative Barber Conable, ranking minority member of the House Ways and Means Committee, for example, was linked to his frustration over the administration's failure to work with him on the 1981 tax bill.)[53]

Beyond its dealings with the parties and congressional "centrists," moreover, the Reagan administration's dealings with interest groups may have sown seeds of future political difficulties. Despite its assault on the "interest group state," the Reagan administration actually augmented the power of some of the business lobbies by expanding the "revolving door" in government, whereby representatives of affected industries are appointed to positions in agencies that oversee their business.[54] Also, the administration's assault on some of the favored programs of environmental, consumer, and antipoverty groups produced a backlash that strengthened the position of many of its opponents.

The administration's hope, apparently is that its combative style and ideological rhetoric about government will pay dividends over the longer run in the form of a more basic political realignment in the country. In this view, by hanging tough, Ronald Reagan is defining the central issue in the 1984 election and thereby laying the foundation for what one observer has termed "the clearest and perhaps most important political choice (the American voters) have faced since 1936."[55]

Based on the evidence to date, however, the prospects for an enduring electoral realignment in the 1984 election are dubious at best. The 1980 election, as we have seen, did not signal a major shift to the right on the part of the American electorate, even though it did provide an endorsement for a significant modification of existing policy. The 1982 election reflected a similar ambivalence, with a surprising portion of the electorate expressing confidence in the Reagan economic program, given the recession then under way, but with significant losses for the Republican Party in both the House of Representatives and in state houses and governorships throughout the country.*[56]

Whatever progress the administration made in 1980 in developing a new governing coalition—of traditional Republican support groups augmented by blue-collar and lower-middle income voters—appears to have been partly offset by the deferral of the social issue agenda of principal concern to many of these new groups, by the economic downturn of 1982–1983, and by the extensive wooing of business groups in the tax and budget battles of 1981. Staffing changes in the White House public liaison position and a new emphasis on school prayer and other social issues signal some recognition of the need to recement the 1980 Reagan constituency. But even if the robust economic recovery continues—which many observers consider uncertain[57]—the prospects for an enduring electoral realignment and for a Republican takeover of the House of Representatives appear slim.

Certainly polling results provide little evidence of a major increase in Republican identifiers in the electorate. The proportion of Republican identifiers, though up somewhat from 1980, stands at about the same level in 1984 as it was in 1972, about 28 percent. Nor is there evidence of a major ideological reorientation. In 1981, according to the Harris survey, about 16 percent of American adults called themselves liberals, about 39 percent conservatives, and about 40 percent middle-of-the-road. In 1983 the liberal proportion was up two percentage points, the conservative proportion down three percentage points, and the middle-of-the-road proportion about even. On particular issues, a similar pattern held, with majorities sometimes favoring and sometimes opposing conservative positions.† The likelihood is strong,

---

*The Republicans lost seven governorships and nine state legislative chambers in the 1982 election. The 1982 election thus differs markedly from the midterm election preceding the 1936 election in which the Roosevelt coalition was cemented. In 1934 Roosevelt was rewarded with important Democratic gains in Congress.

†By 1983 nearly three-quarters of Americans favored a balanced budget amendment, school prayer, the death penalty (up from 54 percent in 1980 to 72 percent in 1982), and opposed busing of school children and legalizing marijuana. At the same time in 1982, a clear majority also opposed decreases in government social spending (66 percent), opposed increases in military spending (up from 27 percent in 1980 to 58 percent in 1982), favored the ERA (61 percent), and opposed a ban on federal financing of abortions (56 percent). *Gallup Report*, no. 206 (November 1982), pp. 3–20.

therefore, that the 1984 election will yield the same kind of ambiguous mandate as the 1980 and 1982 ones, with the outcome affected heavily by temporary economic conditions but not by basic changes in the outlook of the electorate or their attitudes towards government. To the extent this occurs, the alienation of the moderates will not have yielded a new governing coalition willing to endorse a larger dose of the Reagan program than the current centrist coalition would provide.[58]

The Impact on Administrative Institutions and Processes

As important as the contribution a presidency makes to the capacities for on-going political coalition building are its impacts on the central management processes and institutions of government—the civil service, the executive office of the president, the budget process, and the like. Quite apart from the substance of particular presidential agendas, these processes determine the capacity of the political system to function in ways that the public and elected officials consider appropriate. They constitute the infrastructure of political life; and, as such, they are all too often taken for granted, by both political leaders and those who evaluate their performance. Presidents have strong incentives to sacrifice the infrastructure when it stands in the way of their policy goals. Over time, however, such behavior can seriously undermine the capacity of the political system to deliver what is demanded of it.

As the "steward" of this infrastructure, the Reagan administration leaves a mixed legacy. On the positive side, the administration has increased presidential control of the budget process and facilitated more effective budgetary interaction with Congress, which has developed its own improved budget procedures. In the handling of executive branch policy development more generally, the cabinet committees and the Legislative Strategy Group have achieved more clarity about goals and priorities than attained by most administrations. Finally, the Reagan administration has brought to fruition the regulatory review procedures inaugurated by the Ford administration and elaborated under Carter, thus extending to the regulatory arena the integrative perspective hitherto characteristic only of budget and legislative deliberations.

Against these achievements, however, must be balanced a number of developments or considerations that raise serious questions about President Reagan's impact on the governmental infrastructure of the nation. We examine these developments below in three principal areas—the budget process, the administration's dealings with the permanent government, and the efforts to alter the Constitution by making it a vehicle for particular social preferences.

The Budget Process. Serving as it did as the centerpiece of the administration's entire program, the budget became an important vehicle for expanding presidential control over policy. In the process it also became politicized as never before, and consequently lost considerable credibility. The loss was costly not only for the president's relations with Congress (as discussed earlier), but also for the institutional health of the Office of Management and Budget (OMB), the presidential staff agency ultimately responsible for developing the president's budget each year. Despite the undisputed competence of Stockman, the budget director, and despite the prominence of the agency as a whole under Reagan, the permanent OMB staff has lost certain of its functions thanks to the practice of "top-down budgeting," which, in a context of heightened political sensitivity, threatens professional norms and institutional capacities. Contrary to the normal practice of percolating budget recommendations up through the organization from the "examining" staffs and divisions, under Stockman the staff has often been reduced to "running numbers" to service the director's decision making. With attention focused on the "macro" budget perspective and "across the board" actions, the role of OMB careerists and their program-specific knowledge has diminished, thus increasing the chance that good programs get tossed out along with the bad.[59]

This ad hoc use of the OMB career staff and resulting depletion of its program-specific expertise is, in turn, part of a broader failure to devise ways to institutionalize the new top-down approach to budgeting. In formal terms, the budget cycle continues to follow the pre-Reagan practice of soliciting agency input, which is then reviewed by OMB staff. But since these formal routines are increasingly irrelevant to the major decisions made by the director and the president, the role of the departmental and OMB personnel remains ambiguous at best, superfluous and costly at worst.[60]

The administration has also failed to come to terms with the "hidden budget" and uncontrollables identified earlier in this chapter. Some progress was made in the regulatory area through the review process noted, though the reaction to the administration's regulatory relief program in Congress shortcircuited efforts to provide a legislative underpinning to OMB's review function. In addition, the initial use of reconciliation in 1981 gave the administration some leverage over entitlement programs. At the same time, however, the "uncontrollable" share of the budget actually grew between 1981 and 1984 (particularly when long-term defense obligations are included), while the administration's preference for tax subsidies over direct outlays led to further growth in "tax expenditures."[61]

Finally, the Reagan administration has been inconsistent in its use of the congressional budget process, with its actions determined by tactical judgments based on the politics of the season. In 1981 the White House allied itself with the budget committees and used the reconciliation process to drive budget actions. But by 1983 the administration was prepared to give up on the Budget Committees and take its chances with the appropriations process instead. As one close student of budgeting put it, the Reagan administration's handling of budgetary politics has resulted in "a few budget victories but no durable means of support from those in Congress who share its guardianship values."[62] Although it succeeded in changing the terms of debate through its budget and tax victories in 1981, the administration has made only limited progress in institutionalizing a set of budget procedures likely to protect and extend its accomplishments.

The Career Civil Service. The same general lack of attention to institutional processes that characterizes the administration's handling of the budget has also been apparent in its treatment of the career civil service more generally. The numerous RIFs and transfers, as well as the administration's disavowal of any legitimate purpose for many ongoing federal programs, have taken a toll on staff morale and created considerable ambiguity about the responsibilities of federal bureaucrats. At the same time, the reliance on an administrative strategy to achieve policy objectives sometimes put agency staff in the awkward position of having to carry out instructions they felt were inconsistent with the statutes under which they are operating. Judicial rejection of many of the administration's regulatory interpretations testifies to the dilemma facing the career bureaucracy. Finally, the administration's tendency to appoint to subcabinet positions persons with strong ideological convictions and its efforts to plug information leaks from the bureaucracy has further undermined the opportunity for the bureaucracy to provide professional input that can influence policy decisions.[63]

Writing Policy into the Constitution. Perhaps the clearest indication of the predominance of policy objectives over institutional legacy lies in the administration's endorsement of measures to amend the Constitution in order to advance its social-issues agenda in such areas as school prayer and the balanced budget. More than any other institution, the Constitution has a specially protected place in American political life that most observers agree should be tampered with only in very unusual circumstances and for exceptional purposes. Whatever the merits of the social policies now being readied for constitutional enshrinement, therefore, serious questions must be asked about the institutional sensitivity of an administration that would readily alter the constitution to advance them.

Programmatic Viability

Beyond its impact on the basic institutions for achieving consensus and carrying out public functions, the Reagan administration has left a programmatic legacy that will continue to influence governance in America for some time to come. In a sense, of course, the substance of this legacy is the subject of the rest of this book; but here we are concerned not so much with its substance as with its political dimension—that is, with the contribution that this administration's programs have made to public confidence in government and, hence, to the future governability of the country. The positive aspects of this contribution—the curbing of inflation, the federalism initiatives, the slowing of federal regulatory growth—are amply documented elsewhere in this volume. Here, with all due caveats about the necessarily tentative nature of such judgments, we point out three reasons why, on balance, the Reagan administration's programmatic contribution may ultimately prove less durable than at first appears and may therefore raise questions about the political effectiveness of this presidency.

In the first place, having promised a government that will try less and therefore achieve more, the Reagan administration has contributed in its own way to the "politics of misplaced hopes" so characteristic of the past two decades. In making budget and tax reductions its principal domestic priorities, and in achieving some celebrated victories on these fronts in 1981, the administration projected an image of unusual efficacy; but since (for reasons discussed elsewhere in this book) the administration's budget strategy was never sufficient to bring expenditures into line with revenues, the upshot has been an escalating federal deficit, which grew from $79 billion in FY 1981 to $208 billion in FY 1983, and which the president's own budget projects, optimistically, to be close to $180 billion a year over the next three years. For the public at large, this outcome cannot help but appear puzzling indeed: on the one hand, there is a popular president doing battle against the behemoth of federal spending and apparently succeeding; but on the other hand, there is a deficit that continues to grow nevertheless. The administration, to date, has managed to fend off responsibility for this troubling state of affairs by assuming a "what, me worry?" posture and by pointing an accusing finger at Congress. Against the hoopla of the administration's early victories, however, the "fiscalization" of the domestic policy debate, the continuing dominance of budget problems on the nation's political agenda, will undoubtedly take its toll on public confidence in the administration's program and in the capabilities of the political system generally.[64]

This is particularly true, moreover, in view of what must certainly appear, in retrospect, to have been a significant missed opportunity to make serious headway on the main source of domestic budgetary growth—the middle-class entitlement programs such as Medicare—in the administration's first year in office, when the administration chose instead to patch over the budgetary realities with a combination of "unspecified savings" and rosy economic assumptions. The reluctance since then to forge the kind of centrist coalition that will be needed to make progress on these budgetary problems only adds to the political difficulties. Although this may all be part of a larger strategy to build the political support needed to break the political logjam on the entitlement programs, the dangers to credibility and public confidence in government in the interim are considerable.

A second-order threat to the political viability of the administration's program arises from other areas of "missed opportunity," where the administration alienated interest groups prepared to do business with it and surrendered opportunities for more significant policy advance. For example, as discussed above and in chapters 5 and 9, a bipartisan consensus had formed around the need for regulatory reform by the time the administration entered office; but instead of building on this consensus, the administration too often politicized the regulatory reform effort, undercutting the position of potential moderate allies and activating opponents. In the process, it lost a number of opportunities to enshrine its regulatory changes in legislative form and opened its regulatory reform program to successful challenge in the courts. Similarly, in its efforts at intergovernmental reform and the expansion of partnerships with the private, nonprofit sector (see chapters 7 and 8, respectively), the administration has stated some widely applauded goals but pursued them in ways that alienated potential allies. Although it is too soon to know what organized forms the alienation may take, it is not too soon to note that potentially formidable allies are potentially formidable foes and that the failure to enlist the support of those most intimately concerned with particular reforms does not bode well for the long-term viability of the changes.

Finally, the Reagan administration's promotion of the "politics of detachment"—detachment of the government from the problems of the nation and detachment of the presidency, or at least this president, from the problems of the government—may create its own backlash. By taking so strident an antigovernment posture, the administration was clearly taking advantage of a strong antigovernment mood in the nation. The problem, however, is that virtually every public opinion poll taken at the time of the 1980 election and since has demonstrated that the public's antigovernment mood is nicely balanced by a progovernment mood: people register eagerness to reduce government involvement in the abstract but insist on retaining a significant governmental role in programs affecting them. If the electorate has rejected the old government-is-always-good philosophy of traditional liberalism, it has certainly not embraced the government-is-always-bad philosophy of tradi- tional conservatism. Perhaps the most positive contribution this administration has made to American governance has been to force public attention to the hard choices lying between these two extremes. But it has yet to articulate a roadmap to traverse this middle ground.[65]

Conclusion

Both by constitutional design and political necessity, governance is a joint enterprise in America. With power dispersed, values disparate, and authority shared among multiple institutions, political leadership requires not simply the articulation of goals but also the mobilization of support, the mustering of alliances, and the building of collaborative relationships with the other major centers of political power.

The Reagan administration has made substantial progress toward effec- tive governance in at least some of these terms. Committed to a major re- orientation of national policy, enjoying a considerable electoral mandate, yet confronting serious obstacles to the exercise of political power, the admin- istration developed a strategy of governance that fit well both its own ideology and the prevailing realities of American politics—a strategy that featured swift, preemptive action, a radical narrowing of the relevant policy agenda, centralization of executive branch policy management in the Executive Office of the President, and heavy reliance on the unusual communications skills of the president himself.

Viewed against the obstacles it faced, the achievements of this admin- istration are considerable. It made fiscal restraint the principal domestic prior- ity. It slowed regulatory expansion. It put a lid on revenue growth. And it set in motion a massive defense build-up.

Viewed against the long-term operation of the political system, however, the record of this administration is far more mixed. While contributing im- portantly to popular confidence in the "governability" of the nation and strengthening at least one of the political parties, the administration failed to create a durable political coalition to sustain its achievements or even take full advantage of the opportunities it enjoyed. To the contrary, it often acted in ways that alienated potential moderate allies, unnecessarily mobilized op- position, and weakened or abused institutions and processes needed to make the government operate. What is more, having taught the lesson of restraint, it did not come forth with a politically viable program to bridge the gap between the government the population apparently still demands and the one the administration's revenue and defense policies seem able to provide.

Rather than relying on collaboration with the existing political powers-that-be and accepting the joint character of governance in America, the administration seems to be putting its faith in a far more radical, and uncertain, political strategy—one that seeks to change the basic constellation of political power in the nation through a major electoral realignment. Given the extraordinary personal popularity of Ronald Reagan and the economic recovery that is well underway as the 1984 election approaches, there is at least the chance that an unambiguous electoral mandate of this sort is possible. But a more likely outcome, whoever wins the 1984 election, is for continued fragmentation of effective political power, and hence continued need for meaningful cooperation across partisan and institutional lines. In short, what will be needed as always are not the skills of the partisan ideologue, but those of the collaborative politician and political leader—skills that Ronald Reagan has sometimes demonstrated, but that his administration has often neglected to apply.

CHAPTER 3

THE ECONOMY
THE KEY TO SUCCESS

Isabel V. Sawhill
Charles F. Stone

Ronald Reagan took office with high hopes that a combination of tax and spending cuts, monetary restraint, and regulatory relief would eliminate the problems of inflation and sluggish growth that had plagued the economy during the 1970s. The president believed that his economic program, with its emphasis on limiting the role of government and providing incentives to the private sector, would rapidly restore sustainable, noninflationary growth.

Inflation did indeed decline, to its lowest level in over a decade. However, the battle against inflation was a costly one, causing a deep recession in 1981–1982 and an unemployment rate close to 11 percent. In 1983, the economy began to expand with the promise of still better times ahead, but achieving that promise will require that federal budget deficits be brought under control in a timely fashion.

This chapter evaluates whether the administration's diagnosis of the problems facing the American economy in 1981 was sound; whether its program was well designed to deal with those problems; whether the 1981–1982 recession was an unavoidable cost of lowering inflation; and whether the president's program has improved the prospects for long-term growth.[1]

Economic Developments: 1981–1984

Candidate Reagan was successful in exploiting the widespread public perception that standards of living were lower in 1980 than they had been

69

four years earlier.* Moreover, when President Reagan took office at the beginning of 1981, unemployment stood at more than 7 percent, consumer prices had risen by 24 percent over the previous two years, and interest rates were high and volatile.

The president proposed to solve the nation's economic problems with a four-point program of tax cuts, less growth in federal spending, regulatory relief, and a slower and steadier growth in the money supply. The first three elements were intended to provide greater incentives for people to work, save, and invest productively so that the economy would expand. Slower growth in the money supply was designed to lower inflation.[2]

Critics argued that monetary restraint would lower output and employment before having much effect on inflation and that a combination of monetary restraint and fiscal stimulus was the wrong mix of policies for bringing down interest rates and encouraging economic growth. The administration responded that inflationary expectations would quickly dissipate once people recognized its steadfast commitment to lowering inflation and that the need to endure a period of economic slack could thus be avoided. The administration argued further that its spending, tax, and regulatory policies, although aimed primarily at improving long-term growth, would also increase output in the short run. The promise of a painless victory over inflation and renewed economic prosperity was thus premised on a new view of how the economy would respond to these policies.

Because he believed that lower inflation and higher real (inflation-adjusted) growth could be achieved simultaneously and that future budget savings that had not yet been fully specified would be enacted, President Reagan was able to propose both a large cut in taxes and a rapid buildup in national defense while still projecting a balanced budget by 1984. He was largely successful in getting the Congress to accept his spending and tax program. The Federal Reserve had begun to slow the growth of the money supply following the appointment of Paul Volcker in 1979 and continued to do so. In spite of this cooperation from the Congress and the Federal Reserve, the predicted economic recovery failed to materialize. Interest rates began to rise, and the economy headed into a recession as the ink was still drying on the 1981 spending and tax legislation because slower money growth was already working to depress economic activity. By the end of 1982 real gross

---

*The purchasing power of the average family's income declined between 1976 and 1980, but income per person (after taxes and adjusted for inflation) was still rising because families were getting smaller.

national product (GNP) was lower than it had been three years earlier and the unemployment rate had risen to nearly 11 percent, its highest rate since the Great Depression.

The prospect of balancing the budget in the foreseeable future also disappeared once the administration realized the full impact of its tax and spending decisions and incorporated them, along with more realistic economic assumptions, into its budget forecast.

Despite these adverse developments, one of the president's expectations was realized. The rate of inflation fell rapidly after 1980. Consumer prices, which had risen more than 12 percent in 1980, rose less than 4 percent in 1982. Interest rates began to fall as well. By the beginning of 1983 the economy began to recover from the recession, with consumer spending leading the way. Unemployment fell rapidly and the inflation rate remained below 4 percent. By 1984 the income of the average family, after correcting for inflation, was 3 to 4 percent higher than it had been in 1980 (see chapter 10).

Nevertheless, the recession had been so deep and so prolonged that this rise in family income was less than half the average gain experienced over comparable periods during the last thirty years. Furthermore, a full year into the recovery the unemployment rate remained higher than when President Reagan took office. Finally, although interest rates fell, they did not fall as fast as inflation. Real interest rates actually rose between 1980 and 1984.

High real interest rates have made borrowing expensive and have discouraged investment. The Reagan business tax cuts offset the effects of high interest rates for some categories of investment, especially business plant and equipment, but not for all. High interest rates have also made U.S. financial assets attractive to foreigners, increasing foreign demand for dollars and driving up the value of the dollar relative to other currencies. The strong dollar, in turn, has made U.S. goods more expensive in international markets. This situation has aggravated the problems of industries, like automobiles and steel, that already faced strong international competition and created problems for other industries, like agriculture, that normally enjoy a strong international market. Nevertheless, high interest rates and a strong dollar have not limited the overall strength of the recovery, despite their hurting specific sectors.

Clearly, the Reagan Economic Recovery Program has not achieved all that it promised, but given the normal tendency of presidents to promise more than they can deliver and given the difficult problems President Reagan inherited, his own promises are not the only standard by which he should be judged. It is equally important to ask whether the Reagan program offered a reasonable diagnosis of what was wrong with the economy and a reasonable set of policies to deal with those problems—a question to which we now turn.

Diagnosing the Problem

Every administration is in favor of price stability, high employment, and economic growth. But agreement on exactly how these goals should be defined is another matter.[3] Everyone agrees that reducing inflation from double-digit figures is important, but not everyone would pursue this objective with equal zeal or insist that a zero rate of inflation should be the ultimate objective. High employment is usually defined as the rate of unemployment consistent with no *additional* inflation, a rate currently believed by many, but not all, economists to be in the neighborhood of 6 percent. Adequate growth usually means achieving a long-term rate of increase in the supply of output at least as fast as that experienced in the past—say 3 to 4 percent per year.

Whatever the targets chosen, the three goals almost inevitably conflict, not only with one another but also with other policy priorities. Differences in how these conflicts are resolved are what most distinguish one administration's policies from another's. For example, environmental regulations may adversely affect the economy's growth rate but be considered essential to protecting human health. Unemployment is obviously undesirable but may be the only way to curb inflation in the short run. How an administration resolves these and other conflicts reveals far more about its philosophy than its economics, but we can assess the skill and intelligence with which it manages the inevitable conflicts and its ability and willingness to educate the public about the hard choices that have to be made.

Whatever one's view about the relative importance of price stability, high unemployment, and economic growth, there is general agreement that the economy did not perform well with respect to any of these goals during the 1970s. Unemployment averaged more than 6 percent in the 1970s after averaging less than 5 percent through the 1950s and 1960s; consumer prices rose four times as much in the 1970s as they had in the 1950s and 1960s; and productivity grew only half as much.[4] While these problems seemed particularly acute when President Reagan took office, they had been building for some time.

The president placed the blame for this disappointing economic performance squarely on the federal government:

> The most important cause of our economic problems has been the government itself. The Federal Government, through tax, spending, regulatory, and monetary policies, has sacrificed long-term growth and price stability for ephemeral short-term goals. In particular, excessive government spending and overly accommodative monetary policies have combined to give us a climate of continuing inflation. That inflation itself has helped to sap our prospects for growth. In

addition, the growing weight of haphazard and inefficient regulation has weakened our productivity growth. High marginal tax rates on business and individuals discourage work, innovation, and the investment necessary to improve productivity and long-run growth. Finally, the resulting stagnant growth contributes further to inflation in a vicious cycle that can only be broken with a plan that attacks broadly on all fronts.[5]

Given this diagnosis of the problem, the solution was clear: less government. To see whether it was the right prescription, we look first at the reasons economic growth slowed in the 1970s and then at the reasons inflation and unemployment rose.

The Slowdown in Economic Growth and Productivity

Americans have come to expect continual improvements in their material standard of living because this is what they have in fact experienced. Since 1948, real output per capita has risen at an average annual rate of 1.9 percent, and real incomes have approximately doubled. Contributing to this rise in incomes were increases in labor force participation (the proportion of the adult population that works) and increases in labor productivity (output per hour). The latter is what permits real wages to rise and results from increases in capital per worker and such factors as education and technology that lead to improvements in overall economic efficiency.

Living standards rose especially rapidly between 1948 and 1973, when output per capita grew at an average annual rate of 2.2 percent. There was little increase in the proportion of the population that worked during this period, but growth in labor productivity was so strong (3.0 percent per year) that living standards rose even as the average number of hours worked declined. Experts attribute about one-third of this growth in labor productivity to greater capital formation and the rest to an improvement in overall efficiency.[6]

Such good fortune did not continue through the 1970s. Output per capita continued to grow but at the slower pace of 1.2 percent per year between 1973 and 1981. Growth in labor productivity slowed to 0.8 percent per year, and it was only because labor force participation increased substantially with the baby boom coming of age and more women working that output per capita continued to increase at a reasonable pace. Part of the decline in labor productivity was due to slower growth in capital per worker, but most of it was due to a decline in overall efficiency, a large part of which has simply not been explained (figure 3.1).

Thus, declining productivity growth was a major contributor to the slower growth of living standards during the 1970s. Was the administration correct

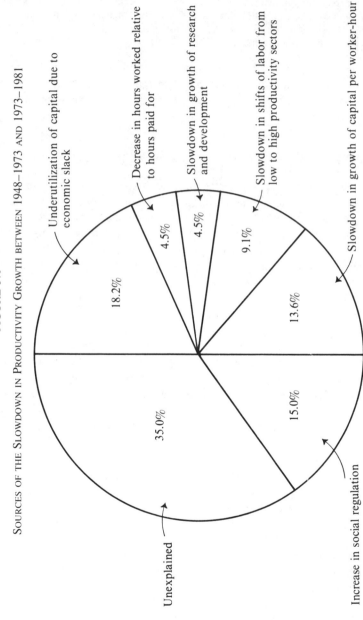

FIGURE 3.1

SOURCES OF THE SLOWDOWN IN PRODUCTIVITY GROWTH BETWEEN 1948–1973 AND 1973–1981

Underutilization of capital due to economic slack

Decrease in hours worked relative to hours paid for

Slowdown in growth of research and development

Slowdown in shifts of labor from low to high productivity sectors

Slowdown in growth of capital per worker-hour

18.2%

4.5%

4.5%

9.1%

13.6%

35.0%

15.0%

Unexplained

Increase in social regulation

SOURCE: U.S. Department of Labor, Bureau of Labor Statistics, *Trends in Multifactor Productivity* (Washington, D.C.: Government Printing Office, 1983), pp. 25–31; authors' estimates of the effects of increased regulation.

that it was the size and intrusiveness of the federal government that was the major cause of the productivity slowdown?

The Size of Government. In the past thirty years, government expenditures at all levels (federal, state, and local) grew more than one and one-half times faster than other spending, rising from an average in the 1950s of 26 percent of GNP to an average in the 1970s of 32 percent (figure 3.2). Taxes to finance these expenditures grew almost as much. Finally, the 1970s was a decade of regulatory activism because of growing concerns about the environment, the health and safety of workers and consumers, and equal treatment for various disadvantaged groups.

These facts do not by themselves tell us whether government has seriously interfered with growth in recent years. One way it might have is through the direct diversion of capital and labor from more productive private uses to less productive public purposes. Opinions differ about how essential most government-financed production is, but one thing is clear: it has not increased substantially over the past thirty years. As a proportion of GNP, total government *claims on real resources* (for such activities as road building and missile production) increased only 1.5 percentage points, and the claims of the federal government actually declined 3.8 points as the relative importance of defense spending was reduced.

Nevertheless, overall government *expenditures* grew because transfer programs, which necessitate taxing some people to provide benefits for others increased from 6.2 percent of GNP to 11.0 percent of GNP, almost exclusively as a result of more generous federal spending for Social Security and other social insurance programs that serve middle-income groups and enjoy widespread political support.

In spite of this growth in transfers, the United States has yet to become a "welfare state" by the standards of the rest of the industrialized world. Total government spending as a percent of GNP is significantly lower in this country than it is in most other industrialized countries. Furthermore, there is no apparent relationship between the size of a country's public sector and its rate of growth. Between 1970 and 1980, among the seven largest industrial nations, only Japan had a smaller public sector than the United States, yet four of the remaining five experienced a faster rate of growth.[7]

Nevertheless, as supply siders properly emphasized, increasingly generous transfer programs, rising tax burdens, and more social regulations may have reduced incentives to work, save, and invest, and lowered economic efficiency. How much did they contribute to slower growth over the past decade?

Labor Force Growth and Saving. As already noted, there was a large increase in the labor force during the 1970s, at a time when taxes and transfers

FIGURE 3.2

THE GROWTH OF GOVERNMENT AND ITS SOURCES

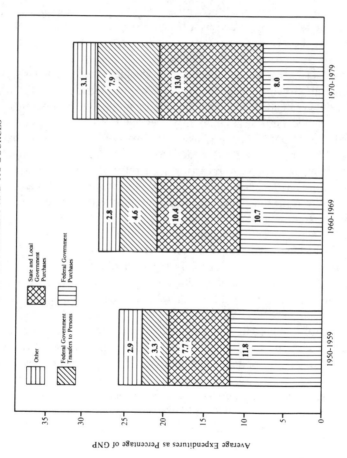

SOURCE: *Economic Report of the President* (Washington, D.C.: Government Printing Office, 1984), tables B-76 (p. 309), B-77 (p. 310).

NOTES: "Other" includes transfers to foreigners, net interest paid, subsidies less current surplus of government enterprises, and state and local government transfers to persons.

were rising. There was also a rise in the overall saving rate of businesses and households. Hence, there is no prima facie evidence to support the view that either work or saving was discouraged. More careful attempts to isolate the effects of taxes and transfers on people's behavior suggest that taxes and transfers do reduce work effort, and may reduce saving, though the effects are far more modest and uncertain than supply-side rhetoric sometimes implies. (This evidence is discussed later in the chapter when we examine the impact of Reagan policies on long-term growth).

Investment. We have also seen that capital per worker grew somewhat more slowly after 1973. The administration argues that this slowdown occurred because effective tax rates on income from capital rose during the 1970s due to the failure to adjust certain costs (such as depreciation charges) for inflation. Once again, this view has merit, but its importance has been exaggerated. First, recent research indicates that effective tax rates on income from capital are less sensitive to the rate of inflation than we once thought and that, if anything, there was a slight decrease in effective tax rates on capital during the 1970s.[8] Second, investment as a share of GNP was no lower in the 1970s than it was during the earlier postwar period. The slower growth in the amount of capital per worker that occurred during the 1970s was due to the dramatic expansion of the labor force, not to less investment.[9] Third, the slower rise in capital per worker accounts for only a small fraction (about one-seventh) of the productivity slowdown. A larger fraction of the slowdown (almost one-fifth) was due to the underutilization of the existing capital stock that occurred because there was more economic slack during the 1970s than during the 1960s (figure 3.1).

To conclude that government policies did not discourage capital formation in the 1970s compared to earlier periods is not to say there was no problem. Given the large increase in labor force participation during the 1970s, more capital formation would have been needed simply to maintain past rates of growth in capital per worker and productivity. Furthermore, some analysts have suggested that much of the capital stock was made obsolete by the sharp increase in energy prices after 1973 and that a higher rate of capital formation would have been necessary simply to restore the productive capital stock to earlier levels.[10]

Regulation. Experts attribute between 10 and 25 percent of the productivity slowdown to the growth of social regulation during the 1970s.[11] As the scope of environmental, health, safety, and consumer protection regulation expanded, businesses were forced to spend money on compliance that could otherwise have gone to producing more goods and services. Although there are obvious benefits from cleaner air, safer products, and a healthier workplace, these benefits do not usually show up in conventional measures of output such as the GNP. Thus, measured productivity declines even when social welfare more broadly conceived is increasing. Of course, in cases where regulations are badly designed, the output foregone in complying with the regulations will be higher than necessary. In such cases, reform rather than elimination of the offending rules is an obvious solution. Beyond this, scaling back regulations entails clear-cut social costs, and the choice between more material growth and, say, a cleaner, safer environment is a matter over which people can disagree. The Reagan administration has apparently come down largely on the side of greater material growth.

All in all, the Reagan administration properly focused on slower productivity growth as a major cause of the disappointing growth in living standards during the 1970s; but it probably placed too much blame on past government policies as the cause of the problem and thus too much hope in its own policies as the solution. Taxes do not appear to have had a major impact on work, saving, or investment, and only a modest portion of the productivity slowdown is related to increasing social regulations.

The Rise in Inflation and Unemployment

As productivity and growth slowed in the 1970s, both inflation and unemployment increased. The administration attributed this unfortunate combination to "stop-and-go" monetary and fiscal policies that alternated between periods of excessive stimulus and periods of short-lived restraint. The implication of this diagnosis is that a different set of monetary and fiscal policies could have produced less inflation as well as more employment and growth. A closer look at our experience with inflation and unemployment since the mid-1960s shows that before 1973 policy mistakes did indeed play an important role, but that much of the disappointing economic performance after 1973 was due to events beyond the control of policymakers.

The events culminating in the double-digit inflation of 1979–1980 can be traced back to the 1965–1968 period, when President Johnson attempted to finance both the Vietnam War and the Great Society without raising taxes. Most economists believed at the time that such a policy was ill-advised, and the inflation it produced was no surprise. The surprise was that inflation hardly fell at all when unemployment rose in response to the restrictive policies introduced in 1969. By this time, inflationary expectations and behavior had taken hold, and it would have taken a deeper recession to restore stable prices than policymakers or the public were prepared to endure. Instead, President Nixon responded to higher unemployment by restimulating the economy and to inflation by instituting wage and price controls in 1971. Most analysts believe that controls merely repressed inflation for a time, and some believe that they actually aggravated the inflation that reemerged when controls were later relaxed.[12]

This account of macroeconomic policy through the early 1970s is broadly consistent with the Reagan critique of past policy and performance, but that critique fits events after 1973 less well. In 1973–1974, and again in 1979–1980, the world economy was rocked by substantial oil price increases imposed by the Organization of Petroleum Exporting Countries (OPEC). These price shocks lowered real incomes in the United States and other oil consuming countries. Policymakers faced a dilemma. If they tried to cushion the short-run effects of these price shocks with expansionary monetary and fiscal policies, they risked inflation and a delay in the economy's adjustment to higher real oil prices and lower real incomes; but if they attempted to extinguish the inflation generated by these oil shocks with restrictive monetary and fiscal policies, they risked recession and unemployment.

Policy did indeed swing back and forth between stimulus, when unemployment seemed the greater evil, and restraint, when inflation seemed the greater evil; but would different policies have produced better outcomes than these stop-and-go policies, given the shocks the economy was experiencing? The nation had no choice but to adjust to more expensive oil, either by keeping the inflation rate down and accepting higher unemployment or by keeping unemployment down and accepting higher inflation. Policymakers at the time chose to accept some of each. In retrospect, some, including President Reagan, may think a different path should have been followed; but it seems very unlikely that any policy could have achieved both lower inflation *and* lower unemployment.

Thus, the inflation and unemployment that Ronald Reagan inherited were not the aftermath of a decade of unrestrained and excessively stimulative policies, but the aftermath of a world oil crisis that had already reduced American living standards and whose inflationary consequences would require still further adjustments in the early 1980s.

Short-run Effects on Inflation and Unemployment

The most positive economic development since Ronald Reagan became president has been the sharp drop in inflation. The president can take some credit for this achievement, but good luck and the Federal Reserve were also on his side.

While the decline in inflation has been welcome, the fight against inflation has been very costly. It has required two back-to-back recessions, and by the end of 1983 had cost the average person more than $1,000 in lost income. We estimate that about half of these costs could have been avoided by tolerating a somewhat less rapid decline in inflation, which still might have been acceptable to the public.

What Caused the Decline in Inflation?

Between 1980 and 1983 consumer price inflation fell from 12.4 percent to 3.8 percent, a drop of 8.6 points. We estimate that nearly 20 percent of that drop occurred because of measurement errors in the official Consumer Price Index (CPI) that led to an overstatement of inflation in 1980; that more than a third of the drop was due to favorable movements in volatile food, energy, and import prices (a substantial part of which would have occurred without a severe recession); and that the rest (nearly 50 percent) was due to the recession (table 3.1).

Until 1983, when the index was corrected, the CPI measured home-ownership costs in a way that overstated their importance. Had the CPI measured homeownership costs better in 1980, the calculated rate of inflation would have been 1.6 points lower and would have more accurately reflected the inflation experienced by most people.

Because food and energy prices rose faster than other prices in 1979 and 1980, they were a major source of the inflation that President Reagan inherited.

TABLE 3.1

WHY INFLATION HAS FALLEN

1980 CPI inflation (December to December):	12.4
1983 CPI inflation (December to December):	3.8
Difference:	8.6

Causes of the decline

	Points	Percentage of Total Decline
Homeownership measurement bias	1.6	18.6
Food, energy, the dollar	2.9	33.7
Economic slack	4.1	47.7
High unemployment	(3.0)	(34.9)
Rising unemployment	(1.1)	(12.8)
TOTAL	8.6	100%

SOURCE: Isabel V. Sawhill and Charles F. Stone, *Economic Policy in the Reagan Years* (Washington, D.C.: The Urban Institute Press, 1984).

The reversal of these adverse price shocks after 1980, together with an appreciating dollar that kept import prices low, reduced inflation by another 2.9 points. Although the decline in oil prices in the early 1980s was caused partly by lower demand resulting from the worldwide recession, the steady weakening since 1973 in OPEC unity and in its control of the world oil market was an independent contributing factor. Sharp increases in oil prices during the 1970s led to conservation efforts and the expansion of non-OPEC oil production, and an estimated two-thirds of the decline in oil prices since 1980 can be attributed to these adjustments rather than to the recession.[13] Similarly, the appreciation of the dollar was due in part to a rise in interest rates caused by large budget deficits and a restrictive monetary policy; but a growing perception by international investors that the United States was one of the few remaining "safe havens" for their savings also strengthened the dollar.

Thus, according to our estimates, perhaps one-third to one-half of the decline in inflation since 1980 would have occurred without a severe recession. The rest must be attributed directly to the economic slack caused by tight money. Empirical research on the effect of unemployment on inflation indicates that the unemployment we have experienced since 1980 has permanently lowered the inflation rate by about 3 percentage points and temporarily lowered it by another 1.1 points.[14] This latter gain, however, will be lost back as the economy returns to high employment.

Some economists believe that these estimates—based as they are on past relationships between inflation and unemployment—are excessively pessimistic because they ignore the effects of the Federal Reserve's new commitment to fighting inflation on people's inflationary expectations and thus on their wage- and price-setting behavior. However, so far there is little evidence of such an effect. All of the slower wage and price inflation of 1982 and 1983 can be explained by high unemployment and the other special factors we have discussed.[15]

What are the implications of this analysis for inflation in the next few years? Has the victory over inflation been a temporary or a permanent one? A reasonable estimate is that about two-thirds of those gains against inflation attributable to highly favorable movements in food, energy, and import prices are transitory and will be reversed over the next several years. Similarly, the temporary part of the drop in inflation due to rising unemployment during the recession will be reversed by falling unemployment during the recovery. At the same time, there will be additional excess unemployment before the economy returns to high employment that should keep some downward pressure on the inflation rate. Putting all these factors together, we can expect a net increase in inflation of perhaps 1 to 2 percentage points between 1983 and 1988. The resulting rate (5 to 6 percent) is above the administration's estimate of 3.9 percent but is still a substantial reduction compared to the double-digit rates of 1980. What were the costs associated with this achievement?

The Costs of the Recession

In 1979, when the Fed set out to curb inflation by slowing the growth of the money supply, the unemployment rate was 5.8 percent. By December 1982 it had risen to 10.7 percent, and it is not expected to return to 6 percent until 1988, even under the administration's relatively optimistic economic projections. Had the unemployment rate remained at 6 percent from 1980 through 1983, the economy would have produced additional goods and services worth $654 billion (measured in 1982 dollars).[16] This foregone output is a major cost that must be set against the benefits of lower inflation. An additional $316 billion of output will be lost between 1984 and 1988 assuming unemployment declines according to the administration's assumptions.

These costs translate into billions of dollars of lost income for workers who were jobless or had to accept shorter working hours or lower wages, as well as more bankruptcies and lower farm and business earnings. Most of the loss in income has been borne by workers (59 percent), with the remainder borne by corporate profits (25 percent) and farmers and small businesses (13 percent).* About one-third of the loss in the pretax earnings of individuals was offset by reduced personal income tax liabilities and increased government transfer payments; hence, disposable income did not fall as much as total income. Nevertheless, the "safety net" programs that cushion income losses during a recession have replaced a smaller fraction of lost income in this recession than they did in past recessions—the direct result of Reagan cutbacks in Unemployment Insurance, Food Stamps, and other assistance programs.[17] Jobless benefits alone were about $8 billion less in 1982 than they would have been without President Reagan's policy initiatives.[18] As a result, a much lower fraction of the unemployed received benefits than in previous recessions—an estimated 45 percent during any month in 1982, for example, compared to 75 percent during 1973–1975 (see chapter 6).

Had there been no recession in 1981–1982, the average person in the United States would have accumulated more than $1,000 in additional income between 1981 and 1983 (table 3.2). Each household would have been about $3,300 richer. Even if the economy recovers in line with the administration's forecast, there will be additional losses in household income due to continuing

---

*The remaining 3 percent represents primarily lower indirect business taxes.

economic slack, with the result that each household will end up paying about $1,000 per point of lower inflation.*

It is important to remember that the figures in table 3.2 are averages; they conceal the fact that recessions are not equal opportunity disemployers. The odds of being drafted into the fight against inflation increase steadily the lower an individual's earnings and family income to begin with. The relative income losses suffered by the working heads of poor families, for example, are four to five times as great as the losses for those heading high-income families, even after adjusting for the cushioning effect of taxes and transfers; and the 1981–1982 recession drove 4.3 million more people into poverty. At every income level, male heads of families experience greater income losses than female heads of families, and black men suffer the most of all.[19] Greater

TABLE 3.2

COSTS OF RECESSION

	Losses in After-tax Income (1982 dollars)	
	Per Household	Per Person
Amount by which actual income is lower that would have been earned with unemployment at 6 percent		
1980	528	187
1981–1983	3,309	1,187
Projected 1984–1986[a]	2,042	746
Cumulative, 1980–1986	5,879	2,120
Amount by which actual income is lower than what would have been earned with a milder recession in 1981–1982[b]		
1980	0	0
1981–1983	1,557	559
1984–1986	1,868	683
Cumulative, 1980–1986	3,425	1,232

SOURCE: Courtenay Slater, "Income Loss Due to the Recession," *Changing Domestic Priorities* Discussion Paper (Washington, D.C.: The Urban Institute, January 1984); Sawhill and Stone, *Economic Policy in the Reagan Years*.
  a. Based on administration's projections contained in Office of Management and Budget, *Budget of the United States Government, Fiscal Year 1985* (Washington, D.C.: Government Printing Office, 1984).
  b. Based on authors' simulation (based on the DRI model) of an easier monetary policy combined with a tighter fiscal policy. See appendix B for details.

---

*This is calculated on the basis of the cumulative costs shown in table 3.2, assuming the recession and continuing slack is responsible for as much as five points of the drop in inflation.

countercyclical assistance targeted on such groups could have ensured that the costs of fighting inflation were more evenly shared.

Of course, if one believes a recession in 1981–1982 was not only inevitable but also necessary to lower inflation, there was no way to avoid some of these costs. However, based on the analysis reported in the next section we estimate that nearly 60 percent of these costs could have been eliminated with a policy that would have brought inflation down more gradually (see the bottom of table 3.2).

To see if inflation could have been brought down without so severe a recession, we examine three alternative policies that might have been pursued after 1980: (1) easier monetary policy (faster growth in the money supply beginning in 1981); (2) easier monetary policy combined with tighter fiscal policy (less government spending and smaller tax cuts in order to avoid large deficits); and (3) an incomes policy (direct action to moderate wage and price increases).

Alternative One: An Easier Monetary Policy. Although large budget deficits are the defining feature of Reagan's economic policy to most people, they are less important to understanding what happened to the economy in 1981-1984 than is the conduct of monetary policy. Suppose the Fed had not been so committed to fighting inflation and had chosen to fight unemployment instead?

One cannot, of course, rerun history to find out what would have happened, but one can simulate economic performance with more expansionary policies and compare the results from the simulation with history. Based on such a simulation,* we found that if the Fed had reversed course and increased the supply of money beginning in 1981, there would have been some economic slack but no recession (figure 3.3). Unemployment would have risen hardly at all from its 1981 base of just over 7 percent. Inflation would have fallen, but more slowly and not quite so far (to 6.6 percent in 1984 versus 4.9 percent under Reagan policies). Although the specifics of any simulation should be treated with a healthy dose of skepticism, there is little doubt that the adverse price shocks of the 1970s would have been absent in the early 1980s regardless of policy and that inflation would have come down from double-digit rates without a recession.

Although it is unrealistic to think that the Fed would have been willing to expand the money supply so much in 1981, there is reason to believe that the recession was deeper than the Fed had wanted or anticipated. In February

---

*We have used the Data Resources, Inc. (DRI) quarterly model of the U.S. economy, one of several large-scale econometric forecasting models that have been widely used for similar exercises.

FIGURE 3.3

ESTIMATED IMPACT OF AN EASIER MONETARY POLICY, 1981–1988

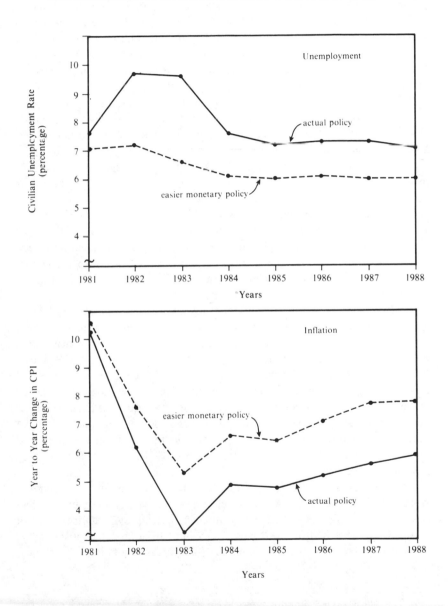

SOURCE: Appendix B, table B.1.

1982 the Federal Open Market Committee, which actually determines the course of monetary policy, forecast that total spending would grow by between 8.0 and 10.5 percent over the year. In fact, spending grew by only 2.6 percent, because rather than spending what little additional money the Fed was providing, businesses and households increased the amount of money they held in their checking and other accounts, perhaps as a hedge against economic uncertainty. Thus, total spending fell more than past relationships between money growth and spending would have predicted.[20]

This development, together with the mounting international debt crisis, apparently worried the Fed enough that it suspended its money targets in the summer of 1982 and announced in October that it would henceforth consider a variety of indicators, including interest rates, in setting monetary policy.

The important point is that had the Fed anticipated, and chosen to offset, this lack of spending earlier, the 1981–1982 recession would have been less severe. This could have happened more or less automatically if the Fed had been focusing more on interest rates and less on the money supply in late 1981, and had therefore expanded the money stock to keep real interest rates from rising as they did. But this would have run counter to monetarist views, and although the Fed has never operated entirely according to monetarist doctrine, it may have felt somewhat constrained by the increased influence of this viewpoint within the administration in 1981.

Alternative Two: An Easier Monetary Policy Combined with a Tighter Fiscal Policy. Even if the Fed had focused more on interest rates, it might still have been so concerned about the stimulus to the economy from large budget deficits that it would not have allowed the money supply to expand. But had there been smaller budget deficits and a weaker economy, the Fed might have allowed greater money growth. Indeed, many economists argue that a policy of smaller deficits and easier money would have been better for growth than the policy we have had, and such a policy might actually have been followed if Jimmy Carter had been reelected or if the Congress had rejected the Reagan budget and tax program in 1981. How would the economy have performed under such a policy?*

Our simulation of such a policy alternative suggests that the economy would still have incurred a serious recession but not nearly so severe a recession as we actually experienced (figure 3.4). Unemployment rises but not above 8 percent. With a less severe recession, inflation falls substantially, but only to 6.4 percent in 1984 compared to 4.9 percent under Reagan policies.

---

*This particular policy alternative is used as a point of comparison for measuring the impacts of Reagan policies in several chapters of this book. It is described in more detail in appendix B.

FIGURE 3.4

ESTIMATED IMPACT OF AN EASIER MONETARY POLICY COMBINED WITH A TIGHTER
FISCAL POLICY, 1981–1988

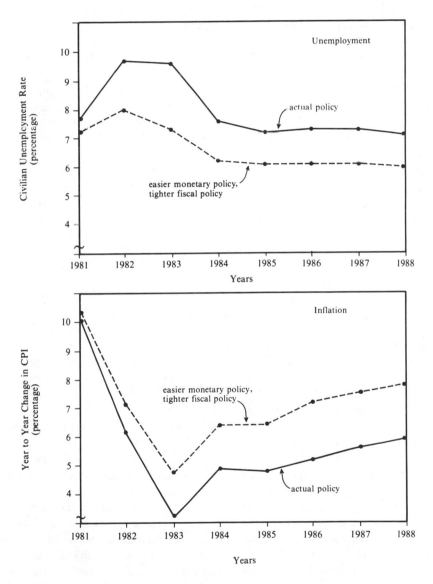

SOURCE: Appendix B, table B.1.

Thus, this policy alternative is more "conservative" than the last one and has the distinct advantage that it eliminates the large structural deficits that currently threaten the economy's long-term growth prospects.

As before, these results should not be taken too literally in all their details. Both sets of results illustrate the general effects to be expected from a whole range of policies that fall under the general rubric of "gradualism"—in contrast to the "cold turkey" approach actually followed between 1980 and 1982.

The advantage of gradualism is that it gives people additional time to adjust to a more slowly growing economy and thus imposes less individual hardship. There are likely to be fewer bankruptcies, less need to renegotiate existing collective bargaining or loan agreements, and more widespread sharing of the costs of unemployment. The disadvantage of gradualism is that it might not have produced an unemployment rate high enough to affect the wage and work rule concessions, management efficiencies, and other changes that have contributed to the recent slowing of inflation. Moreover, there is no guarantee that public opinion and political pressures will allow gradualism to work. The costs are short run and the benefits long run, making it difficult politically to stay the antiinflation course.

Alternative Three: An Incomes Policy. Given the difficulties with both gradualism and cold turkey policies, some economists have long favored an incomes policy as the best way to minimize the costs associated with policies that operate solely by restricting demand. Specific proposals for a tax-based incomes policy (providing rewards to those practicing wage or price restraint) surfaced at the end of the Carter administration, and most postwar administrations instituted some form of wage-price controls or guidelines. Unfortunately, available evidence suggests that incomes policies have had only a temporary effect in slowing inflation, which tends to decline when controls are put in place but to rise once they are removed.[21]

Pessimism about the effectiveness of incomes policies should be tempered, however, with the recognition that they have been used in the past more to supplant than to supplement monetary and fiscal restraint. Thus, incomes policies might have worked better after 1979 when there was a much greater commitment to monetary restraint.

The above discussion of alternative ways of dealing with inflation has significance for the future as well as the past. Despite the substantial reduction in inflation achieved so far, inflation has not been eliminated. All indications are that inflation in the mid-1980s will exceed 5 percent, a rate that would have seemed intolerable barely fifteen years ago. To reduce inflation further will require either more luck, an extended period of economic slack, another recession, or experimentation with new kinds of incomes policies that are more successful than those of the past.

Some economists believe that wages and prices are quite inflexible, especially in a downward direction, with the result that the economy is prone to inflation even when unemployment remains relatively high.* [22] If this is the case, unless the wage- and price-setting institutions that produce this inflexibility (for example, multiyear union contracts) are changed, the only way to maintain price stability over the long run would be to maintain permanent slack in the economy. Perhaps one of the intangible benefits of the experience the nation has just gone through will be greater willingness to change some of these institutional practices.

The Gains from Lower Inflation

Has the reduction in inflation that has been achieved so far been worth the high cost paid in terms of lost output and employment? Is it worth incurring additional costs of this sort to lower inflation still further?

Notwithstanding the widespread belief that inflation is a major problem, there is remarkably little analytical evidence on the costs of inflation. One estimate does indicate that the eventual consequences of lowering inflation by five points would permanently raise the level of real GNP by 1.0 percent. [23] If this estimate were correct, the temporary costs of the last recession would be almost exactly counterbalanced by the permanent gain in output. However, the costs attributed to inflation in these calculations arise as a result of financial regulations and a tax code that lead to increasing inefficiencies with rising inflation. For example, as noted earlier, effective corporate tax rates may vary with inflation, leading to considerable uncertainty about after-tax rates of return on investment. Recent financial and tax reforms, like allowing interest to be paid on checking accounts and lowering business taxes, have reduced many of these inefficiencies and have lowered the costs associated with inflation accordingly. Further reform could reduce them still more, but as long as any remain, inflation will continue to impose some economic costs.

A popular argument against inflation is that it makes everyone poorer by reducing their purchasing power, but this is wrong. Inflation leads to increases in the prices of what people buy, but it also means increases in the

---

*The argument goes as follows: even at high employment, changing patterns of demand will lead to expansion in some sectors and contraction in others. If price increases in those sectors experiencing rising demand are not offset by price reductions in those sectors with falling demand because of wage and price rigidities, the general price level will rise even though there is no net slack in the economy.

prices of what they sell, including their labor. Inflation may hurt some groups relative to others, but it does not make the nation as a whole worse off (beyond the effects already discussed). Unionized workers may gain at the expense of nonunion workers; retirees dependent on Social Security may gain relative to those dependent on their own saving; and people on incomes that are fixed in money terms are certain to lose out to people who are well organized to make sure their incomes rise along with inflation. Thus, inflation may act as an arbitrary redistributional tax. It may also be psychologically and politically unsettling, and these consequences may be as important as its economic costs.

There is one more real and calculable cost of inflation: it induces policymakers to fight inflation, and the costs of fighting inflation are high. For this reason, it is worth trying hard to preserve the gains that have been made against inflation over the past few years, but it may not be worth trying for a further significant reduction by incurring another recession. No government can admit openly that it has adopted a policy of benign neglect toward the existing level of inflation for fear of the political consequences. But neither is any government in the mid-1980s likely to adopt a program that has any real chance of eliminating inflation *entirely*.

Budget Deficits in Recession and Recovery

The recession ended in late 1982. The belated easing of monetary policy was the major reason, but the tax cuts and defense buildup enacted in 1981, which caused fiscal policy to turn sharply expansionary in 1982, also contributed.

Changes in fiscal policy during the Reagan presidency have been dramatic. Deficits averaging well over 4 percent of GNP in 1981–1984, and the prospect of subsequent deficits over 5 percent of GNP by 1988, are without precedent over the postwar period (figure 3.5). When the effects of changing levels of economic activity on the deficit are removed as in the high-employment deficit line in figure 3.5, it is evident that fiscal policy did not turn expansionary until after 1981, when the Reagan spending and tax initiatives began to take effect, and that deficits would not go away even in a healthy economy.*

To isolate the effects of these deficits on economic performance, we compared Reagan budget policy to a policy in which the high-employment budget deficit is in balance.† This comparison shows that Reagan fiscal policy

---

*An expansionary policy is indicated by an *increase* in the high-employment deficit. Note that the high-employment deficit actually *decreased* between FY 1980 and FY 1981.

†Monetary policy remains unchanged. The way in which the budget is balanced is described in appendix B.

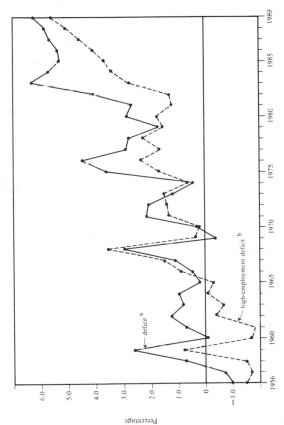

FIGURE 3.5

FEDERAL GOVERNMENT DEFICITS AS A PERCENTAGE OF GNP, 1956–1989

SOURCES: Authors' calculations based on Congressional Budget Office, *Baseline Budget Projections in Fiscal Years 1985–1989* (Washington, D.C.: Government Printing Office, 1984), *The Economic Outlook* (Washington, D.C.: Government Printing Office, 1984), and unpublished data; Frank de Leeuw and Thomas M. Holloway, "Cyclical Adjustment of the Federal Budget and Federal Debt," *Survey of Current Business,* vol. 63, no. 12 (December 1983), pp. 25–40; and Office of Management and Budget, "Total Government Finances," February 1984, and "Federal Government Finances," February 1984.

a. Total federal government deficit (on- and off-budget) as a percentage of GNP.

b. Total federal government high employment deficit as a percentage of high employment GNP. Assumes a 6.0 percent high employment unemployment rate.

has had a small but positive effect on the overall level of spending. It made the 1981–1982 recession a little less severe and the recovery a little faster. By 1984 real GNP is about 1 percent higher (table 3.3).

More importantly, larger budget deficits under Reagan produce higher interest rates, hurting housing, exports, and industries facing strong import competition. Net exports are $12 billion lower in 1984 because higher interest rates produce a greater inflow of foreign capital, strengthening the value of the dollar and raising the price of U.S. goods, so that they are less competitive in world markets. Higher interest rates might be expected to hurt business investment as well, but the stimulus from the business tax cuts is more than enough to offset the effects of higher interest rates in this sector.

On balance, therefore, the Reagan deficits have thus far been good for the economy. They moderated the recession a little, they hastened the recovery, and they strengthened business investment, albeit at the expense of housing and exports. Unfortunately, the effect of the recession on the deficits was not similarly salutary since revenues automatically fall and some types of expenditures (e.g., unemployment insurance) automatically rise when incomes are depressed. These higher recessionary deficits add to the national debt, and the interest on this debt becomes an on-going expense of government. Thus, the large budget deficits forecast for the end of the decade are partly a legacy of the recession incurred at the beginning of the decade. The recession will cast a long shadow in other ways as well.

TABLE 3.3

ESTIMATED IMPACT OF REAGAN FISCAL POLICY
ON THE LEVEL AND COMPOSITION OF OUTPUT
(In 1982 $ billions)

	1982	1983	1984	1986	1988
Real GNP	2.8	20.7	36.2	36.0	23.1
(percentage change)	(0.1)	(0.7)	(1.1)	(1.0)	(0.6)
Consumption	3.7	20.9	36.3	44.5	54.2
Investment	4.2	13.0	19.1	22.6	17.1
Business	4.5	12.7	22.1	33.1	28.4
Residential	−0.3	−3.8	−12.2	−20.8	−26.1
Inventory	0.0	4.1	9.2	10.3	14.8
Government purchases	−4.1	−8.1	−7.1	−3.5	−0.1
Federal	2.9	2.7	4.7	11.6	20.3
State and local	−7.0	−10.8	−11.8	−15.1	−20.4
Net exports	−1.1	−5.1	−12.1	−27.5	−48.1

SOURCE: Authors' calculations from simulations based on the DRI model. See Sawhill and Stone, *Economic Policy in the Reagan Years*, for details.

The Legacy of the Recession

One of the president's implicit promises was that the 1980s would be better than the 1970s. When one looks at the economy's poor performance in the early part of the 1980s, however, it becomes apparent that the economy would have to perform phenomenally well for the rest of the decade to end up performing as well over the whole decade as it did during the 1970s.

Table 3.4 compares three economic projections for the remainder of the decade with what would be required over the same period to match the performance of the 1970s. The comparisons show that the 1980s will almost certainly be a decade of high unemployment, excess capacity, and slow growth compared to the 1970s. Inflation will be lower, but standards of living are not likely to improve as much over the 1980s as they did over the 1970s. To match the performance of the 1970s, real per capita disposable income would have to increase by 3.4 percent a year beginning in 1984, and this is far above most projections for this period.

Table 3.4 tells us nothing about the effects of the recession on *future* growth. In fact, recessions have some potentially beneficial effects on growth. For example, they tend to purge the economy of its worst inefficiencies, selecting out good from bad performers, forcing managers to pay more attention to costs, and encouraging employees to work harder. Also, a lower, and potentially more stable, rate of inflation can create a better environment for business planning and investment (see chapter 9).

At the same time, recessions reduce investment; hence, the capital stock and labor productivity grow less rapidly. In addition, the increase in the number of people too discouraged to seek work—an increase that is typical of a recession—may persist into the postrecession period because work habits and the acquisition of job-related skills have been impaired. This discouragement of work appears to be one of the reasons why the labor force grew so slowly during 1983. Our judgment is that these negative effects, especially the loss of capital formation due to the recession, are important, but whether they offset the benefits of a leaner business sector and a less inflationary environment is difficult to say. Whatever its ultimate effects, the recession is only one factor influencing the prospects for long-term growth—a topic to which we now turn.

Prospects for Long-term Growth

Now that the recession is over and the economy is expanding at a healthy rate, optimism about the future is strong. In order for growth to continue, however, the administration's supply-side policies must work to stimulate the

TABLE 3.4

WILL THE 1980s BE BETTER THAN THE 1970s?

	1970–1979 Average (Percentage)	1980–1983 Average (Percentage)	Required 1984–1989 Average[a] (Percentage)	Projections 1984–1989 Average		
				Data Resources Inc. (Percentage)	Administration (Percentage)	Congressional Budget Office (Percentage)
Civilian unemployment rate	6.2	8.5	4.7	7.5	7.0	7.0
Capacity utilization rate	81.8	76.4	85.4	82.7	NA	NA
Inflation rate	6.5	7.2	6.0	5.2	4.2	4.7
Productivity growth	1.4	1.1	1.6	1.8	NA	NA
Real GNP growth	3.2	0.9	4.7	3.4	4.2	3.8
Real per capita disposable income growth	2.4	0.9	3.4	1.9	NA	NA

SOURCES: Historical data from *Economic Report of the President* (Washington, D.C.: Government Printing Office, 1984), tables B-29 (p. 254), B-45 (p. 271), B-3 (p. 224), B-40 (p. 266), B-2 (p. 222), B-24 (p. 249). Projections from Data Resources, Inc., *The Data Resources Review of the U.S. Economy February 1984* (Lexington, Mass.: Data Resources, Inc., 1984); Data Resources, Inc., *U.S. Long-Term Review Winter 1983-84* (Lexington, Mass.: Data Resources, Inc., 1983); Office of Management and Budget, *Budget of the United States Government Fiscal Year 1985*, (Washington, D.C.: Government Printing Office, 1984); Congress of the United States, Congressional Budget Office, *The Economic Outlook: A Report to the Senate and House Committees on the Budget—Part 1*, (Washington D.C.: Government Printing Office, 1984).

NOTE: Capacity utilization rate is for total manufacturing (FRB series); inflation rate is measured by year-over-year changes in the GNP implicit price deflator; productivity growth is measured by year-over-year changes in the index of output per hour of all persons in the nonfarm business sector.

NA = not available

a. These are the averages required for 1984–1989 if the averages for 1980–1989 are to equal those for 1970–1979.

growth of capital, labor, and productivity. Otherwise, growing demands for output will too quickly bump up against the ceiling of available supply with the threat of renewed inflation.

The focus in this section, then, is on the supply side of the economy—what economists call *potential* output or GNP. This is the maximum output that can be produced once the economy is operating at high employment and both capital and labor are fully utilized.

Over the entire period since World War II, potential output has grown at a rate of 3.6 percent per year. It is not predicted to grow this rapidly over the next decade, primarily because of demographic change that will slow the rate of growth of the labor force. The Commerce Department projects an average growth rate of 3.2 percent through 1988. Analysts outside government are less optimistic. The question focused on here, however, is not how fast potential output will grow but whether it will grow slower or faster as the result of President Reagan's economic policies. In short, is the administration's optimism about the growth of the economy warranted, based on the effects to be expected from its own policies?

Supply-side Effects in the Short Run

The administration promised immediate results from its supply-side policies, and when the economy went into a recession its critics labeled the program a failure. Supporters, in contrast, point to the recovery as evidence that the program is now working. Neither view is right. Supply-side economic indicators, like investment and productivity growth, normally decline during a recession and grow strongly during a recovery. But, if the decline were smaller than usual, or the rebound faster than usual, that would be a sign that supply-side policies are working.

By comparing the performance of various supply-side indicators over the most recent business cycle with their performance over previous cycles and with the predictions of large-scale macroeconomic models, we can get some idea of whether policies to increase saving, investment, and work effort have had an effect.*

The story is mixed. The personal saving rate and the growth of the labor force have, if anything, been slightly lower than what would have been expected based on past cyclical patterns and model predictions.[24] Business saving and investment, in contrast, have been higher than predicted. As

---

*Since most models do not include supply-side effects, or do so only inadequately, underpredictions of the behavior of supply-side variables would suggest that the Reagan program was working.

already noted, this latter result is due to the administration's fiscal policy with its emphasis on accelerated depreciation and other tax cuts for business.

The failure of saving or the growth of the labor force to respond to the drop in personal tax rates that increased the rewards for working and saving could be due to the unusual severity of the recession. The recession may have discouraged people from entering the labor force and may have necessitated that they draw down past savings or curtail current saving even more than usual. Recent saving and work behavior may also reflect the aging of the baby boom generation which has now largely completed its entry into the labor force and is at a stage in its life when child-rearing responsibilities are most likely to deter women from working and when people tend to save relatively little. Finally, the special tax incentives designed to encourage greater personal saving may have failed because they were not well designed for that purpose.[25] A study of the impact of the increased availability of IRAs on personal saving during 1982 indicates, for example, that, for the most part, the increase in IRA contributions during that year reflected simply a shift of funds into IRAs out of other assets, not an increase in saving; but there may be some longer term response once opportunities for such switching are exhausted.[26]

It is such longer term responses that are most difficult to assess. Nevertheless, because they are so critical to the success of the Reagan program, we now plunge into turbulent waters and attempt a quantitative assessment of the eventual impact of Reagan policies on each of the major factors that affect the economy's long-run growth path: capital formation, the size of the labor force, and the efficiency with which each is used.[27]

Capital Formation

The overall impact of Reagan policies on capital formation depends on a number of factors: the excess capacity created during the recession, the business tax cuts, reduced federal outlays on capital goods, greater tax incentives for private saving, and higher deficits (table 3.5). While the business tax cuts are likely to have positive effects, these will be offset, at least to some extent, by the discouraging effect of excess industrial capacity during the first half of the decade and by the federal budget deficits' absorption of saving during the second half of the decade. What one concludes about the effect of Reagan policies on public investment depends on one's assumptions about how productive such investments have been.

Business Tax Cuts. The Reagan business tax cuts were designed to increase the overall rate of private investment, but they did not affect all categories of investment uniformly (see chapter 9). Business plant and equipment received the most favorable treatment, while housing and consumer

TABLE 3.5

ESTIMATED IMPACT OF REAGAN POLICIES ON CAPITAL FORMATION

	Percentage Change in the Stock of Capital during the 1980s	
	Lower Bound	*Upper Bound*
Investment (demand for capital)		
Recession	−2.5	−1.0
Tax incentives for private investment	+2	+4
Public investment	−3	+1
Saving (supply of capital)		
Tax incentives for private saving	0	+3
Deficits	−6	−3

SOURCE: Authors' calculations (see chapter notes).

durables were less favorably treated. This redirecting of investment from "non-productive" to "productive" uses has been dubbed the "Feldstein twist," after the chairman of the President's Council of Economic Advisors, who first argued its desirability. Of course not everyone agrees that building houses is less productive than building factories.

The 1981 and 1982 tax acts reduced the effective tax rate on income from capital by 14 percent overall (from 26.4 to 22.8 percent). Tax rates on new investment in plant and equipment fell by 52 percent. By themselves, these reductions in tax rates could be expected to reduce the overall cost of capital (of which taxes are only one component) by about 3 percent. Other things being equal, businesses would then find it profitable to increase investment by about the same amount (the midrange of the estimates reported in table 3.5), with the increase concentrated in business plant and equipment.[28]

The Effects of the Recession. Other things are not equal, however. In particular, unused capacity and poor sales prospects may discourage businesses from undertaking new projects, regardless of the tax incentives for doing so. We estimate that the 1981–1982 recession brought with it a cumulative loss of $112 to $194 billion (1982 dollars) of investment, reducing the existing stock of capital by between 1.0 and 2.5 percent relative to what it would have been with a more modest downturn in economic activity.[29]

The Availability of Saving. Once the economy is operating closer to capacity, the availability of saving becomes the critical constraint on capital formation. Although the Reagan administration has provided incentives to encourage greater private saving, it has also created large future claims against these savings by allowing the budget deficit to grow.

Several provisions of the Economic Recovery Tax Act of 1981 (ERTA) were directed toward encouraging greater personal saving by raising its after-tax rate of return. However, neither economic theory nor the available evidence provides unqualified support for the view that the response of saving to these new incentives will be quantitatively significant. We estimate an increase in saving of between 0 and 3 percent from this source.[30]

The Effect of Budget Deficits. Offsetting this increase in the availability of saving to finance investment will be the absorption of saving by federal budget deficits that could crowd out private investment. Between 1985 and 1989 the federal government will need to borrow more than $1.3 trillion, with annual borrowing needs reaching over 5 percent of GNP by the end of the decade (compared with 2 percent of GNP for the period 1976–1980).

If nothing else changed, these deficits would reduce the saving available for private capital formation on a dollar-for-dollar basis, but the deficits are so large that further adjustments seem inevitable. For one thing, it is likely that the Congress will take some action to reduce the size of future budget deficits. For another, some portion of any increase in the size of federal government budget deficits may be offset by the surpluses of state and local governments, by inflows of foreign saving, and by an increase in domestic saving in response to higher interest rates.

By one estimate these responses will be very important, with the result that each dollar increase in the federal government budget deficit will lead to only a forty-five-cent drop in investment.[31] This, however, is an optimistic estimate.[32] State and local governments are likely to reduce taxes or increase expenditures rather than allow larger surpluses to accumulate. Capital inflows from abroad, although very large in 1984, may not be either sustainable or desirable. And the domestic saving rate has never shown much variation in response to changed economic conditions.

These uncertainties make it difficult to estimate the likely impact of future deficits on capital formation. We estimate that even if action by Congress, together with increases in foreign and domestic saving, were to eliminate about half the crowding-out problem, deficits would still lower private investment by 1 or 2 percent of GNP, thereby lowering the stock of capital by between 3 and 6 percent.[33] Even when conservatively estimated, these effects are so large that any action taken to lower the budget deficits, especially action that preserves the supply-side incentives introduced in 1981, will greatly increase the likelihood that the overall effect of Reagan policies on capital formation will be beneficial.

Public Investment. Greater absorption of saving by the federal government would not necessarily be bad for growth if that saving were being used to increase productive public investment. However, except for the highway program enacted in late 1982 (largely because of congressional concern about high unemployment), spending for capital improvements has declined under President Reagan. If the popular rhetoric about the high payoffs associated with rebuilding our deteriorating "infrastructure" is true, this decline in public investment has made us a more capital-poor nation. But if public investment is not as productive as private investment and if the Reagan cuts have been concentrated in the least productive programs, as some evidence suggests, then this decline will free up valuable resources for private uses.[34] Given these conflicting views on the productivity of public investment, our lower bound estimate of the effects of Reagan policies is negative, while our upper bound estimate is positive.

In summary, Reagan tax policies have stimulated investment demand, but the budget deficits threaten to absorb so much saving that the net effect of Reagan policies could easily be negative. Translating the effects on capital formation summarized in table 3.5 into effects on economic growth, we estimate that the net effect of Reagan policies could be to lower output by as much as 2.8 percent in 1990 or to raise it by as much as 1.2 percent.[35]

The Labor Force

During the decade of the 1970s, the civilian labor force grew at a very rapid pace. Recessions tended to arrest but not reverse the upward trend, and the downturn of 1981–1982 was no exception. For a variety of demographic reasons, the growth of the labor force is not predicted to be as rapid in the coming decade as it was in the last. But the Reagan tax cuts, together with the reduced availability or generosity of benefit programs, can be expected to encourage greater work effort (more participation or longer hours), thereby increasing the size of the full-time equivalent labor force above what it otherwise would have been. The changes may also encourage people to take greater risks or choose more challenging types of work than they have in the past since the net financial rewards for doing so have increased.

Table 3.6 summarizes the results of a detailed review of the available evidence by Robert Haveman.[36] This evidence suggests that the labor force might increase by anywhere from 0.8 to 2.5 percent as a result of Reagan policies, with most studies arriving at estimates near the lower bound.

More than two-thirds of this effect will be the result of the reduction in marginal tax rates. This effect should not be surprising since everyone has benefited from these cuts, and past research suggests that taxes have a significant effect on the propensity to work, especially among the elderly and married women. The remaining one-third will be due to changes in benefit programs, such as Social Security, Unemployment Insurance, Aid to Families

TABLE 3.6

ESTIMATED IMPACT OF REAGAN POLICIES ON THE SIZE OF THE LABOR FORCE

	Percentage Change in Full-time Equivalents in the Labor Force during the 1980s	
	Lower Bound	Upper Bound
Due to changes in personal tax rates[a]	0.7	1.6
Due to changes in benefit programs[b]	0.1	0.9
TOTAL	0.8	2.5

SOURCE: Robert Haveman, "How Much Have Reagan Tax and Spending Policies Increased Work Effort?" in Charles R. Hulten and Isabel V. Sawhill, eds., *The Legacy of Reaganomics: Prospects for Long-term Growth* (Washington, D.C.: The Urban Institute Press, 1984).
   a. Effects of ERTA relative to an indexed personal tax system beginning in October 1981.
   b. Includes estimated effects of changes in the provisions and outlays for 22 different income transfer, health, education, employment, training, and social service programs.

with Dependent Children (AFDC), and Food Stamps. For many of these programs there has been an increase in the rate at which benefits are reduced as earnings rise. But basic benefits have also been cut, or in some cases eliminated, forcing people to work more to replace the loss of government assistance. This growth in the labor force can be expected to raise output in 1990 by between 0.6 and 1.8 percent.[37]

Overall Efficiency

Economists have emphasized three sources of growth in the overall efficiency of capital and labor: the reallocation of resources from less to more productive uses, improvements in the quality of the labor force due to greater education and training, and advances in knowledge.

Resource reallocation increases efficiency when resources flow from sectors or activities where their contribution to output has become relatively low to sectors or activities where it is higher. Currently, concern centers around the diversion of resources from economically productive activities toward complying with a proliferation of environmental, health, safety, and other social regulations. When properly designed, social regulations improve overall welfare but at the expense of a temporary decline in measured productivity growth. Estimates of the impact of Reagan regulatory policies vary from a finding of "no effect" to evidence that they may have increased the annual rate of measured productivity growth by as much as 0.2 percentage points above what it would have been had the level of regulatory activity that prevailed in the mid-1970s been continued.* This faster rate of productivity growth would produce about 1 percent more output by 1990.[38]

Changes in the quality of the labor force are hard to assess. The administration has reduced real outlays for education and training about 37 percent below their prior levels.[39] Any adverse effects on growth will be moderated to the extent that there is a compensating increase in state and local spending or private expenditures for the same activities. Moreover, it is difficult to estimate how much people's future earning power is improved by whatever additional education and training they receive. Finally, much of any effect will not show up until those now in elementary school enter the labor force in the 1990s. Past research, and our own monitoring of the extent to which state and local governments have been replacing lost federal funds, indicates that the likely effects on labor quality will be minor, but that real output might fall by as much as 0.4 percent by 1990.[40]

The most important source of productivity growth is technological change. The government's role in encouraging such advances is limited to providing a legal environment that will create appropriate incentives for private activity (through, for example, patent laws and permitting joint research ventures under the antitrust laws) and to undertaking or subsidizing basic research. However, because estimated rates of return on research-and-development (R&D) investments are very high—much higher than rates of return on tangible investments—many economists view them as a critical policy lever.[41]

Total R&D spending as a percent of GNP reached a low of 2.2 percent in the late 1970s; it is now rising and is expected to reach 2.7 percent in 1984. The possible contribution of Reagan policies to this increase is a matter of disagreement. Some believe that the 25 percent incremental R&D tax credit passed as part of ERTA in 1981 has encouraged private R&D spending which is currently quite strong. Others contend that the effects have been small or nonexistent. Total federal outlays for R&D have increased slightly since 1980, but all the increases have been in the defense area; nondefense R&D expenditures are lower than they have been in any recent administration. Thus, the benefits of higher federal expenditures depend on whether one believes there are large technological spillovers from defense into the civilian sector. If there are, and if the R&D tax credit has been effective, output could be as much as 0.4 percent higher in 1990 as a result of Reagan policies. Otherwise, output could actually be lower as a result of lower spending on nondefense R&D.[42]

---

*For an expanded discussion of the impact of Reagan policies on private-sector productivity, see chapter 9.

Summary

Our overall assessment of the effects of Reagan policies on long-term growth is summarized in table 3.7. As we have indicated all along, there is considerable uncertainty about all these numbers. Nevertheless, they do serve to focus the debate and to put reasonable bounds on the range of likely effects. They also serve as a reminder of how little is really known about the growth process.

With all their flaws, the numbers are still suggestive. They indicate that, under optimistic assumptions, the net impact of a large number of effects, some negative and some positive, is to increase potential output in 1990 by as much as 4.4 percent. Under more pessimistic assumptions, the net impact is to decrease potential output by 3.4 percent. If the budget deficits can be reduced, and continuing economic slack or another recession avoided, the net effect would definitely be positive.

Figure 3.6 compares the growth path of potential GNP (the economy's capacity to supply goods and services) under these optimistic and pessimistic assumptions with the path that might have been expected without Reagan policies. It also shows the administration's forecast of actual GNP (total demand for goods and services). The administration assumes that the supply of output will rise more or less in line with our optimistic growth path. If it should turn out that our pessimistic scenario is the correct one, and demand grows as forecast, actual GNP will surpass potential in 1986 and the risk of inflation will increase greatly. If the administration is right, we may really see a return to sustained noninflationary growth.

TABLE 3.7

OVERVIEW OF ESTIMATED IMPACTS OF REAGAN POLICIES ON ECONOMIC GROWTH

	Percentage Change in Real Output by 1990[a]	
	Lower Bound	Upper Bound
Capital formation	−2.8	+1.2
Labor supply	+0.6	+1.8
Regulation	0	+1.0
Education and training	−0.4	0
R&D	−0.8	+0.4
TOTAL	−3.4	+4.4

SOURCES: Tables 3.5 and 3.6 and Sawhill and Stone, *Economic Policy in the Reagan Years.* For a similar effort, see William Nordhaus, "Reaganomics and Economic Growth: A Summing Up," in Hulten and Sawhill, eds., *The Legacy of Reaganomics.*

a. This is the total impact on the level of output. If the effects take place gradually over, say, ten years, then the *annual* growth rate would be raised (lowered) by one-tenth as much.

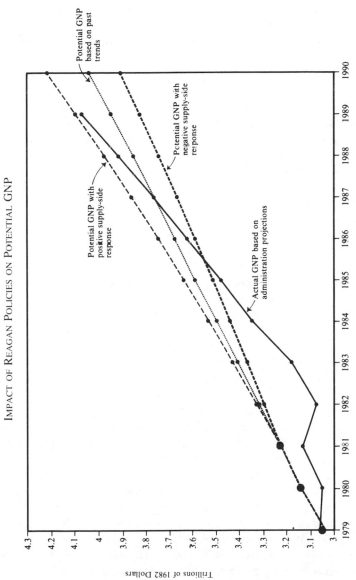

FIGURE 3.6

IMPACT OF REAGAN POLICIES ON POTENTIAL GNP

SOURCE: Office of Management and Budget, *Budget of the United States Government, FY 1985* (Washington, D.C.: Government Printing Office, 1984); authors' calculations.

Conclusion

The Reagan administration's critique of past economic policy and performance properly focused on inflation and inadequate productivity growth as the major problems facing the American economy in 1981. Its diagnosis of the causes of these problems was, however, overly simple. Excessive emphasis was placed on the need to reduce the size of government, when what was really needed was a reappraisal of whether existing programs were providing benefits commensurate with their costs. Tax cuts and regulatory relief were justified as vitally important for restoring productivity, when their likely effects, while in the right direction, were more modest than the administration was suggesting. Finally, monetary restraint was necessary if inflation was to be reduced significantly, but the public was not told that the costs of lowering inflation would be high. Although most economists voiced these objections at the time, the optimism inherent in the Reagan program was seductive. People were willing to suspend their disbelief in the hope that the Reagan economic recovery program would work.

The administration's greatest success has been on the inflation front, but here it must share credit with the Federal Reserve. Moreover, it was a good time to be president: housing, oil, food, and import price movements all helped inflation fall, making policy look even more effective than it was.

A recession in 1981–1982 was all but inevitable. However, an easier monetary policy combined with a tighter fiscal policy would have produced a much milder recession that would have made the average person $500 to $600 richer between 1981 and 1983. Although inflation would not have come down as fast or as far, it would nevertheless have declined substantially—to about 6 percent by 1984. There would have been more growth in housing and net exports and less in consumption.

Whether Reagan policies have been good for growth is debatable. Since much of the president's program was aimed at improving standards of living, not immediately but over the longer run, one would like to be more definitive on this critical issue. However, economists have trouble fully explaining the growth process, and much of the evidence cited in this chapter, while the best currently available, simply cannot support such a judgment.

One thing is abundantly clear from the evidence: no administration can have a major impact on the economy's long-run growth rate. Almost any policy one can think of turns out to have small, usually temporary, effects. Increasing real GNP by 5 percent at the end of ten years, or by an average of about half a point a year, as table 3.7 demonstrates, would be the most one could reasonably hope for. Conversely, reducing the rate of growth by a comparable amount is about the worst outcome one can reasonably imagine.

Whether positive or negative, the effects almost surely lie within this range. Exaggerating the effectiveness of its policies is a political disease that this administration has shared with almost all others. Supply-side economics is no more a panacea for our economic ills than was demand-side economics at an earlier point in our history.

Nevertheless, the administration has, in our view, left three significant legacies for the 1980s. The first is a much lower rate of inflation, but because this rate was achieved at the cost of a deep recession, the decade as a whole will be one of lower growth and higher unemployment than were the 1970s. The second legacy is budget deficits which will cumulate to $1.3 trillion by 1990 unless current policies are changed, and which are the major reason for our somewhat pessimistic conclusions about long-term growth. Our calculations suggest that almost any action undertaken to reduce these deficits will have a positive impact on growth.

The third legacy of the Reagan administration is a less tangible, but possibly important, shift in expectations about what government should or will do.[43] The administration has fostered this climate mostly by virtue of its rhetoric and its ideology, although its stance is also symbolically manifest in its tax and regulatory policies and its willingness to tolerate a long recession. This change in ideological climate does not yet seem to have had a discernible impact on wage- and price-setting practices or, for that matter, on other kinds of economic behavior.[44] Yet public opinion surveys suggest the president has struck a responsive chord with the public, and messages from the Rose Garden about the importance of entrepreneurship and individual initiative may well yet have an impact on the way managers and workers behave and, perhaps, on the economy's efficiency and productivity. The inability of economists to adequately explain the long-term rise and fall of national economies could rest on just such intangibles.

CHAPTER 4

THE BUDGET
A FAILURE OF DISCIPLINE

Gregory B. Mills

More than any U.S. president, Ronald Reagan used the federal budget to articulate and pursue his policies. His initial budget program called for large tax cuts, a rapid buildup in national defense, restrained growth in total federal spending, and a diminishing deficit. Jimmy Carter, if reelected, would have pursued the same objectives, but not to the same degree, nor with such lofty expectations for the economy. The Reagan budget proposals, combined with slower growth of the money supply and regulatory relief, were to promote a vibrant economy which would balance the budget by 1984.

Instead, unprecedented peacetime deficits are both the major budget outcome of the Reagan administration and the dominant pressure for future policy change (table 4.1). How could such deficits arise under the most conservative president of this century, one so devoted to restoring fiscal responsibility to the nation's affairs? This chapter examines the evolving federal budget under President Reagan. How has the budget been altered for both taxes and spending? What are the dimensions of the deficit dilemma, as it places pressure on policy choices and the policymaking process? How enduring are the policy shifts that the president has achieved? What will be the Reagan budget legacy?

President Reagan achieved considerable success on his tax and defense policies. He also succeeded in reducing the growth of nondefense outlays. However, some scaleback of the enacted tax cuts and defense buildup is already underway and will probably continue. And the unremitting need for spending restraint in the face of persistently large deficits will force continuing

TABLE 4.1

FEDERAL DEFICITS

	In $ Billions	Percentage of GNP[a]
Actual		
1981	79	2.7
1982	128	4.1
1983	208	6.4
Projected[b]		
1984	203	5.7
1985	208	5.3
1986	230	5.4
1987	262	5.7
1988	295	5.9
1989	339	6.3

SOURCES: Office of Management and Budget, "Total Government Finances," February 1984, p. 14; Congressional Budget Office, *Baseline Budget Projections for Fiscal Years 1985–1989* (Washington, D.C.: Government Printing Office, 1984) p. 7.

NOTE: Unless otherwise specified, all tables in this chapter include the modest amount of off-budget program outlays. All historical data are derived from Office of Management and Budget (OMB) tabulations that apply consistent accounting assumptions over time. All budget information is by federal fiscal year, ending on June 30 through 1976 and on September 30 in subsequent years. Entries may not add to the totals due to rounding.

a. Subsequent tables show budget outcomes only as a percentage of gross national product (GNP). This is the conventional technique for making comparisons over time periods during which inflation would have caused all dollar magnitudes to rise.

b. Based on enacted policies for FY 1984.

austerity on domestic programs. The downward pressure on spending, along with the general dominance of budget matters in the legislative agenda, promise to remain a lasting consequence of the Reagan budget initiatives.

The President's Success at Achieving His Budget Objectives

Any assessment of President Reagan's success with the budget requires attention both to historical budget trends and to the projected path the budget would have taken during the 1980s without any change in tax and spending policies. With respect to the historical comparison, each presidency is considered here to have a "budget era" that begins with the first full fiscal year of that administration. President Reagan's budget era thus begins with FY 1982. The budget outcomes now projected by the Congressional Budget Office (CBO) for the fourth year of the Reagan era (FY 1985) are compared with the actual budget outcomes in the last year of the Eisenhower era (FY 1961), the Kennedy-Johnson era (FY 1969), the Nixon-Ford era (FY 1977), and the Carter era (FY 1981).* The FY 1985 projections are also compared with estimates of what would have happened if the taxing and spending policies in place by January 1981 had simply been continued through FY 1985.[1] The latter is not intended as a forecast of policy developments under an alternative administration, but rather as a neutral standard of comparison by which to isolate the budget implications of policy change from the effects of economic and demographic conditions. It is referred to throughout as the pre-Reagan policy baseline.

Revenues, National Defense Outlays, and Nondefense Program Outlays

Table 4.2 shows both actual and projected budget outcomes for revenues, national defense outlays, and nondefense program outlays. The major policy developments in each area are discussed in turn.†

Revenues and the Tax Burden. The federal tax burden increased substantially during the twenty years preceding the Reagan administration, from 18.5 percent of gross national product (GNP) at the end of the Eisenhower administration to 20.8 percent at the end of the Carter term. The pronounced increase in the latter part of the period was largely a result of inflation, as price increases tended to push taxpayers into higher tax brackets. In addition to causing this "bracket creep," inflation served to erode the value of fixed-dollar tax advantages.

Periodically through the period, Congress acted to ease the tax burden to some degree by lowering statutory tax rates for both individual and corporate incomes; by liberalizing personal exemptions, deductions, and credits; and by creating "loopholes" through which individuals and corporations could

---

*The following discussion draws heavily from material in Gregory B. Mills and John L. Palmer, *The Deficit Dilemma: Budget Policy in the Reagan Era* (Washington, D.C.: The Urban Institute Press, 1983); and John L. Palmer and Gregory B. Mills, "Budget Policy," in John L. Palmer and Isabel V. Sawhill, eds., *The Reagan Experiment: An Examination of Economic and Social Policies under the Reagan Administration* (Washington, D.C.: The Urban Institute Press, 1982). The outcomes now projected for FY 1985 are based on the budget policies enacted for FY 1984. See Congressional Budget Office, *Baseline Budget Projections for Fiscal Years 1985– 1989* (Washington, D.C.: Government Printing Office, 1984).

†The pre-Reagan policy baseline assumes the policies of January 1981, with full adjustment for subsequent inflation in virtually all nondefense spending programs, no change in tax laws, and real growth in defense outlays of approximately 5 percent in FY 1982, 4 percent in FY 1983, and 3 percent thereafter (consistent with the defense program that Congress had by then adopted). The economic and demographic assumptions are identical to those underlying the projected FY 1985 outcomes of policies enacted for FY 1984).

TABLE 4.2

TRENDS IN FEDERAL REVENUES, NATIONAL DEFENSE OUTLAYS, AND NONDEFENSE
PROGRAM OUTLAYS

	Revenues	National Defense Outlays	Nondefense Program Outlays
	Percentage of GNP		
Actual outcomes, by end-year of presidential budget eras			
Eisenhower (FY 1961)	18.5	9.7	8.1
Kennedy-Johnson (FY 1969)	20.5	9.1	9.7
(without Vietnam-related tax surcharge and defense outlays)	(19.3)	(6.7)	
Nixon–Ford (FY 1977)	19.1	5.2	15.1
Carter (FY 1981)	20.8	5.5	15.7
Projected outcomes for FY 1985, based on:			
Enacted policies for FY 1984	18.7	6.7	14.1
Pre-Reagan policy baseline	21.7	5.8	15.5
Reagan proposals for FY 1982[a]	19.3	6.9	11.0

SOURCES: Office of Management and Budget, "Federal Government Finances," March 1981
and February 1984; Congressional Budget Office, *Baseline Budget Projections*; U.S.
Congress, report of the conference committee on HR 15414 (PL 90–364), June 1968;
Department of Defense (Comptroller), *The Economics of Defense Spending: A Look
at the Realities*, July 1972, p. 149.

a. The "unspecified" outlay reductions that the Reagan administration included in its projections are assumed to come entirely from nondefense programs.

avoid full taxation of their income.* These tax-cutting measures were themselves more than offset, however, by a series of legislative changes that served to further the rise in federal tax burdens. Chief among them were the phased increases in Social Security payroll taxes enacted in 1977 and a windfall profit tax on income from domestically produced oil enacted in 1979.†

From the point of view of the individual taxpayer, the 1960s and 1970s saw a large rise in federal tax rates. For a husband-wife family with two children and with family income at the national median, the sum of the federal income tax and Social Security payroll tax (employee share only) increased

---

*For example, the portion of gross personal income subject to tax declined from 90 percent in 1961 to 81 percent in 1981.

†The taxable earnings base for Social Security was nearly doubled, from $15,300 in 1976 to $29,700 in 1981, and the combined employee-employer payroll tax rate jumped from 11.7 to 13.3 percent.

as a percentage of income from 10.1 to 17.5 percent between 1960 and 1980.* The corresponding marginal federal tax rate, the rate applicable to an additional dollar of income, increased from 20 to 30 percent over the same period.[2] It was largely in response to such rising personal tax rates that candidate and President Reagan advocated across-the-board rate reductions as a cornerstone of his economic program.

Three years of congressional action under President Reagan has indeed reduced the federal tax burden dramatically. From a level of 20.8 percent of GNP in FY 1981, federal revenues are expected to decline to 18.7 percent of GNP in FY 1985 (table 4.2). The president, thus, has succeeded handsomely in his tax-cutting objective. Relative to the pre-Reagan policy baseline, the FY 1985 revenues are projected to be lower by $117 billion, or 3 percent of GNP.[3] This shift was largely the result of a landmark piece of tax-cutting legislation, the Economic Recovery Tax Act of 1981 (ERTA), plus a major revenue-raising measure enacted the following year, the Tax Equity and Fiscal Responsibility Act of 1982 (TEFRA).[4]

Because the federal tax burden was heading toward a peacetime high in 1981 and bipartisan support was mounting for tax relief, one can assume that any administration taking office in 1981 would have initiated some net tax reduction, relative to the pre-Reagan policy baseline. Cuts in both personal and corporate taxes were under active consideration. Some amount of tax increases was also likely, such as a higher gasoline tax to finance road improvements and higher payroll taxes to avert an expected shortfall in the Social Security trust fund. In the absence of the Reagan policies, a possible alternative policy scenario would have been a net tax reduction starting in October 1981 sufficient to offset subsequent inflation-induced bracket creep. This would have kept federal revenues nearly constant as a share of GNP. Compared with this alternative, the post-1980 tax changes resulted in a 1985 revenue loss of $72 billion, or almost 2 percent of GNP.

The Defense Buildup. The twenty years preceding the Reagan administration saw the Vietnam-related rise in real defense outlays through the late 1960s, a subsequent decline through the mid-1970s, and then modest growth beginning in the late 1970s.[5] The latter rise still left the FY 1981 defense share of GNP far below its FY 1961 level. Accompanying this overall trend was a shift in the composition of defense spending. An increasing share of national defense outlays went for current operating expenses in defense-related

---

*The rising tax rates reflected payroll tax increases and the bracket creep caused by inflation and a rising real (inflation-adjusted) standard of living. Over the twenty-year period, the purchasing power represented by the median income increased by more than one-third.

activities, primarily the payroll for active personnel and the operation-and-maintenance cost of existing military facilities and equipment. This meant a declining share of outlays for weapons development and procurement. Concern over the underfunding of defense focused principally on this declining emphasis on the enhancement of future military capabilities.

The desire to modernize U.S. weapons had motivated the reversal in defense spending that began during the Ford administration. President Carter then embarked upon steady real defense growth as part of a strengthened U.S. commitment to the NATO alliance. In the 1980 presidential campaign and in his outgoing budget proposals for FY 1982, President Carter proposed further real growth in defense outlays of about 5 percent.

Ronald Reagan, in contrast, proposed 9 percent annual real growth as part of his FY 1982 budget request—a figure that implied a four-year real increase of more than 40 percent. The purchase of new military weapons was to rise sharply as a share of the defense budget. Congress accepted the president's FY 1982 defense request virtually without revision during 1981. In light of the worsening deficits, however, the administration adjusted its FY 1983 and FY 1984 proposals downward slightly. Congress adopted spending resolutions for both years that further reduced the president's requested rate of growth of budget authority.* However, relative to the pre-Reagan policy baseline, the projected defense buildup under President Reagan will still have increased FY 1985 outlays for national defense by $36 billion, or nearly 1 percent of GNP.[6]

Cutbacks in Nondefense Program Outlays. In contrast to defense outlays, federal nondefense program outlays as a share of GNP rose substantially between 1961 and 1981, especially from the mid-1960s through the mid-1970s. All major components of nondefense program spending shared in the growth: benefit payments for individuals, grants to state and local governments for the purchase of goods and services, and the array of other federal activities, ranging from foreign aid to business subsidies to federal pay. However, the rise in benefit payments to individuals was clearly dominant. Such benefits more than quadrupled in real terms between 1961 and 1981, as they grew from 5.5 to 11.5 percent of GNP.†

---

*Congress does not directly control outlays but rather appropriates budget authority to federal agencies. This authority to make spending commitments does not result in outlays until the Treasury actually disburses funds, such as through payroll checks to federal employees or payments to federal contractors. In national defense spending, budget authority enacted in one year may not result in outlays until several years later, as in the case of long-term weapons procurement.

†Chapter 6 on social policy details the rise in benefit programs.

President Reagan sought a dramatic scaleback in the federal government's commitment to nondefense activities, in order to limit federal spending growth while accommodating a rising GNP share for national defense. The total budget package he submitted in March 1981 (for FY 1982) implied a reduction in nondefense program outlays between 1981 and 1985 of 15 to 20 percent in real terms. Since the proportional cutbacks over this period were to be much smaller in programs considered by the administration to form the "social safety net"—a selected group, most notably Social Security and Medicare, that constituted more than one-half of 1981 nondefense program spending—the implied percentage cuts in all other domestic activities were staggering.* Major targets were means-tested entitlement programs (such as Aid to Families with Dependent Children (AFDC) and Food Stamps) and annually funded grants to state and local governments.

The administration's subsequent budget initiatives continued the assault. Means-tested benefits were again targets. In addition, the FY 1983 budget highlighted management savings and the shift (along with reductions in federal aid) of many federal program responsibilities to state and local governments under the "New Federalism" scheme.† The FY 1984 budget featured a freeze on total annually funded nondefense spending and some suspension of cost-of-living adjustments (COLAs) in federal salaries and transfer programs automatically indexed for inflation. The FY 1985 budget offered less ambitious cost cutting, in response to congressional resistance on many of the earlier proposed cuts, combined with mounting political anxieties over the 1984 election.

The outcome of congressional action on the president's proposals has been a major degree of domestic spending restraint. Measured against the pre-Reagan policy baseline, 1985 nondefense program spending has been reduced by $56 billion.[7] This constitutes a proportional reduction of nearly 10 percent (in contrast to the 15 to 20 percent envisioned in the FY 1982 proposals), and amounts to about 1.5 percent of GNP. Although this restraint was far more than most thought possible when President Reagan took office, it was far less restraint than he sought (one-half, by OMB's estimate). It was also far less than he needed to control the deficit in the face of the tax cuts, the defense buildup, and the economy's performance. Most notably, the administration found that "fraud, waste, and abuse" were neither as pervasive

---

*In fact, the administration did propose in May 1981 a major tightening of Social Security benefits, leaving some doubt as to whether the social safety net was indeed to be "preserved and maintained." However, little more than a week after the president unveiled his Social Security plan, the Senate voted 96 to 0 to reject it.

†See chapter 7 on federalism and the states for details.

nor as subject to policy control as expected. Nevertheless, the domestic program budget has been scaled back to a level, in proportion in GNP, similar to that of the mid-1970s.*

Restraint in Total Outlays and the Deficit

Through the Nixon-Ford era, the decline in real defense outlays was more than offset by the accelerating growth of nondefense programs. This, along with a slight increase in interest payments on the federal debt, led total federal outlays to grow substantially, at a pace exceeding the growth of revenues (table 4.3). These developments caused rising federal deficits. During the Carter era, total outlays rose further, as the upturn in defense spending was coupled with a surge in interest rates that elevated dramatically the government's interest costs. Even with more moderate nondefense spending growth, total outlays reached record peacetime levels in 1981. The deficit nevertheless declined as a share of GNP, as bracket creep also pushed revenues up to record levels.†

President Reagan's original budget proposals prescribed a substantial downturn in total federal outlays, to 19.4 percent of GNP in 1985—the level of outlays at which the budget could be balanced, given the administration's proposed tax cuts and economic assumptions. Despite the planned defense buildup, total federal outlays would be returned to their GNP share in the early 1960s. The reduction was to occur not only through large domestic spending reductions, but also via a marked drop in interest outlays as a percentage of GNP, to be accomplished by a projected lowering of interest rates and arrested growth in the stock of federal debt.

---

*Some net spending reductions were to have been expected under any administration. For instance, Social Security benefits would almost certainly have been restrained as part of necessary legislation to restore the solvency of the program's trust fund. Other possible actions included some limits to hospital reimbursement costs in Medicare, some scaleback of employment and training programs, and less generous cost-of-living adjustments in federal retirement programs. Such measures might have been offset in part by higher outlays, as with possible antirecession spending initiatives.

†During the 1980 presidential campaign, Ronald Reagan cited those developments as evidence of an excessive, uncontrolled diversion of resources from the private sector. However, to the extent that much of the spending growth came in fact through interpersonal transfers (from taxpayers to either recipients of benefit payments or holders of government securities), the spending growth did not constitute a direct claim on private output, as mentioned in chapter 3 on the economy. Furthermore, an important segment of the rise in the government's actual purchases of goods and services was coming through renewed defense growth, a trend which Mr. Reagan of course welcomed.

TABLE 4.3

TRENDS IN TOTAL OUTLAYS AND THE DEFICIT

| | Revenues | Outlays | | | Surplus (+) or Deficit (−) | Structural Surplus (+) or Deficit (−)[c] |
		National Defense and Nondefense Programs[a]	Interest on Federal Debt[b]	Total		
		Percentage of GNP				
Actual outcomes, by end-year of presidential budget eras:						
Eisenhower (FY 1961)	18.5	17.9	1.3	19.2	−0.7	+1.8
Kennedy–Johnson (FY 1969)	20.5	18.8	1.4	20.2	+0.4	−0.4
Nixon–Ford (FY 1977)	19.1	20.4	1.6	22.0	−2.9	−1.6
Carter (FY 1981)	20.8	21.1	2.4	23.5	−2.7	−1.2
Projected outcomes for FY 1985, based on:						
Enacted policies for FY 1984	18.7	20.8	3.2	24.1	−5.3	−3.7
Reagan proposals for FY 1982	19.3	17.9	1.5	19.4	−0.0	+0.0
Projected outcomes for FY 1989, based on:						
Enacted policies for FY 1984	18.9	21.1	4.1	25.2	−6.3	−5.7

SOURCES: Office of Management and Budget "Federal Government Finances"; Congressional Budget Office, *Baseline Budget Projections*, and *The Economic Outlook* (Washington, D.C.: Government Printing Office, 1984); Frank de Leeuw and Thomas M. Holloway, "Cyclical Adjustment of the Federal Budget and Federal Debt," *Survey of Current Business*, vol. 63, no. 12 (December 1983), p. 39.

a. Includes off-budget outlays.

b. Includes interest paid on tax refunds and offsetting interest collected from federal agencies and the public.

c. Estimated at a 6 percent unemployment rate and expressed as a percentage of the corresponding estimate of GNP.

Contrary to President Reagan's intentions, total federal outlays are now higher as a share of GNP than in 1981.* Since federal revenues have fallen in GNP share, the result is a huge federal deficit, now projected to be higher in 1985 than in 1981 by about 2.5 percent of GNP. This deficit level (5.3 percent of GNP) stands well above any peacetime precedent.

Why will the deficit be so much higher for 1985 than it was when President Reagan took office? Since this happened despite a fall of one and a half percentage points in nondefense program spending as a share of GNP, the deficit-increasing factors amounted to some four percentage points of GNP: the fall in the federal tax burden, some two percentage points; the rise in the defense budget, about one percentage point; and the rise in interest outlays, also about one percentage point. The shifts in taxes, national defense, and nondefense programs have been a direct result of the enacted changes in policy. The rise in interest outlays is due to both the policy changes and the combination of high unemployment and low inflation that came with the 1981–1982 recession.

The underlying imbalance between federal tax and spending policies is best shown by the structural or high-employment deficit. As explained in chapter 3, this measure assumes a standardized, high-employment state of the economy. It thus removes the distortions to budget estimates caused by the sensitivity of both revenues and outlays to the general level of economic activity. During the quarter century preceding the Reagan administration, the structural deficit rarely exceeded 2 percent of its corresponding high-employment GNP. However, if current policies are unchanged, the structural deficit will reach 3.7 percent of GNP in 1985 and 5.7 percent in 1989.[8] This is the extent of deficit that will remain even with strong economic growth.

The significance of such structural deficits is their likely adverse impact on the pace of capital formation. The larger deficits since 1981 have already reversed the postwar decline in federal debt as a percentage of GNP (figure 4.1). If this rise continues, one likely outcome is a fall in the ratio of private capital to GNP.[9] Depressed growth in the capital stock can be expected, in turn, to lower attainable levels of economic output in the years to come and thus threaten the standard of living that future generations might otherwise enjoy.[10]

---

*Abstracting from demographic changes and the performance of the economy, the enacted changes in policy have virtually no net effect on the amount of total FY 1985 outlays. When measured against the pre-Reagan policy baseline, the restraint in nondefense programs (− $56 billion) is offset by the increase in defense ($36 billion) and interest ($19 billion). The policy-induced rise in interest payments stems from the tax cuts and defense buildup, which serve to increase the federal debt more than the domestic spending cuts serve to reduce it.

FIGURE 4.1

FEDERAL DEBT HELD BY THE PUBLIC,
FY 1954–FY 1989

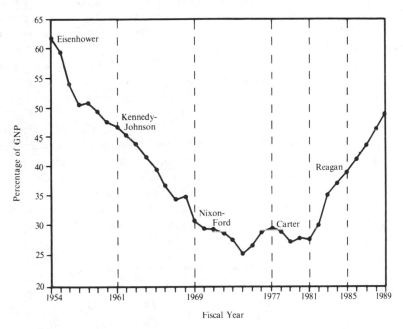

SOURCE: Office of Management and Budget, "Federal Government Finances," February 1984, pp. 102–103; Congressional Budget Office, *Baseline Budget Projections for Fiscal Years 1985–1989* (Washington, D.C.: Government Printing Office, February 1984), p. 27.

NOTE: Actual data through FY 1983; subsequent data based on enacted policies for FY 1984.

Implications of the Enacted Budget Changes

The most striking budget development under President Reagan is thus the severe, structural disparity between federal outlays and revenues. The economic pressures posed by the deficit suggest forthcoming legislative action of sufficient magnitude to render the current budget structure only a transitional state. With so much attention focused on the deficit and with the expectation of continuing budget change, one might easily lose sight of the shifts in tax and spending policies that have occurred thus far under President Reagan. Nevertheless, it is important to understand these shifts. They are not only the Reagan imprint on the budget to date; they also establish the context for future policy action.

Changes in the Composition of Revenues, National Defense Outlays, and Nondefense Program Outlays

Recent budget developments have changed not only the *levels* of revenues and outlays, but also their composition. Whatever judgments are made about the merits of these changes, they have clearly led to a shifting of the tax burden and a reordering of spending priorities.*

Revenues. Changes in the relative importance of different sources of revenue are shown in table 4.4. Most notably, the federal tax structure now relies less than it did in 1981 upon those sources that draw revenue disproportionately from the higher-income population.

The individual income tax is the largest single federal revenue source. As a progressive form of tax, it takes a larger proportional bite from the income of higher-income persons. This tax now constitutes a smaller share of both GNP and revenues than in 1981, due largely to the across-the-board reductions in tax rates.[11] Without the Reagan policy changes, revenues from the individual income tax would have risen as a share of GNP, even if the personal tax had been indexed for inflation after October 1981.

TABLE 4.4

THE SHIFTING COMPOSITION OF FEDERAL REVENUES

	Actual FY 1981	Projected FY 1985[a]	Actual FY 1981	Projected FY 1985[a]
	Percentage of GNP		*Percentage Distribution*	
Individual income taxes	9.9	8.4	48	45
Corporate income and windfall profit taxes	2.9	1.8	14	10
Social insurance taxes	6.3	6.9	31	37
Excise taxes (excluding windfall profit taxes)	0.6	0.8	3	4
Estate and gift taxes	0.2	0.1	1	1
Other receipts	0.8	0.7	4	4
TOTAL	20.8	18.7	100	100

SOURCE: Congressional Budget Office, *Baseline Budget Projections*, p. 17; Office of Management and Budget, "Federal Government Finances," February 1984, pp. 9, 11, 13, and 18.

a. Based on enacted policies for FY 1984.

---

*For nondefense programs, the policy shifts underlying the changing composition of federal spending are examined in detail in subsequent chapters of this volume. These policy developments, along with those in taxes and defense spending, are also discussed at length in Gregory B. Mills and John L. Palmer, eds., *Federal Budget Policy in the 1980s* (Washington, D.C.: The Urban Institute Press, 1984).

The other major progressive taxes are those falling on corporations, most importantly the corporate income tax and the windfall profit tax. Here again, the projected tax yield has fallen as a share of GNP and total federal revenues. This drop would have occurred to some extent even without the Reagan policy changes, as moderating inflation would have caused taxable profits (including windfall oil profits) to fall relative to GNP. The liberalized depreciation provisions resulting from ERTA, however, caused an even sharper decline in taxable corporate income.

Social insurance taxes and other excise taxes, the less progressive federal tax sources, have risen as a share of GNP and total revenues. Payroll taxes for Social Security and Medicare would have become more prominent even without any policy change, through previously scheduled increases in the taxable earnings base and the combined employer-employee tax rate. But the Social Security legislation of 1983 raised payroll tax revenues even further, principally through expanded Social Security coverage and higher tax rates for the self-employed. Excise taxes were raised substantially through congressional action in 1982. TEFRA tripled the telephone tax, doubled the cigarette tax, and raised airport and airway taxes; Congress also enacted the five-cent-per-gallon increase in the gasoline tax, effective in 1983.

The distributional impact of the recent federal changes has been reinforced by tax changes at the state and local level. The fiscal pressures of the 1981–1982 recession and federal spending cutbacks have led many states and localities to increase their own taxes—most notably property and sales taxes—whose burdens also fall disproportionately on lower-income persons. The total government tax burden has thus become even less progressive than examination of the federal changes alone would suggest.*

National Defense Outlays. Spending for the development and procurement of military hardware, especially modernized weapons, is now a significantly larger share of GNP and total defense outlays than it was in 1981 (table 4.5). Even without the Reagan defense buildup, this shift would have occurred to some degree, as the process of defense modernization had been underway since the mid-1970s. But the Reagan buildup intensified it. The projected 1985 pattern of defense budget authority implies continuing support for weapons purchases—about 80 percent of what is shown in table 4.5 as procurement of military hardware. The costs of new weaponry thus seem destined to grow to an even higher share of defense outlays in the late 1980s.

---

*The pattern of fiscal adjustments at the state and local level is detailed in chapters 7 and 8. The net effect on households of the composite changes in government tax policy is to increase the disparities in disposable income between lower- and higher-income families, as discussed in chapter 11.

TABLE 4.5

THE SHIFTING COMPOSITION OF NATIONAL DEFENSE OUTLAYS

	Actual FY 1981	Projected FY 1985[a]	Actual FY 1981	Projected FY 1985[a]
	Percentage of GNP		Percentage Distribution	
Department of Defense—Military				
Military personnel[b]	1.7	1.8	32	27
Operation, maintenance, and construction of military equipment and facilities[c]	1.9	2.0	34	30
Research, development, testing, and evaluation	0.5	0.7	10	10
Procurement of military hardware	1.2	2.0	22	30
Other defense-related activities[d]	0.1	0.2	2	3
TOTAL	5.5	6.7	100	100
Addendum:				
Procurement—budget authority	1.7	2.7	27[e]	35[e]

SOURCES: Office of Management and Budget, "Federal Government Finances," February 1984, pp. 27, 60; Congressional Budget Office, *Baseline Budget Projections* and unpublished tabulations.
  a. Based on enacted policies for FY 1984.
  b. Includes accruals for military retirement contributions, allowances for pay raises and benefits, and family housing.
  c. Includes special currency program.
  d. Largely atomic energy defense activities.
  e. Percentage of budget authority for national defense.

The increased budget commitment to weapons acquisition has been furthered by the administration's emphasis on sophisticated, state-of-the-art hardware—a strategy for enhancing our military capabilities that has stimulated strong bipartisan criticism from former Defense secretaries and high-level military officials, congressional advocates of renewed military strength, and long-time students of the defense budget.[12] Such critics see several risks. First, the more sophisticated a weapon system, the less proven and reliable are its capabilities. Second, state-of-the-art military technology is not only expensive to develop and test, but also subject to production uncertainties that may drive long-term funding upward in unexpected and largely uncontrollable ways. Third, when such weapons come into use, they generate large continuing costs for operation and maintenance; at a minimum, they demand increased skills among military personnel.

These issues are of particular concern if restraint in the total defense budget is deemed necessary in reducing the deficit. To accommodate the current scale of weapons development and production, other defense capabilities may be compromised. The search to find budget savings will tend to focus on those defense activities where reductions in budget authority can most readily translate into lower outlays—for example, spare parts, support equipment, and munitions that support the readiness of our conventional (i.e., nonnuclear) forces. The risk in scaling back the purchase of these items is that our land, air, and sea forces might become less able to quickly move into combat if needed. In addition, these forces might be rendered less equipped to sustain a prolonged combat effort.

Nondefense Program Outlays. The federal nondefense budget provides for central government activities, support to individuals, and support to businesses, institutions, and lower (subnational) units of government (table 4.6).

Central government activities include the core administrative and regulatory functions of the executive branch, the conduct of foreign relations, the Postal Service, the operations of the legislative and judicial branches, and federal employee retirement. Such funding has been reduced modestly relative to GNP, largely through cutbacks in the federal work force.

Social Security dominates the category of federal support to individuals, which includes both income support and services. With the rising number of elderly persons, and despite some benefit restraint enacted in 1983, Social Security has grown faster than the sum of other nondefense programs during the Reagan administration, though not as rapidly as GNP. Medicare outlays, in contrast, will outpace GNP by a wide margin. The effect of rising medical costs, in addition to an expanding elderly population, offsets the modest policy restraint in Medicare enacted thus far under President Reagan. Other forms of social insurance have declined slightly as a share of both GNP and the nondefense budget. This decline reflects deep cuts in unemployment insurance and guaranteed student loans and modest changes in railroad retirement and non-means-tested veterans programs.

Assistance to low-income and disadvantaged persons, the remaining subcategory of support to individuals, includes means-tested entitlements such as Medicaid, Food Stamps, and AFDC, as well as annually funded benefits and services that include health care, employment and training, housing, nutrition, education, and rehabilitation. Significant spending cuts have occurred in both entitlements and annually funded programs, with the principal exceptions of Medicaid and Supplemental Security Income (cash support for the low-income aged, blind, or disabled). The spending reductions, borne especially by the working poor, have served to reinforce the distributional pattern of the tax cuts.

The remaining domestic outlays provide support to businesses, institutions, and state or local governments. Subsidies to commerce and research—

TABLE 4.6

THE SHIFTING COMPOSITION OF NONDEFENSE PROGRAM OUTLAYS

	Actual FY 1981	Projected FY 1985[a]	Actual FY 1981	Projected FY 1985[a]
	Percentage of GNP		Percentage Distribution	
Central government activities	1.7	1.4	11	10
Support for individuals				
Social Security	4.8	4.7	30	33
Medicare	1.3	1.7	8	12
Other social insurance	1.4	1.0	9	7
Assistance to low-income and dis-advantaged				
Medicaid	0.6	0.6	4	4
Other[b]	3.1	2.4	20	17
Support to businesses, institutions, and lower units of government				
Commerce and research[c]	1.4	1.0	9	7
Natural resources and infrastructure	1.6	1.2	10	9
TOTAL	15.7	14.1	100	100
Addendum:				
Total grants to state and local governments[d]	3.3	2.7	21	19

SOURCES: Congressional Budget Office, *Baseline Budget Projections* and unpublished tabulations.

a. Based on enacted policies for FY 1984.

b. Food Stamps, Aid to Families with Dependent Children (AFDC), Supplemental Security Income, veterans' pensions, child nutrition, and many minor benefit and service programs.

c. Farm price supports and other agricultural programs; activities of the Departments of Commerce and Education, Government National Mortgage Association, Small Business Administration, Export-Import Bank, and National Aeronautics and Space Administration; health, energy, and other scientific research.

d. Includes Medicaid, AFDC, and other benefits paid to individuals where funds are provided through state and local governments.

including agricultural programs, credit assistance, and support for education and science—have experienced a dramatic funding decline, with the major exception of farm subsidies. The downward shift in federal spending for the final subcategory, natural resources and infrastructure, also reflects significant policy restraint—achieved through a diminished federal role in the environment, transportation, and community and regional development. In large part, federal support for natural resources and infrastructure is provided through state and local governments. The reductions in such intergovernmental support, combined with the restraint in forms of low-income assistance that also flow through these lower units of government, translates into a marked drop in total grants to state and local governments.

Budget Dynamics and Policy Control

The structural deficits projected under current policy are generally acknowledged as unacceptable. The desire to reduce them raises another important set of questions as to whether the recent budget shifts themselves have made more difficult the task of restoring budget equilibrium. How have recent budget developments affected the ease with which further policy changes can produce a sustainable combination of revenues and outlays?

Indexing and the Restoration of Revenues. For better or worse, bracket creep has served historically as a stabilizing feature of the federal budget. Any structural deficit tended to diminish as inflation and real economic growth—combined with the progressive rate schedule of the individual income tax—served to increase revenues faster than GNP. As long as outlays grew no faster than GNP, diminishing structural deficits and subsequent surpluses were the inevitable result.

Because the 1981 tax act included the scheduled indexing of the individual income tax in 1985, the federal government will reap no further revenues from inflation-induced bracket creep. In important respects, this is a favorable development. Bracket creep has served as a back-door source of revenue, allowing presidents and Congress to avoid explicit financing decisions; the sponsors of new program initiatives could find funding through the revenue dividend provided by inflation. The proponents of indexing have correctly argued that an unindexed personal tax thus discouraged fiscal discipline—a situation that may well have contributed to the 1981 peacetime highs for both federal outlays and federal revenues. But the revenue yield of bracket creep was certainly not converted entirely into more spending. Congress did grant taxpayer relief during the 1970s, which moderated the growth in federal income taxes without a rise in structural deficits. Indeed, bracket creep allowed the debate over tax policy to proceed in an environment whereby necessary tax relief could be offered as an inducement for genuine tax reform, without congressional inaction exposing the economy to the risk of growing deficits.*

Whatever the merits of indexing, once it becomes effective the projected tax burden will rise only slightly as a share of GNP. For higher taxes to

---

*Bracket creep has even served as a form of macroeconomic stabilizer. During periods of inflation caused by excess demand, the inflation-induced upward movement of the tax burden has acted to restrain aggregate demand by reducing consumer purchasing power.

contribute markedly to a smaller deficit, there must now be deliberate policy action.

The Controllability of Federal Outlays. Under President Reagan, two opposing developments have occurred with respect to the controllability of spending. On the one hand, the budget has evolved in ways that pose increasing "technical" limits to future spending restraint, with a rising share of outlays required simply to honor prior fiscal commitments. But on the other hand, the Reagan administration has demonstrated that the congressional budget process can be used to achieve major program cutbacks and that the political obstacles to spending restraint are not nearly as insurmountable as formerly viewed.

The declining budget share that can technically be considered subject to subsequent policy control results from the rise in interest outlays and the rise in program outlays necessitated by prior contracts and obligations (table 4.7). The latter development stems from the defense buildup, accentuated by the procurement emphasis within the defense budget. The trends in both interest and defense have already caused the "untouchable" portion of the budget to rise substantially since 1981, and under current policies this climb will continue through the rest of the decade.*

The remainder of federal budget outlays is directly controllable through legislative action. For most of these outlays, however, restraint requires a change in basic program legislation rather than simply a reduction in the annual funding level. Before the Reagan administration it was considered extremely difficult to achieve the basic legislative changes needed to control entitlement benefits, farm price supports, revenue sharing, or other forms of spending enabled through multiyear program authorizations. The requisite consensus-building within Congress had to occur in the course of time-consuming congressional hearings, committee deliberations, and floor debate. Initiatives for program restraint were typically thwarted in this process, as committees resisted any threat to their jurisdictional prerogatives and interest groups rose to defend their vested interests.

In this area recent developments have served to enhance the controllability of spending. With David Stockman as the chief tactician, President Reagan acted quickly in 1981 to remove the cloak of invulnerability surrounding entitlements and other semipermanent forms of spending. By exploiting the budget procedures established through congressional reforms in 1974, the Reagan administration packaged together numerous changes in basic

---

*Although prior funding commitments can be canceled, in principle, such reversals have never occurred to any extent.

TABLE 4.7

CONTROLLABILITY OF FEDERAL BUDGET OUTLAYS

	Actual FY 1981	Projected[a]	
		FY 1985	FY 1989
	Percentage of Total Budget Outlays		
Outlays that are virtually beyond policy control			
Interest on federal debt	11	14	16
Program outlays resulting from prior contracts and obligations[b]			
National defense	6	10	13
Nondefense programs	10	8	7
SUBTOTAL	27	32	36
All other outlays, controllable through changes in:			
Basic program legislation			
Nondefense programs	45	43	39
Current-year annual funding			
National defense	16	16	17
Nondefense programs	12	9	8
SUBTOTAL	73	68	64
TOTAL	100	100	100

SOURCES: Congressional Budget Office, *Baseline Budget Projections*, pp. 20, 28; Office of Management and Budget, "Federal Government Finances," February 1984, p. 98.

NOTE: Estimates do not include off-budget outlays, except that FY 1985 and FY 1989 figures are adjusted to include outlays for the strategic petroleum reserve, which was shifted to off-budget status after 1981.

a. Based on enacted policies for FY 1984.

b. The 1985 and 1989 estimates are derived from OMB projections through 1985 of President Reagan's budget for FY 1985.

program features and shepherded these to enactment through a series of up-or-down votes.* Although there has been some congressional backlash to this perceived heavy-handedness, President Reagan has demonstrated that the reformed congressional procedures can be a powerful tool for spending restraint.[13]

The Prospects for Deficit Reduction

Of the budget shifts that have occurred under President Reagan, which will endure to establish the Reagan budget legacy? To restate the point made

---

*These procedures had been similarly used in 1980 under President Carter but to achieve much smaller spending reductions.

at the outset of this chapter, large and growing federal deficits are the principal budget consequence of the recent developments. The permanence of the other federal budget outcomes—the lowered tax burden with its shift toward less progressive sources, the increase in defense spending with its emphasis on weapons purchases, and the spending restraint in virtually all domestic programs—will depend on the policy response to the projected deficits.

The Political Economy of Deficit Reduction

The nature of forthcoming budget changes depends of course on the occupant of the White House, the performance of the economy, and the emerging trends in public opinion. If President Reagan enters a second term, he will probably continue to favor domestic spending cuts over defense restraint and push for tax increases only as a last resort. This notion implies an even more pronounced shift in the composition of program spending, with only modest reversals of the enacted shifts in defense outlays and taxes. A Democratic president, in contrast, would presumably seek a more dramatic reversal of the enacted shifts in defense outlays and taxes but less in further domestic spending cuts.

Adverse economic developments would certainly focus more attention on the budget but with uncertain implications for any congressional action on the deficit. An overheated economy, with rising inflation and interest rates, would presumably strengthen the inclination to exercise fiscal restraint. The expected response is less clear if the economy stumbles. On the one hand, a faltering economy—caused perhaps by weakening in the trade- or credit-sensitive sectors, with deficits perceived as a contributing factor—might also increase the call for deficit reduction. But on the other hand, the onset of recession might be used as an argument against budget tightening—or even as an argument for further, countercyclical fiscal stimulus.

With respect to public opinion, available survey evidence shows clear contradictions in the expressed budget preferences of the American public.[14] People are unwilling to cut spending but also are unwilling to accept the level of taxes and/or deficits that is implied by continued spending. If spending must be cut, the public sees the defense budget as the principal target, but people prefer more growth in defense spending than Congress has adopted. People do not like "welfare spending," but they feel the president's cuts in social programs have gone too far. Although domestic restraint is more acceptable in non-means-tested programs than elsewhere, most people feel the Democratic leadership yielded too much to the president in reducing Social Security benefits in 1983. If more federal revenues must be raised, people are generally willing to forgo scheduled tax reductions to close the deficit, but sentiment runs strongly against increases in personal tax rates. And this quandary is coupled with mixed public sentiment as to who bears principal responsibility for the deficit—the Congress, the Reagan administration, prior administrations, or the Federal Reserve.

Such public ambivalence provides little incentive for the president or Congress to "be out front" in the offensive against deficits and thus face the retribution of voters or political opponents by initiating benefit cuts or tax increases. There is a growing consensus among elected officials that deficits may impose widely shared long-term economic costs and that smaller deficits would enhance the nation's long-term economic prospects. It is conceivable and even likely that, in a smoke-filled room or under secret ballot, leaders from both parties could agree on a credible deficit reduction plan. The problem comes in assuming responsibility for the authorship of such a scheme and providing the leadership necessary for its passage.

How much deficit reduction would be necessary for a serious attack on the structural deficit? And what would this require in terms of shifts in spending or tax policies? There is no clear consensus on either question. The illustrative policy target used here is a FY 1989 structural deficit of 2 percent of GNP, or about $100 billion. Such an objective is clearly ambitious, since it compares with a projected 1989 level of about $300 billion under current policies. The remaining structural deficit, however, would still constitute a higher share of GNP than that experienced in nearly every year since World War II, although attainment of such a deficit target would be sufficient to reverse the projected rise in the debt-to-GNP ratio depicted in figure 4.1.

To achieve the implied two-thirds reduction in the projected structural deficit for FY 1989—from roughly $300 billion to $100 billion—one needs a combination of reductions in program spending and increases in revenues that amount annually to about $150 billion in FY 1989. The remainder necessary to achieve the target would come from the associated savings in interest outlays due to the slower accumulation of federal debt—assuming that the policy measures take effect in FY 1985 and build progressively through 1989. Such action would be well beyond that implied by President Reagan's call in early 1984 for a down payment on projected deficits.

The Policy Choices

What are the policy choices and tradeoffs thrust upon the president and Congress if they are to achieve $150 billion of reductions in program spending and increased revenues for FY 1989? Such a deficit reduction will require concerted effort on all policy fronts. national defense spending, nondefense program spending, and revenues.[15] The discussion starts here by addressing outlays, since the general presumption is that revenue measures should be adopted only to the extent that feasible spending cuts are insufficient. Table 4.8 shows an illustrative list of outlay reductions as compared with projected outlays under policies already enacted.

National Defense Outlays. Defense restraint is typically cast in terms of a sustained, multiyear reduction in the rate of growth of budget authority enacted by Congress through its annual defense appropriations. The congressional policy adopted for FY 1984 calls for 5 percent annual real growth in budget authority. Each sustained percentage point reduction in this growth rate, beginning with 1985, would result in an annual outlay savings by 1989 of about $14 billion below the level implied by enacted policy.

TABLE 4.8

OUTLAY SAVINGS FROM ILLUSTRATIVE POLICY ACTION

	Estimated Reduction in FY 1989 Outlays	Addendum: Projected Outlays[a]		
		FY 1984	FY 1989	Growth
	Billions of Dollars			
National defense				
Limit annual real growth in budget authority to:		235	408	173
5 percent	0			
3 percent	−28			
0 percent	−68			
Social Security[b]		179	250	71
Eliminate COLA for one year[c]	−8			
Reduce COLA to CPI increase minus two percentage points	−19			
Medicare[d]		64	120	56
Limit provider reimbursement[e]	−5			
Limit provider reimbursement and expand patient cost-sharing[f]	−12			
Other non-means-tested entitlements[g]		74	87	13
Eliminate COLA for one year	−3			
Reduce COLA to CPI increase minus two percentage points	−5			

SOURCES: Congressional Budget Office, *Reducing the Deficit: Spending and Revenue Options* (Washington, D.C.: Government Printing Office, 1984); and Congressional Budget Office, *Analysis of the President's Budgetary Proposals for Fiscal Year 1985* (Washington, D.C.: Government Printing Office, 1984).
a. Based on enacted policies for FY 1984.
b. Also includes railroad retirement.

One of the major difficulties in achieving defense restraint is that the future path of defense outlays is already affected to a significant degree by prior spending commitments. Thus, even if defense appropriations during 1985–1989 were enacted with no real growth in budget authority, FY 1989 outlays would still represent a real increase over FY 1984 (and

TABLE 4.8 (*continued*)

	Estimated Reduction in FY 1989 Outlays	Addendum: Projected Outlays[a]		
		FY 1984	FY 1989	Growth
Medicaid and other means-tested entitlements[h]		61	81	20
Adopt the proposals from President Reagan's FY 1984 budget[i]	− 3			
Farm price supports and other mandatory spending		22	34	12
Freeze target prices for farm price supports at 1984 crop-year levels	− 6			
Annually funded nondefense spending		156	198	42
Eliminate annual inflationary adjustments for two years	− 12			
Limit annual inflationary adjustments to 2 percent for five years	− 23			
TOTAL PROGRAM OUTLAYS[j]		791	1,176	385

c. Assumes no cost-of-living adjustment (COLA) as scheduled for January 1985; under current law, the scheduled COLA would reflect changes in the Consumer Price Index (CPI); no COLA restraint thereafter.

d. Projected outlays do not reflect offsetting receipts from Medicare premiums.

e. Assumes fee schedules for physicians and limited increases in prospective payment rates for hospitals.

f. Assumes the above measures, plus increased premiums for Supplementary Medical Insurance and expanded coinsurance for hospital care.

g. The largest programs in this category are civil service retirement, military retirement, unemployment insurance, and veterans' compensation.

h. In addition to Medicaid, the largest such programs are Aid to Families with Dependent Children (AFDC), Food Stamps, Supplemental Security Income, veterans' pensions, guaranteed student loans, and child nutrition.

i. For Medicaid, assumes expanded patient cost-sharing and reduced matching funds to states. Also includes tightened eligibility for AFDC and Food Stamps and a six-month delay in the COLA for veterans' pensions.

j. Does not include offsetting receipts or off-budget outlays.

would still exceed the FY 1989 level projected in the pre-Reagan policy baseline) because of the substantial volume of prior contracts and obligations.

Some knowledgeable observers have advocated extending from five years to six years the budget authority now planned for 1985–1989, at least in part because the present spending momentum is seen as protection against any ill effects on our defense posture.* A more ambitious plan is to hold budget authority at a constant real level, which would save $68 billion in 1989 outlays compared with projections based on policy already enacted; this is the very upper bound of what anyone has suggested as possible savings. A more moderate position is held by other defense analysts, who argue that the real growth in defense budget authority can be scaled back to near 3 percent with no ill effects.[16] This would result in a $28 billion savings in 1989 outlays but would still allow defense outlays to rise as a share of GNP by another half a percentage point during 1985–1989.

To implement such restraint, one must face the tradeoff between current and future military capabilities. As cited earlier in this chapter, many defense experts have argued that, even under President Reagan's requested defense budget, there is a worsening squeeze between current readiness and future modernization. To the extent that one wishes to bring total outlays down well below the president's request, one must scale back commensurately the purchase of new weapons or risk reducing the size and preparedness of our present military forces.

Such a tradeoff can be eased in the context of overall defense restraint by some improvement in the management of defense operations. The lack of adequate managerial control over the purchase of military equipment from defense contractors has been highlighted in recent disclosures of the overpricing of spare parts. Those familiar with defense procurement readily admit that lack of accountability and weak cost-saving incentives pervade the system with respect to both defense managers and the private contractors.[17]

Unless one is willing to consider major reductions in the number of defense personnel or the readiness of combat forces, the prospects for defense restraint—beyond management savings—hinge importantly on the need to identify weapon systems where low-priority purchases can be stretched out, scaled back, or simply canceled. For both political and bureaucratic reasons, there are no easy targets. Every weapon system scheduled for production has a lobby of military officials eager to acquire the most up-to-date fighting equipment, members of Congress protective of the weapons-producing jobs in their districts, and industry representatives anxious to keep the business

---

*Former President Gerald Ford is a leading proponent of the stretch-out scheme.

they have. Nevertheless, some weapon systems are indeed of questionable merit, as identified by the CBO and other nonpartisan observers.[18]

Nondefense Program Outlays. What is the range of possibilities for additional spending restraint in nondefense programs? As a frame of reference it is worth noting that the cuts enacted thus far under President Reagan will amount to about $75 billion in FY 1989. An equally large additional amount would reduce aggregate program outlays by approximately another 10 percent from the levels now projected under enacted policies.

As discussed, the greater part of nondefense outlays can be restrained only through changes in basic program legislation. This is the case for all benefit entitlements, plus other "mandatory" spending such as farm price supports. The remaining, annually funded spending is controllable through the yearly process of congressional appropriations. It is this latter category that has experienced the larger proportional reductions thus far under President Reagan—a 16 percent cut by 1989, measured against the pre-Reagan policy baseline. In comparison, the mandatory spending programs have received a projected 1989 cut of 6 percent.[19]

The mandatory spending programs thus remain the largest and fastest-rising segment of the nondefense budget, due to the current size and projected growth of Social Security, Medicare, and other non-means-tested entitlements. For Social Security and other cash benefit programs, the form of restraint most often discussed is a limit to annual cost-of-living adjustments (COLAs) below that required to reflect changes in the Consumer Price Index (CPI).* The largest share of savings from any such plan would come from Social Security. Following the hard-fought bipartisan legislation of 1983, however, it remains unclear whether Congress will want to make any further Social Security cuts, unless the program's trust fund once again faces a shortfall.

For Medicare, proposals to restrain outlays have focused on limits to reimbursement rates for hospitals and doctors, or expanded patient cost sharing. Because major policy action must be taken by the early 1990s to bolster the Medicare trust fund, many experts have argued that measures to restrain spending or raise revenues should be phased in through the late 1980s to soften their impact on patients, health care providers, and taxpayers.[20]

---

*One proposal under consideration, cosponsored by House Budget Committee Chairman James Jones, is to retain annual COLAs but at an adjustment rate that is two percentage points less than the CPI. A less restrictive plan would be to simply forgo COLAs in such programs for one year.

For means-tested entitlements, there is broad congressional and public sentiment that programs serving the low-income population have already borne enough of the burden of necessary federal spending restraint. Medicaid is the possible exception, where prior cuts have been modest and where (as with Medicare) medical cost inflation continues to drive outlays rapidly upward. President Reagan has proposed expanded patient cost sharing and some reduction in the federal matching funds received by states. He has also recommended further tightening of eligibility for AFDC and Food Stamps and COLA restraint in means-tested veterans' pensions. Such proposals, thus far rejected by the Congress, constitute the probable upper bound for savings in this area.

The remaining major form of mandatory spending is farm price support payments. There is considerable consensus that, in this area, the degree of federal intervention is undesirable and should be reduced. Here, as with benefit entitlements, the pending proposals are ones that allow outlays to be restrained through inflationary erosion, rather than explicit cutting. The president and Congress have proposed to freeze at a prior-year level the target prices used as the basis for computing the subsidy for each farm product.

In the area of annually funded nondefense spending, the most frequently discussed strategy for restraint is an across-the-board freeze or partial inflation adjustment for the appropriated amount of annual budget authority, perhaps coupled with some limit on pay increases for federal workers. The appeal of the freeze approach is that it spreads the sacrifice broadly and uniformly. The disadvantage is that it would not allow spending patterns to change in response to shifting program priorities. For this reason some variants of the freeze proposal would apply the freeze at the aggregate level of annually funded spending, rather than on a program-by-program basis. In whatever form it is implemented, a freeze could probably not be fully sustained for as long as five years, as real funding levels would drop by more than 25 percent over the period—constituting an even larger additional proportional reduction than has already been enacted for such programs. A more reasonable expectation is a shorter freeze or one that would allow annual inflation adjustments to proceed, but at some rate below the pace of price change.

Revenues. One might reasonably expect the attainable 1989 outlay savings to be in the range of $50 billion to $100 billion, acknowledging that ambitious and sustained action will be difficult to take on all spending fronts. This expectation suggests that as much as $100 billion in increased annual tax revenues may be necessary to reduce the structural deficit to 2 percent of GNP by the end of the decade. Such an increase in revenues would restore the 1989 federal tax burden nearly to its level in 1981, when President Reagan assumed office.

What are the policy issues raised by the need for so much additional revenue? The debate over higher taxes has focused on both incremental policy changes and major structural overhaul of the tax system. The former options include modest upward shifts in existing tax bases or tax rates; the latter include new forms of personal consumption taxes or a dramatic simplification of the personal income tax through both a vastly broadened tax base and a lower and more uniform tax rate. Congress could in principle raise more revenue through broad, sweeping strokes than through a host of minor revisions in the tax code, but the vested political interests in the current tax system and the logistical complexity of implementing wholesale reform give great inertia to the existing tax law. The near-term revenue raising to be achieved by Congress is thus more likely to come from an array of modest changes to current tax provisions. The advantages and disadvantages of possible revenue-producing alternatives are discussed below. Table 4.9 shows the estimated revenue increase to be expected from various options.

The search for more revenue may bring Congress first to a number of possible "loophole" closings to broaden the tax base for personal and corporate income taxes. The base-broadening options have the advantage of generally not raising marginal tax rates. In addition, such measures can serve to remove the preferential treatment now accorded on questionable grounds to some forms of economic activity. However, the base-broadening options also provoke strong interest-group opposition. In addition, they typically yield relatively modest amounts of additional revenue; one has to assemble a long list of such measures even to achieve $50 billion in higher 1989 revenues.

The limited potential savings to be achieved from base-broadening options virtually guarantees consideration of higher excise taxes, especially on alcohol and cigarettes. These taxes would tend to fall disproportionately on the low-income population. Nevertheless, to the extent that the disincentives created for such forms of consumption are considered a legitimate use of tax policy, the adverse distributional consequences may well be overlooked. One proposal for the resulting revenues is to earmark them for the Medicare trust fund as part of a necessary program-refinancing package that might also include higher payroll taxes.

Unless the base-broadening measures are more extensive than now seems likely, the additional revenues from the minor excise taxes will still leave the need for at least some increases in income tax rates. Such changes would probably take the form of surcharges on the income tax liabilities of individuals or corporations. For individuals, a repeal of (or limit to) indexing would be

TABLE 4.9

REVENUE INCREASES FROM ILLUSTRATIVE POLICY ACTION

	Estimated Increase in FY 1989 Revenues	*Addendum: Projected Revenues*[a]		
		FY 1984	FY 1989	Growth
		Billions of Dollars		
Individual income taxes		294	478	184
Base-broadening measures—				
Eliminate income averaging	7			
Limit itemized interest deductions[b]	8			
Eliminate deductability of state and local sales taxes	8			
Tax accrued interest on life insurance reserves	8			
Tax some employer-paid health insurance[c]	8			
Increase taxation of entitlement benefits[d]	11			
Rate increases—				
10 percent surtax (on tax liability)	48			
Limit indexing[e]	24			
Repeal indexing	65			
Corporate income (and windfall profit) taxes		71	89	18
Base-broadening measures—				
Lengthen building depreciation period from 15 to 20 years	5			
Require full basis adjustment for investment tax credit	6			
Rate increases—				
10 percent surtax (on corporate income tax liability)	9			
Repeal reduced rates on first $100,000 of corporate income	10			
Excise taxes (excluding windfall profit taxes)		29	29	0
Double the excise taxes on alcohol and cigarettes	6			
Excise tax on domestic and imported oil ($2 per barrel)	9			
Broad-based tax on domestic energy (5 percent of value)	20			

TABLE 4.9 (*continued*)

	Estimated Increase in FY 1989 Revenues	Addendum: Projected Revenues[a]		
		FY 1984	FY 1989	Growth
		Billions of Dollars		
Social insurance taxes		237	382	145
Increase the Hospital Insurance payroll tax rate by 0.5 percentage point	22			
Other taxes		32	38	6
TOTAL		663	1,016	353

SOURCES: Congressional Budget Office, *Reducing the Deficit*; and Congressional Budget Office, *An Analysis of the President's Budgetary Proposals.*
NOTE: Because some of these measures are inconsistent with the adoption of others or are variants of each other, it is not appropriate to sum the revenue gains. In addition, the separate estimates of increased revenue are computed under an assumption of no other change in tax policy. Because of the interaction between tax provisions in establishing the actual revenue yield, any combination of measures may not yield the sum of the indicated revenue gains.
a. Based on enacted policies for FY 1984.
b. Assumes a limit of $7,500 for joint returns ($3,750 for others) to itemized deductions for interest on home mortgages, auto loans, credit card balances, and other consumption borrowing.
c. Assumes taxation of monthly employer contributions exceeding $200 for family coverage and $80 for individual coverage. Estimated revenue gain includes $2 billion increase in payroll taxes.
d. Assumes taxation of 50 percent of Social Security benefits and Tier I railroad retirement benefits, and full taxation of unemployment and workers' compensation.
e. Limit indexing adjustments to reflect CPI increase minus two percentage points.

another way to effectively raise tax rates, although action to repeal or limit indexing seems unlikely if President Reagan is reelected; he has repeatedly stated his unwillingness to consider such changes. Any rate increases would raise substantial amounts of revenue. With respect to distributional effects, surcharges on tax liability are distributionally neutral, but repeal of (or an across-the-board limit to) indexing would disproportionately burden lower-income taxpayers. In addition, the increase in rates would tend to discourage work and saving. The high visibility and pervasive impact of such revenue increases would make them politically unpopular, though perhaps palatable as temporary tax changes.

Major excise taxes on energy consumption would also raise substantial amounts of revenue and have been considered as a next step beyond surtaxes and the numerous lesser tax changes. (For example, President Reagan proposed a five-dollar-per-barrel excise tax on oil, along with a 5 percent income surtax, as part of an earlier "contingency tax" plan.) While energy taxes would encourage energy conservation, they are regressive. In addition, any oil tax might have significant short-term regional effects, burdening especially the oil-dependent northeast states.

Perhaps as much as $100 billion in higher 1989 revenues could be achieved through a combination of base-broadening measures, surtaxes, and higher excise taxes. However, to the extent that surtaxes (or a limit to indexing) would be adopted as temporary solutions, the search would have to continue for either further interim measures or permanent major changes.

This search may lead to further consideration of a national sales tax (or a value-added tax). As with other taxes on consumption, these would encourage saving but would fall disproportionately on low-income households. The adverse distributional effect could be reduced somewhat by excluding from the taxable base such items as food, medical care, and housing, but this would require a higher tax rate to yield a given amount of higher revenue. European countries have experience with the value-added tax, a form of sales tax levied on the increased value of a product at each stage of its production. Implementation in this country of such a new tax poses substantial administrative startup problems. The same would be true of a national sales tax, which also has the disadvantage of exploiting the retail sales tax base that has historically been left to state and local governments.

This brings us to the structural reform of annually collected personal taxes. Two types of proposals have surfaced. One would move the existing individual income tax closer to a flat tax (a tax with the same rate for everyone). Such options would flatten and lower the rate structure, with elimination of virtually all itemized deductions and exclusions.* An alternative type of proposal would relate individual tax liabilities to personal consumption, calculated as the difference between income and saving. Such a personalized consumption tax or "tax on consumed income" has the virtue of encouraging saving. Its distributional character would be set through the pattern of deductions and rates.

Policy discussions of these major reform alternatives to the personal income tax typically view them primarily as a means of simplifying the tax code or improving economic incentives—not as a means of raising revenue

---

*A leading candidate in this regard is the "fair tax" proposal authored by Senator Bill Bradley (Democrat of New Jersey) and Representative Richard Gephardt (Democrat of Missouri), under which rates would range from 14 to 30 percent. The proposal would retain the exclusions for Social Security and veterans' benefits and the deductions for mortgage interest and charitable contributions, among others.

above the current tax yield. However, if eventually enacted, they could produce enough revenue to replace a system already augmented by base broadening, surtaxes, and other interim supplementary provisions. These reforms thus offer some promise of permanently restored federal revenues. But even if enacted by the next Congress (1985–1986), such major reforms require lengthy lead times. A multitude of technical policy issues must be resolved, the administrative mechanism for revenue collection must be set in place, and individual taxpayers must be allowed time to adjust their financial arrangements in anticipation of the forthcoming changes.

Conclusion: The Reagan Budget Legacy

Were it not for the large structural deficit, it might be tempting to conclude that federal taxes and spending have been permanently shifted to a new steady state—one that is different from the 1981 status quo in exactly the ways that Ronald Reagan intended. However, the presence of huge deficits introduces a major instability to the budget structure, making further policy changes of significant magnitude virtually inevitable.

With respect to the level of the tax burden and defense spending, forthcoming budget action seems destined to moderate the policy movements initiated under President Reagan. Indeed, this process has been underway since the fall of 1981. The tax burden will no doubt rise in the coming years, perhaps close to its 1981 level relative to GNP. In addition, the defense buildup will be further restrained, reflecting a widening consensus that the pace of military spending is excessive. The increasingly critical view toward the defense budget is suggestive of the scrutiny applied to domestic programs following their rapid growth from the Great Society through the mid-1970s. Even with continued defense restraint, however, the level of defense outlays will rise as a percentage of GNP throughout the 1980s as a result of the surge of budget authority in the early part of the decade.

The composition of taxes and defense spending may also continue to shift in the course of deficit reduction efforts. Tax increases are likely to occur in virtually all revenue sources during the remainder of the decade. However, the desire to sustain private investment and economic growth makes it unlikely that corporate income taxes will be increased by the full extent that they have been thus far reduced. The necessary revenue raising seems more likely to occur in individual income taxes and excise taxes. An important byproduct of large deficits, in the context of longer-term developments in tax policy, may well be to strengthen the case for major tax reforms, such as a wholesale broadening of the taxable income base or a shift of the tax base from income to consumption.

As for the composition of defense outlays, the difficulty of arresting the momentum of weapons procurement will mean increasing policy tension between current military readiness and future weapons modernization. Such a budget squeeze will generate further pressure for management improvements in the Pentagon. This is similar to the mounting support for tax reform and is reminiscent, once again, of the outcry over fraud, waste, and abuse that accompanied the growth of domestic spending.

Concern over deficits can only imply further spending restraint in non-defense outlays. This lends support to President Reagan's notion that by cutting taxes, and thereby trimming Congress' "allowance," one can force spending discipline. There is some desire to restore funding in programs that have been cut. But such restorations, and perhaps temporary countercyclical measures, are likely to be the only domestic spending initiatives considered. The major specific targets for near-term restraint will probably be health care financing, farm subsidies, and non-means-tested retirement benefits, with uncertain prospects for further action on Social Security. To the extent that an across-the-board freeze in annually funded spending is a politically convenient form of restraint, such programs will probably be cut further in real terms. For low-income entitlements, there seems little appetite for additional tightening, with the possible exception of Medicaid.

The continuing policy change will undoubtedly strain the procedures of budget policymaking. The legislative debate in Congress has already become "fiscalized." The budget is now a major preoccupation of the legislative agenda, and congressional dismay over this development has provoked calls for further reform of the budget process. Most proposals seek either to impose binding constraints on fiscal choices or to realign power within the Congress and between the executive and legislative branches. An example of the former is the constitutional balanced-budget requirement, which may yet prove irresistible to politicians and voters. Some greater fiscal discipline is indeed necessary, but a constitutional requirement could be a very blunt instrument. Such an arbitrary policy stricture would at best encourage accounting gimmickry; at worst it would remove a desirable degree of policy discretion. Likewise, the granting of presidential authority to exercise a line-item veto on annual funding bills offers little hope for spending restraint. Although this proposal is seen primarily as a means of cutting domestic outlays, the controllable amount of spending in annually funded domestic programs is less than 10 percent of total federal outlays. Even if liberally exercised, such veto power would scarcely alter the budget imbalance that future presidents now seem destined to face.

More generally, it is unlikely that changes in procedure alone would allow policymakers to reach the decisions they now seem unable to make. The inability to take sufficient action on the deficit does not reflect a failure of the budget-specific policymaking apparatus nor even a lack of political will. Rather it reflects the difficulty of shielding our elected officials when they are called upon to make major decisions that are unpopular but needed. Our very system of government, through its shared power and political accountability, virtually ensures that such choices cannot be made easily. Given this inherent policy inertia, it is perhaps more striking that the budget could become so unbalanced than that its equilibrium is now hard to restore.

This point raises a final question as to whether Ronald Reagan was acting responsibly in pursuing such dramatic budget shifts. Certainly in retrospect his policy goals were not internally consistent. His original economic forecast was a conveniently chosen set of assumptions that gave the president's program its seductive appeal. This "rosy scenario," as it came to be called, offered the promise that we could simultaneously reduce inflation and stimulate growth; that we could have large cuts in tax rates without a massive revenue loss; that we could strengthen our defense and yet restrain total outlays by attacking domestic fraud, waste, and abuse; and that we could balance the budget without economic sacrifice.[21]

Both Democrats and Republicans expressed considerable doubt about these premises of the administration's budget program. Howard Baker, Republican leader of the Senate, characterized the president's program at the time as a "riverboat gamble." Should the country have embarked upon so large a set of tax cuts and so large a defense buildup? Should the administration have at least proposed a broader initial set of domestic spending cuts, as David Stockman now concedes?[22] Granted, the president was clearly moving taxes and program spending in directions the country welcomed. Nevertheless, it is difficult to escape the conclusion that President Reagan, who had campaigned in vigorous support of fiscal responsibility, has exposed the budget and the economy to very large risks, which were clear even without the benefit of hindsight.

CHAPTER 5

NATURAL RESOURCES AND THE ENVIRONMENT
MORE CONTROVERSY THAN CHANGE

Paul R. Portney

President Reagan's professed allegiance to the philosophy of laissez faire was evident in many of his proposed policies for natural resources and the environment. Business would no longer be shackled by rigid and cost-ineffective environmental regulations; wilderness areas would be opened up for energy and mineral exploration and production; the Department of Energy (DOE) would be abolished; and the government would no longer intervene so heavily in agricultural markets.

Not only did the Reagan administration espouse these goals; clearly it considered them a strong and publicly popular part of its program. Yet three years later public opinion polls suggest that the conduct of environmental and natural resource policy in President Reagan's first term has become a political liability as he campaigns for a second. And this is in spite of the evidence, which suggests that less happened, for good *and* for ill, than either the administration promised or the public believes. Why so much controversy and so relatively little accomplished? And what does all this portend for the future?

The answers are complex and somewhat difficult to sort out. They are further complicated because *personas* have been as important as policies in many of the major controversies, and often the two have been intertwined. At the Department of the Interior, for example, Secretary James Watt, until his resignation under pressure in late 1983, displayed a dramatic ability to wring the maximum controversy out of a given policy. At the Environmental Protection Agency (EPA), Administrator Anne M. Burford and Assistant

Administrator Rita Lavelle and other officials, until their forced resignations or dismissals in early 1983, became equally controversial, though not for their personalities as much as for mismanagement and alleged improprieties.

This chapter attempts to separate issues from people, concentrating primarily on the substantive policy changes the Reagan administration has attempted to make and the outcomes achieved. Major attention is devoted to environmental policy as reflected in actions at the EPA and to policy on public lands and water resources as reflected in actions at the Interior Department. Energy and agricultural policies are also discussed but in somewhat less detail.

Environmental Policy

Most major environmental statutes were in place long before the Reagan administration took office. Nevertheless, shortcomings in these laws and/or the way they were being implemented posed serious problems for federal environmental policy even before the widely reported difficulties began to arise at President Reagan's EPA.

Background and Opportunities

The year 1980 marks not only the advent of the Reagan administration; it also marks the end of what has come to be widely known as the "environmental decade." During the period 1970–1980, eight major laws were passed or substantially amended to form the corpus of this country's current environmental protective efforts.* All passed Congress with substantial bipartisan support, reflecting the desires of the voting public which consistently supported environmental protection.[1] The implementing regulations required to translate these legislative mandates into specific controls were delegated to the EPA, which was itself created by President Nixon in 1970.

The EPA grew throughout the decade. In FY 1972, its first full year of operation, the agency had 7,835 full-time employees and an annual operating budget of $450 million. By FY 1981 its work force had grown to 11,500 full-time employees, while its annual operating budget had increased to $1.35 billion. By FY 1981 the agency was also spending more than $3 billion per

---

*These laws were amendments to the Clean Air Act (1970 and 1977), amendments to the Federal Water Pollution Control Act, now known as the Clean Water Act (1972 and 1977), the Federal Insecticide, Fungicide, and Rodenticide Act and the Noise Control Act (1972), the Safe Drinking Water Act (1974), the Resource Conservation and Recovery Act and the Toxic Substances Control Act (1976), and the Comprehensive Emergency Response, Compensation, and Liability Act, better known as the Superfund (1980).

year subsidizing the construction of sewage treatment plants around the country. As the agency grew it also won general respect for the enthusiasm and professionalism with which it did its job.

In spite of this relatively successful start, however, four types of problems began to develop with the basic environmental statutes and the way they were being implemented.[2]

First, the earliest and most important statutes—the Clean Air and Clean Water Acts—were extraordinarily and unrealistically ambitious. They directed the EPA to establish ambient (outdoor) air and water quality standards; develop a nationwide monitoring network to track progress toward these goals; issue discharge standards and permits for all new plants and develop a process to enforce them; initiate regulation of toxic air or water pollutants posing serious health threats; and attend to many other responsibilities as well. At the same time, the EPA was given new responsibilities for the regulation of noise, drinking water, hazardous wastes, pesticides, and other toxic substances. In virtually every case where Congress called for standards to be set, very short deadlines—usually 120 or 180 days—were established.

The extent of this agenda led almost inevitably to missed deadlines. By 1980 the EPA had yet to act on 643 proposed changes in state-established controls on existing air polluters. Four major air quality standards, to be revised every five years according to Congress, had been on the books since 1971. Thousands of water pollution permits, hastily written in the first place to meet a congressionally imposed deadline, had expired and needed review and renewal. Virtually no progress had been made in regulating hazardous air pollutants and little more in the case of toxic water pollutants. No new source performance standards had ever been issued for a number of major air-polluting industries nor effluent guidelines established for important water-polluting industries. Regulation of hazardous wastes and toxic substances under the two major statutes passed in 1976 had proceeded at a snail's pace. Moreover, the constant addition of new responsibilities prevented the EPA from reviewing progress under the existing laws.

Second, compliance with the standards that had been issued was spotty, and enforcement practices left little reason to believe the situation would soon improve. According to the National Commission on Air Quality, for example, violations of some air quality standards were widespread,* although it is

---

*For instance, in 1980, the air quality standard for ozone (the major ingredient of smog) was being exceeded in 489 counties with a combined population of 144 million. In twenty-one of these counties, the standard was being exceeded by at least 50 percent (and in Los Angeles, by 325 percent).

difficult to know exactly how much confidence to place in these data because
the monitoring upon which they are based is well recognized to be deficient.*,3

Similar problems pervaded the monitoring of individual polluters. According to the EPA, by 1977, 92 percent of the approximately 20,000 major
air polluters were in compliance with their pollution limits. However, the
GAO found that the polluters out of compliance were the largest ones—in
New Jersey, for example, less than 1 percent of the sources violated their
hydrocarbon emissions limits, but the same 1 percent were responsible for a
quarter of total hydrocarbon pollution in the state. Also, in only 3 percent of
the cases was determination of compliance based on an actual test of emissions
at the source.[4],† And violations were apparently much more widespread with
respect to water pollution permits. The GAO also expressed concern about
enforcement. In one EPA region, for example, of 321 major air polluters not
in compliance in 1977, only half had ever had any enforcement action taken
against them.[5]

A third problem revolved around the substance of parts of the major
statutes. For instance, under parts of the Clean Air and Clean Water Acts,
ambient standards are to be set with "margins of safety" to protect human
health. This might make sense if "safe" levels exist below which even
sensitive individuals experience no harm or discomfort (and if scientists could
identify these so-called thresholds). Yet scientific research suggests that there
may be no level of any pollutant for which the EPA sets standards which is
safe in absolute terms. If so, standards would have to be set at zero under a
literal reading of the laws, a prospect unappealing to all concerned.

The search for a threshold and the implicit prohibition on balancing risks
with economic and other considerations had led to some very controversial
air quality regulations.[6],‡ For example, compared to a somewhat less strict
standard for ozone advocated by President Carter's own Council of Economic
Advisers staff, the standard actually adopted by the EPA in 1979, and still
in effect, implied additional expenditures in pollution control of $2,000–
$4,000 for each person-hour of exposure.[7] Similar results from other studies

---

*There are only about 5,300 air pollution monitors in all of the United States, no more than
a handful of which are in remote locations, even though air pollution is thought to have serious
effects on agricultural crops, forests, and visibility in national parks. The General Accounting
Office (GAO) (which has the authority to audit the environmental monitoring done in the United
States) has raised serious questions about the quality of the data emanating from these monitors.

†Tests of actual emissions still account for less than 5 percent of all compliance determinations, according to information provided by the EPA.

‡Interestingly, this type of balancing is implicitly permitted or explicitly required in other
environmental statutes.

raised difficult questions about the cost-effectiveness of some environmental health protection.

A fourth problem awaiting the Reagan EPA was inefficient regulation. Rather than pursue reductions in pollution where they could most inexpensively be had, the EPA in the 1970s often pursued a policy of "uniform rollback" whereby all sources were forced to reduce emissions by the same percentage, irrespective of how difficult or expensive this might be for some. Even worse, in certain cases Congress or the EPA allowed sources no latitude in selecting the means of pollution control. New coal-fired power plants, for example, had to reduce sulfur dioxide emissions by expensive chemical treatment of the emissions themselves rather than by using lower sulfur coal, even though the Congressional Budget Office (CBO) has estimated that by the year 2000, $3.3 billion could be saved annually using the latter approach.[8]

Many other studies indicated potential savings of as much as 90 percent through more efficient pursuit of environmental goals. In recognition of these possibilities, efforts begun under President Ford were accelerated in the Carter administration to introduce incentive-based regulatory techniques designed to realize these savings. But although some progress had been made along these lines in air pollution control, the techniques had not been extended fully to new plants and virtually not at all to water pollution control or other areas of regulation.

Against this background the Reagan administration took office. In view of its philosophical bent and the problems it inherited, the administration could have been expected to take advantage of four major opportunities for improvement in environmental policy:

- To review carefully the effectiveness of existing regulations.

- To improve the monitoring of environmental quality and pollution emissions, beef up the enforcement program, and upgrade the scientific research upon which the EPA based standards.

- To propose changes in the Clean Air, Clean Water, and other acts that would permit costs and benefits to be balanced in setting standards.

- To expand through administrative and perhaps legislative means the use of flexible, incentivelike approaches to environmental regulation.

Interestingly, a blueprint for these and other changes was provided the president-elect in late 1980 by his transition Task Force on the Environment, one member of which was William Ruckelshaus.

Policies and Actions

One cannot discuss the policies pursued and actions taken at the EPA without viewing them in the framework of the president's initial appointments to the agency. First of all, appointments were quite late in coming. Anne M. Gorsuch (later Burford) was not confirmed as administrator of the EPA until the first week in May of 1981, and it was months (and, in one case, years) before the assistant administrators who run the operating programs were officially in place. In addition, those eventually appointed to the top positions at the EPA had little management experience or familiarity with the major environmental programs. Even this inexperience need not have spelled disaster. Had the appointees brought with them expert aides or relied for background information on EPA's career staff, they might have succeeded in mastering their programs after a time. Unfortunately, this was not the course chosen.

The administrator chose to rely for advice on a small, closed circle of confidants, a pattern repeated by most other top officials in the agency as well. Contacts with regulated industries were frequent; meetings with environmentalists and other interested parties were almost nonexistent. Coupled with the emphasis being given to "regulatory relief" (rather than reform) and the substantial cuts in the EPA's budget, this way of doing business only heightened public concern that an undoing of regulatory safeguards was nigh.

In early 1983, however, there was a sharp change at the EPA. Twenty top officials—including the administrator, deputy administrator, general counsel, and all but one of the assistant administrators—resigned or were fired. The generally agreed-upon causes were allegations of impropriety at the EPA, which began to surface not much more than a year into the Reagan administration.

In early 1982, for example, as the EPA prepared to revise its regulations governing the maximum allowable lead content of gasoline, Administrator Burford, in a private meeting, reportedly told officials of one refinery that she would not enforce the existing standards after a certain date.[9] In an unrelated incident, she suspended rules banning the disposal in landfills of drums containing hazardous liquid wastes. Thereupon, one Denver company—represented by an attorney who was at the same time a consultant to Mrs. Burford and in line to be a top official at the EPA—dumped thousands of barrels into landfills until, eighteen days later, congressional pressure forced the administrator to reverse her decision and reimpose the ban. Finally, Rita Lavelle—the official in charge of the EPA's hazardous waste programs—was accused of having improperly participated in the settlement of a suit involving her former employer and its role in placing hazardous wastes in a California dump. She was later charged with, convicted of, and sentenced to six months in prison for perjuring herself concerning her role in this matter.

It was during this time that documents were shredded at the EPA and guards were posted to prevent the disappearance of other key papers. Administrator Burford was held in contempt of Congress for refusing to turn over to oversight committees subpoenaed records pertaining to the conduct of the Superfund program for hazardous waste cleanup. Other officials at the EPA were under investigation for, among other things, using government employees to help manage their outside financial interests. Under the weight of all this, the EPA leadership fell like a house of cards.

A definitive assessment of this two-year drama is not yet possible. But several things are already certain. First, as noted, the initial appointees to the EPA were novices who did little to overcome their inexperience. They built no bridges to the EPA's career staff, members of Congress, the environmental groups, or others to whom they could turn for advice and support. Second, they often showed very poor judgment in their dealings with industry groups. An open and balanced process had been established for environmental rule-making and was followed carefully prior to 1981. It was ignored between 1981 and 1983. Finally, the initial appointees became embroiled in conflicts of interest. Even though some conflicts were minor, they took place at an agency where no such charge had been made in its ten-year history. Coupled with concerns about the overall commitment of these officials to environmental protection, this controversy eventually proved intolerable to the public and, therefore, the administration.

The difference between the initial appointees and those who replaced them in the spring and summer of 1983 could not have been more stark. William Ruckelshaus, the first administrator of the EPA and a former official at the Justice Department and the Federal Bureau of Investigation, was named administrator once again. The new deputy administrator, Alvin Alm, had held high-level positions at both the EPA and the DOE. Ruckelshaus and Alm recruited assistant administrators who all had previous experience with the regulatory programs they were to manage or comparable positions in related areas. All moved quickly to take control of their programs.

Not surprisingly, in view of the chaotic management situation at the EPA through early 1983, the substantive policy changes under Burford were few and far between. In particular the recommendations of the transition Task Force apparently were ignored.

By far the most significant development concerned the EPA's budget, which the administration, with the active support of Administrator Burford, sought to cut substantially. Table 5.1 suggests the magnitude of these cuts for the air and water quality, hazardous waste, and toxic substance programs

TABLE 5.1

Budget Trends, FY 1980–FY 1984
(In 1982 $ millions)

Program Area	Program Funding					Percentage Change		
	1980	*1981*	*1982*	*(Estimated) 1983*	*(Requested) 1984*	*1983– 1984*	*1981– 1984*	*1980– 1984*
Water quality	400	341	251	197	138	−33	−59	−65
Air quality	336	252	230	204	175	−14	−31	−48
Hazardous waste	128	151	111	112	100	−10	−34	−22
Toxics	104	100	82	67	61	−9	−40	−41
TOTAL	968	844	674	580	474	−19	−44	−51

SOURCE: Congressional Budget Office, "The Environmental Protection Agency: Overview of the Proposed 1984 Budget," Staff Working Paper, April 1983, p. 5 (based on data obtained from the EPA). Data for 1980 supplied separately by Congressional Budget Office.

NOTE: Data for 1980, 1981, and 1982 indicate actual obligations (contracts awarded, orders placed, or other commitments requiring subsequent payment). Data for 1983 and 1984 indicate budget authority (the amount made newly available for program obligations). Percentage changes were calculated from annual budget figures before rounding. Budget figures have been rounded to the nearest million and may not produce identical percent differences.

which constitute the bulk of the EPA's regulatory activities. Measured from FY 1980, the last full year of the Carter administration, real overall spending at EPA was to have shrunk more than 50 percent by the end of FY 1984. Spending for water quality was to have been reduced nearly two-thirds; the smallest reductions have been for hazardous waste control which is, even so, scheduled to be down 22 percent from 1980 levels.

Reductions in staff parallel the budget changes (see table 5.2). Between 1981 and 1984 the number of full-time employees in the four major regulatory

TABLE 5.2

Staff Trends, FY 1981–FY 1984

Program Area	Number of Employees				Percentage Change *1983–1984*	Percentage Change *1981–1984*
	1981	*1982*	*1983*	*1984*		
Water quality	2,781	2,273	1,953	1,663	−14	−40
Air quality	1,754	1,576	1,375	1,351	−2	−23
Hazardous waste	726	586	643	626	−3	−14
Toxics	716	634	627	606	−3	−15
TOTAL	5,977	5,069	4,598	4,246	−8	−29

SOURCE: Congressional Budget Office, "The Environmental Protection Agency," p. 5 (based on data obtained from the EPA).

programs will have fallen nearly 30 percent, with two of every five positions in water quality eliminated. Between 1983 and 1984 alone, the positions devoted to water quality are scheduled to be reduced by 15 percent.

When the budget reductions are apportioned among the three functions of abatement and control, enforcement, and research and development, all are seen to have suffered about equally.[10] Spending on enforcement will have fallen nearly 40 percent; spending on research and development and abatement procedures, by 46 and 38 percent, respectively; and the number of employees devoted to enforcement of air and water quality, hazardous waste, and toxic substance regulations, by more than a third.

Federal aid to states for the operation of EPA-mandated programs also has been substantially reduced. Between 1981 and 1984 the proposed decline was 44 percent—28 percent to come between 1983 and 1984.[11] Since these funds help support the states' monitoring and enforcement efforts, it is not surprising that a 1983 survey found 40 percent of the states polled to have reduced their monitoring activity. There were 162 fewer air pollution monitors in operation at the time of the survey than the year before, and the total planned state monitoring network had shrunk by 439, or 8 percent.[12]

Some of the budget cuts have reasonable justifications. For example, the EPA has virtually eliminated its noise control program. Although a potentially serious problem, noise does not travel across national, state, or local boundaries as air and water pollutants typically do. Thus, many contend noise control is handled more appropriately at lower levels of government (although the EPA could usefully coordinate these efforts). The administration also has reduced substantially grants to states and local governments to subsidize the construction of sewage treatment plants. This grant program had long been criticized by environmentalists as well as policy analysts. The grants were restricted to construction costs alone, with the not surprising result that very expensive plants often were built which local governments could not then afford to operate properly.

However, many of the cuts have hit programs and functional areas where, according to the Reagan administration's own transition task force, more emphasis was required—basic research, monitoring, enforcement, and improved analytical capabilities. In addition, the budget of the Council on Environmental Quality (CEQ)—the White House advisory office on environmental matters—was reduced from $3.1 million in FY 1980 to $0.7 million by 1984. This action precluded CEQ's involvement in many issues in which it had previously been active, not to mention the expanded role envisioned for it by the task force.

Legislatively, the Reagan administration has been dormant in the environmental area. The Clean Air Act was to be reauthorized in 1981, providing an ideal opportunity for the administration to signal the kinds of reforms it favored in the regulatory statutes. But it proposed no amendments. Instead, Mrs. Burford issued a list of "principles" to which the administration wished to see others adhere if they proposed revisions to the act. Some of these were sound (e.g., eliminating the requirement that new power plants use only technological means to reduce sulfur emissions). However, the whole list was ignored, and the administration was dismissed as a serious player in the reauthorization debate. A similar reticence characterized the administration's posture with respect to the scheduled 1982 reauthorization of the Clean Water Act. Both acts still await formal reauthorization but, in view of the problems at the EPA alluded to earlier, the chances have to be much slimmer than they were in 1980 for the administration to win the kinds of changes that are needed.

Regarding economic incentives, the record of Burford's EPA was disappointing. Despite persistent efforts by the agency's analytical staff—one of the few branches of the EPA to remain strong and untainted during the Burford regime—the administrator and particularly the heads of the program offices remained skeptical of or hostile toward this potential innovation in regulation. For example, little support was evinced initially for allowing air pollution permits to be transferred from old to new sources of pollution (even though the potential savings in control costs and reductions in pollution were considerable); nor did top officials in the water pollution program or other programs make any effort to embrace innovative regulatory techniques. In fact, by pushing one incentivelike program (called "netting") that could actually increase air pollution in some areas, the EPA inadvertently undermined even those parts of the emissions trading program that ensured pollution reductions, because legal action put the whole initiative on hold.[13] Other areas fared little better between 1981 and 1983. To take but one example, an action taken that might have been considered a real accomplishment was delegation to the states of responsibility for managing several important regulatory programs. But the cuts in EPA grants to the states to run these programs occurred at the same time, leaving them little with which to work.

The discussion so far has focused on the EPA under Administrator Burford. In every respect much more can be expected of the current leadership. Most importantly, credibility and effective management have been returned to the EPA. Meetings with environmental and citizen groups, state and local officials, members of Congress and their staffs, and other interested parties again have become routine. Some money has been restored to the EPA's budget. Total obligations for immediate removal of hazardous wastes and initiation of actions at national priority dump sites, for example, are projected to increase in FY 1984 to $192.5 million (more than 100 percent). Due in part to Ruckelshaus's efforts, the administration requested $1.2 billion for the EPA's operating budget for FY 1985, up from $1.1 billion in FY 1984.

Another development that can be expected is improved sophistication in the way the leadership at the EPA approaches legislative reform. Administrator Ruckelshaus has signaled an interest in at least the qualitative balancing of benefits and costs in setting standards for regulation of hazardous air pollutants. This principle might be extended to other environmental statutes where it is now implicitly or explicitly prohibited. One step has already been taken in this direction in a pending decision concerning a lead smelter in Tacoma, Washington— where the agency has attempted to poll local residents to determine their willingness to accept possible economic hardship in exchange for reduced health risk from the smelter's arsenic emissions. Although extremely controversial, this type of effort can be useful if the EPA is to assess the levels of protection wanted by the public.

The picture is also brighter for cautious expansion, through administrative means, of flexible approaches to regulation. In his confirmation hearings, Ruckelshaus endorsed the EPA's "bubble policy," which permits increases in air pollution from one source in exchange for equivalent or greater reductions at another nearby source so long as other stringent conditions are met. Efforts are now underway to expand this emissions trading approach to other areas where it can reduce the costs of meeting predetermined environmental goals.

There are other positive signs at the agency as well. Some stability has been brought to the enforcement program (which underwent three different reorganizations in 1981–1982), and renewed emphasis is being given to ascertaining compliance and penalizing violators. The very serious monitoring problems identified above also are under review. Finally, as illustrated by the recent emergency suspension of all uses of the pesticide ethylene dibromide (EDB) on grain products, the EPA is again willing to make difficult decisions if scientific evidence points toward possibly serious health hazards.

Public Lands and Water Resources

Similarities exist between the Reagan administration's environmental policies and those concerning public lands and water resources. Both have been controversial, both have involved personalities as well as proposals for programmatic change, and both have resulted in surprisingly few changes in the situation as it existed in 1980—in spite of (or perhaps because of) the furor engendered by the proposed policy changes.

Differences also exist. In contrast to the initial EPA appointees, almost all those chosen to manage the Department of the Interior had extensive knowledge of the programs they inherited and a very clear idea of how these programs should be changed. Also, controversies concerning public lands and water resources were more philosophical than those arising at the EPA, where budget reductions and regulatory relief seemed the only general principles. In fact, had the issues at Interior not become *so* highly politicized, an interesting substantive debate might have evolved in the early 1980s over the appropriate direction of natural resource policy for the rest of the twentieth century.

Background and Opportunities

The Department of the Interior has a relatively modest budget ($6.5 billion in FY 1984). With these funds it takes care of many of the nation's natural resources. It administers the leasing of energy and mineral resources, oversees water resources development, has regulatory responsibilities for the reclamation of surface mines and the protection of endangered species, and has custodial responsibility for much of the land owned by the federal government. This last responsibility gives the Department an importance disproportionate to its annual budget.

There can be no mistaking the importance of public lands in the United States. They account for nearly 637 million acres—28 percent of the 2.26 billion acres that make up the total land area of the United States. More than half the lands in Nevada (86 percent), Utah (64 percent), Idaho (64 percent), Alaska (60 percent), and Oregon (53 percent) are owned by the federal government; Wyoming (49 percent), California (47 percent), and Arizona (44 percent) are not far behind.* These public lands, including the Outer Continental Shelf (OCS), are rich in petroleum, natural gas, coal, and nonfuel minerals including copper, zinc, and lead. They are also home to the national forests and the 48 national parks and 286 monuments, historic sites, national seashores, and other units that constitute the National Park System, visited 300 million times in 1980. Since the designation of Yellowstone as the first national park in 1872, the parks, national forests, wilderness areas, and other public lands have been among the most distinctive and admired features of the United States.

Conflict is inherent in the management of public lands. This is precisely because land can often be put to alternative uses. Scenic wilderness areas can be rich in energy and mineral resources; economically productive forests can

---

*For detail see appendix A, table A.1.

be host to considerable recreational activity; rangelands can be valuable watering areas for wildlife; and the habitat of an endangered species can be suitable for commercial development or off-road recreation. Balancing these competing interests—providing for "multiple use" as it is generally called—is the difficult job that often falls to the Interior Department and, to a lesser extent, the Department of Agriculture (of which the Forest Service is a part).

Beginning with the Wilderness Act of 1964 and culminating in the Alaska National Interest Lands Conservation Act of 1980, Congress passed numerous pieces of natural resource legislation in the decade and a half preceding President Reagan's election.[14] Many were intended to clarify the procedures under which both multiple-use and special-purpose lands were to be managed. In addition, new regulatory functions were given to the Interior Department; huge additions were made to the national parks, forests, wilderness areas, and other functional systems; and the procedures governing energy and mineral leasing on public lands were substantially revised. Like the "environmental decade" it overlapped, this activist period was largely bipartisan in nature. Most major pieces of legislation had broad support and passed rather handily.

Against this backdrop, and given its philosophical bent, several opportunities presented themselves to the new Reagan administration vis-a-vis public lands and water resources.

First, there were some excellent opportunities to reduce federal spending and/or increase revenues—opportunities on which there was a large measure of expert consensus. For instance, the administration could have reviewed many federal water projects planned or under construction by the Bureau of Reclamation and the Army Corps of Engineers and eliminated those not passing the same benefit-cost test being applied to new federal regulations. Fees for grazing on public lands could have been made commensurate with those charged by private parties, and fees for the use of inland waterways and visitors' charges at parks and other facilities could have been raised so that beneficiaries bore a larger share of the costs of operating these facilities. Finally, the government-subsidized flood insurance available to those building on ecologically and geologically delicate barrier islands could have been eliminated, thus reducing government expenditures while protecting the continent from ocean erosion.

A second opportunity was presented by the federal energy leasing programs—to initiate leasing on the OCS and in the Naval Petroleum Reserve in Alaska and to renew coal and onshore oil and gas leasing after congressionally and judicially imposed moratoriums. It was important to begin leasing these energy resources in a way that inspired public confidence in the mechanisms developed to do so. Such action could smooth the way for continuing energy development on public lands and thus be consistent with the Reagan administration's emphasis on production rather than conservation as a solution to energy problems. Notably, the Carter administration foresaw substantially increased leasing activity in its hoped-for second term.

A third opportunity concerned the disposition of some federal lands. Long-time observers of public land management had noted that the federal government owned at least some lands that, because they were surrounded by private properties, were difficult to manage and perhaps not worth the trouble.[15] Some thought might have been given to the sale or exchange of carefully selected properties (those with little significant aesthetic, ecological, or economic potential) to private individuals. Other federal lands with much greater state or local than national interest might have been considered for sale or exchange to those levels of government. Elsewhere, private parties owned some lands (called inholdings) within national parks or other areas that were probably more appropriate for public ownership to prevent uses inconsistent with activities on the surrounding public lands.

Finally, the Reagan administration might have tried to alter somewhat the balance between commercial versus natural uses of the federal estate.* Many important public holdings are managed under a multiple-use mandate, a task requiring delicate balancing. All administrations strive to achieve the balance they see fit, and those preceding Reagan's were no exception. However, President Reagan's election, and particularly his large margins in the western states, appeared to reflect at least the perception that the balance had tipped too much in the direction of natural uses. This perception was shared even by some sympathetic to the environmental movement. In an otherwise scathing denunciation of the Reagan administration's policies regarding public lands, for example, one environmentalist wrote:

> Preservation of nature, as though it were a rare artwork, became an end unto itself in the 1970s. The observable fact that the web of life is an intricate multiple-use arrangement was, in some quarters, obscured by the ideological fantasy that the only decent and harmonious natural relationships are nonconsuming ones.[16]

In short, there existed an opportunity to restore some of the balance that, in the Reagan administration's view, had been lost.

Policies and Actions

The Reagan administration took office with a much more ambitious agenda in mind than even this list of opportunities would suggest. As reflected

---

*"Natural" here means wilderness preservation, recreation, and all other less commercial uses.

in "progress reports" issued by Secretary Watt at the end of 1981 and 1982, the administration's six goals were to:

- Enhance energy and mineral production on public lands.

- Improve the national park, wilderness, and wildlife refuge systems.

- Increase the supply and improve the management of water resources.

- Improve relations between the federal government and state and local governments (the "good neighbor" policy).

- Improve the conditions on Indian reservations and U.S. territories.

- Improve the management of the Interior Department.

Themes which cut across these goals, as emphasized in speeches by President Reagan and then-Secretary of the Interior Watt, included more reliance on the private sector and an end to the "lock-up" of federal lands.

These goals may seem innocuous on their face; they turned out to be anything but that in practice. Their pursuit by the administration involved a great number of initiatives, almost all of which were controversial. In addition, Secretary Watt himself became an issue, in part because his personality and style could not be divorced from his policies. In order to understand the turmoil over natural resource policies from 1981–1984, it is necessary to treat several particularly contentious issues in some detail.

Leasing Policies. The Carter administration, as noted, had pledged stepped-up leasing in a second term. Thus, it was not so much that leases were issued which ignited the controversies during 1981–1983 as it was the scale of the program and certain of its aspects. For example, less coal probably would have been proposed for leasing in a second Carter administration than was proposed by Reagan, because the Carter philosophy was to estimate total national coal needs at a particular time, determine the amounts forthcoming from private mines and existing federal leases, and issue new leases to make up the difference. While perhaps sensible in principle, this method proved very difficult in practice, as such large-scale central planning exercises often do.[17]

Skeptical of government planning, Secretary Watt changed the goal of the coal leasing program to one of providing adequate inventories for private companies which would then determine their own production schedules in accord with national needs as they saw them. This reorientation led to a substantial increase in coal leasing activity. According to the Interior Department, 55 leases were issued in 1981 and 1982, comprising nearly 120,000 acres; comparable figures for 1979 and 1980 (when a partial moratorium was still in effect) were 26 and 20,000, respectively.[18] The tonnage of leased coal increased accordingly, from 211 million tons in 1979–1980 to 1,900 million in 1981–1982.

On April 28, 1982, the administration held the largest coal lease sale in history—1.6 billion tons on more than 16,000 acres in the Powder River Basin of Montana and Wyoming, bringing in $55 million in payments. The Powder River sale was quickly and harshly criticized by many, including some proponents of expanded leasing. Some of the leases were located in or adjacent to environmentally sensitive areas, yet little analysis appeared to have been done of potential environmental impacts. More importantly, the wisdom of dumping such large amounts of coal on an already very depressed market came into question. At the time the Powder River leases were issued, in the major coal states there were still 16 to 17 billion tons of recoverable coal on federal lands that had been leased previously but not yet exploited. Only 104 million tons had been produced on these lands in 1982—at this rate the already leased coal would last 160 years. The administration never satisfactorily answered the critics' question as to why such a "fire-sale" disposal of a valuable resource was necessary when the coal already leased would take so long to exploit.

Finally, irregularities appeared to surround some lease sales. Specifically, complaints arose that the Interior Department had (a) redrawn the boundaries on one particular tract so that it would only be attractive to one bidder, thus preventing competition; and (b) not only leaked information about the minimum acceptable bids to private parties prior to the sale but also changed the bidding system less than two months before the sale, in such a way as to reduce the bonuses received by the federal government. Fueling the controversy were a GAO report concluding that the Powder River tracts were leased at $100 million below their fair market value and a similar report by a House Appropriations Subcommittee that put the figure at $60 million.[19] Subsequently, Congress mandated that a federal commission be created on fair market value policy for federal coal leasing which issued its report in February 1984. (It was his ill-considered remark on the composition of the commission that led to Secretary Watt's resignation in late 1983.)

In two respects, the Coal Commission report acknowledged the difficult task the Interior Department faced in leasing the Powder River Basin. It pointed out the difficulty of determining fair market value, especially when no federal coal had been leased for ten years; it also emphasized that some tracts would never interest more than one bidder, hence competition would inevitably be absent. In most other respects, however, the report was critical of the administration's actions concerning the sale. The commission found, for example, that "the experiment with entry level bidding (the new bidding system) was a failure."[20] It also suggested that the leaking of minimum acceptable bids to industry representatives prior to the sale be referred to Interior's Inspector General or the Justice Department for investigation. Overall, the commission concluded as follows:

> the Interior Department probably offered excessive amounts of Federal coal reserves in a declining market and that this, in turn, probably lessened the prospect of receiving fair market value. At the very least, the Interior Department made serious errors in judgment in its procedures for conducting the 1982 Powder River lease sale and failed to provide a sound rationale for many of its actions.[21]

In March 1984, Secretary Watt's replacement, William Clark, announced that he would accept almost all the recommendations in the Coal Commission's report and change the leasing program accordingly. No major lease sales would be conducted through the end of 1984 while these changes were being made.

Similar controversy surrounded the administration's oil and gas leasing, particularly on the OCS. Whereas Cecil Andrus, Carter's Secretary of the Interior, had proposed to offer approximately 55 million acres on the Shelf for leasing between 1980–1985, Secretary Watt proposed to offer nearly 1 billion acres between 1983–1987 (even though there was no serious expectation that it would all be taken up). The Interior Department also rewrote regulations giving industry more discretion governing the selection of tracts to be offered. Similar criticisms arose as in the Powder River case:

- With so much OCS acreage being offered at once, it would be impossible to analyze potential environmental impacts.

- States were given little or no consultative role in the selection of tracts to be offered.

- By "dumping" so much acreage on the market during such a short period of time, the administration was destined to drive down the per-acre price—a charge similar to that levied against the coal leasing program.

Partially in response, Secretary Clark announced that he would reduce the acreage offered for lease and encourage increased participation in leasing decisions by interested parties. Nevertheless, he remained committed to the areawide leasing approach pioneered by Mr. Watt.

Wilderness Policy. One reason given by Secretary Watt for rapidly expanded leasing was lessened U.S. dependence on foreign energy supplies. The same reason was given for another controversial initiative—opening up wilderness areas for mineral and energy exploration. One of the Reagan administration's first actions was issuance of mineral leases in a New Mexico wilderness area and consideration of similar actions in a number of others, including Montana's Bob Marshall Wilderness Area, one of the original national forest areas in the wilderness system. Following an emergency order from the House Interior Committee, which was subsequently upheld by a district court, the Marshall area was withdrawn from further consideration. Having quickly blocked any such activity there, the House then tried to extend this temporary protection to all other designated wilderness areas. Secretary Watt eventually was forced to abandon these efforts in the face of a series of appropriations riders which prevented the department from processing leases in designated wilderness areas. As of January 1984, no new leases can be issued in wilderness areas. Thus, nothing was accomplished as a result of the wilderness initiative other than the galvanization of opposition. The same could be said of a more recent proposal to issue the first oil and gas leases in national wildlife refuges in more than two decades. Secretary Clark dropped the proposal soon after he succeeded Mr. Watt.

Even if handled skillfully, the proposed expansion of commodity production in wilderness areas was bound to be controversial. Was it justified by the energy and mineral content of these areas? Apparently not. Several recent studies have assessed the energy potential of the federally owned lands, including those designated as wilderness areas.[22] Their general conclusion is that most public lands are already available for oil and gas exploration and that a relatively small fraction of the economically recoverable oil and natural gas deposits exists in designated wilderness areas. A recent study by the U.S. Geological Survey (USGS)—a branch of the Interior Department—appeared to confirm these previous studies. It found that even if all potential future wilderness areas are included with present ones in eleven western states, only 3 percent of undiscovered potentially recoverable oil and 5 percent of natural gas are likely to be found there.[23] The Office of Technology Assessment (OTA) analyzed the mineral potential of the public lands and emphasized that, while in some instances it was great, other noncommodity uses often were more valuable.[24]

This is not to say there are no wilderness areas meriting commodity production. If selected carefully and openly, some activity may well be appropriate. Similarly, wildlife preservation may be compatible with energy development. For example, since the 1950s the National Audubon Society itself has permitted natural gas development in its Rainey Wildlife Sanctuary in Louisiana. The wilderness policies of the Reagan administration were unsuccessful due as much to the clumsiness with which they were pursued (with little or no public or congressional involvement) as to the basic concepts behind them.

Privatization. Another failed initiative involved the proposed sale of selected publicly owned lands, the impetus for which was provided not by Secretary Watt but by President Reagan himself. In 1982 he announced the creation of the "Asset Management Program" (the official name of the land sales program) and an interagency Property Review Board whose job it would be to identify the surplus federal lands to be sold. Thirty-five million acres (5 percent of the federal estate) were considered for sales which the administration hoped would bring in several billion dollars per year.

The program was poorly received from the start and subsequently abandoned. Those interested in open access to public lands for recreation and other purposes attacked the program as akin to selling off one's capital to fund day-to-day operating expenses. Considerable skepticism was also evinced by those from whom the administration had expected support—corporations and ranchers, and even Republican governors and congressmen. They objected for three major reasons: because some states and localities had been receiving free federal land for recreational areas and activities through limited disposals which would be terminated by the sales program; because businessmen and ranchers were troubled by the uncertainties surrounding the program (Would they have first crack at the lands? Would the lands be sold in an open auction? Would they have access if others bought the lands?); and because of the possible inconsistency of the program with major public lands legislation and the lack of consultation prior to its announcement.

In the 1982 report of the Department of the Interior, the program was not mentioned by name—instead it was reported that Interior had, ". . . identified 2.7 million acres of publicly owned land already included in land-use plans as surplus to federal needs."[25] It neglected to say that the identification was for purposes of sale. Since then, the administration has reneged both on promises to send legislation to the Hill necessary to conduct some of the sales and on a commitment to work with Congress on sales of certain Bureau of Land Management (BLM) lands. In 1983 the BLM offered 30,000 acres for sale, of which one-third were sold for a total of $2 million; and it has established a target of 200,000 acres to be sold during FY 1984.

Other Actions. The administration did seize on one opportunity identified above, as it worked closely with Congress to pass the Coastal Barrier Resources Act of 1982. This measure prohibits the use of any federal funds to develop barrier islands or other delicate areas, thus ending federally subsidized flood insurance for these areas. In this initiative, and in an innovative effort to encourage private corporations to protect wetlands, the administration had support from the environmental community.

Administration efforts to reduce funds for the purchase of lands for new parks and wildlife refuges, however, lacked this support, although they have proved relatively successful nonetheless. In contrast to requests during the late 1970s averaging $180 million per year for the Land and Water Conservation Fund (which helps finance both federal as well as state and local land purchases), the administration requested $27 million, $60 million, and $55 million, respectively, for fiscal years 1982–1984. Congress appropriated much more, but the administration has obligated only a fraction of those monies. Instead, it has concentrated on increasing the funding for the maintenance of existing parks, citing a responsibility to improve what Watt called their "deplorable" condition before adding new ones. The unwillingness of the Interior Department to acquire new lands became an important point of criticism. However, as Watt himself noted in this connection, the Carter administration in its second "austerity" budget for FY 1981 had requested less for land acquisition than did President Reagan for FY 1983 or 1984.

Facilities at many national parks did indeed need improvement—although the extent of the disrepair attributable to previous administrations appears to have been exaggerated in certain of Secretary Watt's statements on the subject.[26] Furthermore, although the park system has grown rapidly, there still may be parcels worth acquiring, either for new parks or for additions to or buffer zones around existing ones. However, even some conservationists admit that some inferior units were recently added to the national park system in what came to be known as the "park barrel" bill. This suggests that the acquisition process might appropriately be slowed to ensure that only meritorious units are added. As for proposed reductions in the Land and Water Conservation Fund (LWCF), the CBO recently identified (without necessarily endorsing) elimination of the state share of the LWCF as a possible budget reduction target on the grounds that many of the properties purchased by the states with federal support benefit primarily state residents.[27] In view of the relatively good fiscal condition of many states compared to the federal government, a reduced federal contribution is worth serious consideration. In any case, the controversy has become somewhat moot with Secretary Clark's announcement that very modest increases would be sought in the FY 1985 budget to make selected purchases of new park lands.

The Reagan administration's water resource policies have had both positive and negative results. On the positive side, the administration has moved carefully to settle disputes over the water rights of Indian tribes in the West. And at its outset the administration wisely began pressing some beneficiaries of federal water projects to begin sharing a larger part of project costs—where President Carter had suggested 10 percent local sharing, the Reagan administration talked of a 35 to 50 percent local share and secured some commitments for such sharing on Corps of Engineers' projects. On the negative side, this intent was never matched with a push to codify a new sharing formula, however, and in early 1984 the administration appeared to back away from increased local cost sharing. Moreover, the administration virtually abolished the three institutions responsible for the planning and analysis of water projects,* as well as the "Principles and Standards" by which those projects were evaluated. In addition, the administration has been slow to assert federal water rights on public lands even where this would appear to be required for multiple-use management.

The administration also reorganized part of the Interior Department in a useful way by combining personnel from the USGS, the BLM, and other offices concerned with energy activities. This reorganization is likely to improve the analysis and management of oil, natural gas, and coal leasing. On another front the administration rewrote or attempted to rewrite regulations governing many Interior Department programs. These programs include surface mining reclamation, endangered species protection, coal leasing, hard rock mining, and rangeland management. Generalizations are difficult, but the pattern in many of these cases was the proposal of very substantial change in existing rules, followed by considerable controversy and then the issuance of final rules that often were not very different from the original ones.

Secretary Watt Himself

Until his resignation on October 9, 1983, public land and water resource policies were inextricably linked to the personality of the man responsible for their conception and implementation. Many of the policies pursued between 1981 and 1983 were inherently controversial, but they became more so because of Secretary Watt. In one sense the controversy was surprising in that Watt had work experience on Capitol Hill, at Interior, and at the Federal Power Commission. Thus, he might have been expected to understand well the sophistication with which major changes in policy must be handled.

And, indeed, he may well have had that understanding. But he made little or no effort to use it in advancing his proposals. Many of the "rules" governing policy formation were ignored. Meetings with public interest groups came to a halt and career officials at Interior thought to be sympathetic to such concerns were ignored. Procedures to assess environmental impacts before acting were abandoned. Perhaps most important, and ultimately most damaging, consultation ceased with state government officials and relevant congressional committees or subcommittees and their staffs.

---

*These were the Water Resources Council, the River Basin Commissions, and the Office of Water Research and Technology in the Department of the Interior.

All this seemed to flow from Secretary Watt's unshakable belief in the rectitude of his mission. His speeches decried environmentalism, whose practitioners, he believed, did not represent the true beliefs of most Americans. In public remarks and private interviews, indeed, he went so far as to liken environmentalists to Nazis and suggest that he himself was persecuted by them for his fundamentalist religious beliefs as well as his policies. The problem Watt's attitude came to cause himself (and the administration) was that his style created a backlash that came to stand in the way of achieving his substantive objectives. Baiting his environmental and other critics appeared to become as important as the pursuit of the policies to which they objected, and the latter came to suffer at the expense of the former. While he succeeded in keeping the Beach Boys and other "undesirable elements" away from a Fourth of July concert, many of his budgetary initiatives were rejected; while he railed against the "lock-up" of the public lands, his attempts to open them to commercial activity were largely failures; while he derided the balanced representation that is traditional on public commissions, he lost his job and part of his leasing program along with it.

From one who was so skillful in some respects—reorganizing the department, quieting the Sagebrush rebels (people from western states who objected to what they felt was the insensitive management from Washington of publicly owned lands), and nurturing recognition of the inevitability of cost sharing in water projects, for example—the failures are surprising. They stem from an inability, or at least an unwillingness, to even *appear* to listen to opposing arguments before acting. As it was, one writer identified Watt as one of the three individuals who has most influenced contemporary thought and behavior toward nature.[28]

Energy Policy

If events within the United States during the 1970s helped shape policies regarding public lands and the environment, those elsewhere in the world necessitated the development of this country's first conscious policy on energy. And, unlike the previous two areas discussed, "crises" and controversy with respect to energy were more prevalent in the 1970s than they have been since the Reagan administration took office.

Background and Opportunities

Two distinct events marked the energy crisis of the 1970s. In October 1973, at the start of the Middle East War, Arab states embargoed oil shipments to the United States. At the time of the embargo, the price of oil sold by the

Organization of Petroleum Exporting Countries (OPEC) was $3.01 per barrel; by March 1974 when the embargo was lifted, it had risen to $10.95—an increase of 231 percent in six months. This change awakened in the OPEC producers a sense of their collective market power. The nominal price of oil rose only slightly over the next four years, standing at $12.70 per barrel by the end of 1978. By the end of 1979, however, the price had nearly doubled (to $24.00) as a result of the interruption in Iranian oil production following the overthrow of the Shah. By the end of 1980 the price stood at $32.00 a barrel, having increased more than ten times in a seven-year period.

Between 1973 and 1980 energy policy went through several stages, beginning with Project Independence, a short-lived effort to make the United States wholly self-sufficient in energy. Other energy plans were formulated, the DOE was created by consolidating parts of existing federal agencies into one entity, and other important legislative and administrative actions were taken affecting the supply of and demand for energy. In a major step in early 1979, President Carter established a gradual schedule by which the price of domestic crude oil would begin to rise, reaching the world price by September 1981. This measure obviated the need for the government "entitlements" program established in 1973 to share the artificially cheap domestic oil among all refiners. In addition, a windfall profits tax—technically more in the nature of an excise tax—was enacted in 1980 to recapture some of the gain that befell oil producers as prices were deregulated. In 1978 Congress passed the Natural Gas Policy Act (NGPA), which gradually deregulated some natural gas prices between 1978 and 1985 but imposed *new* price controls on gas sold in intrastate markets. Congress also passed the Energy Emergency Conservation Act (providing standby gasoline rationing powers), the Energy Policy and Conservation Act (creating an oil stockpile called the Strategic Petroleum Reserve and mandating fuel economy standards for autos), and the Energy Security Act of 1980 (creating the Synthetic Fuels Corporation to help finance the development of liquid fuels from coal, oil shale, tar sands, and other sources).

Several energy opportunities lay before the Reagan administration.* The first concerned natural gas. Under the NGPA, price controls would remain in effect on "old gas" even after all newly discovered natural gas was decontrolled in 1985. In addition to the new controls it had imposed on intrastate gas, the NGPA had other serious shortcomings as well.[29] In view of these

---

*The discussion here does not include energy production on public lands which has already been discussed.

and the administration's free-market bent, a push for complete decontrol was attractive.

The administration also was suspicious of mandatory energy conservation programs and subsidies for energy supply. Thus, an opportunity existed to review carefully the efficacy of such programs and eliminate those doing little good. Included for review was the Synthetic Fuels Corporation (SFC), eventual appropriations for which could reach $88 billion. Because it represented the most radical departure from the "market test" espoused by the administration, the future of the SFC was uncertain. Finally, an opportunity existed to improve energy security and emergency preparedness through a variety of means, including accelerating purchases for the Strategic Petroleum Reserve. It stood at about 90 million barrels at the end of 1980 (only slightly more than 10 percent of the level Congress had envisioned when it created the reserve) in spite of considerable congressional pressure to increase its size.

Other energy policy opportunities could be, and were, identified by different observers. Indeed, because of its faith in the market, the administration favored the complete elimination of the DOE; and President Reagan's first Secretary of Energy, James Edwards, made that his goal. Also envisioned were the relaxation of EPA and Interior Department regulations to increase energy production. Because there was much less consensus on these goals, however, they had to be considered more controversial. So, too, did the boost the administration proposed to give to nuclear power.

Policies and Actions

In several respects the Reagan administration's actions in the energy area have been reasonable ones. One of President Reagan's first actions, for example, was to advance by eight months the expiration of remaining controls on the price of domestically produced crude oil. Since President Carter had initiated decontrol in 1979, this action was more symbolic than substantive. Nevertheless, it terminated a controversial program in which even many initial supporters had lost faith. It also looked very good when soon followed by declining world oil prices and unprecedented disarray in OPEC, even though their causes were basically independent of it. By mid-1983, the world oil price had fallen to $29 per barrel, down 15 percent from its 1982 high of $34.

Natural gas deregulation proved more difficult. In contrast to crude oil price controls (which conferred substantial benefits on OPEC producers by increasing demand, but hurt domestic producers), some domestic suppliers benefited from controlled natural gas prices and opposed their decontrol, as did many gas users. Also, natural gas is transported and distributed by companies which would remain regulated and thus not benefit from decontrol. The divergent views of producers, consumers, pipeline owners, distribution companies, and state regulatory bodies, thus, greatly complicated decontrol of natural gas prices at the point of production.

In view of the political complexity of the issue, the bill proposed by the administration early in 1983 (and still before Congress as of the summer of 1984) is a sensible one. It would abolish price controls on all natural gas after 1985—even on "old gas" for which controls would continue under the 1978 NGPA. One feature of the bill, however, seems inconsistent with the administration's espoused philosophy of minimal government. It would void voluntary, long-term contracts between companies producing natural gas and the pipeline companies that carry it. These contracts have prevented the pipeline companies from taking advantage of recent decreases in the price of natural gas and for that reason have been frustrating. Even so, such abrogation of private contracts would be an unusual step for a conservative administration.

As a result of considerable congressional prodding, the administration has also made real progress in building the Strategic Petroleum Reserve. By January 1984 it exceeded 360 million barrels, up more than 300 percent from the reserve inherited from the Carter administration. Acquisitions for the reserve have been facilitated by falling oil prices. They have also been helped by the fact that expenditures for this purpose do not show up in the federal budget. (Though still very real, they were moved off budget by mutual agreement of the Congress and administration in 1981 and claimed as a budget cut.) This lack of political visibility helps protect the acquisitions during austere budget periods.

The administration has done less well elsewhere on the energy security front. Virtually no planning has been done, for example, to prepare for a possible oil supply interruption in the Middle East or elsewhere. In fact, President Reagan vetoed the Standby Petroleum Allocation Act of 1982, which would have authorized (though not required) federal rationing of petroleum and other energy commodities in the event of an emergency. The weight of expert opinion supports President Reagan's belief that rationing by price is the most effective way to deal with emergency shortfalls in supply. However, even laissez faire proponents like former energy czar William Simon were forced to accept nonprice rationing to protect the economically disadvantaged during a previous supply disruption. Thus, a contingency plan for income or other assistance to the needy would enhance the political acceptability of price rationing in the event of severe shortage and in view of the need to ensure essential energy supplies to all, irrespective of income.[30]

Several aspects of the Reagan administration's energy budgets bear mention. The first relates to the changing composition of the overall budget of the DOE.

The share of the total DOE budget devoted to nuclear weapons research and production has increased substantially over the past four years, from 38 percent in FY 1981 to a proposed 62 percent in FY 1985 (see table 5.3). Since the share devoted to general science (high energy physics, for example) has remained about constant, the entire increase in weapons programs has come at the expense of civilian energy expenditures. Proposed FY 1985 spending for these latter programs is 25 percent less than four years previously.

The second aspect of the DOE budget relates to proposed changes in the amount and composition of spending for energy technologies, the major component of civilian energy expenditures (table 5.4). Note first that overall spending for energy technologies proposed for FY 1985 is 44 percent less than was spent in FY 1981, the last Carter budget. Conservation, solar and other renewable energy sources (such as wind power), and fossil energy programs accounted for 66 percent of the more than $4 billion spent in FY 1981. By FY 1985, their proposed combined share is 37 percent of the

TABLE 5.3

DOE TOTAL BUDGET
(In $ millions)

	Program Funding		
	FY 1981	*FY 1984*	*(Requested)* *FY 1985*
Civilian energy			
Energy technologies[a]	$ 4,704	$ 3,105	$ 2,988
Direct energy	297	1,007	885
Regulation and			
preparedness	354	138	126
	$ 5,355 (57%)	$ 4,250 (37%)	$ 3,999 (32%)
General science	504 (5%)	641 (5%)	746 (6%)
Atomic defense	3,618 (38%)	6,718 (58%)	7,806 (62%)
TOTAL	$ 9,477 (100%)	$11,609 (100%)	$12,551 (100%)

SOURCE: Subcommittee on Energy Conservation and Power, Committee on Energy and Commerce, U.S. House of Representatives, January 31, 1984.

NOTE: Data for 1981 indicate actual obligations (contracts awarded, orders placed, or other commitments requiring subsequent payment). Data for 1984 and 1985 indicate budget authority (the amount made newly available for program obligations).

a.   The energy technology budget includes all the programs listed in table 5.4, plus electric energy systems, energy storage systems, management, environment, and support research.

TABLE 5.4

DOE Energy Technologies Budget
(In $ millions)

	Program Funding		
	FY 1981	FY 1984	(Requested) FY 1985
Conservation	$ 802 (19%)	$ 431 (18%)	$ 400 (17%)
Nuclear fission/nuclear waste disposal	1,008 (24%) 0	675 (41%) 320	618 (41%) 328
Nuclear fusion	394 (10%)	471 (19%)	483 (21%)
Solar and renewables	771 (19%)	215 (9%)	191 (8%)
Fossil energy	1,134 (28%)	330 (13%)	273 (12%)
TOTAL	$ 4,109	$ 2,442	$ 2,293

SOURCE: Subcommittee on Energy Conservation and Power, Committee on Energy and Commerce, U.S. House of Representatives, January 31, 1984.
NOTE: Data for 1981 indicate actual obligations (contracts awarded, orders placed, or other commitments requiring subsequent payment). Data for 1984 indicate budget authority (the amount made newly available for program obligations).

$2.3 billion requested. Nuclear fission, fusion, and waste disposal expenditures were scheduled to increase from 34 percent to 65 percent of all spending for energy technologies over the same period. Even though congressional appropriations have consistently exceeded administration requests, sometimes by an order of magnitude or more, funding for energy conservation and renewables is still down very sharply from 1981.* It would probably be even lower were it not for Energy Secretary Donald Hodel's reemphasis on conservation and renewables.[31]

Some reduction in expenditures on conservation may have been appropriate. In spite of the political popularity of the solar and energy conservation programs, for instance, there has been little careful analysis of their efficacy. Between 1973 and 1980 energy use as a proportion of the gross national product (GNP) had fallen by 20 percent. While most experts attributed this improved performance primarily to higher prices, tax credits for insulation and weatherizing as well as other conservation programs may have played some role. In view of the demonstrated economic advantages of some conservation programs,[32] a careful review should have preceded such drastic

*For instance, in FY 1984 the administration requested $176 million for conservation, and solar and other renewables while Congress appropriated nearly $650 million.

budget changes. But such a review, even though warranted, did not take place. Rather, the administration eliminated certain programs immediately and proposed to phase out almost all solar and energy conservation programs by 1986.

One program that has consistently received strong support from the Reagan administration is the breeder reactor, included in table 5.4 under Nuclear Fission. For example, the administration had proposed $270 million in FY 1984 to continue funding for the Clinch River Breeder Reactor, a demonstration project which President Carter tried unsuccessfully to terminate throughout his administration. When Congress finally turned against the Clinch River project in 1983, the administration backed a proposal that purported to increase substantially the private financing for the project, hoping to save it. This compromise was criticized as essentially risk-free for private investors, because the guaranteed rates of return were so high, and in the fall of 1983 the Clinch River project was ended.[33] But the FY 1985 DOE budget request still includes about $310 million for other research related to the breeder. On a related matter, the administration successfully supported passage of the Nuclear Waste Policy Act of 1982. This legislation establishes a schedule and financing mechanism for the construction and licensing of nuclear waste repositories and requires DOE to submit a proposal for construction of such a storage site at a specific location.

A final issue of some significance is the fate of the SFC, a key element in the Carter administration's efforts to improve energy security. Its initial authorization of $20 billion (to cover four years) was to provide financial assistance to private firms producing synthetic fuels. After four years, Congress was to decide whether to authorize another $68 billion, but the possible additional authorizations have been reduced to $15 billion by the Reagan administration. When the Reagan administration took office, Edward Noble— the president's nominee for chairman of the SFC—expressed an interest in closing down the SFC, just as Secretary Edwards had pledged to abolish the DOE. More recently, however, Noble and some other supporters in the administration have warmed to the SFC's mission, only to encounter a new problem. Because of a fall in world oil and other energy prices, private firms are backing out of SFC-sponsored projects left and right—even with the federal subsidies, many of the projects are now viewed as unprofitable. To date, only one project has been funded by the SFC in the three years of its existence. The administration must now decide whether, in view of large deficits and the current lack of enthusiasm among private firms for federally subsidized projects, it will spend the money already appropriated for the SFC, much less request additional budget authority.

Agricultural Policy

The complexity of agricultural policy generally keeps it out of the limelight. Nevertheless, in FY 1982 and FY 1983 a dramatic escalation in the cost of agricultural support programs brought them unusual attention. Of particular interest was the Reagan administration's Payment-In-Kind (PIK) program which, although designed to keep federal spending down, actually increased it.

Background and Opportunities

Many federal programs affect agricultural production. Whether the programs provide for direct government purchases or generous loans, payments to farmers to idle land, immunity from antitrust actions, or other measures, almost all the programs have been in place in some form since the 1930s. Although price stability is often cited as a goal of the programs, the protection of farm incomes is by far their most important role.[34]

During the 1970s, agricultural markets generally became more competitive. In addition, the acreage diverted as a result of federal policies also fell. In the 1970–1972 period, for instance, about 55 million acres per year were withheld from production. By 1978–1980 this figure had fallen to about 9 million acres. The reduction was due in part to a fundamental change in the market for U.S. agricultural production. Between 1940 and 1970 agricultural exports never exceeded $7 billion in any one year. Between 1971 and 1980, by contrast, exports *averaged* $23 billion annually and reached $41 billion in 1980. Increased export demand helped increase the prices received by farmers, especially at the beginning and toward the end of the decade.

Upon taking office, the Reagan administration announced its intention to reduce government involvement in the agricultural sector further by eliminating deficiency payments to grain and cotton farmers (equal to the difference between market price and a preestablished "target" price), and by reducing price supports for dairy products (which, unlike other support prices, had increased during the 1970s). In this, most experts agree that the administration correctly perceived an important opportunity. A major impetus for the administration's intentions was the reduction of budget outlays on agriculture. Its goal was total annual outlays on the order of $1.5 to $2.0 billion, $0.4 billion of which would go for dairy price supports.[35] Since expenditures for price support programs had been running at about $4 billion in the late

1970s (in 1983 dollars), the administration was aiming to cut the programs by one-third to one-half.

After initially freezing the support price for milk, the administration tried to reduce all support prices during debate over the Agriculture and Food Act of 1981, the basic legislation establishing farm policy for the next four years. It succeeded in reducing the real support price for milk, which was scheduled to fall by about 7 percent between 1980 and 1983. However, Congress increased the support prices for corn, wheat, rice, and cotton in the 1981 act, but probably by less than it might had there not been active opposition by the administration. Given subsequent developments, the administration no doubt wishes it had fought even harder.

Economic and meteorological events in 1981–1982 combined to aggravate agriculture's difficulties. Yields were at near record levels in both years— 12 to 15 percent above 1980 levels. At the same time, the worldwide recession and the very strong dollar resulted in significant declines in export demand.* The combination of increased supply and decreased demand meant that government payments to farmers increased substantially, as did grain stocks under loan to or owned by the federal government. For instance, while end-of-the-year corn stocks averaged about 1.3 billion bushels between 1977 and 1980, they were 2.3 billion bushels at the end of 1982, and were expected to be 3.4 billion bushels by fall 1983 when the U.S. Department of Agriculture (USDA) made its March 1983 estimate. In spite of some modest 1982 acreage diversion programs, stocks were growing much too rapidly for an administration wishing to keep down commodity loans, payments, and grain storage costs. Price support outlays grew to $12.0 billion (in 1983 dollars) in FY 1982. This was only an indication of difficulties yet to come.

The administration's response to the rapidly deteriorating budget problems in agriculture was the PIK program, announced in January 1983. The intent behind acreage diversions (including PIK) is to reduce supply, increase prices, and hence reduce loans, deficiency payments, and crop storage costs. The PIK program was designed to do this by enabling farmers who had participated in a congressionally mandated acreage diversion program to idle an additional 10 to 30 percent of their land. In exchange they would not be given cash (the usual practice in acreage diversion), but rather would be paid in shipments of the same crops they refrained from growing—corn, wheat,

---

*The growing budget deficits contributed to this problem. Reducing the size of the deficits might permit some reduction in interest rates which would in turn weaken the dollar in comparison to other currencies. This action would stimulate exports and thus reduce government payments to farmers.

rice, cotton—from stocks owned by the government. Some producers were given the option of idling all their lands.

Two problems plagued PIK. First, as some experts had warned, the terms of the program were so generous (farmers received 80–95 percent of the grain they could have grown on the idled land), that twice as many acres were idled as the administration estimated—77 million acres in all. This response made it far and away the largest acreage diversion program of all time, exceeding the previous high, 64 million acres in 1962, by 20 percent—an embarrassing event in an administration pledged to extricate government from agriculture.

Second, as PIK transfers to farmers were reducing bloated grain and other stocks, a severe drought struck the farm belt, reducing grain and soybean yields by 25 percent and cotton yields by 33 percent. As a result, current surplus stocks of corn and soybeans are now below the minimum levels considered necessary to guard against the possibility of a poor harvest.[36] At the same time, PIK-induced acreage reductions have pushed prices for corn and soybeans considerably higher in 1984 than they were a year ago. While this is good news for some farmers, it is bad news for consumers, who can see even higher prices if harvests are poor in 1984.

All this caused the cost of agricultural price supports to skyrocket to $18.8 billion in FY 1983—only $3 billion less than *cumulative* expenditures during the four years of the Carter administration. Moreover, the crops that were given away—publicly owned crops, in essence—themselves had a value of $12 billion.[37] In addition, because enrollment in the program was so great, government stocks were sometimes inadequate to supply participating farmers. In these cases, the government had to buy crops at premium to give to farmers in exchange for not growing them. In one instance, for example, the land that was idled turned out to be under nine feet of water.[38] In view of these and other problems, it is no surprise that the program became unpopular.

The administration abandoned the PIK program for all commodities but wheat in 1984. Some acreage diversion programs are slated to continue, but the hope is that increased demand resulting from economic recovery will reduce deficiency payments and grain storage costs. To discourage over-production again, certain support prices have been reduced. The administration has budgeted $11.0 billion for agricultural support in FY 1985, nearly 30 percent more than expenditures for this purpose in any year between 1977 and 1981.

Assessment

Generally speaking, much less has been accomplished in natural resource and environmental policy than either the Reagan administration had intended or than is suggested by the many controversies surrounding the policies and their purveyors.

The Environment

In the environmental area, the first two years of the Reagan administration were characterized by extreme controversy and little policy action, primarily because of the extraordinarily poor initial appointments to the EPA. Inexperience and suspicion of (or hostility toward) the EPA's career staff and traditional constituencies spelled disaster in the political arena; management problems and almost across-the-board budget cuts damaged programs already underfunded.

By any standard, including the administration's, the number of enforcement actions taken by the EPA against violators has fallen considerably during the Reagan administration. Although this policy *may* have encouraged some polluters to increase their emissions, this is by no means clear. As noted, data suggest that even firms subject to enforcement actions often remain out of compliance for long periods of time, a situation that is not unique to the Reagan administration. However, the very existence of regulations may induce other firms to come into compliance, independent of enforcement efforts. It may even be that the decline in enforcement action is, in fact, a reflection of a push for negotiated settlements (rather than sanctions) to bring firms into compliance.

It also appears that business spending for pollution control, in terms of actual outlays and as a percentage of total fixed investment, has declined during the Reagan administration.[39] But this trend is probably due at least in part to factors independent of Reagan's environmental policy—namely, completion of initial pollution control investments by the major industries and the effects of the deep recession in 1981–1982.

In any case, whether the health and welfare of the citizenry have been adversely affected is much less clear. What data we have on air pollution, from the national monitoring network, indicate that overall air quality in the United States continues to improve.[40] No confident assessment about water pollution trends is possible, due to the moribund condition of the monitoring network. But what data do exist seem to suggest maintenance of the status quo.

Little action was taken in 1981–1982 at the EPA to begin cleaning up the thousands of abandoned hazardous waste disposal sites the Superfund was created to address. During the period of inactivity some citizens have been exposed to risks they might otherwise have avoided. But the extent of the risk will never be known for sure because of the long latencies between exposure and effect and the confounding influences of other determinants of ill health.

The real damage lies in the opportunities not taken in environmental policy during 1981 and 1982. These included improvements in monitoring, the enforcement program, the scientific research upon which the EPA draws, and the extension of economic incentives and other flexible tools to supplement traditional regulatory techniques. An opportunity also existed (and was missed) to work for fundamental changes in the major environmental laws, changes that might have rationalized the process by which environmental standards are set.

The new leadership team at the EPA, which has already gone a long way toward rebuilding staff and morale, is ideally suited to begin work on such an agenda. But it is a much more difficult task given the history of the first two years than it would have been if started in early 1981. An election year dampens administration and congressional enthusiasm for all but the most cosmetic changes in environmental policy. The budgetary situation facing the administration today and in the foreseeable future is far worse than the one inherited in 1981. And the difficulties through early 1983 have probably dissipated much of the public support the administration might otherwise have had for a reexamination of the basic environmental laws.

Interior

Policy change was more significant at the Department of the Interior than at the EPA—but less than the Reagan administration apparently intended and less, in spite of all the *Sturm und Drang*, than many of the administration's critics feared.

There was a substantial burst of leasing activities during the administration's first two years. But the problems and irregularities that resulted, coupled with depressed markets for energy and minerals, have combined to slow the leasing programs at least temporarily. In spite of the administration's intention to greatly increase public land sales, such transactions have been no greater than in previous administrations because of adverse public and congressional reaction. Nor has the Reagan administration had much success expanding oil and natural gas leasing in wilderness areas. Some initiatives have been launched to promote mineral extraction on private lands within or near wilderness areas, although little activity has yet taken place. Finally, some major budget and organizational changes were made at the Interior Department, although even here no truly fundamental change can be claimed to have taken place.

Energy

In energy policy, the administration has certain accomplishments to its credit. By speeding up deregulation of domestic petroleum prices and proposing complete decontrol of all natural gas prices at the wellhead, the administration has acted in accord with the recommendations of most energy analysts. The higher prices that will result should spur new exploration and stimulate conservation as well. With congressional prodding the administration also has taken advantage of reduced prices of imported oil to accelerate additions to the Strategic Petroleum Reserve, which now contains enough oil to replace all imports for a period of about 100 days at current levels. Areas in which administration policy is open to more criticism include a virtual total lack of planning for potential disruptions in the supplies of foreign oil and drastic cuts in the budget for conservation programs without, in all cases, careful review.

Agriculture

Bad luck with the weather and an ill-conceived acreage diversion program combined to make the Reagan administration one of the most interventionist in the history of agricultural policy. Acres diverted were at an all-time high, by a wide margin, as were price support outlays for farmers. However, at least part of the problem is that agricultural policies now in place are poorly suited to the problems of modern agriculture.[41]

The administration has done better in working to reduce support prices and government purchases, a policy that experts applaud. Particularly important will be efforts to restore some semblance of competition to the dairy industry, which now benefits from virtually every restraint of trade imaginable—all sanctioned by the government.[42] The 1985 farm bill may be the occasion for discussions about fundamental restructuring of U.S. agricultural policy which will provide an opportunity to pursue a substantially less active government role.

The Overall Picture

When all four areas are considered together there are, as always in such things, similarities as well as differences in policy.

The most notable similarity is a reliance on administrative discretion rather than on legislative changes as the preferred policy instrument. The probable reason for this course of action is that it is always more difficult to push legislation through Congress than to act by administrative decree, even more so when the proposed changes are drastic. But there is a price to pay;

subsequent administrations can reverse policies more easily. It is unlikely indeed that the Reagan administration will have fundamentally altered the course of policy in these areas, because it has achieved little legislative change. A second common element is the gap between what was promised and what has been delivered. The DOE, for example, has its second secretary and is actively involved in forming administration policy. And the federal government is more, not less, involved in agriculture (although it is searching for ways to extricate itself).

The most conspicuous difference is the type of criticism received. In the areas of energy and agriculture, criticism of the administration has usually focused on policy substance rather than conduct. The same cannot be said of environmental and natural resources policies. Perceived vindictiveness or incompetence led ultimately to the replacement of the top officials in both areas with more seasoned and less controversial appointees. A second difference is in the relative success of the policies pursued. Here the breakdown is different. Energy and Interior have had some successes. The administration has been able to both accelerate decontrol of crude oil and gasoline prices and shift more emphasis away from solar and conservation initiatives toward nuclear programs. The administration has also presided over a substantial (but perhaps short-lived) increase in the amount of federally owned coal that has been leased, as well as an increase in OCS acreage leased for oil and gas exploration. When weighed against the administration's own goals, however, even the successes are few and far between. An administration espousing a free market approach has become the custodian of the greatest agricultural land diversion program in history and has made little progress in furthering the use of economic incentives as tools of environmental policy.

CHAPTER 6

SOCIAL POLICY
CHALLENGING THE WELFARE STATE

D. Lee Bawden
John L. Palmer

In his January 1982 State of the Union address, President Reagan reflected with pride on the accomplishments of his first year in office in the
area of social policy. Observing that he had inherited a system in which
"available resources are going not to the needy but to the greedy," he cited
some $44 billion dollars in cuts already obtained in social programs and
announced his intention to realize another $63 billion in savings over the next
several years. He also took aim at the "jungle" of federal categorical grants
for social services and education (among other areas), characterizing them as
wasteful and inefficient and promising to propose "a single bold stroke" that
would return "some $47 billion in federal (grants-in-aid) programs to state
and local government, together with the means to finance them." Finally,
the president reiterated his often-voiced confidence that "the economic program we have put into operation will protect the needy while it triggers the
recovery that will benefit all Americans."

The views expressed by the president in this State of the Union address
are remarkably consistent with the philosophy he espoused as a presidential
candidate and with the policies he continued to propose while in office.
Together they constitute a coherent ideological attack on the principles that
have governed social policy in this country for the last half century. In
particular, the president has called into question prevailing assumptions about:

- the extent to which the public—any "public," local, state, or federal—is responsible for the social and economic well-being of its

individual members. The historical trend has been toward an increasing assumption of responsibility at all levels of government, but particularly the federal level. President Reagan, however, has suggested that the federal government is often ill-suited to determine public responsibility and that, insofar as it must address this issue, the federal government should conclude that it be "not nearly so responsible as formerly."

• the appropriate goals of social policy. Public debate over this issue in recent years has been preoccupied with questions of equality, whether of condition or of opportunity, but the word "equality" is conspicuously absent in this administration's rhetoric (having been supplanted by "freedom").

• the most efficient means—level of government and type of program—for discharging public responsibility, however defined. Here both the president's public statements and his proposals suggest that the presumption should favor state and local governments as the most efficient vehicles for delivering whatever largesse the public purse has to offer, and that, in general, the federal government should look more to the private sector for the answers to social problems.

These views about the appropriate role of government derive from the president's faith in the capacity of most individuals to fend for themselves within a free-market economy and his faith in the capacity of that economy to function efficiently with minimal (compared to the recent past) federal intervention. The opposite side of this faith is that the federal government is a pernicious influence on individual, community, and corporate initiative and charity. In characterizing the federal government as more of a problem than a solution, the president clearly struck a popular chord with the country; on the strength of this chord, he succeeded in (among other things) abolishing a number of federal social programs and redirecting others.

These broad-brush characterizations of the Reagan experiment leave unanswered a number of fundamental questions about both the president's intentions and his accomplishments. Did he intend a wholesale abandonment of the social activist tradition inaugurated with President Roosevelt's New Deal and brought to full flower in President Johnson's Great Society? Or is he—as he has styled himself—a conservative "in the Roosevelt tradition," responding to a new era of hard times and proposing only to prune the excesses that had crept into federal social programs over decades of material prosperity? And what were his real priorities when push came to shove: that is, when he encountered (as all presidents do) a not completely compliant Congress? To what extent were his aims principally budgetary—to shrink the "bloated" federal budget—and to what extent ideological—to get the federal government out of certain kinds of "inappropriate" activities? Finally, what difference has it all made? What impact has he had on the people most directly affected by federal social policy?

This chapter reports what we have in the way of answers to these questions. It first provides an overview of President Reagan's aims and accomplishments in shrinking the overall "scope" of federal social policy. Next, because it is impossible in a chapter of this length to interpret the significance of the changes in each program area, we focus our assessment of impact on two of the most important and controversial topics: (1) the "social safety net" and related issues of poverty and dependency, and (2) civil rights and equal opportunity policies. (Appendix C provides more detailed summaries of legislative proposals, outcomes, and their consequences for the major social programs.) These two topics provide reasonable measures of the president's intentions in regard to the "goals" of federal social responsibility: preservation of the social safety net is the one existing policy to which he has publicly paid allegiance; civil rights and equal opportunity policies—requiring very little federal spending—constitute one of the few major social policies not in conflict with his budgetary goals. Finally, we sketch the impact of the administration's policies on the "means" by which federally funded social services are delivered.*

The Scope of Public Responsibility

Perhaps the best way to address a question as abstract as the "appropriate scope of public responsibility" is through budget policy; willingness to spend constitutes public acceptance of responsibility. The appropriate scope of public responsibility in any area can be viewed as the priority that spending in this area has over other claims on the public purse. But assessing priorities is no straightforward matter; real and pressing budgetary concerns frequently obscure deep philosophical differences, and decisions made on the basis of legitimate recognition of constraints on public willingness to spend may come to be justified on the basis of a broader philosophical consensus than exists. Whether this has in fact happened in the case of President Reagan's social policies we cannot say; however, we can certainly note that the president, at least initially, parlayed a general public nervousness over the scale of domestic

---

*The sketch is brief because many topics germane to this issue—federalism, the role of the private sector—are covered elsewhere in this volume.

spending into a specific mandate. And we can attempt to place this interpretation of a mandate in the broad historical context of public expenditures for social purposes, so that we can at least see whether a consensus seemed to be in the making when the president took office.

Historical context in this case begins in the 1930s. Until the advent of the New Deal, federal spending in the social arena was virtually nonexistent; destitute individuals—the unemployed, the disabled, the old, those incapable of earning their own living—were dependent for support on their families, private charities, and local and state government. In the social and economic convulsion of the Great Depression this piecemeal system of support fell apart, giving way to a massive assumption of responsibility for social welfare by the federal government. Many of the New Deal social programs proved, as indeed they were intended, to be temporary responses to emergency conditions. However, one category, embodied in the Social Security Act of 1935, permanently altered the federal policy landscape. This landmark legislation inaugurated the Social Security and the Unemployment Compensation "social insurance" programs, as well as federal contributions to state-run, means-tested programs for the elderly, blind, and disabled, and for women with dependent children ("welfare," narrowly defined).

Together, these programs constituted the germ of what the Reagan administration has labeled the "social safety net." Although the phrase has been variously defined both by the administration and by others, it invariably includes the core New Deal programs. Thus it can be viewed as having two tiers: the upper, comprised of insurance programs (primarily funded through payroll taxes); and the lower, comprised of means-tested ("welfare") programs for those either who have no social insurance at all or are not adequately protected by social insurance programs.* Over the years both tiers have expanded steadily, even though the welfare component was originally anticipated to wither away, rendered unnecessary by the working together of the social insurance programs and a revitalized economy. To this core of programs, predicated on temporary or permanent inability to work, were added a whole range of federal programs addressed to various purposes, including alleviation of poverty, promotion of civil rights and equal opportunity, and access to adequate health care. In consequence, federal spending for social purposes mushroomed, growing overall at a much faster rate than the economy (as measured by the gross national product, GNP) and than similar spending

---

*Throughout this chapter we use the term "social safety net" broadly to refer to the entire set of so-called "benefit payments to individuals" programs (but not discretionary grants to state and local governments) which are listed in footnotes b and c of figure 6.2. Most of these are open-ended entitlement programs.

of state and local governments. (See figure 6.1 for a comparison of the growth in domestic expenditures, the bulk of which were for social purposes, between 1929 and 1979.)

This growth occurred in two distinct phases. The first was the New Deal itself. Then, after a hiatus through the 1950s, total federal social program spending more than doubled as a percentage of GNP between the early 1960s and mid-1970s. The vast bulk of the *dollar* growth in federal spending for social purposes occurred in those programs—mostly "entitlements"—providing cash or other forms of support directly to individuals and families. The "social insurance and other" programs not targeted on the low-income population accounted for the lion's share of this growth, rising from well under 4 percent of GNP in the mid-1960s to well over 7 percent by the mid-1970s (see figure 6.2). But "low-income assistance" programs also grew in importance—from under 1 percent of GNP to nearly 2 percent over this same period. The fastest *percentage* growth occurred in the proliferation, under the Great Society, of "other grants," programs that primarily provided federal assistance to state and local governments and nonprofit agencies to deliver education, social, health, and employment services to prescribed (usually "disadvantaged") populations. Despite their rapid growth, however, spending for these programs remained relatively low, never exceeding 1 percent of GNP.

Excepting Medicare (a social insurance program very much in the spirit of the New Deal), the new programs created in the 1960s and early 1970s never accounted for more than one-fifth of total federal social program spending.* Thus, the growth of this spending over the past twenty years must be regarded as primarily a legacy of the New Deal.

Accompanying the growth in social programs was a considerable expansion of their scope and a blurring of the distinction between the upper and lower tiers of the safety net. For example, Social Security, initially intended to supplement private pensions and savings for the retired, became the dominant source of income for many of the elderly; with the establishment of a minimum benefit in 1961 and the increasing favoring of low-wage workers in its benefit formula, the program took on more of a welfare character. Also, extension of coverage to new population groups—the disabled and early retirees—diluted the program's original focus. Similarly, the unemployment insurance program changed its coloration, becoming increasingly long term

---

*These new programs accounted for essentially all the "other grants," about half the "low-income assistance," and a small fraction of the "social insurance and other" spending levels in figure 6.2.

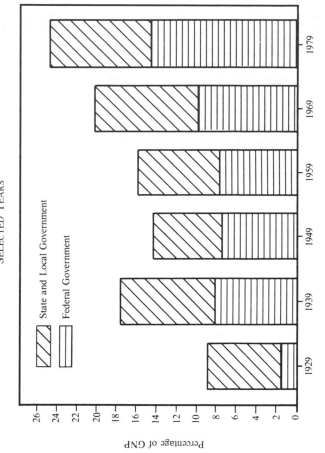

FIGURE 6.1

GOVERNMENT DOMESTIC EXPENDITURES FROM OWN FUNDS AS A PERCENTAGE OF GNP,
SELECTED YEARS

SOURCE: Advisory Commission on Intergovernmental Relations, "Significant Features of Federalism," 1981–1982 ed. (Washington, D.C.: Advisory Commission on Intergovernmental Relations, 1983), table 1.

FIGURE 6.2

FEDERAL SOCIAL PROGRAM SPENDING AS A PERCENTAGE OF GNP

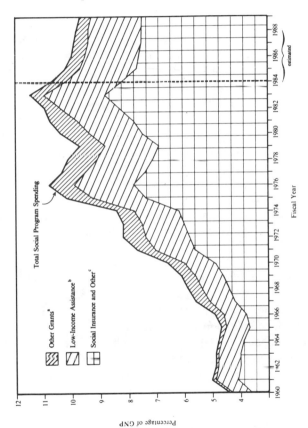

SOURCES: Office of Management and Budget "Federal Government Finances," February 1983. "Federal Grants-in-Aid to State and Local Governments," March 1983, and "Payments for Individuals," February 1983; Congressional Budget Office, unpublished tabulations; and authors' calculations.

NOTES: Figures for 1985–1989 are projections based on 1984 policies.
   a. Includes Compensatory, Vocational, and Adult Education, Education for the Handicapped, Rehabilitation Services, Health and Social Services, Refugee and Entrant Assistance, and Employment and Training Programs.
   b. Includes Medicaid, Aid to Families with Dependent Children (AFDC), Veterans' Pensions, Supplemental Security Income (SSI), Food Stamps, Student Financial Assistance, Housing Assistance, Child Nutrition, Special Supplemental Feeding Program for Women, Infants, and Children (WIC), and Low-Income Energy Assistance.
   c. Includes Medicare, Social Security, Unemployment Insurance, Guaranteed Student Loans, Veterans' Compensation, Medical Care, and Readjustment Benefits.

in coverage and acquiring, in 1979, an income-tested dimension.* At the same time, the lower-tier, means-tested programs were broadening their coverage to encompass new population groups. More and more people were receiving multiple program benefits, and liberalization of eligibility requirements—in particular, the treatment of earned income—meant that benefits were extending up the income scale toward the middle class.

The Great Society heyday of the social safety net programs—and federal social programs in general—coincided with a period of unprecedented economic prosperity; as that prosperity waned, so too did the rate of growth in social spending. While advocating more concern for efficiency in government and attempting several measures to trim major entitlement programs (most notably Medicare and Social Security), President Carter also proposed major expansion of the welfare state through new federal spending commitments for welfare reform, national health insurance, public service employment, and low-income housing assistance. Had he been successful, federal spending for social programs undoubtedly would have continued to grow significantly faster than the economy, as the expansions would have been more costly than the savings. Carter's achievements, however, were much more limited than his aims; in consequence, federal social spending as a percentage of GNP ceased its upward trend during his tenure in office.

In contrast, under President Reagan, with his overriding emphasis on reducing the scope of the federal role and cutting the domestic budget, federal social program spending has begun to decline as a percentage of GNP.† Table 6.1 presents a consolidated picture of the annual impact, by FY 1985, of the spending cuts sought by the president in his FY 1982-1984 budgets and of those actually achieved, relative to the spending levels that would have prevailed had the policies the president inherited been continued. Several programs were proposed for elimination, among them public service employment, the Work Incentive program (WIN), and community services. Others were proposed for reductions of 20 to 65 percent, often in conjunction with consolidation into block grants or other major transformation. Notable examples

---

*Beginning in 1979, unemployment compensation was taxed as ordinary income for individuals with income above $20,000 ($25,000 for married couples).

†As is evident in figure 6.2 it rose significantly, but temporarily, in FY 1982 and 1983 (despite the fact that the initial budget cuts under President Reagan began to take effect in FY 1982). This resulted from the deep recession and the automatic rise in spending in many entitlement programs in response to higher unemployment and lowered incomes. This sensitivity of social spending to the state of the economy also largely explains its modest decline as a percentage of GNP in FY 1977–1979 and subsequent rise in FY 1980 and 1981. Abstracting from the performance of the economy, there was no particular trend during the fiscal years of the Carter era.

TABLE 6.1

<small>ESTIMATED OUTLAY CHANGES IN FY 1985 RESULTING FROM REAGAN
ADMINISTRATION PROPOSALS AND CONGRESSIONAL ACTIONS THROUGH FY 1984</small>

Program	Projected Outlays under Pre-Reagan Policy Baseline (In $ billions)	Proposed Changes[a] Percentage of Baseline	Enacted Changes Percentage of Baseline
Retirement and Disability			
Social Security	200.6	−10.4	−4.6
Veterans' Compensation	10.7	−8.4	−.9
Veterans' Pensions	3.8	−2.6	−2.6
Supplemental Security Income (SSI)	8.1	−2.5	+8.6
Other Income Security			
Unemployment Insurance	29.8	−19.1	−17.4
Aid to Families with Dependent Children (AFDC)	9.8	−28.6	−14.3
Food Stamps	14.5	−51.7	−13.8
Child Nutrition	5.0	−46.0	28.0
Women, Infants, and Children (WIC)	1.1	−63.6	+9.1
Housing Assistance[b]	12.3	−19.5	−11.4
Low-Income Energy Assistance	2.4	−37.5	−8.3
Health			
Medicare	80.4	−11.2	−6.8
Medicaid	24.9	−15.7	−2.8
Other Health Services	1.8	−44.4	−33.3
Education and Social Services			
Compensatory Education	4.1	−61.0	−19.5
Head Start	1.0	c	c
Vocational Education	.8	−37.5	−12.5
Guaranteed Student Loans	4.1	−22.0	−39.0
Other Student Financial Assistance	4.5	−68.9	−15.6
Veterans' Readjustment Benefits	1.1	−9.1	−9.1
Social Services Block Grant	3.4	−41.2	−23.5
Community Services Block Grant	.7	−100.0	−37.1
Employment and Training			
General Employment and Training	5.7	−43.9	−38.6
Public Service Employment	4.8	−100.0	−100.0

(continued)

TABLE 6.1 (continued)

ESTIMATED OUTLAY CHANGES IN FY 1985 RESULTING FROM REAGAN
ADMINISTRATION PROPOSALS AND CONGRESSIONAL ACTIONS THROUGH FY 1984

Program	Projected Outlays under Pre-Reagan Policy Baseline (In $ billions)	Proposed Changes[a] Percentage of Baseline	Enacted Changes Percentage of Baseline
Job Corps	.7	− 42.9	− 7.7
Work Incentive Program	.5	− 100.0	− 35.1
TOTAL	436.6	− 17.2	− 8.8
Addendum:			
Payments to Individuals			
Social Insurance and			
Other[d]	326.7	− 11.5	− 6.5
Low-Income Assistance[d]	86.4	− 27.7	− 8.2
Other Grants[d]	23.5	− 58.7	− 42.1

SOURCES: Congressional Budget Office, "Major Legislative Changes in Human Resources Programs Since January 1981" (staff memorandum), August 1983; Office of Management
and Budget, *Fiscal Year 1982 Budget Revisions* (Washington, D.C.: Government
Printing Office, March 1981), *Budget of the United States Government, Fiscal Year
1983* (Washington, D.C.: Government Printing Office, 1982), and *Budget of the United
States Government, Fiscal Year 1984* (Washington, D.C.: Government Printing Office,
1983); The White House, *America's New Beginning: A Program for Economic Recovery* (Washington, D.C.: February 18, 1981); and authors' calculations.

a. For discretionary programs the proposed reductions are estimated by comparing the lowest
outlays proposed by the administration for FY 1985 from its FY 1982, FY 1983, and FY 1984
budgets to the estimated outlays for FY 1985 under pre-Reagan policies. For entitlement programs
the savings that would be attributable to enactment of all the various specific (actually or
conceptually) nonoverlapping program changes proposed by the administration in its FY 1982,
FY 1983, and FY 1984 budgets (and, in the case of Social Security, the proposal forwarded to
Congress subsequent to the FY 1982 budget) are separately estimated and summed.

b. The administration proposed a virtual halt to the expensive rehabilitation and new construction housing assistance programs, in favor of greater reliance on rent subsidies. However,
because the budget authority granted in the former programs is converted into outlays over a
lengthy time period, actual outlay reductions relative to prior policies in the short run are quite
modest.

c. Total reductions amount to less than $50 million.

d. See figure 6.2 for definitions. Note, however, that the "other grants" category in this table
does not include the few small discretionary programs listed in footnote a of figure 6.2.

here are low-income housing assistance, the Special Supplemental Feeding
Program for Women, Infants, and Children (WIC), Aid to Families with
Dependent Children (AFDC), Food Stamps, compensatory and vocational
education, and general employment and training. A final category of programs, including Social Security, Medicare, Medicaid, Supplementary Security Income for the aged and disabled (SSI), and unemployment insurance,

were all also proposed for cuts, in many cases sizable, but without as major a transformation in scope or structure.

The net effect of President Reagan's proposed reductions would have been to reduce annual federal spending for social programs by FY 1985 by over $75 billion (about 2 percent of GNP), or more than one-sixth below prior policy levels. The plethora of discretionary grant programs, the clearest legacy of the Great Society, would have fared the worst by far as a group, being slated for reduction by three-fifths of their prior policy levels. Low-income assistance payments to individuals also would have been reduced by well over one-fourth. Finally, the social insurance programs would have been cut relatively less—a little more than one-tenth—presumably reflecting both the administration's stronger commitment to the original New Deal concept of a social safety net and the political power of their primary beneficiaries—the middle class in general, and the aged in particular.

Congress granted the president (in the Omnibus Budget Reconciliation Act of 1981) most of the social program spending cuts he requested in his FY 1982 budget. Except for action on Social Security, however, few further cuts were taken in the FY 1983 or 1984 budgets. As a result, the enacted reductions by FY 1985 will total a little under 10 percent from prior policy levels—about half what the president requested. The pattern of reductions across the broad types of programs is similar to what he sought, with the greatest relative reductions by far in the discretionary grant programs, and the smallest in the social insurance programs. Purely in terms of his aims, however, the president was least successful in cutting the programs providing benefit payments to low-income individuals, ending up with less than one-third of the reduction he sought (in contrast to more than half and nearly three-quarters of what he sought in the social insurance and discretionary grant programs, respectively). Despite his FY 1983 and 1984 budget proposals for additional deep cuts in this lower tier of the social safety net, these programs were left entirely alone, as a consensus seemed to emerge in Congress and the country that the 1982 budgetary actions went as far as was warranted in reducing aid to the poor.

Social Welfare Goals

As noted previously, the Great Society represented public acceptance of a significantly larger federal responsibility for the general social welfare than had characterized our New Deal past or than characterizes our New Federalism present. This extension of responsibility occurred along two dimensions.

The first dimension was acceptance of more generous responsibility for income support, through both the expansion of existing programs and the creation of new ones (as outlined earlier). In so liberalizing the notion of federal social responsibility, the Great Society was inching its way toward the goal of greater equalization of incomes—although as an explicit goal this never attained any broad currency (and, indeed, proved a real political liability when it seemed to be explicitly espoused—as, for example, in George McGovern's demogrant proposal).

The second dimension occurred in the direction of equality of opportunity. The Great Society also constituted acceptance of federal responsibility for being more inventive about extending opportunities to those segments of the population that—for whatever reasons—remained outside the American social and economic mainstream. Commitment to this second goal was reflected both in the proliferation of special programs for "disadvantaged" populations and in the prominence of civil rights and affirmative action on the Great Society's legislative and regulatory agenda. The commitment was reinforced by the "social engineering" philosophy of the (by then) booming social service professions, as large numbers of social scientists joined the federal government in an effort to design and administer regulatory policies and service delivery programs (e.g., compensatory education, training, and nutrition programs) that would enable all members of society to compete economically on a more equal basis.

Neither of these two notions of equality was seriously challenged by Presidents Nixon, Ford, or Carter: both have been rejected by Reagan. In the three previous administrations the disagreements came over questions of style and means; both Nixon and Ford kept a low profile in the civil rights arena, and both leaned (as befits Republican presidents) in the direction of more decentralized administration of social programs. All three administrations, of necessity in a deteriorating economy, became increasingly preoccupied with problems of program efficiency and effectiveness. President Reagan has voiced support for civil rights and sung the tunes of both federalism and efficiency, but his proposals for change constitute a large-scale rejection of the goals of the Great Society.[1]

The Social Safety Net, Poverty, and Dependency

As noted, the preservation of a "reliable safety net of social programs for those who have contributed (to social insurance programs) and those who are in need"[2] has been one social policy for which President Reagan has voiced consistent support.* The president, nevertheless, has proposed a number of policy changes that would both narrow and lower the net substantially, apparently reflecting both philosophical and budgetary concerns. Also, the administration has anticipated that the safety net will shrink somewhat of its own accord, as a revived economy and its "workfare" proposal push more people in the direction of self-support.†

The president's proposals have had mixed results. He has been quite successful in removing the least needy from the welfare rolls; but he has been thwarted by Congress in many of his benefit reduction efforts. The recession has actually *increased* the number of families and individuals needing assistance, and the workfare program has never really materialized. On the question of "results" in a larger sense—that is, the impact of all the administration's policies on the problems to which any social policy is presumably addressed— the scorecard is less equivocal. In 1982, the official poverty rate reached its highest level since 1965, when President Johnson launched the War on Poverty. There seems little reason to expect a very substantial reduction in poverty or in long-term welfare dependency in the near future.

In the pages that follow, we explore these issues in more detail. To obviate the need for tedious recitation of administration proposals and congressional actions, we confine ourselves in the text to the broad thrust of the administration's policies and their outcomes. The reader is encouraged to refer to the program descriptions, summaries, and results in Appendix C.

Upper Tier. Somewhat ironically, the expansion of the upper tier of the safety net that transpired over the twenty years preceding the Reagan administration reflected a "liberal" abhorrence of the notion of a "dole" which derived from President Roosevelt and which has come to be viewed as a predominantly "conservative" sentiment. Of welfare (means-tested) programs, Roosevelt observed in 1935: "The federal government must and shall quit this business of relief. To dole out relief is to administer a narcotic, a subtle destroyer of the human spirit."[3]

---

*However, Martin Anderson, Reagan's first chief domestic policy advisor, has stated that "providing a safety net for those who cannot are are not expected to work was not really a social policy objective. The term 'safety net' was used . . . to describe the set of social welfare programs that would not be closely examined on the first round of budget changes because of the fierce political pressures that made it impossible to even discuss these programs without involving a torrent of passionate, often irrational, criticism," and that "the term, safety net, was political shorthand that only made sense for a limited period of time." See Martin Anderson, "The Objectives of the Reagan Administration's Social Welfare Policy," in D. Lee Bawden, ed., *The Social Contract Revisited: Aims and Outcomes of President Reagan's Social Welfare Policy* (Washington, D.C.: The Urban Institute Press, 1984), p. 113.

†Workfare is the term applied to programs that require welfare recipients to work in specially created public jobs for more pay in order to retain eligibility for cash assistance

To the inheritors of Roosevelt's mantle in the 1960s and 1970s, the evil identified by Roosevelt was to be avoided by expanding the net of the social insurance programs to "catch" those who would otherwise fall through to a demeaning dependence on welfare. Accordingly, Medicare was established to address the (often financially catastrophic) health problems of the elderly; unemployment benefits were extended automatically (under the Federal/State Extended Benefits Program) and supplemented routinely through legislative action during times of recession; and Social Security benefits were extended to younger and less drastically disabled populations. All these program changes were intended to strengthen the ties between the middle-class workforce and those at its margin, but the net effect of the changes was to extend benefits to individuals who might otherwise (and this is the sticking point for both liberals and conservatives) have been able to support themselves through work.

Examination of President Reagan's proposals in the social insurance arena suggests that the element of choice is what has proved most galling to the administration. Compared to the lower tier of the safety net, the social insurance programs actually fared quite well in the administration's hands, but the hands invariably fell heaviest on those who might be considered to exercise some choice about whether to work. For example, the administration introduced much more stringent screening procedures for recipients of Social Security Disability Insurance (SSDI) benefits, on the presumption that the doubling in SSDI rolls over the previous ten years had been produced by either malingering or lax management.* As a result, caseload investigations and benefit terminations increased fourfold from 1980 to 1982 and program costs were cut by 10 percent. Similar doubts about beneficiaries' will to work prompted major cutbacks in the Unemployment Insurance (UI) program, including the curtailment of extended benefits and the provision of less generous supplemental benefits than in the recessions of the 1970s. As a result, in 1982 at the height of the recent recession, an average of only 45 percent of the unemployed received UI benefits, compared to 76 percent in 1975, also a peak recessionary year.[4] And, under the administration's initial proposals for the Social Security program, benefits for early retirees also would have been immediately cut back by 40 percent. This proposal was rejected by Congress in favor of a much more gradual reduction beginning in the next century.

---

*In response to growing concern about the "explosion" in the SSDI rolls over the prior decade, Congress mandated tighter review procedures shortly before Reagan took office. However, the new administration implemented these with a zeal that quickly became controversial with Congress, the courts, and the states (who generally administer the procedures).

This shrinkage in social insurance coverage for those at the margin of
: workforce was accompanied by a shrinkage in benefits at the upper-income
d of the workforce. Here, the administration found a willing ally in Con-
ess, which initiated or supported the reinstitution of a means test for guar-
iteed student loans (which were heavily subsidizing the college education
f high-income students), partial taxation of social security benefits for those
vith high incomes, and greater taxation of UI benefits for the middle class.
The net result of all this shrinkage has been to narrow the aims of the social
insurance programs to more closely approximate their New Deal origins.

Although all the changes have undoubtedly been deeply felt by selected
beneficiaries of the upper-tier safety net programs, as we noted earlier, their
overall budgetary impact has been quite modest; spending reductions in upper-
tier safety net programs will total only 6.5 percent by 1985. Interestingly,
although the perceived need for overall federal budget cuts undoubtedly played
as large a role in motivating the president's proposals as did the philosophical
concerns touched on earlier, the president initially made no move on his own
to curb the fastest growing (and second largest) of the social insurance programs: Medicare. This was left to Congress, which mandated a change in
hospital reimbursement procedures that amounted to the largest reduction in
social program spending resulting from a single action since the administration
took office.

Lower Tier. Until the 1960s, the lower tier of the social safety net was
dominated by programs providing cash benefits to categorically defined low-
income populations (single-parent families with children, the aged, the disabled, and veterans). In the 1960s and 1970s, however, the benefits were
diversified and the categories broadened, reflecting an increased sense of
federal responsibility for the totality of the low-income experience, as well
as increased confidence in the capacity of federal programs to shape that
experience. Thus came into being in-kind programs such as Food Stamps (the
only program to serve all low-income people), Medicaid, child nutrition, a
variety of new subsidies for housing, and low-income energy assistance (LIEA).
At the same time, eligibility requirements for the existing means-tested cash
programs were liberalized: the AFDC program, for example, acquired a (state-
option) component for unemployed, two-parent families; and the program's
"penalty" for earned income was softened by the "30 and a third" rule.*
Also, assistance for the aged, blind, and disabled was federalized and became
more generous under the Supplemental Security Income (SSI) program.

---

*Prior to 1967 ADFC recipients' benefits were reduced dollar for dollar if they acquired
any earnings. The rules were then changed to "disregard" the first $30 and one-third of all
subsequent earnings per month in determining benefits.

In determining eligibility for all these programs, federal planners evidenced great concern for the preservation of work incentives, which translated into the extension of low-income benefits to "the working poor." That is, there was more concern that those on the margin of the workforce not be discouraged (by loss of benefits) from augmenting their income through work than that those on the margin might choose not to work (because their benefit levels were more closely equivalent to their potential earnings).

The Reagan administration has exactly reversed these concerns. In advocating a tighter targeting of benefits on the "truly needy," the president is espousing a return to the concept of restricting public assistance to those segments of the population that cannot reasonably be expected to work.* This policy shift was reflected in the series of proposals that, taken together, would have reduced outlays for the means-tested programs by 28 percent in real terms. As outlined below, these proposals generally fall into two basic categories: restricting eligibility standards and offsetting the benefits from multiple programs.

As regards the first set of proposals, the administration has been quite successful in restricting eligibility to remove the least needy from the welfare rolls. Elimination of the "30 and a third" rule and various other changes in the AFDC program, for example, have caused an estimated 400,000-500,000 families (about 11–14 percent of the total caseload) to lose their AFDC eligibility.[5] (Since Medicaid eligibility is closely tied to AFDC eligibility, most of these families also lost Medicaid benefits.) Similarly, upwards of 1 million persons lost their eligibility for Food Stamps, primarily because a limit was put on the allowable income levels of participants.[6]

In AFDC, as in most other means-tested programs subject to cuts, the chief vehicle for restricting eligibility—raising the "tax" on earnings—reduced benefits to remaining recipients with other income and removed people from the rolls. For example, a working AFDC mother with three children earning $450 a month (a below-poverty-level wage) in an average-benefit state would previously have received a monthly AFDC benefit (in 1984 dollars) of about $230; her benefits now have been reduced to about $50 per month after four months of employment. An estimated 300,000 families have experienced such benefit reductions to varying degrees.[7]

There is no question that these and other such changes have led to greater targeting of program benefits on the poor—from 49 percent in 1981 to 54

---

*Two White House aides have defined the truly needy as "unfortunate persons who, through no fault of their own, have nothing but public funds to turn to. . . ." See Robert B. Carlson and Kevin R. Hopkins, "Whose Responsibility Is Social Responsibility?" *Public Welfare*, vol. 39, no. 4 (Fall 1981), p. 10.

percent in 1982 according to recent testimony by Reagan budget director David Stockman[8]—but, administration claims to the contrary, there is also no question that the poor are not better off as a result. The administration has suggested that benefits were *retargeted* on the poor, implying that aid was taken from the less needy and given to the more needy.[9] In fact, this is not the case; in no entitlement programs were real (inflation-adjusted) benefits increased for the most needy when eligibility levels were reduced.

With respect to the second set of proposals—reducing the accumulation of multiple program benefits—the administration's accomplishments appear negligible, for several reasons. First, the goal was evidently being realized to some extent before the administration took office.[10] With the growth in federal means-tested benefits during the 1970s, the states were increasingly electing not to adjust AFDC benefit levels or their supplements to federal SSI benefits upward to keep pace with the rapid inflation. Consequently, basic real benefit levels—the best measure of public assistance to "the truly needy"— under the AFDC and SSI programs were falling for most recipients.* Even in the face of growing Food Stamp, LIEA, Social Security, and public housing programs, real cumulative basic benefits for both AFDC families and the poor elderly fell substantially over the 1970s.†

Second, the administration was largely unsuccessful in obtaining congressional approval for its numerous proposals to offset the benefits of various means-tested programs against one another. As a consequence, both basic AFDC and SSI benefit levels and multiple program basic benefits for AFDC and SSI recipients have performed better under the Reagan administration than over the 1970s. Multiple basic benefits have declined less rapidly for AFDC recipients and leveled off for SSI recipients in nonsupplementing states(see figure 6.3). The large reduction in inflation since 1981—for which the administration deserves some credit—is the principal factor here, but Congress also played a role in initiating action to raise real basic SSI benefit levels (by 6.6 percent) to soften the blow of Social Security reductions on the poor elderly. Had Congress accepted all the administration's proposals

---

*The basic, or maximum, benefit level is the amount provided to a family or individual who is totally dependent on public assistance. About half of all SSI recipients receive this amount, as do nearly nine-tenths of AFDC recipients (before the Reagan budget cuts, the figure was four-fifths). See the program summaries in Appendix C for details on benefit levels in SSI and AFDC.

†For the typical AFDC family, combined AFDC, Food Stamp, and LIEA benefits declined nearly a fifth, from 88 percent of the official poverty threshold in 1970 to 71 percent in 1981. Similarly, a typical combination of benefits—SSI, Social Security, Food Stamps, and public housing—for the poorest elderly declined almost 15 percent from 1974 (when SSI was begun) to 1981, mainly because of a drop in the real value of public housing. With state supplements for SSI falling 20 percent over this period, SSI beneficiaries in supplementing states realized even larger declines.

FIGURE 6.3

BASIC MONTHLY BENEFITS FOR MEDIAN FOUR-PERSON AFDC UNIT AND SINGLE
SSI UNIT, SELECTED YEARS *(Constant 1981 Dollars)*

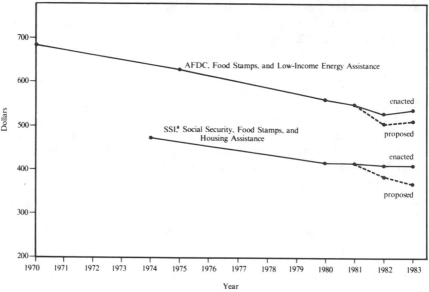

SOURCE: *Timothy M. Smeeding, "Is the Safety Net Still Intact?" in D. Lee Bawden, ed., The
Social Contract Revisited: Aims and Outcomes of President Reagan's Social Welfare
Policy* (Washington, D.C: The Urban Institute Press, 1984).
  NOTE: Data points represent available information. The trend lines were drawn by interpolation.
  a. The first full year of operation for the SSI program was 1974.

for cutting means-tested programs, however, the safety net for "the truly
needy" would have declined more sharply than in the 1970s (as also depicted
in figure 6.3).*

    Poverty and Dependency. The one clear measure (although admittedly
imperfect) of the effect of all these program changes on people is the official
poverty rate.† This rate declined markedly from above 20 percent in the early

---

    *Congress did enact an administration proposal to allow states to count Food Stamp benefits
as income for calculating AFDC benefits to the extent that the value of the stamps exceeds that
portion of the AFDC needs a standard attributed to food costs. No states have exercised the
option so far; if they did it would reduce AFDC benefit levels by as much as a third in those
(principally southern) states with low needs standards.
    †The official poverty rate refers to the proportion of the total U.S. population who live in
households whose money income (as defined by the Census Bureau) falls below a particular
dollar level, which is adjusted annually for inflation. In 1984 this threshold is about $5,300 for
a single individual and $10,600 for a family of four.

1960s, when it first became a focus of attention, to nearly 11 percent in the early 1970s, after which it remained relatively stable through 1979. Pointing to the stronger economy in the 1960s than in the 1970s, the Reagan administration has generally downplayed the role of public transfers in reducing poverty and has emphasized the role of economic growth.* In fact, both have played an important role in the past, though neither appears likely to be as effective in the future.

The antipoverty effectiveness of the various public transfer programs is often underestimated for a couple of reasons. First, only money is counted as income in calculating the official poverty rate; food, medical, and housing assistance—the fastest growing programs over the previous twenty years—do not affect it.[11] If all in-kind benefits were counted as income (at their cost to the government), the poverty rate in 1979 would have been 6.8 percent, substantially lower than the official rate of 11.7 percent.[12] Second, the poverty rate is strongly affected by demographic change—in particular, over the last 20 years, by the increase in the proportion of the low-income population who have little potential for earnings or other sources of private income (see table 6.2). Most notably, between 1960 and 1980 the proportion of the poverty population living in (nonaged) female-headed households doubled (reflecting the increase of female-headed families from 7 percent to 12 percent of all families over the same period). Also, the proportion of the adults in poor male-headed households who were disabled increased, as more and more of the able-bodied worked their way out of poverty. The official poverty rate actually would have been an estimated two percentage points lower in 1979 were it not for these and other changes in the demographic composition of the population since 1967.[13]

The influence of these factors is illustrated in figure 6.4, which shows the poverty rates since 1965 based on three different measures—pretransfer income, money income, and adjusted income (which includes in-kind benefits received and taxes paid). Comparison of these rates demonstrates that the sharp reductions in poverty in the 1960s were caused by the combination of rising pretransfer incomes resulting from strong economic growth and rapidly growing transfers, whereas the relatively stable poverty rates of the 1970s resulted from the offsetting of these still rising transfers by reductions in pretransfer income, attributable to poorer economic performance and demographic shifts.

*The president carried this theme a bit further in early 1984 when he said, ``Back in the '60s, the early '60s, we had fewer people living below the poverty line than we had in the later '60s after the great War on Poverty got under way. And there has been from that moment on a steady increase in the level of poverty. . . .'' (editorial page, *Washington Post*, March 24, 1984). While the president confused the facts, he clearly was arguing that government actions had been ineffective in reducing poverty.

TABLE 6.2

STATISTICS ON THE POVERTY POPULATION FOR SELECTED YEARS
(Percentage)

Poverty Measure	1960[a]	1970	1980	1982
Incidence of poverty[b]				
All persons age 65 or over	35.2	24.5	15.7	14.6
Persons less than 65 in household with female heads	50.4	37.4	35.2	38.7
Persons less than 65 in households with male heads	17.8	7.5	7.9	9.9
Composition of the poverty population				
All persons age 65 or over	13.9	18.5	13.2	10.9
Persons less than 65 in households with female heads	21.2	34.0	42.2	41.2
Persons less than 65 in households with male heads	65.0	47.5	44.6	47.9
TOTAL	100.0	100.0	100.0	100.0

SOURCE: U.S. Department of Commerce, Bureau of the Census, *Money Income and Poverty Status of Families and Persons in the United States: 1982*, Current Population Report, Series P-60, no. 140, table 15.

a. Based on 1960 household composition and 1959 income data.

b. Incidence refers to the proportion of the total population in each age-household category that is classified as poor.

The relative antipoverty effectiveness of the various transfer programs in moving people out of poverty, as measured by the adjusted income concept, is illustrated in table 6.3. The cash social insurance and the in-kind programs have had a major impact, and the means-tested cash programs much less (not surprisingly, since the latter involve many fewer dollars). In 1965, for example, these three types of programs removed from poverty 23.5 percent, 16.4 percent, and 3.3 percent, respectively, of those people who were poor based on their incomes exclusive of the programs' benefits. By 1976 these percentages had increased on average by two-thirds. The effectiveness of the transfer program in alleviating poverty then changed little for the remainder of the 1970s, when the expenditures were no longer expanding relative to the economy.

After two decades of rapid decline followed by comparative stability, all measures of the poverty rate rose rapidly starting in 1980. By the end of 1982 the official rate was nearly as high as at the beginning of the War on Poverty (figure 6.4), and over 9 million more people were officially in poverty

TABLE 6.3

ANTIPOVERTY EFFECTIVENESS OF MAJOR INCOME TRANSFERS, SELECTED YEARS,
1965–1982

| Year | *Percentage of Pretransfer Poor Persons Moved Out of Poverty by Various Public Transfers* | | | | |
	Cash Social Insurance Transfers	*Cash Means- Tested Transfers*	*All Cash Transfers*	*In-Kind Transfers*	*All Transfers*
1965	23.5	3.3	26.8	16.4	43.2
1976	37.6	6.2	43.8	28.1	71.9
1978	37.6	5.9	43.5	NA	NA
1980	35.2	8.5	43.7	NA	NA
1982	33.8	3.8	37.6	25.8	63.3

SOURCE: "Poverty in the United States: Where Do We Stand Now?" *Focus*, Winter 1984,
Institute for Research on Poverty, University of Wisconsin.
NA = not available.

FIGURE 6.4

TRENDS IN THE INCIDENCE OF POVERTY AMONG ALL PERSONS ACCORDING TO THREE
MEASURES OF INCOME

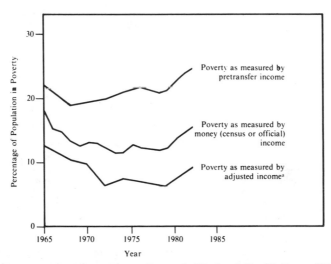

SOURCE: "Poverty in the United States: Where do We Stand Now?" *Focus*, Winter 1984,
Institute for Research on Poverty, University of Wisconsin.
a. This definition of income includes in-kind benefits and adjusts for direct taxes and the
underreporting of cash benefits.

in 1982 than in 1979.* This dramatic shift resulted primarily from the mild recession and high inflation of 1980, followed by the deep recession and budget cuts in the first two years of the Reagan administration. Macroeconomic conditions and Reagan administration budget cuts were about equally responsible for the 3.3 percentage-point increase in the official poverty rate (from 11.7 to 15.0) over this period.†,14 A marked reduction also occurred between 1980 and 1982 in the antipoverty effectiveness of cash transfer programs—particularly for the means-tested programs, presumably reflecting the relatively deeper cuts in AFDC (see table 6.3).‡

Unfortunately, because of the trends described earlier, the administration's argument about the efficacy of economic growth as a remedy for poverty appears overly optimistic. Simply put, the problem is that a growing majority of the poor are in households that benefit little from economic growth. The one group that can be expected to benefit substantially—households headed by nonaged males—constitutes less than half the poor and already has a relatively low incidence of poverty. The economic recovery now under way undoubtedly will reduce the overall poverty rate from its recent high,§ but one study estimates that it would take about 11 years of sustained 3 percent per year real growth in pretransfer incomes just to reduce poverty from its 1982 rate of 15 percent down to its 1979 rate, assuming transfer income were at the levels prevailing prior to the Reagan budget cuts.15

The probable outcome of the second prong of the administration's strategy to reduce poverty—increased work requirements and incentives of various sorts—appears no more sanguine. Congress refused to endorse the administration's proposal to make workfare mandatory for adults eligible for AFDC (in the case of mothers, those who youngest child was over age three), leaving the program optional for the states. So far, only about half of the states have

---

*Of this 9 million, 5.5 million were added since 1980. Another relevant measure of the poverty problem—the posttransfer ''poverty gap''—appears similarly grim. Defined as the amount of money it would take to raise the incomes of all poor families to the poverty level after counting cash transfer from existing programs, the poverty gap rose from $31 billion in 1980 to $45 billion in 1982.

†The pattern of change in the incidence of poverty across various population groups between 1980 and 1982 is also consistent with the pattern of budget actions and what might be expected from a recession (see table 6.2). The incidence of poverty for the aged, most of whom are not in the labor force and whose SSI benefits increased, actually *declined*. In contrast, the incidence of poverty for both female-headed and two-parent families increased sharply.

‡Many recipients depended upon a combination of AFDC benefits and earnings to remain out of poverty, since no state provided AFDC benefits above the poverty level. These are the recipients who experienced large benefit cuts or were entirely removed from the rolls.

§The poverty rate for 1983 will not be known until late 1984 when the Census Bureau releases its analysis.

taken any steps to implement the program, and most did so just on a demonstration basis in a few counties. The idea is unlikely to catch on further; the federal government provides only partial funding for administrative or capital costs incurred in creating jobs, and the program has substantial opposition in the social welfare community.[16] A recent study by the U.S. General Accounting Office has strongly questioned the program's likely effectiveness.[17]

The work incentives embodied in the reductions in eligibility levels for means-tested programs appear slightly more promising than workfare. Research does show that work effort and earnings should increase for those who are eliminated from eligibility.* But because the principal way in which the administration reduced eligibility levels was to increase benefit reduction rates, those remaining covered by the programs have less incentive to work. For example, elimination of the $30 and a third income disregard in AFDC after four months on the job imposes a 100 percent implicit tax on earnings— since benefits are reduced $1 for each $1 of income (after the initial disregard for child care and other work-related expenses). Consequently, the net effect of eligibility restrictions on work incentives is unlikely to be substantially positive.

The only comprehensive assessment to date of the labor supply effects of the changes in all social programs under the Reagan administration concludes that their likely effect by 1985 will be to increase work effort by an average of well under 1 percent, with the response differing across relevant population groups (see table 6.4). The largest positive work response is estimated to come from nonaged, disabled individuals who are eliminated from, or denied access to, the Social Security disability program. Expected outcomes for other groups range from no change to very small positive responses, except for female heads of families. These women are likely to register a slight decrease in overall work effort in response to the rise in benefit reduction rates, which are estimated to more than offset the effects of lowered eligibility cutoffs.

Finally, neither strengthened work incentives nor an improved economy is likely to make much of a dent in what the administration itself has acknowledged to be a (perhaps the) major welfare problem: long-term welfare

---

*Critics of the administration's policies charged that a large percentage of the AFDC recipients eliminated from eligibility (because they had substantial earnings) would be likely to quit their jobs and come back on the rolls at the maximum benefit level. This does not appear to be occurring. Preliminary results from surveys indicate the so-called recidivism rates of such AFDC families are ranging from roughly 10 to 20 percent a year after their removal from the rolls. These are hardly any larger than those of AFDC recipients who left the rolls before the 1981 changes.

TABLE 6.4

ESTIMATED CUMULATIVE LABOR SUPPLY EFFECTS BY 1985 OF SOCIAL PROGRAM
CHANGES UNDER THE REAGAN ADMINISTRATION

Population Group	Change in Full-time Equivalents in the Labor Force (Thousands)
A. Age 62 and over	0 to +100
B. Disabled, under age 62	+200 to +400
C. Female family heads with children	−60 to +30
D. Age 16–24 (not in B or C)	0 to +150
E. Women age 25–61 (not in B or C)	0 to +200
F. Men age 25–61 (not in B)	0 to +100
TOTAL	+140 to 980[a]

SOURCE: Robert H. Haveman, "How Much Have Reagan Tax and Spending Policies Increased Work Effort?" in Charles R. Hulten and Isabel V. Sawhill, eds., *The Legacy of Reaganomics: Prospects for Long-term Growth* (Washington, D.C.: The Urban Institute Press, 1984).

a. This range is from 0.1 percent to 0.9 percent of the labor force.

dependency. Again, the problem arises partly from the shifting demographics of the welfare population. One study of a representative sample of the population over ten years found that, from 1969 to 1978, two of five new AFDC recipients remained on welfare for five years or more, and that new female AFDC recipients apply for aid primarily because of the departure of a husband or the birth of a child out of wedlock.[18] Increasingly, this change in family status is caused by the birth of a child to a very young mother: teen-age out-of-wedlock births tripled from 1960 to 1979 for both blacks and whites (the black rate was, and remains, over five times the white rate). Women who were teen-agers when their first child was born (whether or not the mother was married then) account for over half of all AFDC expenditures.[19]

In a recent assessment of the Reagan administration's welfare policies, Blanche Bernstein, former director of welfare for New York City, faults the Reagan administration for not addressing these causes of long-term poverty and welfare dependency.* As she notes, the administration has given weak support, at best, to family planning and counseling and sex education in schools—programs addressed to the problems of teenage childbearing and the breakup of families. On the more positive side, the administration has taken actions to improve the private income support available to poor mothers through tougher enforcement of child support payments by absent fathers and

---

*Overall, Bernstein gives the administration a mixed grade on its welfare policy changes. See her chapter on "Welfare Dependency" in Bawden, ed., *The Social Contract Revisited.*

by requiring stepparents' resources to be considered in determining AFDC benefit levels for stepchildren and their mothers.

Because of the president's emphasis on self sufficiency, the administration might have been expected to emphasize human capital investment programs—programs primarily intended to increase future productivity in the workforce—as a means of addressing poverty and long-term welfare dependency and to balance, over the long term, the cuts in income transfer programs. Instead, the administration proposed to reduce expenditures for these programs (education and training, public service employment, nutrition programs, Medicaid, and social services) by nearly 40 percent. Some of these programs were of questionable value and were ripe for pruning. However, in its proposals the administration appeared to distinguish little among more or less effective programs, even though evaluation research has demonstrated significant differences in effectiveness.[20] Congress proved more selective, resisting deep cuts in or restoring the budgets of some well-regarded programs (such as Job Corps, compensatory education, and WIC) and ratifying the administration's proposed cuts in others of more dubious merit (such as public service employment).* In the final analysis, Congress granted the administration about half of its proposed cuts—an average expenditure reduction of 23 percent for all human capital programs.

Civil Rights and Equal Opportunity

By the time Ronald Reagan came to office, protection of civil rights and promotion of equal opportunity had been at the forefront of the domestic policy agenda for nearly two decades.[21] New federal institutions had been established to implement a labyrinth of laws, executive orders, court decisions, and administrative rulings to protect the civil and economic rights of minorities in particular, but also of women, the aged, and the handicapped. Ronald Reagan is the first president in the post-World War II period to reverse this trend of an increasingly active government role in ensuring the rights and opportunities of its citizens and redressing the consequences of past discrimination. Thus, understanding the significance of the "Reagan record" in this arena requires a brief look at some recent history.

---

*Previous research had shown that the Jobs Corps program had a very favorable benefit-cost ratio, that the WIC program had been effective in improving the health of low-income pregnant women and infants, and that compensatory education programs had improved the educational performance of disadvantaged children. Research on public service employment, on the other hand, indicated that it had little positive effect on participants' future earnings and that a substantial proportion of the jobs would have been funded by state and local governments in the absence of federal financing. (See footnote 20.)

Background. From Reconstruction through nearly the first half of this century, the executive branch was largely silent on the issue of civil rights. Truman was the first president to take explicit action to protect the rights of black citizens, appointing the President's Committee on Civil Rights (a precursor of the U.S. Commission on Civil Rights), proposing a civil rights bill (rejected by Congress), and issuing an executive order that eventually ended segregation in the military.

During the Eisenhower years, a significant civil rights agenda began to emerge, sparked by the Supreme Court's *Brown v. Board of Education* decision of 1954. President Eisenhower strongly supported court-ordered school desegregation, issued an executive order requiring nondiscrimination in government employment and by government contractors, and proposed legislation to enforce the voting rights of minorities. Under Eisenhower, the Civil Rights Act of 1957 was passed—elevating the relatively low priority of civil rights enforcement within the Justice Department to the status of a Civil Rights Division; and transforming the President's Committee on Civil Rights into the Civil Rights Commission, a quasi-independent body charged with advising the president and Congress on federal laws and policies concerning discrimination. But as late as 1960, no action had been taken by the executive branch regarding racial discrimination in housing or any aspect of discrimination against women, the aged, or the handicapped.

By the time President Kennedy took office in 1961, the grass-roots civil rights movement in the South had attracted national attention. Whether of necessity or by inclination, the Kennedy administration responded by proposing major civil rights legislation and expanding enforcement of the rights of minorities. While Kennedy's strong support for desegregation of the Universities of Mississippi and Alabama received the most national attention, the most significant policy initiative of the Kennedy administration was what eventually became the Civil Rights Act of 1964. This legislation provided, among other things, for the establishment of the Equal Employment Opportunity Commission (EEOC) to process complaints of discrimination in employment, and widened the interpretation of sex discrimination in employment.

If a strong national commitment to civil rights was born during the Kennedy administration, it came of age during the Johnson administration. President Johnson's strong leadership, buttressed by a growing public awareness of pervasive discrimination, resulted in a significant expansion of the meaning of civil rights and equal opportunity. Affirmative action as a means of redressing the ills of past discrimination became an accepted practice and was given a large push by the establishment of the Office of Federal Contract Compliance Programs (OFCCP) in the Department of Labor. (This office was charged with issuing affirmative action guidelines for the hiring of minorities and women by government contractors and with monitoring progress under the guidelines—goals and timetables not being required until 1971.) Also, under Johnson's urging, Congress passed the Civil Rights Act of 1964, the Voting Rights Act of 1965, and the Fair Housing Act of 1968 (prohibiting for the first time racial discrimination in the private housing market).

By the time Richard Nixon came to office, the issue of civil rights and equal opportunity had become more complex, encompassing institutional racism and sexism and not just individual acts of discrimination. Due in part to momentum from the Johnson administration, three obscure, though important, changes were enacted during the Nixon administration: the EEOC was given the power to sue firms that used discriminatory practices; the OFCCP was permitted to use a variety of sanctions against discriminating federal contractors; and the Fair Housing Act was amended to prohibit sex as a basis for discrimination. However, neither President Nixon nor his successor, President Ford, assumed a leadership role anywhere near that of Johnson in making civil rights a national priority.

Under President Carter, civil rights recovered its visibility on the domestic agenda, becoming linked at the same time to the administration's foreign policy (human rights) initiatives. Although little new legislation was enacted during the Carter administration, administrative actions served to extend significantly the federal reach in the civil rights area. The EEOC, for example, established a program specifically addressed to combat systemic discrimination in firms and institutions; the OFCCP broadened its activities to include pre-award reviews of government contractors; and the Justice Department substantially increased "pattern and practice" suits, especially in housing. Perhaps of longer-term consequence were Carter's judicial appointments; of the 298 federal judges appointed by the president, 23 percent were minorities, 15 percent were women, and many had records of considerable sensitivity to issues of civil rights and equal opportunity.

The federal government's commitment to civil rights and equal opportunity, thus, had generally broadened and intensified during the seven consecutive administrations, three Republican and four Democratic, preceding the Reagan administration. Toward the end of the 1970s, however, various commentators, politicians, and private citizens had begun to question whether the government had gone "to far, too fast," especially regarding affirmative action measures. A number of critics contended as follows:

- affirmative action was a form of reverse discrimination, requiring the present generation (chiefly, white males) to pay for the sins of past generations;

- paperwork and associated costs incurred in complying with OFCCP guidelines were excessive;

- affirmative action resulted in the hiring of unqualified women and minorities, reducing overall worker efficiency;

- enforcement methods used by the government were heavy-handed and unnecessarily confrontational; and

- many of the regulations and requirements were unnecessary because racial and sexual discrimination had all but disappeared.

Echoing many of these complaints, the Reagan administration moved to reverse historical trends in the civil rights area:

- by reducing federal involvement in regulating the behavior of individuals and organizations regarding civil rights and equal opportunity, and encouraging voluntary compliance;

- by requiring proof of intent to discriminate before taking remedial action; and

- by rejecting the use of quotas, numerical goals, and timetables as a means of redressing the present consequences of past discrimination.

A Reduced Federal Role. The enforcement of civil rights and equal opportunity under the Reagan administration reflects the same philosophy of a limited federal role applied to other areas of domestic policy: federal budgets have been cut and more reliance has been placed on the private market. Total real outlays for all civil rights and equal opportunity enforcement throughout the federal government declined 9 percent from FY 1981 to FY 1983. Adjusting for inflation, budgets for the EEOC and OFCCP were reduced 10 and 24 percent, respectively, resulting in staff reductions of 12 percent in the EEOC and 34 percent in OFCCP. The budget of the Civil Rights Division of the Justice Department remained about the same, but the number of the staff declined 13 percent.

The administration's narrow interpretation of the federal role in this area has translated generally into reduced litigation and disciplinary action in the areas of employment, education, and housing. In employment, the number of administrative complaints filed by the OFCCP against government contractors dropped from 53 in FY 1980 to 18 in FY 1983 (with a low of 5 in FY 1982), despite an increase in compliance reviews (table 6.5). Although investigations of complaints rose 50 percent, the administration has argued that only identifiable victims should be compensated and, consequently, the

TABLE 6.5

OFCCP ENFORCEMENT ACTIVITIES, FY 1980–FY 1983

Activity	1980	1981	1982	1983
Complaint investigations	1,726	2,136	2,589	2,375
Compliance reviews completed	2,627	3,135	3,081	4,295
Administrative complaints filed	53	15	5	18
Debarments	5	1	0	0
Back pay awarded ($ millions)	9.3	5.1	2.1	3.6
Number of recipients	4,336	4,754	1,133	1,758

SOURCE: Lynn C. Burbridge, "The Impact of Changes in Policy on the Federal Equal Employment Opportunity Effort" (Washington, D.C.: The Urban Institute, November 1983), table 3.

amount of back pay awarded has fallen from more than $9 million in 1980 to less than $4 million in 1983.

Employment discrimination cases brought by the EEOC and the Department of Justice have also declined by half from 1980/1981 (July to June) to 1982/1983, while the number of complaints brought by individuals has increased by nearly 50 percent.[22] The EEOC has succeeded in greatly reducing the backlog of pending cases (from 38,000 in September 1980 to 3,800 in June 1983), but the proportion of all cases with "no-cause" findings has increased by a third. In 1983 the number of cases recommended to the EEOC general counsel for possible litigation had declined slightly from 1980, but the number approved by the commission and filed in court declined by 60 percent.[23] In keeping with the administration's emphasis on voluntary action, the EEOC has developed a plan to provide technical assistance to firms to encourage voluntary compliance with equal opportunity laws regarding employment.

In education, the Civil Rights Division of the Justice Department under President Reagan has eschewed legal, nonvoluntary means—particularly mandatory busing—to desegregate schools, insisting only on the removal of "official impediments" to desegregation. The Justice Department has filed only one school desegregation case, and has not required system-wide remedies for desegregation if only a portion of a school district has been intentionally segregated. The Department has also argued for program-specific sanctions in lieu of the previous practice of terminating funds for entire institutions when discrimination has been found in federally assisted programs.

In a similar vein, the president (and the Justice Department) supported a suit brought by Bob Jones University and Goldsboro Christian Schools against his own Treasury Department challenging the denial of tax breaks to them because of their racially discriminatory practices (social rules prohibiting interracial dating and racially discriminatory admissions practices, respectively). The Supreme Court ruled in favor of the Treasury Department, eight to one.

The administration also has been similarly unaggressive in the housing area, having filed only six fair-housing suits during the first 30 months in office (compared to 46 cases filed by the Carter administration over a comparable time period).[24] The Department of Housing and Urban Development has recently proposed strengthening the Fair Housing Act to allow the Department of Justice to file suit in cases of discrimination against individuals, but at the same time has eliminated previously required certifications that recipients of federal funds comply with civil rights laws.

Intent vs. Effects. Court decisions over the past several years have invariably held that the "effects" of apparent discrimination—as manifested by a significant underrepresentation of a particular group being promoted within a firm or agency, being hired as new workers, or being buyers or renters of houses in particular areas—were sufficient cause for the government to require the offending parties to take an affirmative remedy "tailored to the extent of the violation." If the "effects" could not be ascribed to anything other than discrimination (could not be ascribed, e.g., to education and experience necessary to qualify for jobs, or income to afford housing), and/or if (hiring, promotion, sales) practices were inherently discriminatory, then the federal government filed so-called "pattern and practice" suits to remedy the situation. The intent to discriminate did not have to be proven—only the fact that the practices were discriminatory in effect. The Reagan Justice Department has abandoned these pattern and practice suits, requiring instead that intent to discriminate be proven in order to require remedial action or impose sanctions.*

The issue of intent also surfaced in the debate over reauthorization of the Voting Rights Act. The administration opposed an amendment (subsequently passed by Congress) clarifying that proof of discriminatory intent is *not* required in cases brought under the Act or in the Justice Department's review of voting rule changes by local districts.† However, the net result of

---

*Under Title VIII of the Civil Rights Act, HUD could recommend only pattern and practice suits—not individual complaints—to the Justice Department. This was one reason for the proposed amendment to the Fair Housing Act permitting the Justice Department to file suits in individual cases.

†The administration eventually dropped its opposition to the amendment after Senator Dole, backed by a majority of the Senate, announced his support for it.

this reliance on "intent" has been to reduce discrimination litigation by the government, since it is much more difficult to prove intent than to demonstrate the effects of discriminatory practices.

Quotas, Goals, Timetables. The most heated debate, both among the general public and in government, is over affirmative action—giving preferential treatment to a subgroup of the population whose current circumstances *as a group* have been adversely affected by past discrimination. Proponents of affirmative action argue that it is the only quick way to make workforces of firms and agencies or enrollments of schools representative of the populations from which they draw. Opponents argue that affirmative action is simply another form of discrimination, and that "two wrongs don't make a right." The administration takes the latter view. William Bradford Reynolds, assistant attorney general for civil rights in the Justice Department, has contended that, since those who benefit from affirmative action are not necessarily those who have personally suffered from past discrimination, no justice is really being served by affirmative action.[25] And Attorney General William French Smith argued that goals and timetables entail reverse discrimination and are, therefore, unfair to the majority (presumably white males).[*,26]

In employment, the principal tools of affirmative action have been numerical quotas or goals for hiring or promoting workers from groups underrepresented in the workforce and timetables for accomplishing the goals. The administration opposes quotas, goals, and timetables, even if voluntarily established. In two highly publicized cases which established quotas for promotions in the Detroit and New Orleans police departments, the Justice Department interceded to overturn the consent decrees. (The Supreme Court refused to hear the Detroit appeal, leaving the quotas in place; the New Orleans challenge is now before the Fifth Circuit Court of Appeals.) As further evidence of misgivings about affirmative action, the administration suspended—eight days after President Reagan assumed office—new, and stricter, affirmative action guidelines for the OFCCP, issued by the Carter administration. More than three years later, new guidelines have yet to be officially issued, but a draft that has been circulated would exempt more government contractors from filing affirmative action plans, relax the standards for minority representation in employment, and award

---

*In response to testimony by Reynolds at hearings before the House Judiciary Subcommittee on Civil and Constitutional Rights, Representative Don Edwards (D-Calif.) offered the following counter argument: "You and I are white male attorneys. We came from families with some money and were educated in the right schools. Unless we behaved very stupidly, the family and institutional support systems guaranteed places for us. We benefited from a racial spoils system." See Rochelle L. Stanfield, "Reagan Courting Women, Minorities, But It May Be Too Late to Win Them," *National Journal*, vol 15, no. 22 (May 28, 1983), p. 1120.

back pay as a class remedy only "in an extreme situation."[27] (In general, the Justice Department has not favored class action suits, in line with its philosophy that compensation should be made only to identifiable victims of discrimination.)

The administration's opposition to quotas also lies behind its opposition to busing as a means of integration. In a similar vein, the administration has generally backed away from requiring that dual systems of higher education be dismantled, although the record here is mixed. The Justice Department, for example, rejected as inadequate Virginia's plan to further integrate its historically dual college system, and also filed suit against Alabama for the operation of its college system. Also, the EEOC (which is a part of the executive branch, but is semiautonomous) has openly disagreed with the administration's position on numerical goals and timetables and has, in fact, rejected the Justice Department's internal affirmative action plan, which did not include goals and timetables.

Regarding the administration's own employment record, the Civil Rights Commission published a report comparing the sex and ethnicity of Reagan's presidential appointments with those of Carter. Appointments through the first two years of the Reagan administration were 8 percent female and 8 percent minority (4 percent black); Carter's appointments were 12 percent female and 17 percent minority (12 percent black).[28] The Commission had generally criticized the Reagan administration's civil rights policies, and the president in turn fired three of the six members and tried to fire two others. Finally, a new eight-member commission was created with members whose civil rights views are more in accord with those of the administration.

Conclusion. In 1982 President Reagan said, "One charge I will have to admit strikes at my heart every time I hear it. That's the suggestion that we Republicans are taking a less active approach to protecting the civil rights of all Americans. No matter how you slice it, that's just plain baloney."[29] Nevertheless, administration appointees have forcefully articulated the view that the enforcement of civil rights and equal opportunity had gone too far in recent years, resulting in remedies that discriminate against the majority population, causing racial resentment among whites, and creating a burdensome set of rules, regulations, and procedures.[30] The administration has contended that the government is primarily responsible to assure that individuals *qua* individuals are protected against present, *intentional* discrimination, and is responsible for correcting the consequences of past discrimination only when individual victims can be identified. Regardless of the merit of these views, they have clearly entailed—and produced—a major change in the definition of federal responsibility for the enforcement of civil rights and equal opportunity.

The Question of Means

As our earlier discussion suggests, concern for the efficiency with which the federal government spends its social program dollars is not new.[31] Nixon, Ford, and Carter all had harsh words on the subject of a wasteful and unwieldy federal bureaucracy, and many of their initiatives—Nixon's block grants and Carter's efforts to control hospital costs and welfare fraud, waste, and abuse, for example—are echoed in the proposals of the Reagan administration. What is new is the tying of concern for efficiency to an overall reduction in available federal resources for social program spending. Nixon's version of federalism, for instance, while deemphasizing the social engineering philosophy and much of the rhetoric attendant on the equality theme, actually increased the federal funds flowing to the states for many social purposes. And although President Carter became increasingly committed to cost control (social program spending as a percentage of GNP was projected to decline under Carter's last budget), he showed no disposition for cutting away at the foundations of the welfare state—indeed, he wanted to expand it.

In the interests of efficiency, however, President Reagan has proposed far more sweeping changes than contemplated by either of his predecessors in the devolution of responsibility to state governments and private enterprise, and in the approach to those program responsibilities that remain in federal hands. In so doing, the president has evidenced a notion of efficiency that goes well beyond the commonly understood one of providing the same goods at lower cost (or better goods at the same cost). In fact, under this administration, "efficiency" has significantly changed the nature of the "goods." In the subsections that follow,, we explore these changes along the three dimensions mentioned above: devolution of responsibility to state governments (the New Federalism), reliance on the private sector, and program management.

Federalism

The principle of devolution within the public sector was initially embodied most clearly in the administration's block grant proposals, which would have consolidated more than ninety categorical programs into four block grants, with a 20 to 25 percent reduction in federal funding.* In defense of these proposals, the administration argued that efficiency would be served by increasing state administrative flexibility, by reducing overhead costs (at both the federal and state levels), and by better matching services to needs, since

---

*See chapter 7 for a detailed discussion of the material in this section.

states were closer to (and presumably more knowledgeable about) needy populations. Congress eventually acceded to a less ambitious consolidation with an average 15 percent reduction in funding. The result has been a modest reduction in service levels and some (not readily generalizable) shifts in the pattern of services and recipients. The sizable reduction in federal financial assistance was partially offset both by reduced state overhead costs and—to a surprising extent—by state replacement of federal funds with their own (in marked contrast to the response to federal funding reductions for the jointly financed entitlement programs, discussed below).

Although the administration's original block grant proposals proved too large a dose of New Federalism for Congress to swallow, by far the most ambitious federalism proposal (embodied in the president's January 1982 State of the Union message) never even made it to Congress, succumbing early to the opposition of the states. Under this proposal, the federal government would have relinquished to the states all financial and policy-setting responsibilities for two major welfare programs—AFDC and Food Stamps—and would have compensated the states by taking over Medicaid. Also, most federal discretionary grants-in-aid to states for education, training, health, and social services would have been eliminated, as would federal excise taxes. States would have assumed full responsibility for any public activities in these areas, and replaced the lost federal aid through their own tax increases as they wished. The probable outcome of this more ambitious "swap and turn-back" proposal (as it came to be known) was widely anticipated to be the termination of any public responsibility for a broad array of social problems. In view of many observers, this outcome was not entirely unanticipated or unsought by the administration.

Rebuffed in this grand vision of federalism, the administration settled for a mixed bag of carrots and sticks that would encourage states to control expenditures more tightly under the jointly funded entitlement programs. Thus, for example, the administration imposed interest penalties on states that borrowed from the federal government to cover deficits in their Unemployment Insurance trust funds. Similarly, in the Medicaid program, the administration supported reductions in federal matching payments as a penalty for those states that failed to hold spending within prescribed ceilings for growth (after failing to get a cap on federal financial participation). Concomitantly it increased state flexibility in several areas, most notably in reimbursement procedures. The combination of these two measures appears to have led to some significant slowing in the overall growth of the Medicaid program. However, federal interest in increasing administrative flexibility for the states was largely jettisoned in the case of the AFDC program, in favor of federal cost savings pure and simple. Detailed federal prescriptions for eligibility and income counting undoubtedly added to the states' administrative burdens, but they also contributed significantly to the slowing of overall AFDC program growth.

In general, the states have been cooperative partners in the administration's efforts to restrain spending in all of these jointly funded entitlement programs. The result has been a substantial cost savings to both levels of government, coming primarily from reduced assistance to program beneficiaries.

Reliance on the Private Sector

While doubts about intentions have clouded the administration's advocacy of federalism, intentions have been quite clear from the outset with regard to the role of the private sector. Here there has been a forthright effort at complete divestiture of specific chunks of public responsibility and at radical redesign of others. The administration has attempted, for example, to deregulate wage rates and occupational health and safety conditions on the grounds that federal objectives are more likely to be achieved by the voluntary and more flexible approaches of a less-fettered private sector. (Actual changes in these and other regulatory areas have been very modest.)* And many of the proposed cuts in the services programs—or wholesale elimination, as in the case of legal and community services—were advanced with the rationale that these services could and would be provided more efficiently by the private sector without federal involvement. However, most of the nonprofit organizations that would be the primary vehicle for private provision were themselves heavily dependent on dwindling federal support. Thus, the nonprofit sector in general was hardly in a position to expand services and, in fact, cut back in many of the areas strongly hit by federal budget reductions.†

Strong confidence in the efficacy of the private sector and market mechanisms has also led the Reagan administration to propose major changes in policies where the federal government retained substantial responsibility. In addition to eliminating public service employment, the administration persuaded Congress, for example, both to cut and to redesign general employment and training programs, emphasizing partnership with private employers. (Thus, the Comprehensive Employment and Training Act has been superseded by the Job Training Partnership Act.) The new program will serve both fewer people and people who are less disadvantaged (because of the proclivity of

---

*See chapters 5 and 9 for more detail.
†See chapter 8 for a full discussion of the impact of President Reagan's policies on nonprofit organizations.

private employers to "cream" for the most employable of the eligible populations). It is too soon to ascertain whether the new programs will in fact
prove more effective—as the administration claims—for the population still
to be served.

Of potentially much greater impact on public/private collaboration were
the administration's wide-ranging plans to substitute vouchers for more direct
public provision of benefits or services.[32] Prior to 1980, the federal government had made limited use of vouchers to assist certain populations to obtain,
from the private market, food (the Food Stamp and WIC programs), higher
education (various forms of student financial assistance), and jobs (a small
employer tax credit program for disadvantaged populations). Although the
general concept of vouchers has received considerable support across the
political and ideological spectrum, specific proposals have generally encountered widespread opposition, primarily because of the considerable uncertainty
about their likely consequences. Thus, of the administration's many proposals
for greatly expanded use of vouchers in the areas of housing, elementary and
secondary education, health care, and housing, only in housing—where extensive field testing of the idea has taken place—has the actual use of vouchers
been successfully promoted. Even here, Congress approved only a demonstration program, apparently out of concern that, although housing vouchers
do assist poor people in paying their rent and are less expensive than the
alternative approach of subsidizing construction, they do little to ensure the
availability of an adequate supply of low-income housing.[33]

Program Management

Finally, where the administration has been less dependent on Congress
for action—that is, in the actual management of programs—the pursuit of
efficiency has produced some cost savings. Not surprisingly, given the business background of many of its appointees, the administration's efforts have
focused on improving financial management, most notably in the housing,
student loan, and employment and training programs. Many of these reforms
were widely regarded as long overdue; in any case, they embody minor savings
in comparison to the budget cuts.

Savings through improved federal program management in other areas
also proved quite modest, though for different reasons. To judge from its
rhetoric, the administration arrived in Washington convinced that errors and
fraud were rampant in many of the entitlement programs. In fact, however,
what had indeed been a serious problem ten years earlier was already under
much better control by 1981. As a result of steps taken by previous administrations, payments in error as a percent of total payments in the AFDC and

Food Stamps programs, for example, which were above 16 percent in 1973, had by 1980 been reduced to about 7 percent and 10 percent respectively.*,[34] Error rates in the Medicaid and Unemployment Insurance programs had been similarly brought into line, and default rates in the largest student loan program (Guaranteed Student Loans) had been reduced to under 5 percent. The cost-effectiveness of attempts at much further improvement in these areas thus appears questionable. In the one program that clearly warranted considerable additional effort to reduce inappropriate payments—Social Security for the disabled—the administration has (as noted elsewhere in this chapter) clearly gone overboard, eliciting strong criticism from Congress, the states, and the courts for being too severe in its screening and review processes. On the whole, however, the Reagan administration has achieved substantial management savings in social programs, although the potential for such savings has proven to be far less than generally perceived by the public.

Conclusion

In answer to the various questions posed in the introduction to this chapter regarding President Reagan's intentions and accomplishments in the social policy arena, we offer the following conclusions. The president clearly did seek to turn back the social policy clock, in some extreme cases (e.g., AFDC) to a pre-New Deal time. By and large, however, it was more recent history that sustained the most strenuous efforts at repeal. Given his way, the president would have eradicated most of the hallmarks of the Great Society and would have shrunk the social insurance programs to a scope more nearly approximating their New Deal origins. On the civil rights front the president would have scrapped the federal government's role as a "commanding general" in the war for equal opportunity, in favor of something more like a reluctant sergeant; broad goals, quotas, and timetables would have been replaced by individual disciplinary action according to rather narrowly interpreted rules.

---

*Error rates are computed by comparing the sum of overpayment to eligible recipients and payments to ineligible recipients to total payments. The federal share of this sum is currently about $2 billion for AFDC and Food Stamps.

An interesting perspective on fraud, waste, and abuse in welfare programs can be gained by examining analogous data for personal income taxes. The Internal Revenue Service calculates the "tax gap," which is defined as "the difference between the total amount of income tax which is voluntarily paid for a given tax year and the correct tax liability for that year" (based on *legally* earned income only). The "tax gap" as a percentage of actual taxes paid has risen from 23 in 1973 to 26 in 1981, when it represented some $75 billion. (Statement of Philip E. Coates, Acting Commissioner of Internal Revenue, before the Finance Committee, U.S. Senate, June 23, 1983.)

As it turned out, Congress and the courts have been considerable moderating forces on the president's intentions. Congress acted to protect many of the Great Society programs and to hold together the bottom tier of the safety net. As a result, by and large, the most ineffective programs were deeply cut or eliminated, while the programs more generally acknowledged as effective were left unscathed or reduced only modestly. And, although the president had, as any president has, considerably more latitude in the civil rights area than in the social spending programs, Congress and the courts have provided a substantial check here, rejecting the administration's most ambitious efforts at narrowing the laws or their interpretation. Although the president did succeed in realizing many of his philosophical preferences in the civil rights area through purely administrative action—not subject to court or congressional scrutiny—subsequent presidents can use their administrative flexibility in service of other philosophical preferences.

Thus, there is a sense in which the actual changes in social policy under the Reagan administration do not appear all that dramatic or permanent; many, in fact, can be viewed as logical extensions of existing trends. A period of consolidation in social spending and social programs had clearly already begun in the 1970s, with the growing emphasis on program efficiency and reform of the federal-state grant system. The annual real growth rate of federal social program spending was more than halved under President Carter from its levels under Presidents Kennedy through Ford. The policies adopted under President Reagan so far will lower this growth rate a bit more,* but only enough to return social program spending as a percentage of GNP to its level of the mid-1970s. (Appendix table A.2 shows these overall growth rates, as well as those for the different categories of programs, and figure 6.2 shows the GNP percentages.)

But to rest with this assessment, we think, would be to miss much of the larger social policy legacy of this administration. In fact, the long cycle of dramatic growth in the social activism of the national government that began with President Roosevelt's New Deal has ended. President Reagan has shifted the national social policy agenda from problem solving to budget cutting;[35] and as long as the federal deficit remains a serious problem (which is likely to be long indeed, see chapter 4), there is little room for the agenda to shift back.

---

*This growth rate was 7.9 percent under Presidents Nixon and Ford. It dropped to 3.9 percent under President Carter. Over the 1981–1985 period, as the budget reductions are phased in, it is estimated to be 1.5 percent. It will then increase to an estimated 2.5 percent for the rest of the decade under current policies and (favorable) economic assumptions.

Somewhat ironically, despite this shift in agenda, social spending looks like the Achilles' heel of the president's overall budget policy. Because none of the recent program cuts have addressed the basic entitlement and indexed nature of the major social programs, their continued real growth—particularly that of Social Security and Medicare—places more pressure on taxes and defense for solutions to the deficit problem.* Further, the potential for savings in social programs through efficiency gains has been largely exhausted, and public and congressional support for additional cuts in low-income assistance appears to have waned. Thus, any sizable future reductions in social spending will probably necessitate more fundamental changes in the social insurance programs.

Finally, no discussion of the administration's social policy legacy can end without mention of one of the primary presumed targets of any social policy: the poor. Insofar as the administration has made no progress in alleviating poverty and long-term welfare dependency, these problems must be regarded as part of its legacy. It is a legacy, to be sure, that is common to previous administrations, and perhaps the administration's economic policies will prove to have the desired ameliorative effect. But right now we can take scant comfort in these reflections. The bare fact remains: so far under this administration, the poor have continued to get poorer, and their long run prospects do not appear to be appreciably improved by the administration's policies.

---

*The real annual growth rate of the social insurance programs has declined only from 4 percent in the Carter era to 3 percent under current policy projections and will result in no reduction in their spending total as a percentage of GNP.

CHAPTER 7

FEDERALISM AND THE STATES

AN EXPERIMENT IN DECENTRALIZATION

George E. Peterson

Most domestic policy in the United States is implemented by state and local governments. A national government that sets out to change domestic priorities must therefore have a strategy for working with the state and local sector. As it happens, the Reagan administration has had at least two strategies, which sometimes have warred with each other for priority.

The narrower strategy has been to enlist state and local governments as partners in the effort to restrict public spending. The administration has had uppermost in its mind obtaining savings in the federal budget, but the president has made it clear that he believes domestic spending is excessive at all levels of government and that it is desirable to revamp the structure of federal grants-in-aid and regulations to eliminate the bias toward spending throughout the public sector.

At the same time, the administration set for itself the broader goal of devolution of domestic policy authority. One of the president's most consistently articulated criticisms has been that the national government has usurped responsibilities and authority that belong to the states. He entered office promising to redress this imbalance by setting the states free to pursue their own policy goals under their own management and by bringing government "closer to the people."

The two strategic goals of public spending reductions and devolution of political authority are, in principle, fully compatible with each other. They are held together by the conservative expectation that governments directly accountable to local voters will choose to spend less than a central government where the voters' will is filtered through interest groups. From the federal government's perspective, few budget-cutting devices are as effective as simply terminating federal grants-in-aid or shedding federal involvement in intergovernmental programs, as the administration sometimes has done in the name of devolution. Nonetheless, in practice conflicts have arisen between the goal of expenditure reduction and the goal of devolution. Congress and the states thus far have rejected the more sweeping proposals for achieving both ends at once, such as the New Federalism proposals to turn over domestic program responsibility to the states while drastically reducing federal aid. In effect, the administration has been forced to decide whether its first priority is the federalism initiative or expenditure restraint.

There is no doubt that the administration has resolved this dilemma by giving priority to the budget and to institutionalizing expenditure restraint in federal relations. For the present, it has put aside the goal of explicit devolution. This has led some observers to conclude that the grand design of returning authority to the states was never more than a rationalization for budget cutting, or at most was an ideological preference that quickly receded into the background when it was no longer useful to the federal budget debate.

Such an interpretation underestimates the mark the administration has left on intergovernmental relations. Radical program devolution has not been simply abandoned as a priority by the administration. It has been given a fair public test and found to lack a constituency. In this respect, the Reagan years have constituted a political experiment with a clear outcome. At the same time, however, the administration has been able to overhaul the standard tools of federal relations—the grant and regulatory mechanisms, as well as the tax linkages between the federal and state-local sectors—to reduce the incentives for governments to spend. And for the most part states have joined as willing partners in the effort to contain costs by redesigning social programs with historically high rates of spending.

So there is an irony to the Reagan record on intergovernmental relations. The administration set before the nation a highly ideological program of federalism reform, many of whose recommendations lay outside the mainstream of conventional thinking. The formal New Federalism never got off the ground. The principle of radical devolution of program authority was rejected by Congress, the states, and the electorate. However, the same principle inspired a devolution of management responsibilities (program implementation) that the states have seized upon and that has helped rationalize the operation of intergovernmental programs. Coupled with greater emphasis on expenditure controls in the grant system, the changes have allowed the administration to accomplish more of the mainstream agenda of intergovern-mental management reform than did earlier administrations that had this as their avowed goal.

This chapter discusses the Reagan initiatives and their effects in two parts. The first part considers the impact the administration has had on the system of intergovernmental relations. The second part considers the response of state and local governments to the Reagan initiatives.

The Reagan Challenge to Intergovernmental Relations

Ronald Reagan inherited an intergovernmental system that in many respects was frustratingly out of control. For decades federal spending on grants-in-aid had been growing faster than the rest of the federal budget, and by 1980 the grant system seemed to have lost its focus. According to some counts there were 534 separate grant programs. More fundamentally, there was no consistent rationale guiding the federal government's decisions as to when to become involved in intergovernmental aid or how to regulate the lower levels of government that were its partners in public activities. Indeed, the intergovernmental debate had deteriorated to such a point that the most frequently voiced justification for federal grant assistance was that states and localities had become accustomed to it and could not easily survive without further federal help.

The new president stepped into this confusion with both a budget plan for limiting grant-in-aid expenditures and an ideology for drawing sharp lines of demarcation between the responsibilities of different levels of government. Most of the activity occurred during the first two years of the administration (see table 7.1). The FY 1982 budget and the FY 1981 budget rescissions identified grants-in-aid as the most effective lever for reducing domestic spending and produced the first absolute declines in grant levels in recent history. President Reagan's budget also reintroduced the principle of block granting. As conceived by the administration, block grants simultaneously simplified federal management, transferred programmatic discretion to the states, and reduced federal funding commitments. In his January 1982 State of the Union address, the president revealed the political vision that tied together the various pieces of federalism reform, when he proposed a ten-year program for sorting out government responsibilities under the flag of New Federalism. The nation's basic income support programs, Aid to Families with Dependent Children (AFDC) and Food Stamps, were to be turned over to the states, while the federal government would assume full responsibility for Medicaid. In addition, sixty-one smaller intergovernmental programs were

TABLE 7.1

CHRONOLOGY OF REAGAN INTERGOVERNMENTAL INITIATIVES

Year	Event
1981	• FY 1981 budget rescissions and FY 1982 budget single out grants-in-aid for steepest budget cuts.
	• Immediately after entering office, Reagan appoints Presidential Task Force on Regulatory Relief to recommend deregulation and devolution of regulatory authority.
	• Administration proposes block grant consolidations. Congress passes nine block grants. Most go into effect Oct. 1, 1981.
	• Legislation tightens welfare eligibility and establishes penalty reductions in federal aid for states with rapidly rising Medicaid costs.
1982	• President introduces New Federalism in State of Union address. Plan is debated by Congress and states, eventually disappears from political agenda.
	• FY 1983 budget proposes further block grant consolidations. Congress passes one block grant for job training and employment.
	• Gas tax for highway repairs passed, reversing trend of grant reductions.
	• Administration imposes market interest rates on state borrowings from federal treasury to finance unemployment insurance payments.
1983	• President proposes "mega-blocks" or large-scale grant consolidations. Congress rejects proposal.
	• Legislative amendments allow states to avoid penalty tax increases and interest payments if they bring their unemployment insurance trust funds into fiscal balance.
	• State and local authority to issue tax-exempt single-family mortgage bonds expires at end of year. Legislation is introduced to curb issuance of industrial revenue bonds and to curb tax benefits of government sale and leaseback arrangements.
	• Task Force on Regulatory Relief submits final report.
1984	• FY 1985 budget contains only modest changes in grant structure or funding.
	• Industrial revenue bond and leasing restrictions are incorporated in congressional proposals to reduce federal deficit.

to be packaged together and returned to the states for their sole financing and administration, in return for federal surrender of a comparable amount of tax revenues. If consummated in full, the New Federalism would have severed intergovernmental ties to such an extent that, by 1991, the grant-in-aid share of the state and local budgets would have fallen to 3 to 4 percent, the lowest level since the first year of the New Deal.

The Mainstream Reform Agenda

One way to appreciate the scope of the Reagan reform agenda is to contrast it with the mainstream proposals for intergovernmental reform. By 1980 most observers shared the president's view that the system of intergovernmental relations stood in need of change. Behind the constant disputes over the structure and targeting of grants programs, there even lay agreement on many of the elements of a critique and prescription for reform.

Ever since the implementation of General Revenue Sharing in 1972, presidents had been calling for a slowdown in the explosive rate of growth of spending on federal grants. Repeatedly, presidential budgets planned for reductions in the rate of grant growth. Just as regularly, the intentions of funding restraint were frustrated by congressional politics or by the appearance of a recession which was thought to necessitate a new round of countercyclical grant assistance. Through most of the 1970s, the grants budget pushed higher— in real dollars, as a share of the federal budget, and as a share of state and local revenues. Finally, in 1979 the Carter administration achieved the first reduction in real grant levels, when it began to phase out the antirecession programs it had adopted. In retrospect, 1978 can be read as the high-water mark for federal grants-in-aid. Some observers have interpreted this as signifying that the federal commitment to a slowdown in grants spending already was in place before Reagan's arrival in the White House. At the time, however, it was far from evident that the recent dips in federal grant outlays represented anything more than the dismantling of temporary jobs and public works programs; in fact, under the traditional scenario the onset of a new recession shortly thereafter would have triggered a new set of federal grant initiatives.

There was also nearly universal assent that the burgeoning grant system had become unmanageable. When Budget Director David Stockman lamented in the administration's first budget hearings that, "We are overloaded at the national level. We simply can't make wise decisions on the thousands of issues that come before us," he was echoing a theme sounded by many others, often in almost the same words.[1] Nor did obstacles to effective management exist only at the federal level. More than a decade of research had established just how difficult it was for state or local governments to implement federal programs.[2] The long arm of federal regulatory and grant policy reached down from Washington through federal regional offices, leaving states and localities with onerous obligations but little administrative flexibility to accomplish program objectives. Attempts to simplify and rationalize the intergovernmental system had led to occasional grant consolidations and relaxation of categorical grant restrictions throughout the 1970s, starting with Richard Nixon's proposals for general and special revenue sharing. But the preponderant trend toward grant proliferation and more detailed regulation had not abated.

An additional criticism, which had not been completely accepted by 1980 but had spread well beyond its conservative origins, held that the traditional structure of grant and regulatory programs was ill suited to an era of restraint in public spending. Quite apart from their costs to the federal budget, categorical matching grants gave states or localities an economic incentive to spend more than they would choose to spend without federal intervention. The multiplicity of specific categorical grants opened the way for interest groups to lobby with congressional committees for increased funding or new grant programs, and with sympathetic bureaucrats for regulations that sometimes transformed the meaning of legislation. All these devices combined to sustain public spending and to insulate intergovernmental programs from the scrutiny of taxpayers. By 1980 taxpayer-voters had asserted their preference for less government growth. To many, the categorical matching grant structure seemed an anachronism that should now be replaced by a grant structure that was neutral toward spending or even encouraged spending restraint.

This mainstream agenda for intergovernmental reform was, in one sense, very ambitious. After all, a decade of effort had registered only scant progress toward achieving its goals. It was not, however, a program of fundamental reform. It gave no thought to diminishing the domestic policy role of Washington. It assumed that large parts of domestic policy would remain the joint responsibilities of different levels of government, with the federal government in the role of senior partner. Indeed, when the Advisory Commission on Intergovernmental Relations, the National Governors' Association, and other organizations recommended a partial sorting out of program responsibilities to rationalize aid relationships, they assigned to the federal government the entire responsibility for income support through federal takeover of AFDC and Medicaid. They suggested the possibility of federal withdrawal only from its relatively modest role in local law enforcement, local road assistance, and some education programs. In a word, the mainstream agenda called for management improvements within the framework of existing federal relations.

The Ideological Challenge

Ronald Reagan is the first president since Franklin D. Roosevelt to challenge not just the workings of the intergovernmental system but the prevailing federalist ideology of his time. His alternative vision of federalism can be summarized in three phrases: "separation of powers," "devolution of responsibilities to governments that are closer to the people," and "less spending by all levels of government." Each has powerful antecedents in conservative thought.

The doctrine that under a federal system of government each level of government exercises its assigned powers independently of the other was, until fifty years ago, the accepted legal and practical principle of federalism.* It has now become a dissenting conservative theory of how a federal system should be organized. Even conservative critics acknowledge that a model of formal separation does not fit the facts of the mid- to latter twentieth century, where the different levels of government are bound together by federal grants, federal regulations, and federal standards for services. They argue rather that lines of accountability have been blurred by this overlapping of authority. In proposing to sort out the major government responsibilities so that they were assigned exclusively to one level of government or the other—and in proposing to eliminate, wherever possible, the instruments that tie lower levels of government to Washington—the president was proposing to revive a literal separation of powers, as he had said in his inaugural address:

> It is my intention to curb the size and influence of the federal establishment and to demand recognition of the distinction between the powers granted to the federal government, [and] those reserved to the states or to the people.[3]

Reestablishment of the separation of powers does not, by itself, indicate how much responsibility should be exercised by the different levels of government. Conservative philosophy, however, argues for returning as much authority as possible to those levels of government that are closest to the people. This expression is not without its ambiguities.† As used by the Reagan administration, however, it seems to carry two principal meanings: that in the absence of overriding national needs, local taxpayers and voters should be the ones to decide which public programs they will support and how much

---

*A classic, albeit extreme, statement of the separation of powers is to be found in the 1871 U.S. Supreme Court decision on *Tarbel's Case*:

> There are within the territorial limits of each state two governments (federal and state), restricted in their sphere of action, but independent of each other, and supreme within their respective spheres. Each has its separate departments, each has its distinct laws, and each has its own tribunals for their enforcement. Neither government can intrude within the jurisdiction of the other or authorize any interference therein by its judicial officers with the action of the other.

Quoted in Deil S. Wright, *Understanding Intergovernmental Relations*, 2d ed. (Monterey, California: Brooks/Cole Publishing, 1982), p. 31.

†The political scientist Morton Grodzins once considered six different meanings that "closer to the people" had been asked to bear in political writings. He concluded that, under all of the meanings, the proposition that local government was closer to the people than the federal government was hopelessly resistant to empirical verification. Morton Grodzins, *The American System*, edited by Daniel J. Elazar (Chicago: Rand McNally, 1966), pp. 210–211.

they will spend on them; and that local citizens should have control over the way even federal programs are implemented in their community.* Given the large federal role in domestic policy at present, this distribution of authority can be reached only through devolution of program responsibilities from Washington.

A strict application of separation of powers and devolution of authority is likely to produce an outcome that conservative critics also believe is desirable: less public spending throughout government. Freed from the artificial inducements of matching grants and mandates, state and local governments are likely to replace only selectively the activities the federal government turns back to them, and to search for less expensive ways to meet the local sense of need for public programs. Perhaps the fundamental reason for making government "closer to the people," in the conservative line of argument, is that distant government has forced upon the public more spending than it wants to support.

Testing the Constituency for Devolution

The practical debate over devolution, of course, was not waged at the level of political or even budgetary theory. Despite the president's well-known belief in a weaker role for the federal government and a stronger role for the states in domestic policy, federalism issues had not figured prominently in the presidential campaign of 1980. The New Federalism debate therefore tested for the first time how large a constituency there was for devolution— among directly affected interest groups, among the states and localities that would inherit new responsibilities, and among taxpayers. The results of this test were decisive. They revealed virtually no constituency for a devolution of basic federal authority, but strong support for devolution of implementation responsibilities.

Only ideologues and political theorists debated the New Federalism proposals in their entirety. Others swiftly isolated the separate components targeted for devolution and debated them function by function or regulatory rule by regulatory rule. This process of constituency testing can best be illustrated by the debate over two specific government functions, welfare and regulation.

Welfare. If any part of the New Federalism should have had a natural political constituency, it was the proposal to turn over Aid to Families with Dependent Children to the states. Public opinion polls repeatedly have shown that voters believe that AFDC is too expensive and too many households

---

*In his 1982 State of the Union address that introduced the New Federalism, the president stated that average citizens "feel they have lost control of even the most basic decisions made about the essential services of government."

receive welfare assistance. Politicians and analysts alike have predicted that devolution would produce lower benefit levels and tighter eligibility standards. State operation of the welfare system would eliminate the open-ended federal matching grants that now lower the cost of welfare to the states and stimulate welfare spending; moreover, it could be expected to create a competitive situation wherein each state would have to restrict AFDC benefits for fear of attracting welfare recipients from neighboring states or losing taxpayers to them. Some such mobility exists even under the current system of partial welfare decentralization.* But full state operation of AFDC would greatly exacerbate the states' sensitivity to cost differentials. One empirical study has estimated that average AFDC benefits would fall by as much as 80 percent within five years if AFDC were turned over to the states without federal matching assistance.[4]

Although fear of such an adjustment can help explain the bitter opposition of welfare groups to the turnback of AFDC or Food Stamps, the prospect of lower spending might be thought to strengthen the conservative case for devolution with taxpayers.

In actuality, no taxpayer lobby for turning over welfare to the states has materialized. Opinion polls show that voters—despite their expressed preference for lower welfare spending—believe it is a federal responsibility to set welfare standards and to assist states in meeting welfare needs.[5] State governments also have resisted the transfer of authority. Governors have held that the political constraints on a decentralized welfare system would force benefit levels lower than was in the national interest. They also have opposed elimination of the federal government's role in partially offsetting inequalities in states' fiscal capacity through federal matching rates that are higher for poor states than for rich ones.

Without a constituency for full devolution, the Reagan administration was forced to split its welfare policy into two parts, a national policy of cost control and a local policy that granted states and localities greater discretion over the operation of welfare programs by allowing them to institute work requirements if they chose. An experiment in San Diego County suggests that flexibility in program implementation may be the aspect of devolution that local governments value most highly.† The San Diego County effort began

---

*Oregon, for example, reported losing one-quarter of its Indo-Chinese AFDC population to California after it reduced AFDC benefits. Helen F. Ladd, "Federal Aid to State and Local Governments," in Gregory B. Mills and John L. Palmer, eds., *Federal Budget Policy in the 1980s* (Washington, D.C.: The Urban Institute Press, 1984).

†The experiment holds special interest because it was designed in the late 1970s by Robert Carleson, who earlier designed California's welfare program for Governor Reagan and later was a principal architect of the New Federalism as a White House advisor to President Reagan.

with a citizen mandate to require that welfare recipients who were able to work do so. In a general election referendum, 80 percent of the voters expressed support for requiring welfare recipients to work off their welfare grants. By 1983 San Diego had in operation three new workfare programs— one for AFDC recipients, one for participants in refugee assistance, and one for Food Stamp recipients—made possible by the 1981 amendments to the welfare laws. San Diego officials reported that the modifications to the AFDC program had satisfied voter demand for local control over the philosophy and implementation of welfare. The experiment seems to show that even conservative voters who share the president's values place greater importance on local control of program implementation than on removing the federal government from program participation or program funding.

Regulation. One of the most innovative efforts of the Reagan administration was to extend the concept of devolution to regulatory policy. The president's executive order on regulation sets out a framework both for regulatory relief and for return of regulatory responsibility over private activity to states and localities.[6] As one writer has noted, the policy carries a "rebuttable presumption" that the best government to vest with regulatory responsibility will be that closest to the people.[7] Just as the turnback of grant programs was intended both to serve federalist principles and to further the substantive goal of spending restraint, so restoring local control over regulation was intended both to strengthen the local and state role in policymaking and to be a vehicle of regulatory relief.

No constituency stepped forward to support the president's calls for delegating to the states the basic choices of regulatory policy. Business would seem to be the natural constituency to support regulatory devolution. However, business has generally opposed efforts to substitute state for federal regulation, and frequently has lobbied for federal preemption of state regulatory standards. For example, when the Reagan administration decided to support federal legislation that would override state laws on product liability, it was at business' behest. Business preferred the certainty of a single set of federal standards to the inconsistent, and often stricter, standards of product liability contained in state laws. Business groups also supported uniform federal regulations for the labeling of hazardous chemicals used in the workplace, in order to head off a movement toward local regulation.

The most successful examples of delegation of regulatory responsibility have come in cases where the federal government retains responsibility for standard setting, but cedes to the states greater discretion in designing regulatory strategies to meet these standards.[8] The Reagan administration has delegated to the states greater responsibility for implementing the rules that govern the operation of surface mines, for example, by changing the condition of delegation from one that required states to have in place programs ''no less stringent than federal rules'' to one requiring state programs to be ''no less effective than federal rules.'' The new performance standards allow states flexibility they did not formerly possess to tailor their regulatory restrictions to take account of differences in climate, geography, and other local conditions. In air quality regulation, the administration has promulgated generic standards that state emission-trading plans must meet, but has dropped the requirement of case-by-case federal review of proposals that fall within its general guidelines. This step has freed states to exercise more initiative in putting together market-based plans, like the sale and purchase of emission rights, which let firms meet air quality standards in a least-cost manner.

The Practical Challenge to Intergovernmental Relations

If the federalism debate set off by Ronald Reagan sometimes seemed to wander far from the work of everyday government, no state or local official doubted the immediacy of the administration's practical challenge to the intergovernmental system.

The administration approached practical reform with two objectives in mind. First, it wanted to lower the growth path of federal spending. Second, it sought to transmit its own program priorities and desire for spending reductions throughout the federal system. To this end, it modified the grant and tax structure to create incentives for state and local behavior consistent with the federal government's domestic priorities. It also sought to shift to states and localities more responsibility for grants management.

Federal Spending. In its attack on domestic spending, the administration has enjoyed more success in cutting grant expenditures than in cutting the rest of the federal domestic budget. In the administration's first year, grants to state and local governments were cut by 13.1 percent from baseline levels (levels that would have existed without a change in policy), or more than double the overall reduction in the domestic budget.[9] Direct grants to states and localities, as distinguished from income support and Medicaid payments to individuals, bore the greatest reductions. Changes enacted during the administration's first year in office, if sustained, were projected to reduce grant outlays of this type by 25 percent from baseline levels by FY 1986. A quarter-century perspective shows that by most measures grant spending indeed has receded markedly from the peak levels reached in 1978. As a proportion of the federal domestic budget, for example, grant spending by FY 1983 had returned to the levels of the early 1960s (table 7.2). Entitlement grants to individuals account for all the growth in grant spending that has occurred since 1978.

TABLE 7.2

AID TO STATE AND LOCAL GOVERNMENTS FOR SELECTED FISCAL YEARS

| | Year | | | | *Percentage Change* |
	1960	*1970*	*1978*	*1983*	*1978–1983*
Aid in current dollars (billions)					
Grants-in-aid	7.0	24.0	77.9	93.0	+ 19.4
To governments	4.5	15.0	51.9	48.2	− 7.4
To individuals	2.5	9.0	26.0	44.8	+ 72.3
Tax expenditures	NA	10.8	19.3	46.8[a]	+ 142.9
Interest exclusion	NA	2.3	6.1	20.4	+ 234.4
Tax deductibility	NA	8.5	13.2	26.2	+ 98.5
Aid in constant 1972 dollars (billions)[b]					
Grants	10.8	27.0	49.5	39.3	− 20.6
To governments	7.4	17.2	32.0	20.4	− 36.3
To individuals	3.4	9.8	17.5	18.9	+ 10.8
Tax expenditures	NA	12.3	12.1	19.8	+ 63.6
Interest exclusion	NA	2.6	3.8	8.6	+ 163.2
Tax deductibility	NA	9.7	8.3	11.1	+ 33.7
Grants as a percentage of:					
Total federal budget	7.6	12.3	17.4	11.7	− 32.8
Domestic federal budget	15.9	21.1	22.9	16.1	− 29.7
State and local revenues	11.6	16.0	21.0	18.3[c]	− 12.9

SOURCES: 1960–1978, Helen F. Ladd, "Aid to State and Local Governments," in Gregory B. Mills and John L. Palmer, eds., *Federal Budget Policy in the 1980s* (Washington, D.C.: The Urban Institute Press, 1984), table 1; 1983, *Budget of the United States Government, Fiscal Year 1985, Special Analyses,* Section H, "Aid to State and Local Governments," *Survey of Current Business,* vol. 64, no. 2 (February 1984), table 3.3
NA = not available.
a. This figure is the sum of individual tax expenditure items, and comparable with previous years. The Office of Management and Budget estimates that the net cost is significantly less, because of the interaction of the individual items.
b. Deflated by state and local implicit price deflator, National Income Accounts.
c. National Income Accounts basis.

Since the first year's budget onslaught, only modest further cuts in grant programs have been made. In current dollars, total grant expenditures dropped in FY 1982, then resumed their long-term growth path at a somewhat diminished rate. Most of the savings realizable from a general tightening of the grants budget now have been accomplished. The fiscal imperative behind the New Federalism, in fact, came from recognition that if further large cuts were to be made in the federal grants budget, there would have to be a fundamental redefinition of the federal role in domestic policy.

In the absence of a redefinition of government roles, the focus of future intergovernmental budgetary debates is likely to shift from the grants side of the budget to tax expenditures on behalf of state and local governments. These have now become by far the fastest-growing costs in the intergovernmental system (table 7.2).*

Reform of the Grant Structure. The Reagan critique of the grant system has gone beyond a desire to reduce federal spending to urge reshaping of the grant structure. One goal has been to consolidate the large number of categorical grants into fewer, broad-based grants. By the administration's count, it has trimmed the number of separate grant programs by more than a quarter since it took office.[10] The largest consolidations took place as part of the FY 1982 block grant reforms, when the administration obtained congressional approval of nine block grants combining some seventy-six different categorical grants. Seven of these new block grants were in the areas of health and social services, one combined a number of small educational grants, and the ninth restructured the community development block grant.

The Reagan block grants embodied in miniature the president's objectives for grant restructuring.[11] They were intended to help restore primacy to the states by channeling funds only to state governments. They gave the states wide discretion in selecting their own program priorities, subject only to restrictions imposed by Congress before final passage of the block grant legislation. They removed most of the regulatory or administrative rules limiting states' choices about how to implement grant-supported programs. And they bundled together many small programs which had been sustained primarily by federal dollars, leaving states with the option of withdrawing altogether from these program areas if they desired. In exchange for the greater flexibility of the block grants, the administration cut funding levels for the programs consolidated into the block grants by approximately 20 percent.

Despite its initial success with block granting, the administration has not succeeded in shifting the grant mix strongly toward broad-based grants. In FY 1984, general purpose and broad-based grants will constitute 20.2 percent of the federal grants budget, slightly less than the 20.7 percent in FY 1980 before the administration took office. In each of its budget proposals, the administration has recommended further block-grant consolidations, including an escalation of the principle of block-granting into mega-blocks. However,

---

*Estimates of the federal tax revenue lost because of tax preferences are inexact and controversial, especially for interest exclusion. There are significant discrepancies between the tax expenditure estimates developed by the Treasury Department, Senate Finance Committee, and Congressional Budget Office. However, all estimates show rapidly rising costs, especially for private-purpose tax-exempt borrowing.

except for a consolidation of job training programs, these subsequent proposals have been rejected by Congress.

The type of categorical grant which receives the harshest criticism in the Reagan assessment is the project grant. Project grants are awarded on a case-by-case basis by bureaucrats or Congress, and therefore are thought to embody the worst aspects of federal intrusion into local decision making. For example, under one type of project grant, cities propose new mass transit projects they want to build and the Urban Mass Transportation Administration selects certain ones to fund, often after extensive reshaping of the local proposals in Washington. Project grants are perceived by the Reagan administration as particularly undesirable because they strengthen spending ties among grant recipients, Congress, and agency bureaucrats.

Without a great deal of fanfare, the administration has gradually substituted automatic formula funding for discretionary project funding and has selectively killed off project grants, so that by FY 1983 the profile of the federal grant mix looked quite different from the way it did in FY 1980 (table 7.3).

One dimension of the grant system of importance to the Reagan reform program is the matching structure. Categorical grants frequently are designed to match state and local spending with federal dollars in a designated proportion. The grant structure thus lowers the "price" to state and local governments of making expenditures on grant-assisted programs. These matching

TABLE 7.3

CHANGE IN MIX OF FORMULA AND PROJECT GRANTS, FY 1980–FY 1983

| | Fiscal Year | | Percentage Change |
	1980	1983	1980–1983
Total number of grants[a]	428	313	−26.9
Project grants[b]	320	210	−34.3
Formula grants[b]	93	92	−1.1
Total obligations[a]			
(in $ million)	82,410	83,970	+1.9
Project grant obligations[b]	17,066	11,728	−31.4
Formula grant obligations[b]	54,430	58,945	+8.3

SOURCE: Compiled by The Urban Institute from unpublished grant classification, Office of Management and Budget.

a. Grants to state and local governments as defined by OMB consistent with budget concept and for which obligations are reported.

b. Project and formula grants do not sum to total because of third category of mixed formula/project grants.

incentives were deliberately built into earlier generations of federal grants, which in part were intended to stimulate more spending on targeted functions than state and local governments voluntarily would undertake.

Economists have ascribed considerable importance to categorical matching grants as stimulants of state and local expenditures. A large number of empirical studies suggest that, if there is no ceiling to federal matching, a one-to-one match increases total spending over the level that state and local governments would support if dependent solely upon their own resources.[12] One of the Reagan administration's goals has been to reduce the grant stimulation to public spending by lowering matching rates, by eliminating the matching principle altogether, or by capping the size of the federal contribution. In this last case, the grant is converted from open-ended matching to closed-end matching. Beyond the ceiling set for federal matching payments, there is no price incentive to further program spending. As can be seen from table 7.4, the administration has made significant inroads into reducing the matching-grant stimulus. Several of the largest federal grants have been refashioned to eliminate or reduce the price subsidy. In some cases, the administration has gone farther to create positive rewards for state and local expenditure restraint.

Sometimes a single change in grant structure can achieve several objectives at once. The consolidation of many matching-grant categorical programs into a single block grant, for example, simultaneously creates the administrative flexibility of the block-grant form, removes the matching-grant stimulus to spending because the amount of the block grant is fixed regardless of spending levels, and may substitute a formula grant for former project grants.

Intergovernmental Tax Policy. Implicit in the withdrawal of federal funding from domestic programs is a realignment of tax burdens. State and local taxes must rise if states and localities decide to replace federal spending. At the same time federal taxes can be cut. The turnback element of the New Federalism proposals explicitly recognized this linkage. It proposed having the federal government withdraw from funding participation in a miscellany of intergovernmental programs, while also abandoning taxes of the same dollar magnitude; state and local governments then could choose whether to pick up the services and tax burdens on their own. A special trust fund would have been created to handle the transition from federal grant funding to full turnback of program choices. Although the turnback proposal never made any headway, the administration has accomplished part of its objective by simply reducing or eliminating federal aid for domestic programs, thereby confronting states and localities with a *de facto* decision whether to raise their own taxes to replace federal funds.

TABLE 7.4

STRUCTURAL CHANGES IN FEDERAL GRANT SYSTEM

Grant Program[a]	FY 1981 Outlays (Billions of dollars)	Principal Changes
Medicaid	16.8	1981 Omnibus Budget Reconciliation Act reduces the grants states otherwise would receive by 3 percent in FY 1982, 4 percent in FY 1983, and 4.5 percent in FY 1984. It allows dollar-for-dollar offset of these reductions by amount states keep spending growth under 9 percent. Offsets are also allowed for states that reduce error rates.
Highway Aid	8.6	No change in matching grant structure. Total federal assistance reduced in FY 1982, then increased sharply with passage of 5 cent additional gas tax.
Aid to Families with Dependent Children	8.5	1981 Omnibus Budget Reconciliation Act reduced eligibility of working households by setting absolute income ceilings, reducing income disregards, and changing treatment of work expense deductions. Administration estimates that changes in eligibility rules removed some 400,000 families from welfare rolls.
Employment and Training Assistance	5.9	Comprehensive Employment and Training Act replaced by Job Training Partnership Act (JTPA). Total funding reduced sharply. JTPA terminates the Public Service Employment program that many cities had used to boost public service provision.
General Revenue Sharing	5.1	No change in structure.
Community Development Block Grant	4.0	Small cities portion of grant (approx. $1 billion) shifted to state administration. Matching requirement eliminated for small cities portion.
Wastewater Treatment Construction Grants	3.9	Effective FY 1985, federal matching share will be reduced from 75 percent to 55 percent for conventional wastewater systems, and from 85 percent to 75 percent for innovative systems. Total funding reduced.
Urban Mass Transportation Grants	3.8	One cent of five cent gas tax increase earmarked for mass transit capital grants. Federal share reduced from 80 percent to 75 percent.
Child Nutrition Programs	3.3	Administration lowered federal subsidy rates for school lunch program, restricted income eligibility for free and subsidized meals. Income eligibility also tightened for Women, Infants and Children Supplemental Food Program and Special Milk Program.

TABLE 7.4 *(continued)*

Grant Program[a]	FY 1981 Outlays (Billions of dollars)	Principal Changes
Compensatory Education	3.3	Funding reduced. Targeting requirements relaxed.
Social Services	2.6	State matching requirement eliminated. Funding reduced. Welfare targeting requirement eliminated.

SOURCES: Office of Management and Budget, *Budget of the United States Government, Fiscal Year 1983, Special Analysis H: Federal Aid to State and Local Governments* (Washington, D.C.: Government Printing Office, 1982); Office of Management and Budget, "State and Local Matching Fund Requirements for Federal Aid," (unpublished report), February 2, 1983; Congressional Budget Office, *The Federal Government in a Federal System: Current Intergovernmental Programs and Options for Change* (Washington, D.C.: Government Printing Office, 1983).

Pressures on the federal budget also have forced the administration to begin to tackle tax expenditures as vigorously as it has addressed grants policy. First priority has been assigned to limiting the costs to the federal treasury of tax-exempt interest on state and local bonds. The right to issue tax-exempt bonds and notes can be thought of as the tax equivalent of receiving an open-ended matching grant. For as large a volume of bonds as a state or locality chooses to issue, the federal government subsidizes a share of the interest costs. This cost sharing lowers the "price" of borrowing, and hence of capital spending, just as a matching grant lowers the price of program spending. States and localities have stretched their imaginations to find new ways to use tax-exempt bonds. They have defined for themselves a "social banker" function, in which they borrow large sums of money at tax-exempt interest rates, then relend the funds at below-market rates for politically popular purposes, such as to provide homebuyers with subsidized mortgages or to lower the costs of business investment within a state.

The federal government has on occasion tried to limit this activity. In 1968 it first placed a ceiling on the size of individual industrial revenue bonds. More recently, it imposed an aggregate ceiling on a state's issuance of single-family mortgage revenue bonds, and placed a calendar limitation of December 31, 1983 on the states' right to issue such bonds. Neither of these measures did more than temporarily retard the growth of private-purpose tax-exempt bonds. By 1983 state and local borrowing for private purposes had

reached some $50 billion. The most controversial pieces of federalism leg-
islation to come before Congress in 1983 and 1984 did not concern grants
reform, but proposals to further curb the ability of states and localities to
issue private-purpose debt. As of the spring of 1984, these proposals have
been consolidated into an extension of states' authority to issue single-family
mortgage bonds, along with a cap on most other private-purpose industrial
revenue bonds of $150 per capita, per year.

State and Local Responses to the Federal Challenge

Once the federal government changes the rules for intergovernmental
programs, the next move is up to states and localities. It has become customary
to consider state and local responses to the Reagan policy changes under the
heading of ''replacement''—whether states and localities have boosted spending from their own resources to replace the federal dollars lost in aid cuts.
Replacement decisions can be examined for individual grant areas or for state
and local behavior in the aggregate. Such an inquiry can, however, impose
too narrow a focus on state and local reactions. Whether other governments
replaced federal funding within a broad category often is of less interest than
whether they maintained or altered former federal program priorities, or whether
they changed the style of managing intergovernmental programs.

Consideration of the replacement choices of state and local governments
has been further muddled by the tendency to run together federal policy
changes of quite different character. For one set of programs, the federal
government altered the grant structure with the express purpose of discouraging growth of state-local expenditures. The programs targeted in this fashion
tended to be the large social programs, in which state expenditure levels
directly determine federal budget outlays through open-ended matching-grant
or borrowing provisions. Through grant changes the Reagan government
sought to impose its new domestic priorities upon the states. A second set of
program changes adhered more closely to the Reagan philosophy of true
devolution. For these programs—exemplified by the block-grant consolidations—the federal government adopted a hands-off attitude toward state decisions whether to maintain, terminate, or alter the formerly joint programs.

The States as Partners in Transmitting Domestic Priorities

When it came to the largest intergovernmental expenditures, and to the
programs closest to the heart of Reagan's promise to reduce government's
role in social policy, the administration performed in the traditional manner
as senior partner in the federalist grants partnership. The change from previous

policy was that the new financial inducements built into the grant structure were meant to achieve expenditure reduction rather than expenditure growth. Table 7.4 identified the principal changes in grant structure which the administration made for each of the largest grant programs. Although the intent to reduce spending stimulation is apparent throughout the changes, the impact was greatest for AFDC, Medicaid, and unemployment insurance. For these programs, the administration sought to impose new regulations or devise federal aid penalties that would actively restrain expenditures. Did the states respond to these incentives and regulations as the federal government hoped?

AFDC. For AFDC, the principal federal strategy was to remove households from the welfare rolls by imposing new restrictions on eligibility.* The states had no choice but to accept these changes in eligibility and earnings rules. They could, if they desired, offset the impact by compensatory actions. If they accepted the federal restrictions without offsetting adjustments, however, they could expect to share in the program savings that resulted.

One option open to the states was to expand their own state-financed general assistance or general relief programs, so as to absorb families displaced from AFDC. Such a replacement carried a high cost. To transfer a family from AFDC to state general assistance at the same benefit level more than doubled the cost to the average state, because of the loss of the federal match. In a monitoring sample of twenty-five states selected by The Urban Institute for geographic, fiscal, and political diversity, no state was found to have relaxed eligibility for general assistance to compensate for federal tightening of AFDC eligibility standards.[13] At least two states—Michigan and New York—moved to cut back their general assistance eligibility, for fear that under the existing program structure, large numbers of those displaced from AFDC would move on to the general relief rolls at state expense.†

A second option open to states was to increase the AFDC need standard. Since federal regulations had limited AFDC eligibility to families with incomes no greater than 150 percent of the state-established need standard, an increase in the need standard could restore families to the eligibility rolls—

---

*The FY 1982 budget reconciliation act (1) imposed an income ceiling on AFDC eligibility of 150 percent of state standard of need, (2) decreased the amount of earnings and other income that could be disregarded in setting benefit levels, (3) required states to use recipients' past actual income rather than expected next-month income in computing benefits, (4) ended payments to strikers, students, and women in the first five months of pregnancy for their first child, and (5) required that part of a stepparent's income be counted as available for recipient's support.

†Michigan's tightening of income eligibility removed an estimated 18,000 households from the general assistance rolls in FY 1982. Average monthly caseloads for general assistance fell slightly in that year, despite high unemployment and displacement from AFDC rolls, after jumping 40 percent in 1981.

but not without triggering cost consequences for the entire AFDC system. In most states, AFDC benefit payments are set as a percentage of the need standard. Therefore, raising the need standard, while restoring to the rolls families made ineligible by the change in federal rules, would at the same time raise benefits payments for almost all AFDC recipients. No state tried to increase its need standard enough to compensate for the federal eligibility changes. A number of states, however, did increase their need standards somewhat. Over time, these actions have mitigated in small part the impact of the federal eligibility restrictions. Although AFDC caseloads fell in most states in FY 1982, when the federal eligibility changes went into effect, caseloads stabilized in FY 1983 and began to increase again in FY 1984.

One implication of this pattern is that welfare eligibility, as well as welfare benefit levels, has become much more dependent upon states' fiscal condition. In a normal economic cycle, welfare rolls swell as the economy moves toward its recessionary bottom. In the most recent cycle, welfare enrollment did not begin to grow until states were well on their way to fiscal recovery, and judged themselves once again able to afford welfare assistance. Overall, the rules rendering some of the working poor ineligible for AFDC are estimated to have cut the welfare rolls by about 10 percent.

Medicaid. The changes in the Medicaid program reflect quite a different approach to intergovernmental cost control. Whereas the AFDC changes took the form of tighter eligibility standards imposed from Washington, the Medicaid changes consisted of a penalty reduction in federal grants for states that failed to restrain costs, plus greater flexibility for states to achieve their own cost reductions (see table 7.4).* States that held their Medicaid spending growth to less than 9 percent could reduce the new federal penalties, dollar for dollar, by the amount they fell below this growth threshold.

In 1982, the year the federal penalties went into effect, thirty states plus the District of Columbia succeeded in holding the growth in Medicaid outlays below the target rate of 9 percent and received incentive rebates. Average Medicaid spending growth, as reported to the federal government for the purposes of matching payments, fell to 6 percent, or about one-third the annual rate of growth over the period 1979–1981, although there are indications this may overstate the extent of actual cost reductions. Preliminary econometric estimates suggest that about one-third of this reduction can be

---

*The reductions in AFDC eligibility also produced some Medicaid savings, since AFDC recipients are categorically eligible for Medicaid.

attributed to the change in price incentives.* The remaining two-thirds is attributable to the program reductions made during the recession and to the greater flexibility accorded states to negotiate their own cost controls.[14]

For the long run the most significant element of cost control built into the federal Medicaid package is the ability of states to negotiate fixed-rate payments with hospitals rather than to reimburse hospitals for reasonable costs. States have seized upon this opportunity to restrict what had been the fastest-growing category of Medicaid expenses. The state of California, for example, appointed a hospital "czar," empowered to negotiate, through competitive bidding, hospital rates with individual hospitals on behalf of the state. States now have the authority to steer Medicaid clients into the lower-cost hospitals where negotiated rates are in effect.†[15] California budget estimates place the first full-year savings from hospital rate negotiation in the vicinity of $400 million.

Unemployment Insurance. Unlike AFDC and Medicaid, unemployment insurance is not operated as an intergovernmental matching-grant program. States are supposed to pay into a federal trust fund the full costs of their unemployment compensation programs through employer payroll taxes. The intergovernmental connection comes from the fact that states are allowed to borrow from the federal Treasury when their unemployment insurance trust funds are in deficit. By July 1983 deficit states owed the U.S. Treasury nearly $13.5 billion.

Before 1982 such borrowing was interest free, and states had little incentive to bring their unemployment insurance programs into fiscal balance. The Reagan administration moved to impose market rates of interest on these state borrowings. Since April 1982 new federal loans have carried a 10 percent annual interest rate. To the "stick" of interest costs the Social Security Amendments of March 1983 added the "carrot" of special incentives for states to bring their unemployment insurance programs into fiscal balance. If

---

*There are broad discrepancies in Medicaid spending as reported by different sources. The 6 percent growth rate referenced in the text is computed from Form 64 quarterly reporting by states to the Health Care Financing Administration. The states possess some accounting flexibility in charging Medicaid costs to different fiscal years. The federal penalty system created an incentive to allocate costs to federal FY 1981 rather than FY 1982, so that a state could qualify for the cost-containment rebate. Thus the official data are likely to somewhat exaggerate the decline in Medicaid spending growth. Census of governments data indicate that in state FY 1982 Medicaid spending growth fell to 11.7 percent from 16.6 percent the previous year.

†For example, in Alameda County, California, 26 percent of Medicaid participants were redirected to contracting hospitals from hospitals where they previously were served.

a debtor state increases the net solvency of its unemployment insurance program by 25 percent (through tax increases and/or benefit reductions), it now can defer most of the interest payments on its debt to the Treasury. If it meets other solvency requirements, it can avoid the federal penalty taxes which are imposed on states that have had loans outstanding for two years or more.

The major debtor states all have restructured their unemployment insurance programs to qualify for the federal incentives (see table 7.5).* The financial and political adjustments required by these actions have been large. In the short run most of the cost adjustment has been borne by increases in employer payroll taxes, but it is probable that, in addition to the one-time reduction in unemployment benefits in several states, the higher level of taxation will effectively constrain future benefit increases and eligibility standards as well.

State Spending and Federal Priorities. Have the federal changes in grant incentives been able to shape the overall allocation of state budgets? The rates of state spending growth in FY 1981 and FY 1982 are compared in table 7.6 for all of the major categories of spending. They reveal a pronounced pattern. The programs singled out for federal grant restructuring show an abrupt slowdown—or, in the case of welfare, an absolute decline—in expenditure growth. Among the other functions, activities fully funded from states' own revenues typically sustained or increased their growth rates, while activities receiving significant federal assistance showed declines, sometimes sharp, in their rates of spending growth. At least in the short run, the Reagan administration achieved its goal of restraining the growth of social programs throughout the intergovernmental system. Further, the states' budget adjustments seem to show that (as the administration intended), if forced to become reliant on their own resources, states would select very different budget priorities from those coaxed from them by past federal aid.

Some qualifications must be kept in mind before concluding that federal actions can so powerfully shape state behavior. First, the administration's efforts to restrain social spending coincided with the recession. States and localities would have made some effort to slow Medicaid, AFDC, and unemployment compensation growth regardless of federal policy—though in past recessions attempts at program restructuring have been overwhelmed by increases in the number of program eligibles because of unemployment growth. Second, the federal initiatives to control costs were reinforced by similar pressures being brought to bear directly upon state governments by taxpayers

---

*The Social Security Amendments were written so as to allow Michigan and Ohio to count the restructurings made in their unemployment insurance programs, even though these took place in December 1982, before passage of the new federal legislation.

TABLE 7.5

STATE UNEMPLOYMENT INSURANCE INDEBTEDNESS AND RECENT LEGISLATION TO
REDUCE STATE DEBTS
(States with largest debts)

State	Outstanding Debt, July 1983 (Billions of dollars)	Date of Legislation	Size of Adjustment (State tax increases plus benefit reductions)	Composition of Adjustment	
				Reduced Benefits (Percentage)	Higher Taxes (Percentage)
Pennsylvania	2.66	July 1983	$2.1 billion over 3 years (1984–1986)	33	67
Illinois	2.43	April 1983	$2.0 billion over 4 years (1983–1986)	40	60
Michigan	2.27	December 1982	$3.6 billion over 4 years (1983–1986)	31	69
Ohio	2.11	December 1982	$.27 billion over 1 year (1983)	19	81
		June 1983	$1.3 billion over 2 years (1984–1985)	22	78
Wisconsin	.65	April 1983	$1.2 billion over 4 years (1983–1986)	37	63
Texas	.52	September 1982	$.25 billion over 3 years (1983–1985)	0	100
		May 1983	$1.0 billion over 6 years (1983–1988)	0	100

SOURCES: State debts from U.S. Department of Labor. Other data: "State Unemployment Insurance: Benefit Availability and Financing Problems," Wayne Vroman before the Budget Committee Task Force on Entitlements, Uncontrollables, and Indexing. State of Montana, September 7, 1983.

and voters. State governments received the same electoral message of resistance to social spending that Congress did.

The perspective of a few years will be needed to judge how greatly recent program changes deflected social spending from its previous long-run path. Both grants-in-aid and state budget pressures were relaxed after FY 1982. In some cases (e.g., highway aid), the federal budget cutbacks of FY 1982 were

TABLE 7.6

STATE GOVERNMENT SPENDING GROWTH AND FEDERAL AID, BY FUNCTIONAL AREA[a]
(*Percentage change from previous state fiscal year*)

	FY 1982		FY 1981	
	Total State Spending	Federal Aid	Total State Spending	Federal Aid
Social programs with grant restructuring				
Welfare Cash Assistance (AFDC)	− 3.2	c	11.0	c
Medicaid[b]	11.7	c	16.6	c
Unemployment Compensation	1.0	c	48.6	c
Function with more than 10 percent federal funding (1981 Federal % of Total Revenue in parentheses)				
Employment Security Admin. (104%)	0.3	− 0.4	13.4	15.2
Highways (55.5%)	− 1.2	− 11.4	1.6	5.7
Natural Resources (23.7%)	7.6	− 3.0	15.5	15.9
Education (14.6%)	6.3	− 6.7	10.2	10.5
Health and Hospitals (11.5%)	9.2	− 3.5	12.2	12.6
Functions without Federal Funding (in order of expenditure)				
Employee Retirement	15.0	d	11.3	d
Interest on Debt	14.9	d	16.0	d
Corrections	15.6	d	14.5	d
Utilities	11.4	d	39.4	d
General Control	14.3	d	5.8	d
Financial Administration	12.1	d	9.9	d
Police Protection	6.7	d	13.0	d
Liquor Stores	4.4	d	4.5	d

SOURCES: U.S. Department of Commerce, Bureau of the Census, *State Government Finances in 1982* (Washington, D.C.: Government Printing Office, 1983).

a. All functional areas with FY 1981 total expenditures of $2.0 billion or more.

b. See footnote, p. 235, for discussion of reporting discrepancies in Medicaid spending. States' Form 64 reporting to the Health Care Financing Administration shows a decline in Medicaid spending growth from 17.8 percent in federal FY 1981 to 6.0 percent in FY 1982.

c. Federal aid change not shown for programs with grant restructuring.

d. No identifiable categorical federal assistance, Census of Governments.

followed by greatly increased aid in subsequent years. Nonetheless, the structural changes to the major social programs should slow the long-run trend of spending, even after the short-term jolt to the system delivered in FY 1982 has subsided.

The administration's success in intergovernmental cost control is not without some ironies. The device that ultimately proved successful in restraining spending was the combination of penalties for high expenditures and incentive rewards for cost restraint. This two-way sharing of program costs and program savings is perhaps the purest embodiment of cooperative federalism, an intergovernmental working style which the administration in principle has repudiated. In not one of the three fields examined in this section did the administration initiate the idea of sharing with states the financial benefits from spending restraint. Its original position was that market rates of interest on federal loans would be sufficient inducement to persuade states to reform their unemployment compensation programs. Congress added the "carrot" of interest deferral and penalty-tax forgiveness if states acted to restore solvency. The administration sought initially to shift to the states all the responsibility for AFDC and Medicaid choices, and all the marginal costs of these programs.* Only after it was dissuaded from this cause by opposition in Congress and by the governors and state legislators did it accept the alternative course of providing positive financial incentives for states that succeeded in controlling program costs.

Block Grants: Devolution in Practice

More than any of the other federal initiatives, the block grants embody the original Reagan philosophy of coupling devolution of program authority with federal funding cuts.[16] For this reason, the states' responses to the block grants constitute a special test of the Reagan approach to federalism.

One issue raised by the block grant consolidation is the extent of state and local replacement of federal aid. In contrast to its active discouragement of spending for the larger social programs, the administration did not attempt to influence state spending decisions within the block grants. These grant areas also were a small enough part of state budgets that, if the states chose to sustain program spending, they could do so without major consequences

---

*The administration originally proposed to convert AFDC into a block grant with no federal matching. Its first proposal to contain Medicaid costs was to convert the program into an incremental block grant—i.e., to limit each state's grant payments to 5 percent annual growth over the FY 1981 base. In both cases, it would have been left to state initiative to decide whether (and how) to keep program expense growth within the bounds of federal aid growth.

for all other budget categories. They therefore offer a purer test of replacement behavior under devolution.

Early studies of the states' adjustments to the block grants reported extremely little replacement.*,[17] Closer inspection of eighteen states' responses through the first two years, however, reveals a significantly different picture.† For most of the block grants most states have replaced at least part of the federal funding losses. A number of states have increased own-source spending sufficiently either to offset the entire dollar loss from federal funds or to preserve the real value of program spending in the face of both inflation and federal grant reductions. The states' block grant responses through state FY 1983 are summarized in table 7.7.

Why has the actual replacement pattern diverged so broadly from that first reported, as well as from the spending retrenchment found in the major

TABLE 7.7

STATE AND LOCAL REPLACEMENT, HEALTH AND HUMAN SERVICES BLOCK GRANTS,
STATE FY 1981– FY 1983
(Number of sample states)

Block Grant	Funding Replacement (Current dollars)			Full Replacement of Lost Federal Dollars (With adjustment for inflation)	
	Full	Partial	Zero or Negative	Yes	No
Social Services	11	4	3	3	15
Community Services	0	0	18	0	18
Maternal and Child Health	8	2	3	4	9
Preventive Health and Health Services	9	1	3	5	8
Alcohol, Drug Abuse, and Mental Health	12	2	0	5	9

SOURCE: George E. Peterson et al., *Block Grants* (Washington, D.C.: The Urban Institute Press, 1984).

NOTE: Data represent actual expenditures by states plus local governments for programs funded by predecessor categorical grants. Full sample consists of eighteen states. Data were collected by The Urban Institute, General Accounting Office, and Association of State and Territorial Health Officials. Where results are reported for fewer than eighteen states, data collection has not been completed.

---

*For example, Nathan, Doolittle, and Associates concluded, "Most of the cuts in grants to state and local governments in the sample were ratified. . . . Most states replaced less than 10 percent of the cuts." (p. 191).

†The eighteen states for which block grant adjustments were analyzed are a subset of The Urban Institute twenty-five-state monitoring sample.

social programs? For one thing, states have shared the replacement burden with local governments and with third parties. States frequently have required local providers to absorb a greater share of program costs, and these providers have done so by raising fees or by sharing in higher local taxes. The programs brought under the block grants thus have been protected from the full brunt of federal aid cutbacks, but not always in a manner that is visible from state budgets. In addition, states sometimes have been able to protect individual services (e.g., day care for children of low-income working mothers or in-home health services) by switching these programs to AFDC or Medicaid coverage, where there is open-ended federal matching assistance. Finally, since the block grants were approved by Congress so late in the federal fiscal year, many states postponed their decisions about replacement and program priorities to FY 1983. For this reason, the steps taken in FY 1982 tend to understate the final adjustments that states made.

The strength of state replacement in the block grants raises questions about our understanding of the price incentives built into categorical matching grants. For an economist, probably the most important feature of block grants is that they eliminate the price subsidy in favor of recipients' spending. The consolidation of categorical grants into block grants, therefore, should serve to restrain state and local spending from own sources. Any replacement at all can be considered surprising in the light of standard economic models.[18]

The experience with block-grant replacement carries an important lesson. Almost all federal categorical grant programs have been capped. Most states already are spending more than the amount necessary to capture the maximum federal contribution. At the margin, therefore, their spending is no longer being subsidized by federal matching incentives. For these cases, the conversion to block grants creates no new price incentives and cannot be counted on to restrain state and local program spending. An asymmetry is at work. It may well be true, as the Reagan theory of grants hypothesizes, that the categorical matching grants offered by the federal government helped induce state-local expenditure growth in the first place. But it does not follow that the process can now be arrested by reversing the grant structure. The state programs are in place. They involve expenditures beyond the federal categorical grant ceilings. The structure of price incentives for most grants cannot be altered by block granting, but requires special penalty arrangements or cost-saving incentives if they are to act as a restraint on state-local expenditure decisions.

Program Priorities under the Block Grants. A basic presumption underlying the block grants was that state program priorities had been distorted by the categorical restrictions and matching incentives built into the federal grant structure. If this presumption is true, once the categorical restrictions are removed and spending incentives neutralized, we should observe a divergence between states' new spending patterns and the patterns formerly in effect.

In the first two years of adjustment to the block grants, states gave no hint that they had a backlog of program priorities or innovations that had been suppressed by the federal grant structure. The states were cautious, even timid in setting new directions. Only one program in all the implementation experience might fairly be termed "new"—a registry of cancer patients undertaken by New York State under the Preventive Health Block Grant. Almost without exception, states restricted themselves to programs with which they had previous experience under the predecessor federal grants. Of course, this conservatism was supported by the funding cutbacks that accompanied the block grant consolidations. In a time of nearly universal funding reductions for grant-assisted programs, it became especially difficult to justify diverting funds to new enterprises.

Nonetheless, states did act to reallocate budgets under the block grants. Some generalizations can be made about the direction of movement. States have emphasized delivery of services to high-need or at-risk populations, as long as these do not have very low incidence in the overall population. Under the Social Services Block Grant, spending on child and adult protective services and adoption/foster care gained budget share at the expense of family planning and day care, even though day care services might be thought to hold the broadest voter appeal. Staff training programs were cut back once brought into budget competition with direct service provision. Under the Low-Income Energy Assistance Block Grant, states have increased the share used for energy crisis services. Many states have combined block grants to forge overall program strategies. One example of such reorientation occurred in Low-Income Energy Assistance. The majority of states, once freed from federal restrictions, cut back on household transfer payments to cover utility bills. Instead, they directed more funds into weatherization and insulation programs meant to produce savings in energy consumption. These programs had the further advantage that they could be combined with monies from the Community Development and Community Services Block Grants to provide jobs for neighborhood residents.

States used the block grants' flexibility to weed out some programs that apparently were being kept alive only by federal "force feeding." None of the states, for example, provided general replacement funds for the community action agencies, which had been set up by the federal government and had always received their funding directly from Washington. Many states would have cut back still more rapidly on funding for these agencies had they not been prevented from doing so by constraints Congress added to the Community Services Block Grant. Lead-based paint, rat control, and school desegregation programs are other examples of strictly federal programs, typically operating without state program involvement and targeted to specialized populations, which were cut back or eliminated by most states except where not permitted by the courts.

In short, states used the block grants, as the administration had hoped, to test for citizen demand for programs as well as professionals' assessment of service need. If the categorical grants chosen for consolidation were selected properly in the first place—in areas where there is indeed no appropriate national interest in state or local spending decisions—the displacement of politically unpopular programs by politically popular ones could be viewed as an unambiguous gain. However, for certain programs—conspicuously, school desegregation—for which state and local support is known to be lacking, and which have been major losers in the budget reallocations, an important national interest may be sacrificed by turning over funding decisions to state and local choice.

Administrative Efficiencies and Cost Savings. Although the block grants were rationalized, in part, on the basis of the administrative efficiencies they were expected to produce, the evidence of actual savings is meager. When able to do so, states did combine parallel lines of administration that had existed for federal and state-funded programs into a single administrative structure (as many states did for programs under the Alcohol, Drug Abuse, and Mental Health Block Grant). These changes produced some efficiency gains. Most participants, however, whether at the state or the local level, saw efficiency gains as small; approximately half the local respondents felt that state regulations were more burdensome than the federal regulations they replaced.

The greatest cost savings came not from pure efficiency gains but from the flexibility the block grants provided states to replace high-cost, high-standard (and presumably high-quality) services funded under federal grants with less expensive services and less demanding standards under state funding. State officials argued that the less expensive services were perfectly satisfactory in meeting citizen demands, and that limited budgets could be stretched further by backing away from "top-of-the-line" quality standards. The state of Texas, for example, lowered its average daily cost for day care from $10.87 to $8.15 under the new Social Services Block Grant, when it was able to drop from its requirements proposed federal standards on staff-pupil ratios and staff training requirements. As a result, it both increased the number of children in day care and decreased total day care spending. The state of Michigan substituted home-based day care for institutional day care, also reducing per-pupil costs. Whether these changes resulted in a deterioration of the quality of day care is not known, but in the eyes of state officials the block grant regulations permitted them to shift to the "economy-class" services they thought appropriate to their budget position.

In other block grants, states also acted to reduce the preferred status they believed federally funded institutions had enjoyed. Several states reduced assistance levels for formerly federally funded community mental health centers to bring their funding support into line with payments the states made to other institutions not receiving federal dollars. Budget savings typically were used to expand program coverage. Whether broader spreading of a limited budget is preferable to a concentration of resources in selected institutions is a matter of professional opinion, but the block grants assigned this decision to the states, which frequently chose to lower the cost structure of service provision and reach a wider geographical constituency.

Tax Burdens and Deficits

Thus far in this chapter, we have treated federalism as a system in which the federal government acts and state-local governments react to the national policies that have been established. For some purposes, however, it is more helpful to think of a consolidated public sector, in which both the federal government and state-local governments have roles that shift over time. This is particularly applicable to the revenue side of public budgets.

Because of the cuts in federal tax rates, most of the responsibility for incremental public sector revenue collection during the Reagan years has shifted from the federal government to states and localities. At the time the president entered office, just less than two-thirds of public revenue collection in the United States occurred at the federal level. From his inauguration through the end of 1983 (the portion of the Reagan term for which figures are available), this proportion was almost exactly reversed. Two-thirds of the growth in public sector revenues came from state and local governments.* The long-term reallocation of revenue-raising responsibilities, of course, is not as pronounced as these figures may imply. Enlargement of the state-local share has not come from a sudden surge in state-local revenue collections, but from the virtual elimination of growth in federal revenues during much of 1982 and 1983. Any serious effort to close the federal deficit will put an end to this unusual imbalance in revenue growth. Nonetheless, it is fair to

---

*Between the first quarter of 1981 and the fourth quarter of 1983, state and local own-source revenues grew by $96 billion or 30 percent, while federal revenues grew by $47 billion, or 7.6 percent.

say that during Reagan's first three years the restructuring of government responsibilities looked far more ambitious when viewed from the public revenue side of the budget than when viewed from the expenditure side.

During 1982 and 1983 state and local tax rates rose at the same time federal rates were cut. For the median-income household in the majority of a sample of twenty-seven cities, state and local tax payments climbed—sometimes sharply—as a percentage of family income between 1981 and 1983 (table 7.8). Tax increases were steepest in the industrial states hit hard by the recession. Local tax policies added to the variability of tax burdens. In this sample and in the nation as a whole, local tax increases outpaced state tax increases. Only in California and Massachusetts, where local government tax increases were constrained by Proposition 13 and Proposition 2½, respectively, did state and local tax burdens decline in relation to family income during this period.

A consolidated public sector budget also shows that state and local governments are now accumulating record surpluses at the same time the federal government compiles record-setting deficits. Unrestricted state and local surpluses (the total excluding pension funds) swung from a $2 billion deficit in the third quarter of 1982 to a $19 billion surplus in the third quarter of 1983. Total surpluses on state and local accounts now amount to roughly 30 percent of the federal deficit (figure 7.1, p. 256).

State and local governments must decide how they will bring their budgets back into approximate balance. They can choose to reduce taxes, especially those taxes that were adopted as temporary measures, or they can make new expenditure commitments. A backlog of deferred spending obligations—most conspicuously for repair and replacement of old capital facilities, and for catch-up wage increases for public employees—ensures that part of the surplus potential will find its way into higher state-local spending. States have begun to relax some of their restrictions on Medicaid, AFDC, and other social programs, as well. At this point, however, it appears that much of the state-local fiscal improvement will be used to grant tax relief.*

---

*As of March 1984, major tax rollback proposals were pending in many states. Michigan Governor James Blanchard had proposed to accelerate a $130 million income tax cut from January 1985 to October 1, 1984 if the legislature accepted his zero-increase budget. Illinois Governor James Thompson had proposed allowing $800 million in tax surcharges to expire June 30, 1984. Wisconsin Governor Anthony Earle and the state legislature were competing to set the earliest possible date for expiration of the state's 10 percent income tax surcharge. Under pressure from the state legislature, Ohio Governor Richard Celeste supported a formula that would trigger an income tax rebate. Pennsylvania Governor Richard Thornburgh proposed a $100 million cut in personal income taxes to take effect July 1, 1984 and a $92 million corporate tax reduction for January 1985. Governor Rudy Perpich of Minnesota proposed termination of the state's 10 percent income tax surcharge effective July 1, 1984.

TABLE 7.8

STATE AND LOCAL TAX ADJUSTMENTS FOR MEDIAN-INCOME HOUSEHOLDS IN TWENTY-SEVEN CITIES

		Median Income[a]	State Taxes[b] (%)	Local Taxes[c] (%)	Change, As Percentage of Income	Principal State and Local Tax Changes, 1980 to 1983
Atlanta	1980	$14,849	3.0	5.6	+1.4	1. Local sales tax rate increased from 1% to 2% in 1983. 2. The nominal and effective property tax rate was increased.
	1983	18,157	3.8	6.2		
Boston[d]	1980	17,801	4.4	6.7	−2.5	1. Proposition 2½ lowered the effective property tax rate. 2. An increase in state income tax personal exemptions and a cap on Social Security deductions.
	1983	21,833	4.5	4.1		
Buffalo	1980	16,984	4.4	6.7	+0.3	1. State income tax rates lowered for taxable income over $17,000; standard deduction and exemptions raised. 2. Effective property tax rate decreased.
	1983	20,879	5.4	6.0		
Burlington, Vt.[d]	1980	20,094	3.3	3.9	+0.3	1. Increased state income tax from 23% to 26% of federal tax. 2. Increased state sales tax from 3% to 4%.
	1983	24,949	3.8	3.7		

TABLE 7.8 *(continued)*

		Median Income[a]	State Taxes[b] (%)	Local Taxes[c] (%)	Change, As Percentage of Income	Principal State and Local Tax Changes, 1980 to 1983
Chicago	1980	19,710	3.1	5.1	+1.3	1. State income tax rate increased from 2.5% to 3% (scheduled to return to 2.5% in July 1984). 2. Local sales tax increased from 2% to 3%.
	1983	22,710	3.4	6.1		3. State sales tax will increase January 1984; food and medicine taxed at lower rate. 4. Nominal property tax rates increased.
Cleveland	1980	16,748	2.5	6.1	+1.9	1. State increase in income tax rates for high income taxpayers; 83.3% surtax in 1983; additional $80 credit or $350 personal exemption. 2. Increase in local wage tax rate from 1.5% to 2%. Additional increase proposed for February 1984.
	1983	19,150	3.5	7.0		3. Increase in state sales tax from 4% to 5%. 4. Increase in effective property tax rate.
Columbus	1980	19,493	2.6	3.9	+1.6	1. State income tax—see Cleveland #1. 2. Increase in local wage tax rate from 1.5% to 2%. 3. State sales tax—see Cleveland #3.
	1983	22,289	3.9	4.8		4. Instituted a .5% local sales tax. 5. Increased effective property tax rate.

TABLE 7.8 (continued)

		Median Income[a]	State Taxes[b] (%)	Local Taxes[c] (%)	Change, As Percentage of Income	Principal State and Local Tax Changes, 1980 to 1983
Dallas	1980	22,202	1.9	2.9	-0.2	1. Property tax millage reduction and increase in homestead exemption.
	1983	26,847	1.9	2.7		
Denver[d]	1980	21,870	3.5	4.8	+0.8	1. State income tax rates are normally indexed but were frozen at 1982 levels.
	1983	26,751	4.6	4.5		2. State sales tax rate temporarily increased to 3.5% from May 1983 to June 1984. Rate scheduled to return to 3% in July 1984.
Detroit	1980	17,129	4.0	6.1	+2.1	1. State income tax rate raised from 4.0% to 6.35% in 1983; scheduled to decrease in 1984 and 1985.
	1983	18,988	5.4	6.8		2. Local wage tax increased from 2% to 3%. 3. Effective property tax rate increased.
Houston	1980	24,656	1.8	2.9	+0.5	1. Effective property tax rate increased (despite millage reductions).
	1983	29,811	1.8	3.4		

TABLE 7.8 *(continued)*

		Median Income[a]	State Taxes[b] (%)	Local Taxes[c] (%)	Change, As Percentage of Income	Principal State and Local Tax Changes, 1980 to 1983
Jacksonville	1980	19,559	2.2	1.1	+0.5	1. State sales tax increased from 4% to 5%, offsetting assessment and millage changes; homestead exemption for the county increased from $15,000 to $25,000.
	1983	24,112	2.8	1.0		
Los Angeles	1980	21,394	3.6	3.5	-0.5	1. Local sales tax increased from 1.25% to 1.75% for the transit district. 2. Property tax under Proposition 13 restrictions; debt portion of tax declined. 3. State income tax fully indexed. 4. 1984 contingent state sales tax increase now not necessary.
	1983	24,984	3.2	3.5		
Louisville[d]	1980	16,779	4.7	3.8	+0.7	1. Local wage rate increased from 2% to 2.2%. 2. Effective property tax rate increased.
	1983	19,772	5.0	4.2		
Miami	1980	14,803	2.3	6.0	-0.8	1. Increase in state sales tax from 4% to 5%. 2. Decrease in property tax rate and increase in the homestead exemption from $15,000 to $25,000.
	1983	18,248	2.9	4.6		

TABLE 7.8 (continued)

		Median Income[a]	State Taxes[b] (%)	Local Taxes[c] (%)	Change, As Percentage of Income	Principal State and Local Tax Changes, 1980 to 1983
Milwaukee	1980	20,769	6.1	5.8	+3.8	1. State income tax is normally indexed for inflation, but brackets were temporarily frozen at 1982 levels and a 10% surtax was added.
	1983	23,342	8.7	7.0		2. State sales tax increased from 4% to 5%.
						3. Effective property tax rate increased despite decrease in mill rate.
Minneapolis[d]	1980	21,287	5.7	4.4	+1.6	1. State income tax surcharge (10%) imposed.
	1983	24,640	9.3	2.4		2. State sales tax rate increased from 4% to 6%.
						3. Decrease in effective property tax rate and an increase in the cap for the homestead credit.
Newark	1980	12,228	2.8	13.5	−1.4	1. State income tax rate raised for taxable income over $50,000.
	1983	14,936	3.2	11.7		2. State sales tax rate rose from 5% to 6%.
						3. Effective tax rate declined.
Newport News, Va.	1980	20,356	4.1	2.9	+0.2	1. Decrease in the effective property tax rate.
	1983	24,692	4.5	2.7		

TABLE 7.8 (*continued*)

		Median Income[a]	State Taxes[b] (%)	Local Taxes[c] (%)	Change, As Percentage of Income	Principal State and Local Tax Changes, 1980 to 1983
New York City	1980	18,510	4.4	7.8	+1.2	1. State income tax rates lowered for taxable income over $17,000; standard deduction and exemptions raised.
	1983	22,579	5.4	8.0		2. Surtax on local income tax. 3. City sales tax increased from 4% to 4.25%.
Philadelphia	1980	17,596	3.9	6.2	+1.4	1. State income tax rate increased from 2.2% to an effective rate of 2.45%.
	1983	19,863	4.1	7.4		2. Local wage tax increased for residents from 4.3125% to 4.96%. 3. Effective property tax rate rose.
Phoenix[d]	1980	22,221	5.2	2.4	+0.1	1. State income tax brackets were indexed beginning 1983.
	1983	26,039	5.6	2.1		2. State sales taxes increased from 4% to 5% in 1983. 3. Effective property tax rates decreased.
Portland[d], Ore.	1980	20,457	3.7	3.5	+3.4	1. Surcharge on state income tax rates for 1982–1984 period; elimination of personal exemption replaced by personal credit.
	1983	22,360	5.0	5.6		2. Effective property tax rates increased.

TABLE 7.8 (continued)

		Median Income[a]	State Taxes[b] (%)	Local Taxes[c] (%)	Change, As Percentage of Income	Principal State and Local Tax Changes, 1980 to 1983
Raleigh, N.C.	1980	23,485	4.3	2.9	+0.4	1. Effective property tax decrease despite a slight increase in nominal rates.
	1983	28,525	5.1	2.5		
San Diego	1980	22,126	3.8	3.3	−0.4	1. Property tax under Proposition 13 restrictions; debt portion of tax declined.
	1983	25,841	3.5	3.2		2. State income tax fully indexed.
						3. 1984 contingent state sales tax increase now not necessary.
Seattle	1980	23,690	3.3	4.4	+1.3	1. State sales tax rate increased from 4.5%, with food exempt from the tax, to 5.4% until March 1983 and rose again to 6.5% for the rest of the year; food was taxable during part of 1983 only.
	1983	26,763	5.4	3.6		2. Local sales taxes rose from .8% in 1980 to 1.3% and then 1.4% in 1983.
						3. Effective property tax rate fell.
St. Louis[d]	1980	16,215	3.4	5.0	+0.6	1. Local sales tax rate increased from 1.5% to 2.5%.
	1983	18,778	3.7	5.3		2. Effective property tax rate fell.

TABLE 7.8 (*continued*)

NOTE: State taxes consist of state income and sales taxes. Local taxes consist of local income, sales, and property taxes.

a. Calculations of median family income were based upon 1980 U.S. Census estimates of each city's 1979 median income. These estimates were updated using percentage changes in state per capita wage and salary disbursements. Projections of state population and state wage and salary disbursements were used for 1983 updates.

b. For state and local taxes, it was assumed that each family consisted of four persons (wage earner, spouse, and two dependents), that all income was in the form of wages or salaries, and that all income was earned within the taxing jurisdiction. Itemized deductions were used in calculating state income taxes where applicable. Where state deductions coincided with federal income tax deductions, the Internal Revenue Service's *Statistics of Income* was used to estimate relevant deductions.

State and local sales taxes were calculated using effective sales tax rates compiled in Donald Phares, *Who Pays State and Local Taxes* (Cambridge, Mass.: Oelgeschlager, Gunn and Hein Publishers, Inc., 1980). Where retail food purchases were added or subtracted from the sales tax base (Washington and Illinois), estimates of food consumption as a percentage of income were derived from the *U.S. Consumer Expenditure Survey, 1980–81* published by the U.S. Bureau of Labor Statistics. All information on state and local tax laws and regulations was obtained from state and local officials.

c. Local property taxes were based upon the U.S. Census estimates of the median-priced house in each city. These estimates were updated to 1983 using the percentage change in housing prices in metropolitan areas published by the National Association of Realtors where available. For areas where these data were unavailable, state housing price data were used.

d. Because the state allows deductions of federal income tax and/or Social Security payment liabilities from taxable income for state purposes, calculations of federal payments were made first. To calculate federal income taxes, previous year state income tax deductions were estimated using effective rates compiled by the Advisory Commission on Intergovernmental Relations, *Significant Features of Fiscal Federalism: 1980–81 Edition.* Local taxes and other deductions were calculated using data from the *Statistics of Income.*

FIGURE 7.1

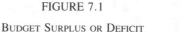

BUDGET SURPLUS OR DEFICIT
(Annual rates plotted quarterly, in $ billions)

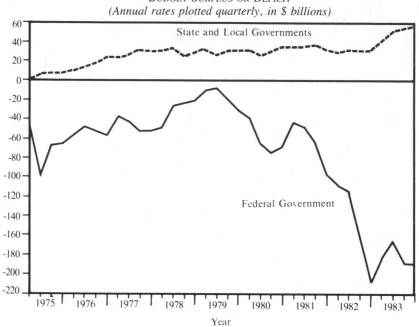

SOURCE: U.S. Department of Commerce, Bureau of Economic Analysis, National Income and
Product Accounts, *Survey of Current Business*, tables 3-2 and 3-3.

The nation now faces the likelihood that the tax pendulum will swing
back in the opposite direction from that of the first three years of Reagan's
term. In fact, the basic choices about future federal roles can be reduced to
a public choice about the ultimate disposition of the federal deficit and state-
local surplus that will materialize without policy changes. In the absence of
further federalism initiatives, the federal tax increases necessary to help close
the federal deficits will be offset in substantial degree by reductions in state
and local tax rates. If the federalism debate is renewed, however, more of
the public spending burden could be thrust on states and localities, in effect
freezing present state-local tax rates, while relieving some of the pressure on
future federal tax revenues.

Summing Up: Reagan in Perspective

Two of the most perceptive observers of intergovernmental relations,
Richard Nathan and David Beam, in their assessments of the Reagan impact

on federalism and the states, have pointed out that the rhetorical garments cloaking Reagan policies have tended to exaggerate the changes actually made. Nathan has noted that political opponents tend to overstate the impact of the budget cuts, as a means of urging resistance to them, while conservative supporters have looked to those impacts for empirical evidence of fundamental fiscal reform.[19] Beam has called attention to a parallel discrepancy between the language and the accomplishment of federalism reform: "No large-scale devolution of federal fiscal or regulatory functions has been accomplished. Indeed, once the heat of battle dissipates, it is possible that the changes that have actually emerged from Congress since 1981 will be regarded as relatively moderate, incremental adjustments to the intergovernmental system."[20]

In the context these authors intended, their conclusions of only moderate impact are appropriate. The budget cuts did not have the fundamentally disruptive effect on state and local governments that some had forecast. A formal devolution of authority over domestic policy to state and local governments, which the president has said is one of his fundamental goals for government, seems no closer today than it was in January 1982, before the president made his New Federalism address, and just as unrealistic.

To measure any president's record against his stated intentions, or against the rhetoric of his supporters, however, is to adopt an unfair standard of performance and one likely to obscure the true extent of change. Intergovernmental relations in 1984 are very different from the way Ronald Reagan found them when he took office. Not all the changes of the Reagan era, by any means, should be attributed to the president or to the administration. Some of the old trends had peaked before the president moved into the White House; others, like the public demand for spending restraint, had been felt by local and state governments long before they found expression in Washington. Still, the administration is responsible for consolidating and accelerating the change in political opinion that has so rapidly "dated" the common assumptions about intergovernmental relations of four years ago.

For a benchmark of the change that has occurred, we may turn to a thoughtful text on federalism, whose second edition was published in 1981.[21] The authors concluded the book with a discussion of the trends then in effect that would shape intergovernmental relations of the future. It is remarkable how few of these have survived the Reagan presidency.

> First, it seems safe to say that the states and localities will become even more dependent upon federal financial assistance in the next few years.

If the Reagan period in office has left any incontrovertible mark on federalism, it is reversal of the trend toward greater financial interdependence

of the different levels of government. The administration may not have succeeded in many of its attempts to eliminate intergovernmental aid programs,
or in its efforts to return responsibilities to the states, but it has succeeded
beyond reasonable expectation in resisting new commitments to intergovernmental assistance. At this point it is difficult to see how the momentum toward
greater fiscal dependence could be restored. A political consensus—stretching
beyond political party, and bridging the gap between Washington and the
states and localities—appears to have been reached that lower levels of government are better off, and the federal system healthier, when they possess
greater self-sufficiency, both in fiscal resources and in policy design.

> (T)he domestic role of the national government will increase . . . (through) the
> assumption by the national government of services previously handled on a shared
> basis (including AFDC and Medicaid).

The forecast that the federal government will take over responsibility for
income-support and health programs may yet turn out to be an accurate long-
term forecast. The obstacles lie as much in the federal budget deficit as in
ideological opposition to an expansion of the federal role. Still, any prediction
of national takeover of AFDC and Medicaid would be made far more cau-
tiously today than before the Reagan term of office. Although the administration has been unable to find a constituency for its proposals to localize
welfare responsibilities, it has enfeebled the constituency for nationalization,
creating at least a temporary equilibrium of the status quo.

This prediction reminds us that, over the long run, the fundamental
expression of Reagan's views on federalism may be his tax and budget policy.
A federal government that faces almost insuperable deficits, given its present
range of responsibilities, cannot realistically contemplate the absorption of
expensive responsibilities from other levels of government. A national government that permanently indexes its income tax revenues will (as indexing
proponents predicted) have to struggle to justify each marginal expansion in
federal functions. The restrictiveness of the federal budget constraint is likely
to force state and local governments to retain at least their present allocation
of service and financing responsibilities, and provides a recurring impetus
toward further devolution.

> A third prediction—one which we think is a very safe bet—is that the predominant
> mode of federal financial assistance will continue to be that of categorical grants.
> Every time Congress begins with a broad grant of authority, it ends up changing
> that broad grant into a series of specific grants as it receives feedback information
> on the use of funds that it finds were politically popular.

Whether the Reagan block grants will, in the end, prove more durable
than those enacted in the past remains a matter of surmise. It is clear, though,

that the politics of the grant structure are changing. The opportunities for pork barrel politics have declined as the number and importance of project grants in the grant structure have shrunk. Block grants have begun to develop a modest constituency of their own, at least among governors and state legislatures who favor them by a wide margin over the categoricals they replaced.

More importantly, the very meaning of a categorical grant is undergoing change. Several of the most important categorical grants have been restructured to remove their matching-grant incentives; some have been tailored so that, at the margin, they discourage further spending. The restrictive federal regulations that once were thought to be the inevitable accompaniment of a categorical grant have been relaxed so as to allow recipients greater flexibility in carrying out the program purposes of the grant. It is an important part of the Reagan legacy to leave an intergovernmental grant structure that is less stimulative and less restrictive than the one the president inherited.

> If ever there was a time of separated functions, . . . as the dual federalism proponents always have assumed, then those days are gone forever . . . . (W)e expect a continued development of the notion of a national community and continued acceptance of the corollary proposition that it is proper for the goals and standards of public services to be set by the national government as a basis for uniform rights of citizens.

If one were to try to give expression to the ultimate purpose behind the mechanics of the Reagan federalism and grants-in-aid proposals, he might say that the president wanted to arrest just this trend toward federal prescription of nationally uniform standards for public services. The failure of state and local governments to deliver equitable services to all of their citizens once seemed remediable only by federal assumption of the responsibility for overseeing service delivery. There are no empirical indices to measure change along this dimension of federalism, but it is an indication of the president's success in persuading the public to reconsider federalist roles that even many of those most concerned about equity in public service provision are today uneasy about vesting responsibility for uniform standard setting with the federal government.

In this respect, as in the fiscal impact of his budget actions, the president has been most effective in halting trends that, as recently as four years ago, seemed to many to be inexorable. He has had less success in articulating an alternative vision of federalism which the public will endorse, or which other political leaders and service professionals will accept as defining a reasonable role for the federal government to play in protecting the national interest in service equity.

CHAPTER 8

NONPROFIT ORGANIZATIONS
THE LOST OPPORTUNITY

Lester M. Salamon

> With the same energy that Franklin Roosevelt sought government so-
> lutions to problems, we will seek private solutions. The challenge before us
> is to find ways once again to unleash the independent spirit of the people and
> their communities. . . . Voluntarism is an essential part of our plan to give
> the government back to the people.
>
> —Ronald Reagan, October 1981

In few areas did the Reagan administration enter office with a clearer sense
of purpose than in its commitment to voluntarism and private action as a way
to respond to national needs. Yet in few areas were its concrete achievements
more difficult to discern. Committed to a new approach to public problems
stressing private initiative instead of public action, the administration never
managed to convert that commitment into a serious program of action. In the
process, it lost an important opportunity that existed in 1980 to develop an
improved partnership between government and voluntary organizations as an
alternative to purely governmental solutions to social problems.

The story of the Reagan administration's performance in the area of
private-sector initiative and voluntary action is not only important in its own
right, however. It is also important for what it can tell us about how the
administration performed where its goals were not simply to cut spending,
but to launch a program of genuine policy change. To tell the story, this
chapter first examines the nature of the opportunity facing the administration,
then reviews the administration's response, and finally analyzes the available

261

evidence on the impact of the administration's policies on private voluntary agencies.

The Opportunity

The unusual opportunity that confronted the Reagan administration in 1981 to improve the relationship between government and voluntary institutions in American life and chart a new course for dealing with the nation's social problems arose from a number of developments over the previous decade: first, widespread dissatisfaction over the perceived ineffectiveness of government programs; second, growing strains that had surfaced in relations between government and nonprofit institutions; third, increasing concerns about a decline in charitable giving; and fourth, the convergence of a useful body of knowledge to guide a major reorientation of policy along lines that the new administration would have found congenial. To put the administration's performance in context, it is useful to explore the nature of this opportunity and the background against which the administration's actions and inactions took place.

Background: The Nonprofit Sector. A useful starting point is the private, nonprofit or charitable sector, since this is the set of organizations most likely to take on the functions that government would no longer perform or perform a different way. More a legal construct than a coherent entity, the nonprofit sector formally includes the 850,000-odd entities listed on the Internal Revenue Service's Exempt Organizations Master File, plus numerous religious organizations and informal groups. These organizations are as diverse as mutual insurance companies and child care centers, college fraternities and major hospitals, art galleries and political parties, religious congregations and nursing homes. What these organizations have in common is that they are private in structure yet not profit seeking. What is more, they perform functions judged to be publicly relevant or socially desirable, on the basis of which they are exempted from federal income taxation. Twenty-six different subsections of the Internal Revenue Code are required to spell out the types of organizations that qualify for tax exemption on this basis.

To make sense of this sector, it is useful to distinguish four major types of organizations: first, those that serve primarily their own members, such as professional associations and social and recreational clubs; second, those that serve essentially sacramental religious functions, such as churches, synagogues, mosques, and other religious congregations; third, those that serve a public or charitable purpose, but do so chiefly by channeling funds to other nonprofits, such as private foundations and United Way organizations; and fourth, those that serve primarily a public or charitable purpose, direct their efforts to a broader public than only the immediate members of the organization, and provide actual services in such areas as health care, education, the arts, and others.

Of these four types of nonprofit organizations, the last is of principal concern here as it provides the clearest expression of the public purpose concept that is the ultimate rationale for tax-exempt status.* Included are hospitals, health clinics, private universities, adoption agencies, nursing homes, day-care centers, neighborhood development organizations, private elementary and secondary schools, museums, art galleries, and symphonies. Also relevant are the funding organizations, but their activities can be examined through the income they provide to the service organizations.

Private organizations of this sort have roots deep in American history. As Alexis de Tocqueville observed in the 1830s:

> Americans of all ages, all stations of life, and all types of disposition are forever forming associations. . . to give fetes, found seminaries, build churches, distribute books and send missionaries to the antipodes. . . . In every case, at the head of any new undertaking, where in France you would find the government or in England some territorial magnate, in the United States you are sure to find an association.[1]

Despite the important social, economic, and political changes that have taken place since de Tocqueville wrote, voluntary organizations continue to play a vital role in American society. Although gauging the scope of that role with any precision is difficult given the available data, some rough measure can be obtained by combining data from a variety of official and unofficial sources.† Based on Internal Revenue Service data, for example, we estimate that the charitable-service component of the nonprofit sector contains approximately

---

*The trade and social organizations are less relevant for our purposes because their services are restricted to members, and are thus not properly charitable or educational in purpose. Reflecting this, contributions to them are not tax deductible though the organizations themselves are tax-exempt. Sacramental religious organizations are also less relevant because, although they provide some services, this is not their primary purpose. Along with churches and funding organizations, this fourth group corresponds closely to what the Internal Revenue Code classifies as Section 501(c)(3) organizations, those serving charitable, educational, scientific, and related purposes. In addition to being tax exempt themselves, 501(c)(3) organizations are also eligible to receive tax-deductible contributions.

†All tax-exempt organizations except churches are required to file for tax-exempt status from the Internal Revenue Service (IRS) and to submit an annual information form, but many never do. In addition, the IRS system for classifying organizations makes it difficult to sort out the organizations that fall within the charitable-service component of the sector or to differentiate types of organizations within this component. The Census Bureau conducted a 1977 survey of exempt organizations, but the data are both out of date and imperfectly representative, since the bureau relied heavily on IRS data to generate its survey list.

375,000 formally constituted entities.* This means that there are almost five times as many nonprofit service organizations as there are special districts and units of general government in the country, and about half as many incorporated nonprofit service organizations as there are for-profit corporations in the service sector of the economy.

Drawing on a combination of government data from the Internal Revenue Service, Census Bureau, and Bureau of Labor Statistics, combined with individual subsector surveys, we estimate that this set of charitable-service nonprofit organizations had expenditures in 1980 of $114 billion and employed just over 4.6 million people. To put it another way, these organizations account for about 5 percent of the gross domestic product and about a quarter of the service employment in the nation. In some fields, nonprofits account for an even larger share of total employment—48 percent in higher education, over 50 percent in social services, close to 60 percent in hospitals. As reflected in figure 8.1, well over half of all nonprofit expenditures and employment is concentrated in the health area, primarily in hospitals. Educational organizations account for another 20 percent of both expenditures and employment, with the remaining 20 percent split among an assortment of social service, civic, and cultural institutions that together constitute more than 80 percent of the organizations in the sector.

This nonprofit charitable-service sector is both large and in a continual process of change: a recent survey we conducted of some 3,400 such organizations, exclusive of hospitals and higher educational institutions, revealed that over 60 percent had been created since 1960.† This continued vitality of the nonprofit sector has somewhat confounded conservative critics of the American version of the welfare state, who have viewed the expansion of state power as inherently antagonistic to the voluntary sector.[2] How, then, can we explain this apparent vitality? What is the function of this set of organizations and how can we account for its durability?

There is, as yet, no generally accepted theory that can satisfactorily answer these questions and explain the workings of the nonprofit sector. But there are five strands of thought that bear on the question. One stresses simple historical accident, the fact that communities came into existence in America before government emerged. Lacking government institutions to handle their collective needs, Americans turned to voluntary associations, which were thus

---

*This figure represents the number of 501(c)(3) organizations recorded on the IRS Exempt Organizations Master File, after deleting religious congregations and funding organizations.

†For details on this survey, see Michael F. Gutowski and Lester M. Salamon, *The Invisible Sector*, forthcoming.

FIGURE 8.1

THE SCOPE OF THE NONPROFIT SECTOR, 1980

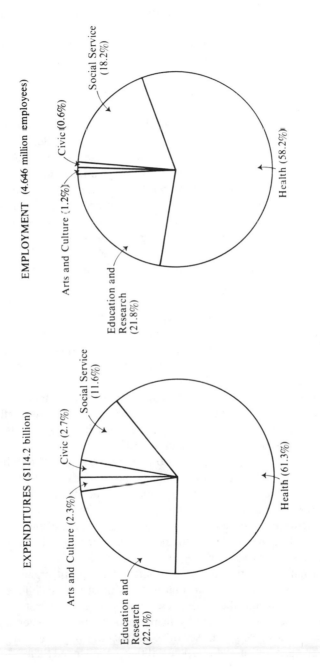

EXPENDITURES ($114.2 billion)

EMPLOYMENT (4.646 million employees)

SOURCES: Expenditure data from Lester M. Salamon and Alan J. Abramson, *The Federal Budget and the Nonprofit Sector* (Washington, D.C.: The Urban Institute Press, 1982), p. 15; employment estimates based on Bureau of Labor Statistics and Census Bureau data.

an established form when governments took shape and remained a significant presence even as government expanded.

A second school of thought focuses on the limitations of both the market and political institutions in providing the levels and types of collective goods and services that various groups within our pluralistic society consider appropriate. The limitations of the market are easy to see: the particular goods and services offered by the nonprofit sector are usually ones which the beneficiaries themselves could not afford and which require some form of collective action to be produced. But as a provider of "collective goods," the government, too, is limited by the need to generate sufficient political support for action, and by the need to make services available uniformly throughout a political jurisdiction. By contrast, nonprofit institutions provide a mechanism for producing "collective goods" considered necessary by one segment of the community even in the absence of full majority support. What is more, the nonprofit sector offers a way to target benefits more precisely, to escape the rigidities of large government bureaucracies, and to offer more personal ties to recipients. The more diverse the community, therefore, or the more entrenched the hostility to government involvement, the more extensive is nonprofit activity likely to be.[3]

A slightly different rationale for the nonprofit sector derives from what has been termed "contract failure," the fact that some goods or services either are so complex or are purchased under such conditions that consumers are unable to evaluate them effectively.[4] This is the case, for example, wherever the individual or organization footing the bill is not the one receiving the service—as is the case with welfare services or care for the aged. Nonprofit organizations have appeal in such cases because, compared with their for-profit counterparts, they presumably have fewer incentives to abuse the trust that consumers necessarily place in them.

Yet another rationale for nonprofit activity arises less from its presumed advantages in producing particular goods and services than from its presumed broader impact on the character of American society. Private, nonprofit organizations are important from this perspective because of the contribution they make to pluralism and liberty, to the preservation of multiple centers of thought and action, and thus to the potential for experimentation and for expression of multiple points of view.[5]

A final explanation of the durability of nonprofit organizations in the United States—and the explanation that has most relevance here—has to do with the relationships that have been forged between nonprofit organizations and government. Overlooked by many theorists of the "alternative-to-government" view of the private sector[6] is the peculiar way in which governments have been carrying out their responsibilities in the United States. In particular, the tremendous growth of government during recent decades has involved less the expansion of direct service delivery than the provision of funds to support the delivery of services by others. Governments at all levels have turned increasingly to a wide assortment of third parties to help them respond to public needs. The result is a pervasive pattern of "third-party government" that effectively blurs the distinctions between the public and private sectors.[7]

In some areas, this creation or use of nonprofits has been dictated by substantive programmatic considerations, such as the desire to create a community-controlled mechanism for providing services and developing leadership in the War on Poverty. In other cases, the use of nonprofits is motivated by considerations of convenience or efficiency, by the fact that nonprofits are already active in a field and able to carry out the functions government wants performed without the need to establish new government delivery systems. Finally, the funneling of public resources into the private sector is often an incidental consequence of the government's decision to preserve choice of service providers for beneficiaries of particular programs (e.g., Medicare). Whatever the specific form, the cooperation between governments at all levels and nonprofit institutions has become extensive: our estimates indicate that by 1980 federal support alone amounted to approximately $40 billion—35 percent of the total revenues of nonprofit charitable-service organizations (table 8.1). By comparison, private charitable contributions to these same organizations from individuals, foundations, and corporations, totaled approximately $22 billion.*

TABLE 8.1

NONPROFIT REVENUES FROM FEDERAL PROGRAMS, 1980

Type of Organization	Federal Support (In $ billions)	Total Expenditures (In $ billions)	Federal Support as Share of Total (Percentage)
Social Service	7.3	13.2	58
Civic	2.3	3.2	72
Education and research	5.6	25.2	22
Health care	24.9	70.0	36
Arts and culture	0.3	2.6	12
TOTAL	40.4	114.2	35

SOURCE: Lester M. Salamon and Alan J. Abramson, *The Federal Budget and the Nonprofit Sector* (Washington, D.C.: The Urban Institute Press, 1982).

*Of the remaining 45 percent of nonprofit income, approximately 5 to 10 percent came from other levels of government. The remainder came from a combination of fees and charges and earned income.

The relationships that have developed between government and nonprofit institutions make it possible to set priorities and generate resources through a democratic political process, while still leaving the actual delivery of services in the hands of private organizatons operating on a smaller scale than government agencies. But these relationships also have a number of problems, stemming in important part from the ad hoc fashion in which the relationships have been forged, with little attention to the careful demarcation of responsibilities. Concerned about accountability in the expenditure of public funds, governments often impose procedures that are administratively burdensome and threatening to the independence and informal character of nonprofits. Payment delays, underfunding of overhead costs, and other such problems further strain the relationships. Finally, considerable sensitivity can arise over who actually determines organizational purposes—the voluntary boards nominally in control or the government program managers who provide the funds.

Although these concerns have a long history in government-nonprofit relations, they intensified greatly in the 1960s and 1970s as the scope of government involvement in fields of traditional nonprofit action increased. Concerns also began to grow about the viability of the philanthropic base of the nonprofit sector. For one thing, political pressures were building to curb perceived abuses of the tax exemption accorded to charitable contributions, particularly as they applied to private foundations. At the same time, the growth of charitable giving was not keeping pace with the growth of overall personal income. Between 1969 and 1979, for example, private giving as a share of gross national product declined from 2.1 percent to 1.8 percent.[8] One reason for this has been continual liberalization of the "standard deduction," and expansion of the number of taxpayers who take the standard deduction to over 70 percent of the total. This is important because taxpayers who itemize their tax deductions, and can therefore claim a deduction for charitable contributions, tend to give more to charity than comparable taxpayers who do not itemize. The increasing use of the standard deduction may thus have dampened the growth of giving.

The 1970s: Development of Voluntary-Sector Agenda. Confronted by these challenges and prompted by the passage of the 1969 Tax Reform Act containing significant restrictions on private foundations, the nonprofit community began to organize a response. The first and most important element of this response was the formation in 1973 of a private, blue-ribbon Commission on Private Philanthropy and Public Needs chaired by John Filer, chairman of Aetna Life and Casualty Company. The Filer Commission undertook a detailed inquiry into the health and characteristics of the nation's nonprofit sector, focusing particularly on the declining base of charitable support and the growing role of government. While acknowledging the dangers that the growth of government posed to the autonomy and character of the nonprofit sector, the commission in its 1975 report urged not that public support be constrained, but that private assistance be encouraged and expanded. Accordingly, the Filer Commission called for the establishment of a permanent national commission on the nonprofit sector, the expansion of corporate philanthropy, and a series of tax changes designed to encourage charitable giving.[9]

While the Filer Commission focused on nonprofit funding, a second effort, housed at the Washington-based American Enterprise Institute for Public Policy Research (AEI), sought to redefine the role of voluntary organizations and other so-called mediating structures such as neighborhood, church, and family within the modern welfare state. Rejecting ultra-conservative hostility to government involvement in serving community needs, this "mediating structures" project developed a way to square the conservative preference for voluntary institutions with existing government-guaranteed protections for those in need. It did so by proposing a much more explicit partnership between government, voluntary organizations, and other mediating institutions, under which government would strive at a minimum to avoid harming such institutions in its policies and seek "wherever possible" to "utilize mediating structures for the realization of social purposes." Thus, for example, proposals were advanced to underwrite the activities of tenant associations in managing inner-city housing, to encourage home-based care for the aged, and to rely on existing community institutions to handle foster care. As the leaders of this project summarized the thinking behind such proposals, "We suggest that the modern welfare state is here to stay, indeed that it ought to expand the benefits it provides—but that *alternative mechanisms are possible to provide welfare-state services.*"[10]

Unfortunately, the proponents of this "mediating structures" paradigm took too little account of the extent to which existing government program structures already used mediating institutions for the realization of social purposes, emphasizing instead the ways in which government harmed such institutions. Nevertheless, by virtue of its explicit acceptance of federal welfare responsibilities and its commitment "not to revoke the New Deal but to pursue its vision in ways more compatible with democratic governance," the AEI project offered a bridge between the conservative and liberal traditions and a program of action around which a conservative president might muster liberal support.

The process of developing a private-sector agenda begun by the Filer Commission and the "mediating structures project" benefited also from two developments occurring toward the end of the decade. The first was the formation in 1979 of a major new national association, Independent Sector, intended to represent all segments of the philanthropic community—funders as well as service organizations—in national policy deliberations and to foster greater awareness of and appreciation for the role of the "third sector."* Potentially, Independent Sector provided a vehicle for mobilizing support behind voluntary action of the sort that the AEI "mediating structures" project had developed. At about the same time, the conservative Heritage Foundation produced its own analysis of the status of philanthropy in America and reached many of the same conclusions as the Filer Commission. The result was to give a conservative stamp of approval to a program of action originally formulated by a moderate-liberal coalition of business, foundation, and voluntary-agency leaders.[11]

By the time the Reagan administration took office in early 1981, therefore, the pieces were in place—both analytically and politically—for a significant redirection of national policy that could place greater reliance on voluntary organizations, rationalize government's relationships with them, and foster a more sensible partnership between government and philanthropic institutions in carrying out public purposes. A consensus had tentatively formed around four key elements of the redirection: first, increased financial support for programs that rely on "mediating institutions" to carry out public purposes; second, tax changes to encourage private charitable giving;† third, a set of management reforms to ease the burdens that existing federal programs often imposed on nonprofit providers; and fourth, increased use of challenge grants and similar devices to encourage organizations to supplement public support with private resources.

To be sure, these strands of thought had yet to coalesce into a coherent program of action. Also, voluntarism still provoked a degree of cynicism among liberals, while conservatives frequently had trouble squaring their fondness for the concept of voluntary organization with their hostility to some of the more activist neighborhood groups that had formed in the 1960s. Nevertheless, the sense of shared concern was striking, insofar as it spanned a considerable range of ideological and political persuasions, and even social and economic positions. Some of the thinking was reflected in the policy initiatives of the Carter administration—particularly in its urban policy, emphasizing as it did the need for a "new partnership" between public and

---

*This association now represents close to 500 foundations, associations of voluntary organizations (e.g., the YMCA, The Salvation Army, Catholic Charities), and corporate giving programs.

†These included provisions to soften the "pay-out" requirements facing foundations, to liberalize the treatment of charitable contributions of appreciated property, and to permit taxpayers who take the standard deduction to claim "above the line" deductions for charitable contributions. The pay-out requirement in the 1969 tax act stipulated that private foundations must pay out in grants either the full value of their earnings or 5 percent of their assets, whichever was higher.

private institutions. However, most of the ideas had hardly been tapped in any serious way. They were thus available for adoption by a new administration, particularly one committed to what the 1980 Republican platform termed the restoration of "the American spirit of voluntary service and cooperation, of private and community initiative."

The Reagan Response

Against this backdrop, the Reagan administration's handling of the nonprofit sector constitutes a significant lost opportunity. Instead of forging a new coalition in support of a positive program of cooperation between government and the voluntary sector, the administration relied primarily on exhortation and on the expected success of its economic program to suffuse the country with voluntaristic spirit. The problem, however, was that the administration's tax and budget actions had serious negative implications—apparently never clearly thought out—for the overall health of the nonprofit sector. Insofar as the administration acted at all with specific regard for this sector, the actions—chiefly establishment of a task force—must be judged tepid at best and wrong-headed at worst. Meanwhile, the administration pushed a set of administrative changes widely perceived as threatening to the nonprofit sector. Thus, the lost opportunity is at least in part attributable to the simple fact that the administration's real priorities clearly lay elsewhere, in the major program of spending cuts, tax reductions, and defense buildup. But the situation is also in part attributable to an unwillingness to face up to the complex realities that characterized existing government-nonprofit relations, exacerbated by the hostility of a few individuals in the administration to particular types of organizations. To see this, it is useful to examine briefly the three major kinds of actions the administration took that touched most directly on the voluntary sector: spending and tax action, the formation of a Presidential Task Force, and changes that occurred or were proposed in the administration of some of the government's relations with the nonprofit sector.

Spending and Tax Cuts. Although the primary motivation for the combination of spending and tax cuts embarked on in 1981 was clearly economic, the cuts came to be defended as well for the contribution they could make to the restoration of voluntarism and private action. This defense was rooted in the conservative theories mentioned earlier, which regard the growth of government as seriously jeopardizing the position of the voluntary sector by robbing it of its "functional relevance." From here it was an easy step to the conclusion that the best way to revitalize the voluntary sector was simply to get government out of the way. In this sense, spending and tax cuts would create a new opportunity for the resurgence of the voluntary sector.

The scale of the opportunity to be thus created for the philanthropic sector was quite substantial, however. In the initial budget proposed for the period FY 1982 to FY 1985, the administration would have cut federal spending in program areas in which nonprofits are active by the equivalent of $115 billion in real terms below what would have been spent had FY 1980 spending levels simply been maintained. The bulk of the cuts would have come in the fields of social services, employment and training, and housing and community development, where we projected that overall federal spending would have declined by 57 percent in real terms between FY 1980 and FY 1985.[12]

By reducing government service provision, these spending cuts promised to increase demand for the services of nonprofit organizations. Never acknowledged, however, was that they would simultaneously reduce the revenues these organizations had available to meet even the pre-existing level of demand. In particular, we estimate that by FY 1985, after adjusting for inflation, the administration's proposed reductions in federal spending would reduce the federal support to nonprofit social service organizations by 64 percent below what it was in FY 1980. For community development organizations the drop would be 65 percent, and for education and research organizations, 35 percent.[13] In addition, some of the programs most clearly oriented toward stimulating private, nonprofit action—such as the community action program, neighborhood "self-help" housing, and some of the demonstration programs under the Comprehensive Employment and Training Act—were targeted for the sharpest cuts. Under the circumstances, the administration's protestations of support for nonprofit organizations and public-private partnership came to have an exceedingly hollow ring to leaders within the philanthropic community, and the potential support within this community for the administration's efforts began to slip quickly away.

The other prong of the administration's economic recovery program—the tax cuts—also had a hidden hook for the voluntary sector. An extensive body of research has found that, among tax payers who itemize their deductions, higher tax rates are associated with a greater willingness to give to charity and lower tax rates with reduced propensities to give.[14] Because charitable contributions are tax deductible, the real "cost" of giving is the difference between what the taxpayer gives and what the taxpayer would have owed the government in the absence of the gift. For someone in the 70 percent tax bracket, for example, the net cost of giving a dollar to charity is only thirty cents, whereas for someone in the 40 percent tax bracket, the cost is sixty cents. In other words, as tax rates fall, the real cost of giving rises, and ample evidence attests that this real cost rise discourages giving.

Preoccupied as it was with the macroeconomic consequences of its tax-reduction proposals, the Reagan administration gave scant attention to these potential negative impacts on charitable giving. What is more, it opposed the proposals advanced by the philanthropic community to offset some of the potentially harmful effects by instituting an above-the-line charitable deduction for nonitemizers and liberalizing the foundation pay-out requirement—both proposals advanced by the Filer Commission and supported by Independent Sector and a broad coalition of voluntary groups. Although both measures passed over administration objections, the above-the-line charitable deduction passed only in watered-down form, with a phase-in provision, a cap, and a termination date. As a result, even after taking account of the increased income the tax act would leave private individuals, we estimated that the 1981 tax act would reduce individual charitable giving approximately $10 billion over the 1981–1984 period below what would have existed under prior law.[15]

Task Force on Private Sector Initiatives

Recognizing somewhat belatedly that a menu of spending and tax cuts hardly added up to a positive program for encouraging nonprofit action, the Reagan administration moved in late 1981 to create a Presidential Task Force on Private Sector Initiatives to "promote private sector leadership and responsibility for solving public needs, and to recommend ways of fostering greater public-private partnerships."[16] Chaired by Armco Steel President William Verity, this task force was to bring together several dozen private-sector leaders to work closely with administration officials in developing an action program. As the president put it at the end of his speech announcing the formation of the task force: "I'm not standing here passing this off to you as solely your task, and the government will wash its hands of it. We intend a partnership in which we'll be working as hard as we can with you to bring this about."

Translating this promise into action, however, turned out to be far more difficult than was initially supposed. Despite the president's apparent personal commitment to the concept, "private-sector initiatives" never caught on as a serious policy effort. Although a special White House Office for Private Sector Initiatives was established, it was more a part of the White House public relations operation than a part of its policy operation, and was at any rate divorced from the budget decision making going on in the Office of Management and Budget (OMB) and the Treasury. Nor did the task force itself ever really jell as a shaper of policy; instead, it functioned the way the White House Office did, as an outreach effort to the press, outside groups, and local officials. If the leadership either of the task force or the White House Office ever seriously addressed the theoretical and policy issues formulated by the Filer Commission, AEI, the Heritage Foundation, and Independent Sector, there is little evidence of it in the actions taken.* The major activity involved amassing a data bank of innovative private-sector initiatives and organizing counterparts to the president's task force in local communities across the country.[17] Although these efforts usefully publicized the concepts of voluntarism and private action to solve public problems, and therefore buttressed the administration's effort to change public thinking about the role of government and involve private-sector leaders in public problem solving, the tangible effects were fairly limited. *Newsweek* was thus exaggerating only in part when it pointed to the delivery of 5,000 copies of Pat Boone's record "Lend a Hand" to radio stations across the country as one of the most substantive accomplishments of the effort.[18]

Administrative Changes

Contributing further to the administration's lack of credibility as the supporter of an effective program of voluntarism and public-private partnership were a number of administrative actions that served to erode further its relations with the voluntary community. The first was the administration's decision to eliminate the government's principal vehicle for promoting community-based voluntary organization, the Community Services Administration (formerly the Office of Economic Opportunity). The second was to appoint as the head of ACTION, the government's voluntary action agency, a particularly ardent conservative who early on began an effort to stop funds from going to liberal, activist organizations. Simultaneously, as part of its budget program, the administration sought to eliminate or significantly scale back the postal subsidy for nonprofit organizations, which would have seriously hampered their direct mail fundraising efforts.

Even more significant for the voluntary sector were two further administrative developments. The first was an effort to restrict access to the federal government's annual work-place charitable drive—the Combined Federal Campaign (CFC). The largest work-place charitable solicitation in the nation, the CFC functioned from its inception in 1957 through the mid-1970s as a mechanism for raising funds for a small number of large charities, such as United Way, the Red Cross, and the American Lung Association. In the

---

*Indeed, the task force leadership pointedly rejected an offer from the American Enterprise Institute to develop a more explicit program of action built around the "mediating structures" paradigm.

1970s, however, a variety of independent charities, many of them minority run or advocacy oriented (such as the Black United Fund and Planned Parenthood), managed to secure access to the CFC, and thus challenged the dominance of the established charities. With United Way support, the Reagan administration moved to reverse this trend, developing a draft executive order that would bar from the CFC any charity that provided abortion or abortion counseling, or that engaged in lobbying or litigation on public policy issues. Leaked to the press in late 1981, this draft executive order sparked a prolonged battle between the Office of Personnel Management (which supervises the CFC) and a broad coalition of independent charitable organizations. This struggle led ultimately to issuance of a slightly revised presidential executive order in February 1983, which a U.S. District Court then declared unconstitutional. In the process, the administration added considerably to the apprehensions of the more liberal elements of the voluntary community.

Even more widespread apprehensions were created by yet another administrative move: an effort launched by the counsel of the Office of Management and Budget to rewrite the accounting principles applicable to voluntary organizations as well as to many other contractors with government. Concerned that public funds were going to support advocacy activity, OMB proposed to revise its Circular A-122, which sets guidelines for organizations that receive government support. Under the proposed revised rules, organizations that engage in "political advocacy" would have to isolate all funds and resources used for this purpose from those used to fulfill their government contracts, if the government contract represented as much as 5 percent of their budget. An organization that engaged in "political advocacy" might therefore have had to maintain separate offices and administrative structures— one for the government contract work and one for the advocacy activity. Not surprisingly, the reaction from the philanthropic community was exceedingly hostile and the administration once again found itself in the middle of an intense battle with many of the organizations that might naturally have been its allies.

Not content simply to ignore the AEI "mediating structures" agenda, the administration thus seemed determined to violate the AEI's basic principle that "public policy should cease and desist from damaging mediating structures." Whether this was conscious policy or simply the working out of the uncoordinated preferences of individual administration appointees, the cumulative effect on the voluntary sector was unmistakably chilling. As Brian O'Connell, president of the broad-based Independent Sector, pointed out in testimony before a subcommittee of the House Government Operations Committee in early 1983, the administration's combination of rhetorical support for voluntarism and budget policies hostile to the charitable sector had made many leaders of voluntary organizations "skeptical, if not cynical, about the president's interest." "Against this uneasy backdrop," O'Connell continued, the administrative changes proposed by the administration, particularly the proposed change in the rules governing political advocacy, "have changed the skepticism and cynicism to bewilderment and hostility."[19]

The Impact

Aside from the question of whether the Reagan administration failed to take actions that might have capitalized effectively on the opportunity that seemed to exist to improve the federal government's relations with the voluntary sector and to develop a new approach to coping with domestic problems, it is important to analyze the actual impact of the actions the administration did take. It is necessary to ask, in other words, not simply whether the Reagan program failed to help nonprofits but also whether it did them real damage. For this purpose, we draw on two principal bodies of data: first, an analysis of the implications for nonprofit organizations of the actual changes in federal spending approved by Congress and the president for the period between FY 1980 and FY 1984; and second, a major survey we conducted of nonprofit, human service, and arts agencies in late 1982 and early 1983 to determine how government budget cuts were affecting nonprofit agencies and how the agencies were responding.

Federal Budget Changes

In FY 1980, the federal government spent $148.3 billion on programs in fields where nonprofit organizations are active.* This figure represented slightly more than one-fourth of all federal expenditures and one-third of all nondefense expenditures. About 35 percent of these expenditures went for health services; about 25 percent for needs-tested income assistance; about 20 percent for "social welfare" (including social services, employment and training, and community development); about 15 percent for education; and the remaining 5 percent for international assistance, arts and culture, and conservation.

As a result of the Omnibus Budget and Reconciliation Act of 1981, the level of federal spending on these programs declined in real terms by about

---

*"Programs in fields where nonprofits are active" includes all programs for which changes in the funding levels are judged to have direct implications either for the demand for nonprofit services or for the revenues of nonprofit organizations. For a fuller discussion, see Salamon and Abramson, *The Federal Budget and the Nonprofit Sector*, pp. 22–25.

5 percent between FY 1980 and FY 1982 after adjusting for inflation. Excluding Medicare and Medicaid, which continued to grow, the drop was a much larger 13 percent. Following these significant reductions in FY 1982, however, Congress generally resisted the further sharp cuts in these program areas proposed by the administration for FY 1983 and FY 1984. At the same time, health care finance programs continued to grow. The result is that, by FY 1984, total federal spending on programs of relevance to nonprofit organizations was down 3 percent below FY 1980 levels with health included, and by 15 percent with health excluded (table 8.2). In short, although less extreme than the administration originally proposed, a significant reduction occurred in federal support in a variety of program areas (particularly social welfare, education, and the environment) likely to affect the demand for nonprofit services.

TABLE 8.2

CHANGES IN FEDERAL SPENDING IN FIELDS WHERE NONPROFIT ORGANIZATIONS ARE ACTIVE, FY 1984 vs. FY 1980, *(In constant 1980 dollars)*

| Program Area | Outlays (1980 $ billions) | | Percentage Change |
	FY 1980	FY 1984[a]	FY 1984 vs. FY 1980
Social welfare	28.5	18.6	−35
Social services	7.3	5.7	−22
Employment and training	10.3	4.1	−60
Community development	10.8	8.8	−19
Education and research	22.0	17.1	−22
Elementary, secondary	7.0	5.4	−23
Higher	10.4	6.9	−34
Research	4.7	4.8	+2
Health	53.0	63.2	+19
Medicare, Medicaid	49.1	60.0	+22
Health services	4.0	3.1	−23
Income assistance	36.4	37.2	+6
International aid	6.9	7.3	+4
Arts and culture	0.6	0.5	−17
Environmental	0.7	0.4	−43
TOTAL	148.3	144.2	−3
TOTAL excluding Medicare, Medicaid	99.2	84.2	−15

SOURCE: Author's calculations based on federal government data from Office of Management and Budget and Congressional Budget Office documents. Figures for FY 1984 are estimates reflecting congressional actions on the FY 1984 budget. Actual FY 1984 spending may differ as a result of changes in economic conditions, different spending rates, and supplemental appropriations.

a. In FY 1980 dollars.

The reductions just outlined had implications for nonprofit revenues, not just for service demands. In particular, if we assume that the share of each program's resources going to nonprofits in FY 1984 was roughly equivalent to the share they received in FY 1980, then the federal budget changes enacted as of the start of 1984 translate into overall reductions in nonprofit support from the federal government of between 1 and 2 percent in FY 1982 and FY 1983, and an actual increase of 3 percent in FY 1984, as noted in table 8.3. However, these figures are somewhat misleading because they largely reflect the impact of the continued growth of Medicare, and to a lesser extent Medicaid, reimbursements to hospitals. With health care excluded, the value of federal support to the remaining types of nonprofit organizations dropped an estimated 27 percent between FY 1980 and FY 1984.

Impact on Nonprofits

Whether these reductions in federal spending actually show up in the balance sheets of nonprofit organizations cannot be determined from top-down budget analysis alone. Too many other factors can intervene along the way. For example, state and local governments may have decided to offset or intensify federal cuts through their own funding decisions; local delays

TABLE 8.3

ESTIMATED CHANGES IN NONPROFIT REVENUES FROM THE FEDERAL GOVERNMENT, FY 1980 VS. FY 1984, BY TYPE OF ORGANIZATION

Type of Organization	Outlays (1980 $ billions)		Percentage Change
	FY 1980	FY 1984[a]	FY 1984 vs. FY 1980
Social services	6.5	4.2	−35
Civic	2.3	1.8	−22
Education and research	5.5	4.6	−16
Health	24.9	30.2	+21
Foreign aid	0.8	0.6	−25
Arts and culture	0.4	0.2	−50
TOTAL	40.3	41.6	+3
TOTAL, excluding Medicare, Medicaid	16.7	12.2	−27

SOURCE: Author's calculations based in part on federal government data from Office of Management and Budget and Congressional Budget Office documents. Data for FY 1984 are estimates based on congressional action in the FY 1984 budget as of the beginning of the fiscal year.

a. In FY 1980 dollars.

may have occurred in putting the cuts into effect because of ongoing contractual arrangements; the *share* of program resources going to support nonprofit service delivery rather than delivery by state or local government agencies may have changed. To gain a clear view of actual impacts, we conducted a major survey of nonprofit charitable service organizations, exclusive of hospitals and higher educational institutions, in sixteen localities across the country. The localities were selected to provide a reasonable cross section of the nation in terms of region, size, economic circumstance, urban and rural character, and philanthropic tradition.[20]

The first conclusion that emerges from this survey confirms our earlier finding that government plays a substantial role in the financing of nonprofit activities in this country. Sixty-two percent of the organizations responding to our survey reported receiving some government support in 1981, and government accounted for a significant 41.1 percent of their total revenues.* This makes government the largest single source of revenues for these organizations, with the other two major sources—fees and service charges (28 percent) and private giving (20 percent)—far behind.

The extent of reliance on government varied widely, however, among different types of agencies. In particular, mental health, legal services, and housing and community development organizations all received more than 60 percent of their total income from government in 1981, contrasted with 15 percent for arts and cultural agencies. But even among the types of agencies in which the government share of total support is smallest, the proportion of agencies receiving some government assistance was substantial. In fact, except for education (chiefly private elementary and secondary education), well over half of all the nonprofits we surveyed in every field received some government support. Government budget decisions are thus very relevant to a sizable segment of the nonprofit community, even though the impacts of the decisions vary markedly.

Between 1981 and 1982, the organizations we surveyed reported a 6.3 percent reduction in their government support (table 8.4). Among some types of agencies, however, the loss of government support was even larger: 29 percent for legal services organizations, 16 percent for housing and community development organizations, 13 percent for employment and training agencies, and 9 percent for social service organizations. By contrast, government cutbacks were far less pronounced among institutional/residential care, health,

---

*Because agencies frequently do not know which level of government is the actual source of the government funds they receive, the figures reported here are for all levels of government.

TABLE 8.4

REAL CHANGES IN NONPROFIT REVENUES AND IN SUPPORT FROM GOVERNMENT BY
TYPE, AGE, AND SIZE OF AGENCY, 1981–1982

Type of Agency	Percentage Change in Government Support	Percentage Change in Total Agency Expenditures
By Primary Service Area:		
Legal services/advocacy	−28.8	−15.5
Housing/community development	−15.6	+1.9
Employment/training	−12.7	−6.3
Social services	−8.8	−4.0
Multiple purpose	−8.1	−1.7
Education/research	−7.3	+0.6
Culture/arts/recreation	−1.3	+5.7
Health care services	−1.3	+3.3
Mental health	−0.1	+6.5
Institutional/residential care	+4.1	+4.4
By Age (year formed):		
Pre-1930	−2.6	+1.9
1930–1960	+1.3	+2.3
1961–1970	−12.7	−4.5
1971–present	−6.7	+1.5
By Size (expenditures):		
Small (under $100,000)	−1.8	+9.7
Medium ($100,000 to $1 million)	−4.9	+2.7
Large (over $1 million)	−6.7	−0.4
ALL AGENCIES	−6.3	+0.5

SOURCE: Michael Gutowski and Lester M. Salamon, *The Invisible Sector* (forthcoming).
   NOTE: In comparing the columns the reader should bear in mind that since government funds
      accounted on average for about 40 percent of total revenue for these organizations, a
      6.2 percent reduction in government support will translate into only a 2.4 percent
      reduction in total agency income.

mental health, and arts and culture agencies. In fact, the institutional/residential care institutions registered an overall increase in the value of their government support, reflecting in all likelihood the continued growth of the federal Medicaid program. When this information is combined with the data on changes in government funding by agency age (in the same table), it is clear that the reductions in government support were most marked among agencies created in the 1960s. In other words, it was the "Great Society" agencies that seem to have suffered most under the Reagan administration. These impacts are all the more notable in view of the fact that the survey was carried out in late 1982, before the full results of the federal budget changes had shown up.*

The evidence, outlined above, of the impact of government budget cuts on nonprofit agencies tells only part of the story of the consequences of this administration's policies toward the nonprofit sector. To understand the rest of it, we need to see what happened to the nongovernment sources of income for these agencies, since one of the central tenets of the administration's Economic Recovery Program was that some or all of the loss of government support could be made up through private charitable contributions.

On the surface, the evidence of overall change in nonprofit expenditures seems to support this optimistic expectation (table 8.4). In particular, although the real value of total government support to these organizations declined by about 6 percent between 1981 and 1982, overall organization expenditures increased by 0.5 percent, even after adjusting for inflation. Real increases occurred in several of the nongovernment sources of support, particularly direct individual giving, fees and charges, foundations, and corporations, all of which grew by more than 5 percent even after adjusting for inflation. Given the economic downturn that had begun when our survey was conducted, this was a notable achievement.

Examination of the absolute dollar amounts in table 8.5, however, makes it clear that the real explanation of the capacity of the nonprofit sector to close the funding gap left by federal budget cuts was not the increases that occurred in private charitable contributions. Rather, the major part of the explanation was the increase that occurred in income from fees and service charges. Almost 60 percent of the income that enabled the average agency to close the gap left by federal budget cuts and achieve a modest 0.5 percent overall real gain came from such fees, and another 6 percent came from endowment and investment income. Thus, earned income, which comprised 55 percent of the nongovernmental income of these agencies in 1981, made up 65 percent of the increase in revenues for the average agency between 1981 and 1982. Private giving from all sources, which comprised 45 percent of the nongovernmental income of these agencies in 1981, accounted for only 35 percent of the increase. In other words, the philanthropic share of agency income actually declined.[21]

Reflecting this situation, not all types of agencies were able to make up for the government cuts. In general, agencies that focus chiefly on the poor

---

*The survey results also compare 1982 agency receipts to 1981 levels rather than the 1980 levels used as a baseline for the earlier budget discussion.

TABLE 8.5

CHANGES IN REVENUE FOR THE AVERAGE NONPROFIT AGENCY, 1981–1982,
BY SOURCE

Source	Income from Source, FY 1981 (In 1981 dollars)	Change in Income from Source, 1981–1982	
		Amount (In 1981 dollars)	Percentage
Government	295,665	−18,530	−6.3
Corporations	21,639	+1,261	+5.8
Foundations	24,253	+1,262	+5.2
United Way	38,165	+712	+1.9
Religious and other federated funders	19,317	+703	+3.6
Direct individual giving	42,747	+3,387	+7.9
Fees, charges	200,001	+13,251	+6.6
Endowment, investments	32,097	+1,323	+4.1
Other	40,134	+891	+2.2
Unallocated	3,595	−599	NA
TOTAL	717,613	+3,661	+0.5

SOURCE: Gutowski and Salamon, *The Invisible Sector*.
    NA = not applicable.

and that have the least access to fee income did the worst (as is apparent from table 8.6). Thus, legal services, employment and training, social services, and multiple service agencies all had above-average reductions in government support and below-average increases in fees and charges. These agencies were also at the high end of the scale in terms of reliance on government support to start with. Although such agencies did manage to increase their private charitable support, the increases were not sufficient to recoup losses in government support. For these types of agencies, therefore, the expectations of the Economic Recovery Program clearly did not work: far from allowing these agencies the support needed to expand their services to fill the gaps left by government cutbacks, the available philanthropic support did not even allow the agencies to maintain prior levels of activity.

A quite different picture emerged for the six types of organizations that posted real increases in expenditures between 1981 and 1982 (mental health, arts and culture, institutional care, health and housing). Typically, these organizations either experienced relatively modest reductions in government support, or relied on government support less than average, or both; they also had access to above-average increases in fees and charges. The one exception is the housing and community development organizations, which started the

TABLE 8.6

CHANGES IN REAL (INFLATION-ADJUSTED) SUPPORT FOR SELECTED TYPES OF NONPROFIT ORGANIZATIONS, 1981–1982, BY SOURCE

(*Percentages*)

Type of Agency	Government	Corporations	Foundations	United Way	Religious and Other Federated Funders	Direct Individual Giving	Fees, Charges	Endowment, Investments	Other	TOTAL
Legal services	−29	+11	+3	+5	+5	+4	+19	−12	−7	−16
Employment/training	−13	+9	−29	−9	+5	+18	+1	−11	+5	−6
Social services	−9	+1	−2	+4	+3	+4	+4	−3	−6	−4
Multipurpose	−8	+25	−3	+1	+3	+7	+4	+14	−10	−2
Education/research	−7	+2	+14	−3	+7	+7	−3	−1	+5	+1
Housing, community development	−16	+19	+7	−5	+3	+50	+45	+37	+4	+2
Health care	−1	+2	+2	0	−12	−2	+7	+16	0	+3
Institutional/residential care	+4	−4	+34	+4	+11	+23	+5	+9	0	+4
Arts, culture	−1	+3	+8	+4	−2	+11	+9	+3	+5	+6
Mental health	0	+16	−6	−2	+49	−20	+29	+2	+130	+7
ALL AGENCIES	−6	+6	+5	+2	+4	+8	+7	+4	+2	+1

SOURCE: Gutowski and Salamon, *The Invisible Sector*.

period with extremely high reliance on government support, experienced sharp reductions in that support, but were nevertheless able to generate alternative sources of support from virtually all other sources. In the process, we hypothesize, they probably somewhat altered their program mix, turning to fee-generating activities such as provision of day-care services and the like.

The picture that emerges from this analysis of changes in the funding base of the nonprofit, charitable-service sector thus casts doubt on both the doomsayers and the Pollyannas. Because the federal cuts were less severe than originally proposed, because not all agencies were equally dependent on government support to start with, and because many agencies managed to increase fees and charges significantly, some types of agencies—particularly those in health-related areas and arts and culture—managed to achieve real growth in expenditures between 1981 and 1982, and to move the average for the organizations examined here slightly into the black. At the same time, however, agencies in fields where the government cutbacks were most noticeable and where access to additional fee income is limited, ended up worse off despite some real increases in private philanthropic support. Finally, although the charitable-service sector as a whole managed to hold its own between 1981 and 1982, it was not in a position to expand its services to fill in for the much larger reduction of direct government services in these fields.

Conclusion

The Reagan administration entered office with a significant opportunity to redefine the way services are delivered in the American version of the modern welfare state and to forge a new model of partnership between government agencies and voluntary groups. Both the political and intellectual roots of such a reorientation of policy had been laid in the 1970s, and a coalition of leaders in the philanthropic and nonprofit communities was eager to push this agenda along. Instead of seizing this opportunity, however, the administration was content to rely mostly on rhetoric, while putting uncritical faith in the workings of its economic program to revitalize the nonprofit sector. In the process, the administration exposed this sector to a period of considerable fiscal strain. Faced with reduced government support—and unable to cover costs from private charity—those agencies in a position to do so turned increasingly to their commercial activities, expanding their reliance on fees and charges. Agencies not in a position to pursue this course found themselves unable to sustain even prior levels of activity, let alone expand enough to meet new demands created by government retrenchment. By emphasizing the importance of private sector initiatives and voluntary action, the Reagan administration has put the philanthropic sector on the agenda of American politics in a forceful way. But by pursuing a serious assault on a broad range of domestic programs that help to sustain the sector financially, without accompanying this with a positive program of action, the administration may have set back its own private-sector agenda for some time to come and discredited voluntarism further as a serious policy alternative.

CHAPTER 9

BUSINESSES
REAGAN'S INDUSTRIAL POLICY

Perry D. Quick

A key theme of President Reagan's economic program was to restore prosperity to American business. He was not alone in his concern that, compared with past performance, U.S. industry had lost vitality. By 1980, irrespective of political affiliation, many Americans had begun to feel that businesses were losing ground and that this, in turn, was losing the United States its position of leadership in the world economy.[*,1]

Much of the thinking was concerned with developing a new "industrial policy" for government to redirect the growth of American industry, either by providing financial assistance or by increasing cooperation among government, management, and labor.[2] The Reagan administration took a completely different approach. Rejecting the notion of an industrial policy as something that "would not solve the problems faced by U.S. industry and would instead create new problems," the Reagan administration set out to remove what it saw as impediments to the working of the free market.[3]

The intellectual foundation of this free-market ideology is Adam Smith's "invisible hand," first described two centuries ago. This basic tenet of economic theory holds that—in the long run and with appropriate qualifications—individual business decisions based on maximizing profits are consistent with

---

*In fact, aggregate measures such as output and employment growth indicated that U.S. economic performance relative to the rest of the world appeared to have improved in the 1970s, and the U.S. share of world trade and world GNP stabilized in the 1970s after two decades of decline.

maximum economic efficiency and growth. But even the strongest proponents of free markets admit that the market does not always work perfectly in achieving either economic efficiency or the other social goals set by a society. While all agreed that some government intervention was necessary to achieve these broader goals, the Reagan administration felt justified in seeking a substantial reduction in government, which in turn would unshackle the efforts of business and improve the well-being of society as a whole.[4]

For this reason, the Reagan administration proposed to move to much greater reliance on the free market as the best way to restore the competitiveness of the business sector. Three major business-oriented policies would be pursued: cutting business taxes, lightening the burden of regulation, and encouraging freer trade. Businesses, however, and the way they reacted to these supply-side measures were strongly affected by the administration's macroeconomic policies, which led to a deep recession followed by a strong recovery, and a large reduction in inflation. We begin, therefore, with a discussion of the costs and benefits of macroeconomic policies for business, then turn to business taxes, regulation, and trade.

Recession, Interest Rates, and the Dollar

The short-term macroeconomic landmarks of the Reagan administration have been a recession that was longer and deeper than the typical post-World War II downturn, reduced inflation, high real interest rates, and a highly valued dollar relative to other currencies. What have been their costs and benefits to business?

Short-run Costs

Obviously, the sharp recession of 1981–1982 had painful consequences for business in the short run.

First, in sharp contrast to the normal cyclical pattern, real (inflation-adjusted) interest rates rose on balance early in the recession and remained high through the recovery.* The resulting high cost of capital had a particularly

---

*Nominal long-term interest rates, not adjusted for inflation, did in fact fall substantially during the recession. The nominal prime rate, for example, declined from 20.3 percent in the third quarter of 1981 to 14.7 percent in the third quarter of 1982. But the real prime rate (estimated as the nominal rate less the GNP deflator) rose from 10.9 percent in the third quarter of 1981 to 12 percent in early 1982, and was still as high as 11 percent by the third quarter of that year. Nominal long-term interest rates also fell over the recession, though not as sharply as nominal short-term rates. Estimations of real long-term rates are somewhat less certain that those of short-term rates, because of difficulties in estimating long-term inflation expectations. However, estimates by the author based on both survey data and past trends of inflation indicated that real long-term rates also remained unusually high during the recession.

discouraging effect on purchases, and therefore production, of consumer durables and capital goods. The high interest costs, combined with the recession-induced squeeze on sales generally, also contributed to the highest levels of bankruptcy since the Great Depression—25,000 firms failed in 1982 and 31,000 in 1983 compared with an annual average over the 1970s of fewer than 10,000.*,[5]

Second, the value of the dollar rose sharply in international exchange markets during 1981 and 1982, primarily because of high U.S. interest rates, but secondarily because investors shifted their funds into dollar assets in response to perceived increased riskiness in other parts of the world.[6] This put U.S. manufacturers at a sharp competitive disadvantage relative to foreigners in both domestic and foreign markets. And problems were compounded by the continuing worldwide recession which shrank overall demand. In previous recessions U.S. manufacturers had been able to cushion some of the impact of slackening domestic markets by maintaining or increasing sales abroad, and the nation's trade balance moved toward greater surplus. From 1980 to 1983, however, there was a sharp swing toward deficit in the merchandise trade balance, representing a shift in annual production from U.S. plants to producers overseas of roughly $40 billion—and about $50 billion for manufactured goods.[7]

Third, recent deregulation in banking and finance, transportation, and communications—which generally preceded this administration—has created a new competitive environment in these service industries. Whatever the long-term effect of these deregulatory actions, they have been accompanied in the short term by dislocation and problems of adjustment. Such problems were foreseen by industry experts. What was not foreseen was the "triple squeeze" of deregulation, the recession, and high interest rates, resulting in significantly reduced profitability, outright losses for many businesses, and worker layoffs and company failures at rates unprecedented since the Great Depression. Profits of financial services companies—banks and other depositary institutions, securities and commodities firms, insurance companies, and investment companies—fell by 75 percent from 1979 to 1982, to their lowest level (in real terms) since 1933. Bank failures increased to their highest level since 1940. Other service industries, like trucking, airlines, and railroads, showed similar patterns of reduced profits and increased failures.[8]

---

*A Small Business Administration survey of bankruptcy judges revealed that the dominant causes of failures reported to the courts in the 1981–1982 period were sharp runups in interest costs, and a cutback in credit availability from the banks, in the face of unexpected reductions in sales revenues.

Two developments—one a Reagan policy initiative, the other a structural trend independent of Reagan policy—mitigated the short-term costs of the recession to some degree. The Reagan initiative was the sharp defense buildup, which by 1982–1983 had already led to an increase in real defense purchases of roughly 10 percent ($15 billion) annually. Defense-related industrial production increased substantially as a result, even in the downturn when all other industries were in decline.* The favorable structural trend was the effect on business investment of rapid developments in communications, computation, and other equipment over the last two decades. The relatively better performance of high-technology investment during a downturn is not new, but its importance for the shape of the cycle has changed dramatically. By 1983, high-tech outlays accounted for 30 percent of total capital spending versus less than 15 percent for heavy machinery and industrial plant—reversing the relative weights of the 1960s. If this shift had not occurred, the contraction in capital outlays probably would have been over 40 percent larger—putting it among the sharpest in the post-1945 period—and the drop in durable goods production possibly 10 to 15 percent larger.[9]

On all quantitative indicators of aggregate performance, the 1981–1982 recession was bad for business in the short run. The loss would have been even greater in the absence of the defense buildup and structural changes over the last decade that made business investment—hence capital goods production—more resilient over the cycle. The 1983 rebound in production and profits, while stronger than expected given high real interest rates, roughly matched the historical pattern for recovery from a deep downturn. A different set of macroeconomic policies—easier money to keep interest rates down, and tax and expenditures policies in closer balance to keep the deficits from growing so rapidly—would still have led to recession. But the recession probably would have been milder; estimates suggest that with a different macroeconomic policy mix the loss in profits during 1981–1983 could have been over $100 billion *less* than actually occurred.†

Long-run Benefits

Despite these large short-term losses, much of the business community has continued to support the Reagan economic program. Three-fourths of

---

*If President Carter had been reelected and followed through on his proposed 5 percent real increase in defense expenditures, our estimates suggest that defense-related production would also have increased during the downturn, but probably only about one-third as much. For the detailed policy assumptions underlying this calculation, see appendix B.

†Profits after tax, current dollars, excluding inventory valuation and capital consumption adjustments. See appendix B.

over 800 executives at large and medium-sized companies surveyed in early 1984 responded that the recession had been a good thing for the country.[10] These executives cited control of inflation and the imbuing of workers and management with a more realistic sense of their competitive prospects as the major positive effects of the recession on private sector behavior. They also noted their view that the recession may have been the short-term price to be paid for putting in place a more rational federal tax and regulatory structure. Did the recession stimulate structural adjustments by managers, workers, and government that will more than compensate for short-term losses and lead to increased efficiency and greater profitability in the long run?

Economic downturns can be viewed as part of what conservative economist Joseph Schumpeter described as the process of "creative destruction" in a capitalist economy. In the period of decline, there are economic hardships leading to new production technologies and shifting consumer preferences. These drive investment out of unprofitable areas and increase productivity. Then, in the subsequent expansion, investment flows into the production of newly desired goods and services and more efficient processes, enriching the society.[11]

Preliminary evidence from the recent recession and recovery suggests such a process may be underway. Reduced wage rate increases and productivity increases combined to produce a marked slowing of growth in labor costs per unit of output. For 1973–1981, for example, U.S. labor costs per unit of output increased at an annual rate of 8.3 percent. By 1983 this had dropped to 2.5 percent. One analyst expects most of this decline to be permanent (table 9.1).[12] If this prediction is borne out, the performance of unit labor costs over the 1980s will be considerably better than that of the 1960s and 1970s. As yet, however, there is no firm evidence of a significant structural shift in either labor compensation or productivity. The decline in the growth rate of hourly wages is no more than might be expected from the recent recession, and the rate of productivity increase was actually substantially lower than the average increase in the first year of the five previous recessions (when productivity increases are typically abnormally high).* In the remainder of this section we discuss some of the important recent factors influencing labor costs and productivity and whatever structural adjustments may be occurring.

---

*The increase in productivity for the nonfarm business sector was 3.5 percent from the fourth quarter of 1982 to the fourth quarter of 1983. Average increase in productivity over the first four quarters of recovery for the preceding five recessions was 4.8 percent. See chapter 3.

TABLE 9.1

PRODUCTIVITY, LABOR COSTS, AND PRICES,
U.S. PRIVATE DOMESTIC BUSINESS ECONOMY,
SELECTED PERIODS 1948–1983, AND FORECAST 1984, 1981–1990
(Average annual percentage rates of change)

Period	Average Hourly Compensation	Product per Hour	Unit Labor Cost
Actual			
1948–1966	5.0	3.2	1.8
1967–1973	6.9	2.3	4.5
1974–1981	9.2	0.8	8.3
1982	7.8	−0.1	7.9
1983	5.2	2.6	2.5
Projected			
1984	5.5	3.0	2.5
1981–1990	5.9	2.7	3.2

SOURCE: John W. Kendrick in "The Implications of Growth Accounting Models," in Charles R. Hulten and Isabel V. Sawhill, eds., *The Legacy of Reaganomics: Prospects for Long-term Growth* (Washington, D.C.: The Urban Institute Press, 1984).

Cost Adjustments. Wage increases had shown no tendency to abate during the 1980 recession, but a marked slowdown in the rate of wage gain began in mid-1981. Even as the economy was beginning to recover in late 1982, wage settlements continued to moderate. Collective bargaining agreements omitted or scaled back regular wage increases, automatic increases to keep pace with inflation, and fringe benefits. Wage freezes or absolute reductions in 1983 were even more prevalent than in 1982 (the year of greatest economic slack). Wages and salaries increased, for both union and nonunion workers, by only 5 percent, and hourly earnings by less than 4 percent, the lowest rate since 1966.[13]

A number of factors contributed to the unwinding of the wage spiral. First, the deceleration in inflation reduced the scale of the inflation adjustments directly and also lessened pressures for catchup adjustments as workers' real wages started to rise in early 1982 after having declined since 1979. Second, the extensive unemployment raised wide concern about job security. Third, the extremely low recorded profits made it clear to all, including the workers themselves, that the shaky financial state of many companies could not withstand a sharp rise in labor costs. Fourth, these depressed conditions were sustained over a longer than usual period—from 1980 through 1982—and thus touched on most of the major union bargaining agreements (in which a three-year cycle had become the rule).[14] Fifth, the growing competition from lower-wage domestic nonunion firms and the intensified competition from foreign firms made it less and less possible for firms to pass on higher labor costs to the consumer. Sixth, government deregulation of industries such as trucking, buses, and airlines further increased the competitive environment. Finally, President Reagan's tough stance with the union of air traffic controllers may well have had its own symbolic "demonstration effect," convincing many managers and workers that when economic conditions change, excessive union pressures can, and must, be withstood.

Whether the recent wage moderation is a temporary phenomenon primarily due to the unusually long period of economic slack, or whether it represents a more fundamental change in labor management relations, remains uncertain.[15] On the one hand, some of the developments that forced the sharp reduction in wage increases over the past two years have already turned around; 1983 was a year of declining unemployment, robust economic growth, and reports of record profits for a number of companies. On the other hand, inflation is still low and certain structural changes—like the increased competition from domestic nonunion and foreign companies—remain.

Those who believe that the early 1980s are a period of transition to a new wage bargaining environment point to changes in the traditional timing and sequence of contract negotiations, to the abandonment in some cases of automatic cost-of-living adjustments, and to the breakdown of industry-wide agreements—increasing the incidence of wage bargains "custom tailored" to the specific labor cost and competitive conditions of individual firms.[16] Since the intensified competitive environment that contributed to these recent developments remains even as the economy recovers, they believe the moderation represents a structural change and will continue. But other observers suggest that the 1982–1983 changes in wage agreements are not as pervasive or fundamental. For example, the 1982–1983 agreements in autos, trucking, rubber, and other hard-hit industries—although sharply lower than their predecessors—still average roughly 5 percent, and not one has a complete wage freeze over the life of the contract. Workers in these unionized industries, except for steel and aluminum, probably will retain their wage differentials relative to nonunion and foreign workers achieved in the 1970s. Moreover, the upward pressure built in by sequences of wage increase clauses set to go into effect over the life of multiyear contracts shows only minor modification. Indeed, the recent slowdown in wage increases is little more than would be expected on the basis of historical relationships between wages and overall economic conditions.[17]

Recent changes in work rules are viewed by many business managers as potentially more permanent and far-reaching, because they allow much more flexible responses to changes in technology and the nature of international competition.[18] In steel, automobiles, rubber, meatpacking, airlines, trucking, and other major industries, for example, unions have acceded to major changes: eliminating unneeded jobs, combining craft jobs and allowing journeymen to perform helpers' duties, allowing management more flexibility in scheduling daily and weekly hours, restricting the privileges of seniority, and allowing individual workers to learn more than one job and rotate jobs among a team. If these changes persist over the longer run they can be expected to improve productivity and the competitiveness of American business.

Another widely noted business response to the combined pressures of increased competition and economic slack is management's new commitment to cost control. Reports abound of industries automating assembly lines and clerical tasks, closing down less productive lines, and introducing tighter control on inventories of materials and unsold finished goods to keep down the costs of nonproductive stocks of working capital. The latest efforts of manufacturers to become "leaner and meaner" and slash their break-even points—the level of sales at which a company can just cover its total fixed and variable costs—are widely perceived as going much farther than the cost-reduction programs that have characterized past recessions. If this is true, it could be pivotal in turning a modest recovery in output into an improved competitive position for U.S. firms and possibly a sharp expansion in short-term profits.

One positive indication that this may be happening is that inventories have been outstripping sales less in this recovery than in earlier recoveries. But there are negative indications as well. For example, total operating costs in manufacturing industries during the latest recession were reduced only about two-thirds as much as they were in the 1974–1975 recession. Moreover, nonlabor costs as a percentage of net sales rose in the 1981–1982 period at about the same rate as they had in the 1974–1975 downturn.[19]

Impediments to Adjustment. To the extent that lowered costs per unit of output reflect underlying structural changes rather than temporary cyclical phenomena, they should improve not only the short-run profitability of American industries, but also their long-run competitiveness. A recent Urban Institute survey and other surveys make it clear that in business executives' view the deterioration of America's basic industries, like steel, autos, machine tools, and rubber, was inevitable and that the Reagan policies were the "medicine we need" to make business and labor more realistic and, thus, accelerate change.* However, although management and workers recognize that adjustments must be made, the severely depressed demand and high interest rates made those adjustments more difficult and painful. Workers found it hard to locate new jobs in other industries, because until recently, few were hiring; management has found capital for improving technology and productive processes scarce and expensive. Moreover, the high purchasing power of the dollar continues to encourage U.S. companies to put their new capacity overseas.

The special characteristics of the recent cycle have also hurt the ability of our new and growing high-technology industries to sustain their international competitive edge. Credit has been scarce and expensive. In addition, the rapid rise in the dollar has given foreign industries a significant price advantage in both domestic and world markets by increasing the relative cost of U.S.-made goods and services. This competitive edge helped foreign competitors to boost output and expand their market shares.

The resulting competitive imbalance is serious enough over the short run, but it has long-term consequences as well. For some well-managed firms that previously were expanding their world market share, the long-term consequences may be fatal. For others, the currency differential has given their foreign competitors the extra margin to boost R&D investment and allow them to reduce or eliminate the previous U.S. technological advantage. More generally, business strategists studying market dynamics have shown that cumulative learning-by-doing effects and economies of scale in production, logistics, and marketing—all of which accrue to companies that gain early and extensive penetration of new markets—are important sources of long-term competitive advantage.[20] Even if the dollar falls in value, this competitive lag will remain. To the extent that the strong dollar and high interest rates have hindered development of new markets by U.S. companies, they have served to counteract the long-term effects of the policy strategies explicitly designed to help business—cutting business taxes, deregulation, and freer trade—to which we now turn.

---

*The Urban Institute conducted an informal survey of key figures in the business communities of four locales—Boston, Detroit, Richmond, and San Diego—in the late spring and early summer of 1983. For details see Marc Bendick, Jr., and Phyllis M. Levinson, "How's Business in the Reagan Era? The Perceived Impact of Federal Policies," Changing Domestic Priorities Discussion Paper (Washington, D.C.: The Urban Institute, December 1983).

Cutting Business Taxes

A major element of the administration's supply-side strategy is the assumption that long-term economic health depends on greater business investment, and that the key to stimulating such investment is to target tax benefits primarily on plant and equipment expenditures.* In pursuit of this goal, the Reagan administration focused on the tax deductions allowed for the cost of wear and tear on plant and equipment (depreciation). Depreciation allowances have always been based on the original cost at time of purchase (historic cost). But this is less than replacement in periods of rising prices because the allowances do not fully reflect the cost of new equipment. Since 1954 the tax system had allowed depreciation to be deducted at a faster rate than would have been the case if the costs were allocated over the actual useful life of the asset. However, the extra value so gained was not sufficient to compensate for the full cost of replacing the machine, because inflation in the late 1970s was more rapid than anticipated.

The need for some measure of business tax relief to counteract the effects of inflation was widely supported in 1980. One much-discussed possibility was to institute a system that adjusted allowable depreciation automatically for inflation. The Reagan administration, however, opted for further acceleration of depreciation, still based on historical cost. This increased the sensitivity of the value of allowable depreciation to the rate of inflation. Thus, although above a certain rate of inflation the allowable deduction would still be below replacement cost, at lower inflation levels the allowable deduction would actually *exceed* replacement cost.

The Size of the Reagan Tax Cut. The Accelerated Cost Recovery System that the Reagan administration advocated—as finally passed by Congress in the Economic Recovery Tax Act of 1981 (ERTA)—divided all equipment investments into only four useful-life classes (3 years, 5 years, 10 years, and 15 years, with the preponderance falling into the 5-year class).† This significantly shortened the depreciation periods for virtually all equipment. For some short-lived equipment (mostly in the 3-year class), the new pro-

---

*See chapter 3 for a discussion of the relationships between taxes, investment, productivity, and long-term economic growth.

†For a more comprehensive description of the initial development of the business tax provisions in ERTA and of alternative approaches to stimulate business investment, see Charles R. Hulten and June A. O'Neill, "Tax Policy," in John L. Palmer and Isabel V. Sawhill, eds., *The Reagan Experiment: An Examination of Economic and Social Policies under the Reagan Administration* (Washington, D.C.: The Urban Institute Press, 1982).

visions increased the investment tax credit as well.* The depreciation period for buildings and other business structures was also drastically reduced.

The new system was so generous that the value of allowable deductions and credits actually exceeded the tax liability on the income that investment in a typical piece of equipment would generate. In other words, for equipment investments the depreciation system had turned from a tax to a net subsidy, and equipment purchases provided excess deductions and credits that could be used to shelter, from tax, income from other sources.[21] The tax package also permitted investing firms with income too low to absorb all their allowable tax benefits to transfer those benefits to other firms with enough income to take advantage of them through sale-leaseback arrangements.

The massive scale of these benefits proved to be short lived. The Tax Equity and Fiscal Responsibility Act of 1982 (TEFRA), passed in response to fears of the large projected budget deficits (and in recognition of the aforementioned problem), reduced the business tax cuts substantially. Further accelerations of depreciation deductions for equipment, scheduled to go into effect in 1985 and 1986, were repealed. TEFRA also mandated that investors in equipment could not depreciate that fraction of the cost equal to half the amount of the investment tax credit (the so-called "basis adjustment"). Finally, the provision allowing firms to lease excess deductions and credits to other firms was repealed. In all, about half the business tax reduction embodied in the 1981 law was eliminated.

This still leaves a business tax burden substantially lighter for most firms than the tax structure in effect prior to ERTA. Even after the "TEFRA takeback," corporate tax liabilities were reduced by $10 billion in FY 1983 and are projected to fall by $17 billion in FY 1986 or by 16 percent relative to what they would have been prior to pre-ERTA law (table 9.2). (There are corresponding investment incentives, plus ERTA's cuts in individual tax rates, for unincorporated business.) What effects are these incentives likely to have on capital formation and the efficiency of investment allocation?

Capital Formation. The new business tax system can be expected to increase capital formation in two ways. First, it substantially reduced corporate taxes and hence raised after-tax business income. Under normal circumstances, a sizable share of such an increase in available funds would be reinvested. It is not clear, however, how effective this impetus to capital

---

*The investment tax credit allows a business to reduce its tax liability by 6 percent of purchases of equipment in the 3-year class, and 10 percent for longer-lived equipment.

TABLE 9.2

SIZE OF CORPORATE TAX CUTS DUE TO ERTA AND TEFRA

	Fiscal Years							
	1981	1982	1983	1984	1985	1986	1987	1988
$ billions	1	10	10	10	16	17	14	14
Percentage of corporate liabilities	2	20	18	14	20	19	14	14

SOURCES: Congressional Budget Office, "Baseline Budget Projections for Fiscal Years 1983–1987"; same publication for FY 1984–1988 and 1985–1989; calculations adjusted for different economic assumptions of different baselines.

formation will be, at least in the short run, because of the legacy of underutilization of capacity from the recession. In December 1983, manufacturing capacity utilization rates were still well below normal levels, and recent experience suggests that attempting to stimulate business capital formation by cutting taxes to increase cash flow for businesses with excess capacity is a bit like pushing on a string. For example, the internally generated funds of U.S. nonfinancial corporations were $30 billion more on average in 1982–1983 than in 1980–1981, but their total capital expenditures averaged $20 billion less. For the first time in two decades, internally generated funds exceeded annual capital expenditures in both 1982 and 1983. Rather than adding new capacity, businesses used the added cash to reduce their short-term borrowings and increase their holdings of financial assets, including purchases of $10 billion of U.S. government securities.[22]

The second way the tax rate affects the amount of capital demanded is through the cost of capital to its potential users, namely businesses. This user cost includes not only the interest costs of obtaining the funds, but also the return forgone by using the capital for the purpose in question rather than other purposes, the wear and tear on the capital (depreciation), and—the relevant item for this discussion—any tax burden associated with its use.

There is no doubt that ERTA, even after the TEFRA changes in 1982, substantially reduced the effective tax rate paid by business—that is, the tax rate paid on the income generated from an additional investment, taking into account all deductions and credits. (See figure 9.1 for a comparison of the statutory tax rate and the effective tax rate with ERTA and with ERTA/TEFRA.) In 1980, the effective tax rate was about 33 percent; in 1982 it had about halved (dropping to just under 16 percent). The effect of this was to reduce the marginal cost of capital to business from 17 cents on the dollar in 1980 to 16 cents on the dollar in 1982 (table 9.3).

FIGURE 5.1

STATUTORY AND EFFECTIVE MARGINAL CORPORATE TAX RATES FOR TOTAL NONRESIDENTIAL BUSINESS

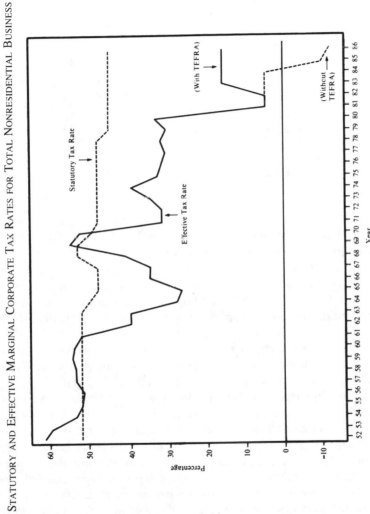

SOURCE: Charles R. Hulten and James W. Robertson, "Corporate Tax Policy and Economic Growth: An Analysis of the 1981 and 1982 Tax Acts," Changing Domestic Priorities Discussion Paper (Washington, D.C.: The Urban Institute, December 1982).

TABLE 9.3

EFFECTIVE FEDERAL CORPORATE TAX RATES AND USER COSTS OF CAPITAL,
1952–1982

Year	Tax Rate (Percentage)	Cost of Capital (Cents per dollar of investment)
1952	61.2	21.3
1955	51.8	19.3
1960	53.4	19.6
1965	26.3	16.6
1970	52.3	19.4
1975	32.1	17.2
1980	33.1	17.2
1981	4.7 (ERTA only)	15.5
1982	15.8 (ERTA/TEFRA)	15.9

SOURCE: Hulten and Robertson, "Corporate Tax Policy and Economic Growth."
  NOTE: These estimates reflect a 4 percent after-tax rate of return and (for 1981 and 1982) a
     6 percent rate of inflation.

To what degree will such a reduction actually stimulate business investment? This question has been much debated but, unfortunately, the range of possibilities still appears very wide.[23] Mid-range estimates suggest that the 8 percent reduction in user cost should raise the desired stock of business capital by 8 percent, or about $240 billion if other factors affecting investment are ignored. Reaching this higher level over a 5-year adjustment period would raise net investment about 10 percent. However, the enormous deficits (forcing government to compete in the loanable funds market with private industry) and high interest rates are having a depressing effect on business investment. As discussed in chapter 3, however, these have not offset the positive effects on investment from the tax cuts reducing the user cost of capital.

Not only the level but also the allocation of investment is important to the long-run productive capacity of American industry. The ERTA/TEFRA tax changes will also affect the distribution of business investment.

Allocation of Investment Capital. Most economists believe that for maximum efficiency the tax law should interfere as little as possible with the free-market allocation of investment among types of assets and industries. Thus, if income from capital is taxed, tax burdens on all assets should be the same, so that investment decisions are not distorted by different after-tax rates of return on assets that are in fact equally productive.

The pre-1981 tax structure had widely varying tax burdens on different forms of investment. The ERTA/TEFRA changes narrowed the range of rates somewhat, but still left a wide variation (table 9.4).

TABLE 9.4

EFFECTIVE TAX RATES ON ILLUSTRATIVE TYPES OF CORPORATE ASSETS
(Percentage)

Asset	1980 Law	ERTA/TEFRA
Office machinery, computers	−26.8	1.3[a]
Agricultural machinery	−6.8	−5.6[a]
Trucks, buses, and trailers	−4.1	.6[a]
Service industry machinery	−1.6	−2.8
Instruments	.4	−3.4
Electrical machinery	9.9	−4.7
Automobiles	10.5	−2.9
Engines and turbines	16.4	−6.4
Telephone and telegraph	34.7	35.5[a]
Inventories	35.6	35.6
Land	39.9	39.9
Industrial buildings	51.8	41.4

SOURCE: Don Fullerton and Yolanda K. Henderson, "Incentive Effects of Taxes on Income from Capital," in Hulten and Sawhill, eds., *The Legacy of Reaganomics*. The effective tax rates in this table include property taxes and personal income taxes and are based on different assumptions about inflation and after-tax rates of return from those that underlie table 9.3. The *relative* shifts are consistent, however, with those in table 9.3.

NOTE: A negative rate implies allowable tax deductions exceed expected income on investment, and the excess could be used to reduce tax liabilities from other income sources.

a. Effective tax rate increased by ERTA/TEFRA.

The major difference in tax burden under the current rate structure is between equipment considered as a class, and land, inventories, and structures. ERTA/TEFRA left rates on equipment near zero or negative. This is in contrast to rates on inventories, land, and structures of between 35 and 42 percent. It should be noted, however, that the reduction in the effective tax rate on structures influenced their user cost more than that of equipment, because depreciation is a much larger part of the user cost of structures.

Distorting differences also remain among different types of equipment, but, with minor exceptions, the spread is less than it was before the 1981 changes. Finally, the negative effective tax rates on some investments (because of the extreme acceleration of depreciation allowances, and in some cases the investment tax credit) encourage tax sheltering through investment in projects of negligible or even negative economic worth. Tax-advantaged limited partnerships registered with the Securities and Exchange Commission, for example, increased from $5.5 billion in 1982 to $8.4 billion in 1983. This growth has stimulated renewed concern in Congress over the economic distortions of the current business tax structure, as well as the burden on the tax system and the potentially deleterious effects on tax compliance more generally.[24]

Nor are the allocational distortions restricted to investment within industries. As is clear from table 9.5, they extend to investment choices among industries. Once again, such distortions existed before ERTA/TEFRA. After ERTA/TEFRA they still exist as distorting influences on long-term productive growth.

Another investment allocation issue is the new tax credit for increases in business expenditures on research and development (R&D), currently scheduled to expire in 1985. In addition to the immediate tax deductibility of such costs, which existed pre-1981, this incremental tax credit grants businesses a 25 percent tax credit of all their R&D spending in excess of the average of the previous three years. The combination, of course, provides significant net tax subsidies. As a result, reported R&D spending expanded in 1982–1983 despite the recession.[25] However, whether actual R&D spending increased, or whether the R&D tax credit simply encouraged firms to label as R&D for tax accounting purposes activities that do not add to the stock of knowledge as R&D is designed to do, is not clear.[26]

In addition to the definitional problems that may allow tax sheltering under the guise of R&D, the tax credit may discriminate in the treatment of different types of firms. For new firms, for example, no more than one-half of their expenditures on R&D is eligible for the credit; existing firms expanding into new lines of business expenditures are not eligible for the credit until they actually enter the new lines of business; and the base-period calculation eliminates the benefit for firms with ongoing research projects at a constant level of effort.

The tax credit aside, the effect of the other aspects of ERTA/TEFRA on R&D is probably negative. First, some capital particularly important to research activities is treated less favorably than under prior law; conspicuous

TABLE 9.5

EFFECTIVE CORPORATE TAX RATES FOR MAJOR SECTORS

Sector	1980 Tax Law	ERTA/TEFRA
Mining	47.9	29.9
Construction	16.2	1.9
Manufacturing	30.8	11.9
Transportation, communications, and utilities	35.0	19.9
Trade	30.1	13.2
Finance and insurance	31.4	16.4
Services	32.2	16.3

SOURCE: Hulten and Robertson, "Corporate Tax Policy."
   NOTE: Effective corporate tax rates assume a 4 percent after-tax rate of return and 6 percent rate of inflation for ERTA/TEFRA.

among the classes of equipment whose effective tax rates were increased by ERTA/TEFRA are computers, as shown in table 9.4. High-technology firms also tend to pay generally higher taxes than do "smokestack" firms. This happens because the latter generate a higher proportion of their total income through investments in depreciable capital, which is heavily benefited by accelerated depreciation and the investment credit. High-technology firms make more intensive use of knowledge and computer software that are not so benefited.[27]

In sum, the business tax cuts in ERTA, even after the partial reversal in TEFRA, add significantly to corporate cash flow; they reduce effective tax rates and, therefore, the cost of capital for many types of assets. This can increase demand for investment capital substantially, as long as capacity utilization is reasonably high and interest rates low enough so that their effect on user cost does not counteract the beneficial effects of ERTA/TEFRA. The efficiency of that investment, however, is not likely to improve significantly because there remains considerable variation in tax treatment of assets of different types. Finally, although the tax credit for R&D expenditures may encourage additional research to some degree, federal revenues are also lost to the extent that other activities are called R&D only for purposes of the credit. In addition, it is possible that the effect on R&D of the ERTA/TEFRA provisions as a whole may be negative because some capital particularly important to research has relatively high tax rates, and because high-technology firms make relatively minor use of depreciable capital.

Lightening the Burden of Regulation

In addition to a strong philosophical aversion to intrusion by government into private markets, the Reagan administration assigned major importance to "a dramatic, substantial *rescission* of the regulatory burden" as necessary to improve the performance of American business.* Sweeping regulatory relief was seen as a significant means to stimulate production by reducing costs and improving cash flow in the short run, and to improve productivity in the long run.[28] What improvements did President Reagan's regulatory initiative achieve, and what were its costs?

In addressing this question it is useful to distinguish between economic and social regulation, because they have different goals and presented different opportunities and problems for the Reagan administration.

---

*This section draws heavily on George C. Eads and Michael Fix, eds., *Relief or Reform? Reagan's Regulatory Dilemma* (Washington, D.C.: The Urban Institute Press, 1984).

Economic regulation typically attempts to control the conditions of entry and prices in specific markets in order to ensure that they are economically efficient. For markets that work tolerably well in achieving economically efficient outcomes, elimination of excessive regulation is an appropriate goal, and current thinking is that competition is more robust and less easy to thwart than was previously understood. Social regulation, in contrast, attempts to achieve broad social goals like a cleaner environment and safer work places. Elimination of social regulation (in other words, relying exclusively on the market) cannot be expected always to achieve these goals. The benefit-cost calculus for society as a whole is more complex in this case and much less likely to be captured by business decisions on profitability. Each will be discussed in turn.

Economic Deregulation

Economic deregulation is obviously consistent with the Reagan administration's *laissez-faire* philosophy. Much of the impetus for such deregulation was built up in the 1970s, however, and as a result, many of the legislative, administrative, and legal changes were made in the years shortly before President Reagan took office; other recent ones were the result of court action initiated before 1981.* The Reagan administration has had only a minor role in continuing this momentum for deregulation. Two initiatives passed during the Reagan years, for example, are deregulation of buses in 1982 and some deregulation of financial institutions.[29] However, the area of "economic" regulation where the administration is perceived to have had the greatest impact is antitrust.

The last fifteen years have seen the erosion of many of the theoretical underpinnings of traditional antitrust. Current economic and legal thinking, for example, no longer automatically equates bigness with badness, or concentrated markets with excess profits.[30] In addition, there are theoretical reasons, and practical evidence, to indicate that cartels and other clandestine forms of price fixing are inherently unstable and do not achieve the goals of their participants over any length of time. These new trends in economic regulatory thinking have led to an increasing bipartisan consensus that the appropriate role for antitrust policy in our technologically complex and increasingly internationalized economy is to promote competition and efficiency

---

*Examples of action predating the Reagan years include the Securities and Exchange Commission action to end the cartel that was setting stockbrokers' commissions in 1975; congressional action to deregulate airlines in 1978 and trucking and railroads in 1980, and to approve the phaseout of deposit interest rate ceilings in 1980.

through a more flexible approach tailored to the circumstances of each case. Three examples show how this administration consolidated these trends.

First, the trend against breaking up monopolies on the automatic assumption that monopoly itself conferred inappropriate market power began in the 1960s. In the later 1960s and early 1970s the Justice Department's Antitrust Division brought a number of cases against large firms holding significant market positions. The most prominent one was against IBM. But by the late 1970s the value of taking action against the large monopoly was increasingly being called into question. The IBM case had become the relic of an earlier age, and the Reagan administration moved swifly to settle it.

Second, the administration's increased willingness to allow mergers also builds on previous experience. Companies seeking to merge have always been able to go to the Antitrust Division for internal advice. Ten years ago, for example, when British Petroleum wanted to buy out Sohio, they availed themselves of the antitrust review process. The division under President Reagan has been even more accommodating in working with companies considering merger, so as to ensure that their plans are consistent with antitrust law. The advice given under the Reagan administration has become more precise and innovative, and has more detailed applicability to the specific circumstances. In early 1984, for example, the assistant attorney general for antitrust offered to conduct industrywide discussion among U.S. steel manufacturers to find ways to shrink and rationalize excess domestic steel capacity in order to make U.S. steel more competitive in world markets. As a result of the administration's attitude, the number of mergers seems to be increasing. In 1983, for example, the number of mergers completed or pending was more than it had been in a decade; there were several consolidations among major oil companies and the Federal Trade Commission approved a joint production and marketing venture between the world's No. 1 and No. 3 automakers (General Motors and Toyota). In 1984 the Antitrust Division approved the merger of the third and fourth largest domestic steel manufacturers (Republic and LTV).

Third, the salutary trend toward reducing the uncertainty created by antitrust advisory opinions not having the weight of law also predates the Reagan administration and has bipartisan support. The two major business areas where the uncertainty is particularly constraining are joint R&D ventures, and products that compete in an international market. With respect to R&D, the Carter administration developed and published guidelines for joint venture activities. The Reagan administration refined these guidelines and has backed legislation to reduce the antitrust liability of such activities if fully disclosed. This legislation is supported by members of both parties in Congress, and passage of some variant is expected in 1984. With respect to export-related activity, the Export Trading Company Act of 1982 (initiated by Democratic Senator Adlai Stevenson, Jr., in 1981) has already reduced potential damages from a private suit from triple damages to actual damages plus court costs.

Social Deregulation

Social deregulation, in sharp contrast to economic deregulation, was specifically a Reagan initiative—indeed, a conspicuous and highly publicized part of the new administration's agenda. The initial Reagan program had seven major elements, all aimed at administrative and organizational changes that would deliver, or at least appear to deliver, quick relief from social regulation.*

Considerable movement did indeed take place during the first year of the Reagan administration, and did result in a number of impacts. In particular, the halt to major new regulatory initiatives added a measure of perceived stability to the business environment. This stability may be more important to business than was the easing of existing regulations, which had already forced regulated industries to incur the necessary compliance costs, and whose rescission was complicated by judicial reversals. As one respondent to our survey put it: "Reagan has at least quit going in the other direction."

Beyond this welcome arresting of new regulatory initiatives, business was the beneficiary of a wide range of other regulatory actions taken by the administration. One of the most notable has been in the realm of enforcement. The Occupational Safety and Health Administration (OSHA), for example, has restricted the discretion of field enforcement personnel with respect to site violations, given them strong incentives not to issue citations that are likely to be challenged, and ordered them to target their inspections more narrowly on firms with high recorded rates of injuries. Beyond these changes, the clear direction of new enforcement policy is to have personnel perform the role of "consultants" rather than "cops," in an effort to create a new environment of cooperation between the agency and regulated firms.

Another area of change has been standard setting. Probusiness shifts in this area include the simple elimination of regulations that promised to impose

---

*The seven were formulation of a cabinet-level Task Force on Regulatory Relief, headed by Vice President Bush; immediate suspension of nearly 200 regulations promulgated just as Carter left office (the "midnight regulations"); imposition of a rigid cost-benefit standard by which all existing and proposed rules were to be judged; appointment of agency heads sympathetic to the President's regulatory values; budget and personnel reductions on a substantial scale within federal regulatory agencies and departments; dismissal or settlement of antitrust actions against parties formerly believed to be in violation of federal laws; and transfer of substantial regulatory authority to state or local governments.

substantial costs on industry. An example is the rescission of the National Highway Traffic Safety Administration's (NHTSA) regulations requiring that new automobiles install passive restraints. In other areas the administration attempted to write more flexible regulations which provided compliance cost savings to industry. The Securities Exchange Commission, for example, promulgated regulations which permitted delayed or sequential sale of individual securities without requiring disclosure with each sale.

The administration failed notably, however, to achieve fundamental changes in the legislative framework of social regulation. Not one of the important pieces of social regulatory legislation was successfully altered, even though several (such as the Clean Air and Clean Water Acts) came up for reauthorization during the administration's first year. By early into the second year, increasing political controversy fueled by the personalities of major appointees and growing resentment in Congress to the administration's new oversight processes and agencies' rulemaking and enforcement policies—put increasing constraints on further action in the social deregulation area. By August 1983, regulatory relief appeared to have ground to a halt as the President's task force disbanded, claiming victory and announcing that its work was done.* What were the benefits and possible costs to business of the actions that were taken?

Benefits. The economic benefits of social deregulation are reductions in the direct costs of compliance with the regulations (resources required to achieve the air, water, health, and other standards specified); the costs of enforcement (resources to monitor whether the standards are being met and, if not, sanctioning procedures and further monitoring to ensure compliance); and the more intangible costs of management time and attention.

Empirical studies that have attempted to quantify the economic costs of regulation vary widely in quality and in their underlying assumptions. They generally indicate that the total resources devoted annually to regulatory enforcement and compliance during the 1970s were as high as 2 to 4 percent of the gross national product. This translates into regulatory costs that are substantial as a share of total business costs. For example, the share of investment devoted to antipollution equipment in iron and steel and other metals industries exceeded 20 percent through the late 1970s, although it has been declining since that time (figure 9.2). Evidence suggests that as much as 10 to 25 percent of the slowdown in productivity growth in the late 1970s may have been attributable to such regulation.[31]

---

*See chapter 5 for further discussion.

FIGURE 9.2

POLLUTION ABATEMENT AS A PERCENTAGE OF TOTAL NEW PLANT AND EQUIPMENT
EXPENDITURES

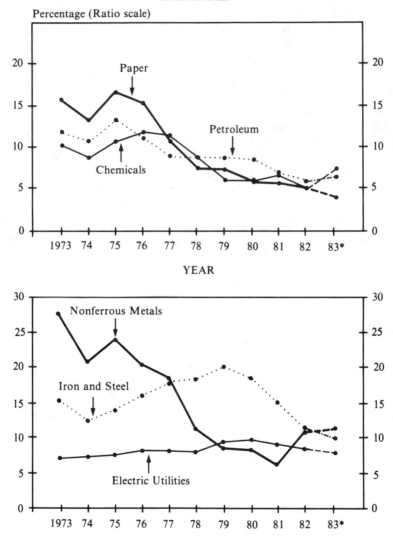

*Planned

SOURCE: George C. Eads and Michael Fix, *Relief or Reform? Reagan's Regulatory Dilemma*
(Washington, D.C.: The Urban Institute Press, 1984).

Somewhat in contrast to this, our survey of business executives suggests that although they find complying with regulations annoying and time consuming, in most instances they do not believe (at least in the early 1980s) that regulations reduce profitability substantially. There are two probable reasons for this attitude. First, much of the cost can be passed on to consumers in higher prices. Second, by the early 1980s business had been taking steps to comply with social regulation for some years, so that the drain on productive resources had diminished considerably. The latter phenomenon probably explains the administration's failure to generate industry support for its proposed revision of the Occupational Safety and Health Administration's cotton dust regulations, for example. At issue was whether OSHA would require plantwide engineering controls to protect textile workers from the effects of cotton dust or would call for the less expensive option of requiring that workers wear individual respirators. Since 80 percent of the mills covered by the regulations had already installed the required control equipment—and because the controls were increasing productivity and improving employee health—regulatory relief proved to be a largely empty box. Indeed, some businesses actually opposed revision, because it revived issues they thought were dealt with already.

Our survey also indicates that businesses tend to discount the potential impact of regulatory relief. There seems to be an abiding belief that regulations are "just a fact of life." In addition, business managers were reportedly skeptical—with great perspicacity as it turned out—that Reagan could quickly undo the major regulations without congressional support.

The most detailed accounting of the savings from regulatory relief during the Reagan administration is that provided in the August 1983 final report of the task force. This report claims one-time savings for American consumers and business of $15 to $17 billion and annually recurring savings of $13 to $14 billion. Roughly two-thirds of the savings were said to accrue to business from the "modification and rescission of unnecessary existing regulation."

Evidence strongly suggests, however, that the effect of much of this claimed saving to business was questionable at best, for several reasons. Some items carried with them (uncounted) increased business costs; some items were savings to one type of business but (uncounted) costs to another; some items were the savings associated with regulations already reversed by the courts or never seriously considered for implementation; and some items were savings to state and local governments rather than to business.[32] Table 9.6 lists some of the task force's most seriously questionable items, which add up to about two-thirds of the total claimed.

TABLE 9.6

Selected Questionable Claims of Business Relief from the President's
Task Force on Regulatory Relief as They Apply to Business

	One-Time Savings (in $ millions)	Annual Recurring Savings (in $ millions)
Total claimed cost savings as a result of "Completed Regulatory Reforms"	15,150– 17,200	13,525– 13,855
Questionable business sector benefits		
Items predominantly composed of transfers among businesses or between businesses and consumers		
Deregulation of interest rate ceilings: (OCC, FRB, FDIC, FHLBB)[a]	6,200	3,600
Equal pension benefits for men and women (DOL) not applied retroactively	—	1,500
Permitting lighter bumper standard (DOT)	*	300
Emissions standards for auto industry paint shops (EPA)	75	—
Rescissions or regulations never seriously considered for implementation		
Passive restraints and automatic seat belts (DOT)	535	1,000
Dual definition of source in application of emissions trading to non-attainment areas (EPA)[b]	1,300	—
Rescissions of regulations proposed but never implemented		
Low tire pressure warnings (DOT)	—	130
Prohibition of use of multi-piece rims on trucks (DOT)	300	75
Mandatory onboard technology for control of HC emissions (EPA)	103	240
Items where savings accrue to state and local governments, not business		
Bilingual education requirements (HHS)	900–2,950	70–155
Regulations implementing block grants (HUD)	—	52
Minimum wage rates: federally supported prevailing wage: Davis-Bacon	—	585
Accessibility of public transportation to handicapped Section 504 of the Rehabilitation Act (DOT)	2,200	—
Regional clearance procedures for federal grant proposals/awards from local governments: Circular A-95 (OMB)	—	50

Note: Based on claimed costs savings from the Report of the President's Task Force on Regulatory Relief, August 1983.

a. The savings from interest deregulation were acknowledged by the administration as not accruing to businesses, but there was no acknowledgment that this increased business costs.

b. On appeal to the Supreme Court as of March 1984.

An example of a claimed savings to consumers that carried with it possible uncounted business costs is the action of the National Highway Traffic Safety Administration in lowering the requirement that an automobile bumper withstand an impact at 5 miles per hour to one at 2.5 miles per hour. Reducing the bumper standards decreased the initial cost of the auto and reduced fuel costs for consumers. But expected increases in insurance and maintenance costs were, by some estimates, at least as much as these reductions, if not more. If the cost increases more than offset the savings so that the total cost of owning and operating an automobile rose, fewer automobiles would be bought. Depending on the reduction in demand, the net impact on producers could be negative.

A similar uncounted business consequence involves the largest single item claimed—the one-time savings of $6.2 million and recurring savings of $3.6 million a year from eliminating deposit interest ceilings. These carried with them, of course, commensurate costs to banks, which now have to pay more for their funds and will pass on at least some of these costs to business borrowers.

Given that additional items are questionable to varying degrees, the actual savings to business from the administration's deregulation efforts in this area are clearly modest. The extent to which even these modest savings can be expected to translate into productivity gains, as resources used for compliance are shifted into production of measured goods and services, is unclear. One analysis has calculated the expected improvement in productivity if the reduction in the annual regulatory burden within five years were $7 billion to $10 billion, and finds that, if these savings are fully realized, annual productivity improvements in the business sector could be as much as 0.2 percentage point.[33] Such an improvement would raise the annual growth in productivity from its current 3.0 percent to 3.2 percent. The long-run significance of this already optimistic estimate is further reduced because a given set of actions will produce only a temporary boost to productivity growth. Additional boosts will come only to the extent that new relief actions are taken. Furthermore, even the regulatory actions already taken may not yield their full potential benefit. Until (and unless) they are codified, many will remain politically, and to some degree legally, vulnerable.

Costs. The potential direct cost to business of reduced social regulation is primarily lost labor from sickness or injury due to unhealthy or unsafe work places. If there has been such an effect, it is too small to be discernible in the statistics. The potential indirect cost to business of the social deregulation efforts under Reagan, however, may be larger.

Social regulation, to the extent that it is effective, generates important benefits to society at large. Air becomes cleaner, water becomes purer, and so on, with attendant effects on health and well-being. The task force's final report stated that the business savings had been gained at no cost in public benefits forgone, and the evidence on this point, though fragmentary, does not support the notion that substantial short-run harm has been done.* However, whether fairly or not, Congress and the public apparently believe that some harm has already been done, and that more potential for future harm is embodied in these policies. This belief has led to a substantial political backlash, which raises the possibility of reversals of the actual cost reductions generated, as well as more stringent, more rigid, more costly regulations in the future. This may be the ultimate real cost to business of the Reagan deregulation efforts.

Our current set of social regulations is unsatisfactory by almost anyone's standards. But the experience of the Reagan administration shows that the public does not equate reform with a total rollback of the regulatory system. In addition, failure to address the legislation that provides the basis for social regulation has made the administrative changes vulnerable to reversal in the courts. Effective reform requires building the expertise and information to permit cost-effective progress, and the political will to work for legislative reform. As a recent study of Reagan's regulatory program notes about the Reagan administration's social deregulation initiative:

> One of the great ironies of the Reagan regulatory relief program is that. . .the debate over regulation has regressed from a productive concern with finding more effective regulatory instruments to an old and somewhat tired debate over goals. In the end...it is likely to be viewed as a costly, time-consuming, and ultimately unnecessary detour on the road to regulatory reform.[34]

International Trade

Just as each of his predecessors since World War II had come into office with free trade as a basic policy goal, President Reagan espoused a strong commitment to liberal trade policy ideals.[35] But given his consistently articulated *laissez-faire* philosophy, there was an expectation that his actions in support of free trade would be stronger and more consistent than those of other presidents. Looking back at the last four years, however, makes it clear that the Reagan administration has followed previous administrations in this policy area with a sharp break between its rhetoric and its actions.[36]

The administration came the closest to adhering to its free-trade objectives by taking action early in its term to reduce export disincentives embodied in

---

*See chapter 5.

U.S. law. For example, the 1981 ERTA legislation eased the tax burdens on Americans working abroad. Other actions in pursuit of freer trade, taken in 1982–1983, included reducing barriers against imports of nonrubber footwear from Korea and Taiwan, fighting against "domestic content" legislation for the automobile industry, and rejecting relief action against Japanese makers of machine tools.

But most other actions moved in the other direction. The administration, for example, pressured the Japanese into "voluntarily" limiting auto exports to the United States for three years and then pushed to extend the limits for a fourth year; reintroduced sugar quotas; extended the Multifiber Agreement and tightened the quotas under it; and adopted combinations of tariff increases and quota restrictions for motorcycles, specialty steel, textiles, pasta, and other products.*,[37] Nor are things likely to improve. Several domestic industries, including carbon steel, machine tools, copper, ferroalloys, and shoes, filed new claims for import relief in 1984—an election year, when administrations have historically been particularly susceptible to protectionist pressure.

What happened to the administration's free-trade initiative? The answer includes several forces which, taken together, produced pressures that would have been extremely difficult for any administration to withstand.

First, structural problems in a number of prominent, labor-intensive, unionized industries (steel, automobiles, textiles) had been building up for more than a decade. These industries had been describing their need for protection as temporary—to allow them an opportunity to return to their fundamentally strong position. And, indeed, their public statements in 1981 were still couched in terms of temporary problems. As the Reagan administration got further into its term, however, the long-term structural nature of their plight was increasingly recognized and pressure for broader, more permanent forms of protection mounted.

Second, a new element of pressure was added by the high-tech industries, which had previously been enthusiastic supporters of free trade, but were beginnning to have second thoughts as they encountered pressure from foreign competition for the first time.

Third, there was an increasing public presumption, partially supported by facts, that only the United States was playing fair. If other countries were engaging in unfair trade practices, U.S. industry should be allowed to retaliate.

---

*In the case of automobiles, the particular approach to import relief—quotas on total number of vehicles without further specification—added to the long-term competitive problems of domestic companies. It induced the Japanese to shift their U.S. sales into the bigger, more expensive, and more profitable midsize markets, where U.S. companies had previously been dominant, and thus put more pressure on domestic companies' profits.

There were two aspects to this pressure. The industries in long-term structural trouble used this argument to push long-term protection (e.g., against the European Economic Community's steel exports). Industries like electronics, in contrast, which still perceived potential benefits from trade, wanted to use threats of protection in order to force the opening of markets abroad.

Finally, the recession and the overvalued dollar intensified all these pressures. Companies like Boeing, which had been consistent lobbyists for free trade, finally began to change position as they lost market share for the first time—mainly because of the U.S.-foreign cost differentials produced by the high dollar.

Would the policies of another administration have been different? The answer is probably not much, at least along the dimensions so far discussed. As indicated in chapter 3, a plausibly different economic policy—with easier money and tighter fiscal policy to keep the deficits down—would have produced a somewhat milder recession, and a somewhat more reasonably valued dollar. But the underlying structural problems in U.S. industry—and, therefore, the intense political pressures—would still have been substantial. In addition, another president would in all likelihood have been considerably more beholden to labor, and therefore more vulnerable to protectionist pressure from highly unionized industries like steel and automobiles. A second Carter administration, judging from actions of the first one, would probably have bargained somewhat harder for fundamental restructuring in return for trade relief, but also would probably have been more willing to expand export subsidies.

One facet of the Reagan administration's policy is affecting trade in a way that is almost certainly very different from what would have happened under another administration. The influence of national security on international trade is much greater than under previous administrations. A conspicuous example of this increased priority, and the consequences of its heavy-handed implementation, is the decision to ban exports to Soviet-bloc countries of high-technology equipment for the Soviet-European pipeline and other purposes. Since the United States failed to coordinate the ban with other exporting countries, the primary effect of the ban was to lose sales in the short term to European and Japanese competitors. It also may have hurt the competitive position of U.S. firms in the long term by casting them as potentially unreliable suppliers, and damaged the U.S. government's reputation and bargaining power generally in international markets. President Reagan's March 1984 decision to increase the Defense Department's role in reviewing export licenses for high-technology products to non-Communist countries with a record of allowing diversions to Soviet-bloc nations indicates that the influence of national security considerations on trade policy is likely to continue.

Conclusion: Are Businesses Better Off?

Ronald Reagan's program was designed to change more than the raw quantitative economic factors affecting business health and vitality. He also sought a psychological impact on individual decision makers. He wanted a program to "break the cycle of negative expectations . . . renew optimism and confidence, and rekindle the nation's entrepreneurial instincts and capabilities."[38]

From the standpoint of the business executives, the administration appears to have delivered on its promise to change business perceptions. Our survey of selected business executives across the country found great praise for the Reagan administration for being "probusiness" and for creating a more positive environment in which to conduct business. This general sense of "a more hospitable climate under Reagan" was expressed even by interviewees who were critical of the administration's handling of particular issues.

There is little doubt that business was and still is skeptical of the more extreme claims of supply-side economics. But executives generally support the tax cuts, believe the administration has cut business regulation and eased environmental standards, and expect the president—*in his second term*—to restore U.S. business competitiveness with Japan and Western Europe and to preside over a sustained economic recovery that is not followed by sharply rising inflation.[39]

What can be said about the accuracy of these impressions? The uncertain effects of Reagan's economic program on the long-term growth of the economy are discussed in chapter 3. With respect to the business sector in particular, the evidence reviewed in this chapter suggests the following effects of Reagan's industrial policy:

- Greater wage and work flexibility from workers induced by the recession, if sustained, could cut costs and improve profits and competitiveness. There is considerable question, however, about the extent to which moderation in wage growth reflects a permanent structural change and therefore will continue, or whether it will begin to erode as the economy moves toward full employment. Moreover, actual reductions in nonlabor costs may not have been as extensive as recent reports about "leaner and meaner" management seem to imply.

- The long and deep recession, combined with high interest rates and the rise in the dollar that severely depressed overseas sales by U.S. firms, could put American companies at a long-term competitive disadvantage relative to foreign companies in industries where learning-curve dynamics and economies of scale in production, logistics, and marketing are important.

- Reductions in business taxes will improve profits and encourage greater investment in plant, equipment, and R&D, which should lead to greater business productivity. The prospects are, however, somewhat clouded by continuing tax distortions in the allocation of investment because of differential tax treatment.

- In antitrust policy, the administration has continued the trend already under way of treating corporate size and market share more flexibly, in line with the emerging needs of a highly complex and increasingly internationalized economy.

- The economic benefits of relief from social regulation are not nearly as great as initially anticipated by the administration, nor are they as large as the benefits claimed in 1983. But the reductions in social regulation that did take place can be expected to give a one-time boost to productivity, and the slowing of the growth of regulation may represent an important source of stability for business planning.

- In trade policy, the administration's rhetoric diverged sharply from its trade-specific actions, which showed no sharp divergence from the pattern of past administrations. Structural problems, the perceived unfair practices of foreign firms, and the short-term devastating impact of the high dollar and high interest rates have overwhelmed any potential progress by pressuring the administration into a number of protectionist decisions. But an alternative administration probably would have done no better, and could have done worse.

Thus, except in the psychological sphere, whose effects on performance cannot be known for years to come, this list adds up to a somewhat qualified success.

And the biggest qualification—how the problem of massive overhanging deficits is to be resolved—will have important implications for business. If there is some attempt to deal with the deficits, the long-term outlook for interest rates will be improved, although business almost certainly will be targeted for further cutbacks in tax benefits. If the administration and Congress allow the massive deficits to continue, the outlook is bleaker. Should the Federal Reserve continue its commitment to tight money, businesses will be forced to bear the consequences of continued high interest rates and an overvalued dollar. Should the Federal Reserve increase money growth to bring down short-term interest rates and the value of the dollar, business profitability and competitiveness might improve in the short term, but the inflation spiral almost certainly would be rekindled.

CHAPTER 10

FAMILY INCOMES
GAINERS AND LOSERS

Marilyn Moon
Isabel V. Sawhill

On October 28, 1980 candidate Reagan posed his now famous question: "Ask yourself, are you better off than you were four years ago?"[1] It was the right question to put to the public at the time. From late 1977 to early 1980, the polls had shown that Americans believed their financial situation was deteriorating although the facts on what happened to average family income do not wholly support this impression.*

Something new also surfaced in the polls of the late 1970s. During previous periods of perceived economic decline, Americans had always expressed optimism about the future, believing that things would get better. During the late 1970s, in contrast, pollsters found a pessimism about the future that had not been expressed before. President Carter attributed this pessimism to "a national malaise"; others linked it to a decade of accelerating inflation.[2]

Whatever the causes of this earlier pessimism about the future, it has all but disappeared in the last few years.[3] Americans are particularly optimistic about the financial prospects for their children. In late 1983, 65 percent of those polled said they expect their children to do better than they have,

---

*If the Consumer Price Index (CPI) is used to measure inflation over the period, then average real income per family was lower in 1980 than it was in 1976. But if the Personal Consumption Expenditure (PCE) deflator is used, then average income was higher in 1980 than it was in 1976. However, the PCE deflator is a better measure of actual changes in real income over this period, since the CPI exaggerated the increase in housing costs (and was corrected in 1983).

317

compared with 47 percent who expressed this view when Reagan was inaugurated.

Views about the last few years, however, are more mixed. In late 1983, just over two-fifths of those asked whether they felt better or worse off than they were when President Reagan took office said they felt worse off—perhaps in response to the effects of the 1981–1982 recession, during which many families had members whose real wages were reduced or who lost their jobs altogether. But almost another two-fifths said they were better off—perhaps because those who kept their jobs were able to reap the benefits of both the Reagan tax cuts and the drop in inflation.

One last finding from the polls is noteworthy. There is a growing perception on the part of the public that the Reagan administration has not been evenhanded in its treatment of different income groups. When Reagan took office, 64 percent of the public said that Reagan cared equally about serving all people. By December 1983 this figure had dropped to 35 percent. Over half of those polled at the end of 1983 thought that Reagan favored the rich over the middle class and the poor. An equally high proportion thought that cutbacks in federal spending for social programs had created serious hardship.

This chapter examines family income trends over the last four years in order to assess the extent to which people are better off or worse off financially since Reagan took office. How much of any change in people's incomes is the result of the Reagan administration's policies, and how much would have occurred no matter who was president? Who has gained and who has lost? The chapter also examines projected trends over the rest of the decade to see whether the prevailing optimism about the future is justified.

Changes in the Level and Distribution of Income, 1980–1984

The past four years have been marked by significant changes in the level, and especially the distribution, of family incomes. We first examine changes in the level of family incomes to determine the extent to which people, on average, are better off. We then look at changes in the distribution of income to discover who has gained or lost in relative terms. We measure a family's economic well-being by looking at how much its members can buy. For this reason, we focus on real disposable income, that is, family income after taxes and adjusted for inflation.*

The Level of Income

On the eve of President Reagan's inauguration, families had an average real disposable income of $20,333. By 1984 this figure had risen to $21,038. Over the 1980–1984 period as a whole, therefore, average income will have increased by about $700, or 3.5 percent.[4] However, because 1980 was a recession year, the level of real disposable income per family was still below its 1979 peak. Moreover, by historical standards this represents a relatively modest gain, compared with average four-year gains of 5.1 percent in the 1970s and 11.3 percent in the 1960s.

We focus on 1980 and 1984 in this chapter; however, important changes occurred in the intervening years. Average incomes declined by $900 from 1980 to 1982 and then rose by $1,600 from 1982 to 1984. The lower average incomes in 1981 and 1982 were the result of the high rates of unemployment, reductions in hours worked, and lower earnings per hour that prevailed during the recession.

The Distribution of Income

Averages, of course, conceal important differences in how various families fared over the 1980–1984 period. A useful way to examine these differences is to divide families into five groups of equal size (quintiles or fifths), ranked from lowest to highest according to their incomes. If all families had equal real disposable incomes, each one-fifth of the population would have one-fifth of the income. As it was, in 1980 the bottom quintile received 6.8 percent of total income, and the top quintile received 37.0 percent.

---

*All figures are expressed in 1982 dollars. Our numbers differ from official Census income figures in that they include the value of Food Stamps, which are practically equivalent to cash, and exclude the taxes that directly affect families and individuals. Moreover, since Census data are not yet available for 1984, our estimates of income for that year are projections using The Urban Institute household income model. These projections are consistent with administration economic forecasts.

We concentrate on families in this chapter, rather than including persons who live alone—"unrelated individuals" as they are called by the Census Bureau. Unrelated individuals have much lower incomes than families do (their average income in 1984 was only $10,398). Since they also have lower consumption needs, analyzing them together with families would distort the profile of economic well-being by overweighting the low-income end of the scale.

From 1980 to 1984, the typical middle class family's income rose from $18,857 to $19,034 or by about 1 percent (figure 10.1).* The average income of the poorest one-fifth of all families declined from $6,913 to $6,391, or by nearly 8 percent, whereas the average income of the most affluent one-fifth increased from $37,618 to $40,888, or by nearly 9 percent. These changes have caused the distribution of income to become more unequal.

Quintile income shares typically have varied little over time. Even concerted efforts to assist the poor or tax away the incomes of the rich have been followed by only gradual and modest changes in the proportion of income received by each quintile. From 1960 to 1979, for example, the share of total income going to the bottom quintile increased by only 0.5 percentage points even though expenditures on government benefit programs directed at those families rose rapidly. (See appendix A, table A.4.)

Since 1980, however, there has been quite a large change in quintile shares for a four-year period (see table 10.1). Families at the top of the income distribution have gained substantially; those in the bottom two quintiles have actually lost all the ground they had gained over the two preceding decades. The share of total family income received by the bottom quintile fell by 0.7 percentage points. In contrast, the share of total family income received by families in the top quintile rose by 1.9 percentage points. This 1.9 percentage point increase may not at first glance seem very large, but it represents a transfer of disposable income to the top quintile from other income groups of $25 billion overall and translates into an extra $2,000 per family for this group. The net result, of course, is that disparities between the incomes of poorer families and those of more affluent families grew markedly over the 1980–1984 period.

The Effects of Policy Changes, 1980–1984

To what extent are these changes in the level and distribution of income attributable to policies that President Reagan put in place, and to what extent would they have occurred whoever was in the White House? This section isolates the impacts of changes in federal benefit programs, taxes, and macroeconomic policy from the impacts of other influences on family income from 1980 to 1984. As we will show, Reagan policies had less influence on the level of family income than they did on its distribution, and even here

---

*The 3.5 percent gain in average incomes cited earlier is based on changes in the *mean* income for all families and, as such, gives more weight to higher-income families than it does to lower-income families.

FIGURE 10.1

PERCENTAGE CHANGE IN REAL DISPOSABLE INCOME FOR FAMILIES, 1980–1984

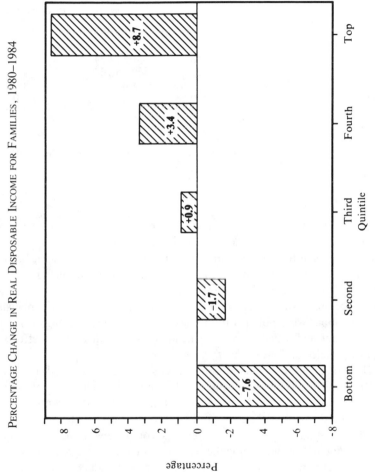

SOURCE: Urban Institute household income model.

TABLE 10.1

REAL DISPOSABLE INCOME BY QUINTILE, 1980 AND 1984
(In 1982 dollars)

	1980		1984	
Quintile	Average Disposable Income	Percentage Share	Average Disposable Income	Percentage Share
Bottom	6,913	6.8	6,391	6.1
Second	13,391	13.2	13,163	12.5
Third	18,857	18.5	19,034	18.1
Fourth	24,886	24.5	25,724	24.5
Top	37,618	37.0	40,880	38.9
All families	20,333	100.0	21,038	100.0

SOURCE: Urban Institute household income model.

other factors were operating that would have led to growing inequality no matter who was president.

A Comparative Benchmark

In order to assess the effects of Reagan policies on family income, one must choose an appropriate benchmark for comparison. It is not appropriate simply to compare the situation in 1984 with the situation in 1980, because the world would not have stood still, nor incomes remained unchanged, had Ronald Reagan not been elected president. Although what would have happened under another administration is unknowable, we make some plausible judgments about what policies might have been pursued if Reagan had not been president and use these as a benchmark for estimating the effects of Reagan's policies on family income.*

The benchmark we have chosen is discussed at greater length in chapter 3 and in appendix B. Several aspects of it are relevant to this discussion. First, since any other administration would undoubtedly have proposed fewer cuts in social program spending, our alternative scenario has federal domestic expenditures continuing to grow largely in accordance with the program legislation and guidelines governing them in 1980. (The major exception is Social Security benefits which we assume would have been reduced no matter who had been president because of the need to protect the solvency of the system.)

---

*We estimate the effects of these policy alternatives with two widely used and well-respected models: the Data Resources Incorporated (DRI) quarterly model (also discussed in chapter 3) and The Urban Institute's Census-based household income model. As with any model based on survey data, the estimates we derive are subject to possible error.

Second, we assume a more moderate defense build-up than has taken place under Reagan. Third, since there was strong bipartisan support in 1980 for some form of tax relief, our alternative scenario retains the personal income tax rates in effect in 1980, but adjusts them fully for inflation starting in October 1981 (when the Reagan tax cuts went into effect). This results in lower taxes than would have occurred with no change in tax law but is a much more modest reduction than the Reagan cuts we examine.

This combination of expenditure and tax policies implies a balanced high-employment budget and a less stimulative fiscal policy; thus the burden of fighting inflation would have fallen less heavily upon the Federal Reserve Board, which could then have pursued a more expansionary monetary policy. The results of the particular monetary policy we assume for comparison would have been lower interest rates and a milder recession, with less reduction in inflation but more growth in the economy over the 1980–1984 period. By 1984 the unemployment rate would have been 1.4 percentage points lower and the inflation rate, 1.5 percentage points higher.

With this benchmark as a point of comparison, we now examine the effects of changes in macroeconomic policy, benefit programs, and taxes on the level and distribution of income from 1980 to 1984. At the end of this section we combine the separate effects into an overall appraisal.

Effects of Macroeconomic Policy

Of all the factors that cause the average family's income to rise or fall over time, changes in the performance of the economy are likely to be the most important for the simple reason that earnings are the major source of income for most families. We estimate that the deeper recession under Reagan policies caused average real disposable family income in 1984 to be $780, or about 4 percent, lower than it would have been under our alternative set of macroeconomic policies. The family income losses associated with Reagan policies during the intervening years—1981, 1982, and 1983—are larger, totaling about $1,800 over the three years.* Although inflation is lower under Reagan policies, even after adjusting for this fact, families are worse off in every year than they would have been under our alternative set of economic policies.

With the stronger economy produced by these policies, the distribution of *earned* income would also be more equal than it is under Reagan. However, stronger growth increases disparities between those without earnings (mainly

---

*See table 3.2 in chapter 3. The per person figures shown there have been adjusted to put them on a per family basis.

the elderly and female-headed families) and those with earnings (mainly husband-wife families) and thus has a slightly disequalizing effect on the overall distribution of income across all types of families in 1984.

Effects of Changes in Federal Benefit Programs

Federal benefit payments—both cash payments, such as AFDC and Social Security, and in-kind transfers, such as Food Stamps and Medicaid—totaled $317 billion (almost half of total federal outlays in FY 1981) before the first round of Reagan budget cuts were enacted. Since then such payments have risen slightly in real terms. But they are about 7 percent lower than what they would have been for FY 1984 if the Reagan budget cuts had not been enacted.[5]

Because these programs provide most of their benefits to those in the bottom two quintiles of the income distribution, and because programs targeting assistance to low-income families (such as AFDC) were cut back more than those serving families irrespective of income (such as Social Security), the net impact of the cuts has been to widen disparities in economic well-being (see table 10.2). Including in-kind as well as cash benefits, the program cuts range from almost 8 percent of income for households with less than $10,000 in annual income to less than 0.2 percent of income for households with more than $40,000 in annual income.* If Congress had acted affirmatively on all the president's budget proposals, the increase in inequality resulting from the program cutbacks would have been even greater, since relative to what was enacted, the *proposed* benefit reductions were more than twice as large and also more heavily concentrated on low-income assistance programs. Moreover, our focus here on the effects of program cuts by broad income groups masks the fact that families actually experiencing the benefit cuts—particularly working AFDC families and the long-term unemployed—suffered much larger reductions in benefits as a proportion of their income.†

Effects of Changes in Taxes

Unlike the program cuts, which served mainly to reduce the incomes of poorer families, the personal income tax cuts served mainly to raise the after-tax incomes of more affluent families. The primary vehicle for this was an equal percentage reduction in tax rates for all taxpayers. But since personal

---

*Note that we have shifted from families to households (families plus unrelated individuals) because the data in table 10.2 are only available on a household basis.

†The proposed and enacted cutbacks and their effects on beneficiaries are discussed in detail in chapter 6.

TABLE 10.2

REDUCTION IN BENEFIT PAYMENTS PER HOUSEHOLD IN FISCAL YEAR 1984
(*In 1982 dollars*)

	Household Income					
	Less than $10,000	*$10,000– 20,000*	*$20,000– 40,000*	*$40,000– 80,000*	*$80,000 or More*	*All Households*
Cash benefits[a]						
Reductions (in dollars)	217	154	67	41	85	112
Reductions as a percentage of household income	4.3	1.0	0.2	0.1	b	0.5
In-kind benefits[c]						
Reductions (in dollars)	158	84	46	56	46	84
Reductions as a percentage of household income	3.2	0.6	0.2	0.1	b	0.4
Total benefits						
Reductions (in dollars)	375	238	113	97	131	196
Reductions as a percentage of household income[d]	7.5	1.6	0.4	0.2	b	0.8

SOURCE: Congressional Budget Office figures and authors' calculations.
a. Includes Social Security, Railroad Retirement, Civil Service Retirement, Veterans' Compensation, Veterans' pensions, SSI, Unemployment Insurance, AFDC, and Low Income Energy Assistance. This category also includes a positive increase through the Federal Supplemental Compensation Program for the Unemployed.
b. Less than 0.1 percent.
c. Includes Food Stamps, Child Nutrition, Guaranteed Student Loans, Student Financial Assistance, Medicare, Medicaid, and Housing Assistance.
d. Totals sometimes differ from the component parts because of rounding error.

income taxes are a higher proportion of the income of more affluent families, the effect of such an across-the-board tax cut is to provide more relief to these families than to poorer ones.

This disequalizing effect was further strengthened by several other provisions in the 1981 tax act. First, the top rate on unearned income was reduced from 70 percent to 50 percent. This also had the effect of reducing the maximum rate on capital gains (a form of income received predominantly by the affluent) from 28 percent to 20 percent. Second, a special deduction for two-earner couples was introduced. Third, no adjustment for inflation over the 1980–1984 period was made in the standard deduction (now called the zero bracket amount), personal exemptions, or the earned income tax credit. Thus, the real value of these tax offsets was eroded through the period, and this erosion was relatively more important for lower-income families, who do not itemize and for whom such deductions and exemptions constitute a relatively large share of income.

The result of the Reagan cuts in federal personal income taxes was to increase average disposable income in 1984 by nearly 4 percent, in comparison with what it would have been under our alternative of an indexed tax system.* The effect, however, varies by quintile (see table 10.3). For the bottom quintile, there is essentially no tax cut at all, but as income increases, the size of the tax cut increases. The typical middle-class family's tax cut increased their after-tax income by 2.8 percent, and the top quintile's tax cut increased their disposable income by almost 6 percent.†

TABLE 10.3

AVERAGE REDUCTION IN TAX LIABILITIES PER FAMILY IN 1984 AS A RESULT OF THE
1981 TAX CUT
(In 1982 dollars)

| | Quintile | | | | | All |
	Bottom	Second	Third	Fourth	Top	Families
Reductions (in dollars)	3	185	529	1,019	2,429	829
Reductions as a percentage of 1984 disposable income	a	1.4	2.8	4.0	5.9	3.9

SOURCE: Urban Institute household income model.
  a. Less than 0.1 percent

*Under this alternative, the average federal personal income tax burden would have risen from nearly 14 percent of pretax income in 1980 to over 16 percent in 1984. The reason for the increase is that there was still considerable inflation in 1980 and 1981 before our alternative indexed system goes into effect. Inflation raises money incomes and moves families *with the same real incomes* into higher tax brackets—a phenomenon known as "bracket creep." Under the Reagan tax cuts, in contrast, the federal personal income tax burden declined to 13.4 percent in 1984 (see table 10.4).

†If we compared actual tax liabilities in 1984 with the liabilities that would have occurred with *no change* in tax law over the 1980–1984 period, the distributional pattern of the Reagan tax cuts would be much the same but the cuts would be larger in absolute size.

Other tax changes enacted in 1981 and 1982 but not included in table 10.3 undoubtedly would have widened disparities in income and wealth even further. These include the sizable tax cuts for business (see chapter 9), the liberalized treatment of Individual Retirement Accounts (IRAs), and the reductions in gift and inheritance taxes.

By sharply cutting federal personal income taxes in 1981, President Reagan hoped to reduce the overall tax burdens of Americans. However, his intentions were thwarted. Even though *federal personal income tax* liabilities as a percentage of income decreased from 1980 to 1984, *the total tax burden* actually increased slightly from 25.9 percent to 26.3 percent (see table 10.4). The reasons for this increase are threefold. First, payroll taxes rose as a result of the Social Security amendments of 1977 and 1983, passed by Congress in order to finance continuing federal obligations for health care and pensions for the aged and disabled. Second, inflation and economic growth, though modest, continued to push some people into higher tax brackets. (As we noted earlier, the effects of inflation were particularly serious for lower-income families because of the eroding value of exemptions and deductions, and this erosion explains why their federal personal income tax burden actually rose.) Third, state and local tax burdens increased somewhat, as the declining economy and reductions in federal aid forced these lower levels of government to increase sales, property, and income taxes to prevent large declines in service levels.*

As a result of all these tax changes, the burden of paying for government has shifted slightly from higher-income taxpayers to lower-income taxpayers. The bottom 40 percent of families are paying proportionally more of their income in taxes, with most of the increased burden falling on the poorest 20 percent of families, whereas the top 60 percent are paying proportionally less of their income in taxes.†

The Contribution of Reagan Policies

We come now to the bottom line: what effect have President Reagan's economic, spending, and tax policies taken together had on the level and distribution of income? We have shown that his economic policies substantially reduced average incomes (by about 4 percent). His spending policies reduced average incomes only a little (the effects are hardly discernible in

---

*See chapter 7 for further discussion and data on state and local tax increases.

†While this is true for the top three quintiles as a whole, as table 10.4 shows, tax burdens declined for the third and fourth quintiles and rose for the top quintile.

TABLE 10.4

TAX BURDENS FOR FAMILIES BY QUINTILE OF PRETAX INCOME, 1980 AND 1984
(Percentage of pretax income)

	Bottom		Second		Third		Fourth		Top		All Families	
	1980	1984	1980	1984	1980	1984	1980	1984	1980	1984	1980	1984
Federal income taxes	0.5	1.2	6.3	6.0	10.5	9.4	14.0	12.6	19.5	18.9	13.9	13.4
Federal payroll taxes	3.2	3.7	4.6	5.2	5.3	5.8	5.3	5.9	4.5	5.0	4.8	5.3
State and local taxes	7.4	7.5	6.4	6.8	6.8	7.1	7.2	7.4	7.7	8.2	7.2	7.6
All taxes	11.1	12.4	17.4	17.9	22.6	22.3	26.5	25.9	31.6	32.1	25.9	26.3

SOURCE: Urban Institute household income model.

the data for all families).* In contrast, President Reagan's tax policies increased disposable incomes by about as much as his economic policies reduced them. The net effect of all these changes is a very slight reduction in real disposable income for all families of about 0.5 percent for the 1980–1984 period (see table 10.5).

Put a little differently, in real terms, actual incomes grew by 3.5 percent, on average, from 1980 to 1984. Under our alternative policy scenario they would have grown by 4.0 percent. Thus, the net effect attributable to all of Reagan's policies is a reduction of 0.5 percent, as shown in table 10.5.

This modest overall impact is a combination of more substantial changes in the incomes of families at different points in the income distribution. As might be expected given the disequalizing nature of the Reagan spending and tax cuts, Reagan policies contributed to a substantial increase in income inequality. Only those in the top quintile benefited from Reagan policies. All other families lost ground, and the ones in the bottom quintile were hurt most of all.

TABLE 10.5

CONTRIBUTION OF REAGAN POLICIES TO CHANGES IN THE LEVEL AND DISTRIBUTION
OF REAL DISPOSABLE FAMILY INCOME, 1980–1984
(In 1982 dollars)

| | Quintile | | | | | All |
	Bottom	Second	Third	Fourth	Top	Families
Percentage change since 1980	−7.6	−1.7	0.9	3.4	8.7	3.5
Percentage change since 1980 under alternative policy scenario	−3.5	1.3	2.6	4.0	7.1	4.0
Difference attributable to Reagan policies	−4.1	−3.0	−1.7	−0.6	1.6	−0.5

SOURCE: Urban Institute household income model.

*The effects of only two of the benefit programs included in table 10.2 (AFDC and Food Stamps) show up in table 10.5 as a difference resulting from Reagan policies. The effects of the Social Security amendments of 1983 are not attributed to Reagan policies. The other noncash programs are not included at all in our measure of income. The major omissions here are Medicaid and Medicare. It is inappropriate to include them in a distributional analysis if the medical benefits from employer-paid health insurance (for which there are no good data) are not also included. Also, there are conceptual difficulties in valuing the worth of in-kind benefits to people.

The benefit cuts included in table 10.5 reduce the disposable incomes of families in the bottom quintile by less than 2 percent, and above the second quintile the effect is negligible.

An equally important finding is that only some of the increase in income inequality from 1980 to 1984 is the result of President Reagan's policies. As table 10.5 shows, under our alternative policy scenario the bottom quintile would still have lost ground, although not by nearly as much. There would still have been growing disparities between upper-middle and lower-middle income families. And most of the improvement for the top group would still have taken place.

Several other factors probably increased income inequality over this period. First, the real value of welfare benefits per recipient has been eroding for some time because states have not adjusted them for inflation, and this erosion presumably would have continued whoever was president. Second, demographic changes have had an adverse impact on the distribution of income. The proportion of both female-headed families and two-earner husband-wife families in the population is rising; since the former group is concentrated at the bottom of the distribution and the latter at the top, their greater numbers contribute to greater inequality.* Third, interest, rent, and dividend income, which flows mostly to higher-income households, increased by 11 percent from 1980 to 1984 (compared with a 3.5 percent increase for all income). This increase was partly due to Reagan policies, but it may also reflect such factors as a rise in interest income associated with financial deregulation. Fourth, and perhaps most important, the early 1980s has been a period of high unemployment by historical standards, much of which would have occurred even under our alternative scenario. Such periods tend to generate increased income inequality among families with members in the labor market.[6] There are two reasons for this. Those at the bottom are the most likely to experience unemployment; and slow growth creates few opportunities for the young, the disadvantaged, and those displaced by changing patterns of trade and technology to find jobs and to advance in the labor market.

Fifth, our estimates did not measure the effects of every policy change attributable to the Reagan administration. Examples of influences not included that might tend to increase income inequality are the cuts in taxes on savings and business incomes; shifts in regulatory policy, such as less stringent enforcement of equal employment opportunity regulations or stricter review of disability cases; and actions taken by state governments and nonprofit organizations in response to the recession and federal cutbacks. Many of these actions do not affect a family's cash income directly (e.g., day care, health care, family counseling), but some do (e.g., state changes in unemployment benefits). Indeed, all the evidence reviewed in this book suggests that a fuller

---

*See appendix A, table A.5.

accounting of changes in family economic welfare would show that over the 1980–1984 period, Reagan policies have increased the degree of inequality in family economic well-being—broadly defined to include services as well as money incomes—by more than we have been able to capture here.

The changes in policies discussed in this section may create incentives that eventually change people's behavior in significant ways. For example, there could be more savings or greater labor force participation in response to lower taxes and transfers, although there is little evidence of such a response to date.* The tax cuts have also contributed to large budget deficits, which will require future changes in taxes and spending with further potentially important implications for the level and distribution of income. Later in the chapter we explore these longer-term issues further. But first we take a closer look at what happened to the incomes of specific types of families and individuals from 1980 to 1984.

Impacts on Different Types of Families

So far we have focused on changes in the economic status of all families by income level. In this section we turn to the question of how five different types of families—husband-wife families with one earner, those with two earners, and elderly, black, and female-headed families—have fared over the 1980–1984 period. Nonelderly husband-wife families are, of course, the dominant group, constituting two-thirds of the 63 million families in 1984.† We also examine a group not yet discussed—"unrelated individuals" who do not reside in family units. This group (accounting for about 10 percent of the population) is a very diverse collection of individuals—such as elderly widows and young singles just starting out on their own.

Nonelderly Husband-Wife Families and Individuals

For the nonelderly husband-wife family, the 1980–1984 period was not one of substantial income growth. The incomes of all husband-wife families rose modestly, but those of two-earner families outperformed those of one-earner families (a 4.3 versus a 2.1 average percentage increase, as shown in table 10.6). The typical middle-class family with only one earner actually experienced a small drop in real income over this period, whereas, again,

---

*The evidence on both short-run and likely long-run responses is reviewed in chapters 3 and 6. The long-run effects are further discussed in the section on the outlook for 1984–1988.

†See appendix A, table A.5, for data on the proportion of all families in 1980 and 1984 represented by the five types discussed in this section.

TABLE 10.6

PERCENTAGE CHANGE IN REAL DISPOSABLE INCOMES FOR FAMILIES AND UNRELATED INDIVIDUALS, 1980–1984
(In 1982 dollars)

Demographic Group	Quintile					All Households
	Bottom	Second	Third	Fourth	Top	
FAMILIES						
Elderly						
1980 average disposable income	5,771	9,801	13,680	19,021	33,548	16,363
Percentage change in disposable income, 1980–1984						
Actual	6.2	6.8	8.4	9.2	11.2	9.5
Alternative policy scenario	5.8	6.1	8.1	8.5	9.3	8.3
Attributable to Reagan policies	0.4	0.7	0.3	0.7	1.9	1.2
One-earner husband-wife (nonelderly)						
1980 average disposable income	8,764	15,126	19,791	25,593	39,182	21,688
Percentage change in disposable income, 1980–1984						
Actual	−10.5	−2.6	−0.5	1.1	8.6	2.1
Alternative policy scenario	−6.9	0.2	1.3	2.5	7.4	3.2
Attributable to Reagan policies	−3.6	−2.8	−1.8	−1.4	1.2	−1.1
Two-earner husband-wife (nonelderly)						
1980 average disposable income	11,030	18,064	22,871	28,165	39,851	24,010
Percentage change in disposable income, 1980–1984						
Actual	−6.7	−0.1	2.5	4.9	10.1	4.3
Alternative policy scenario	−1.7	2.3	3.7	4.5	8.0	4.6
Attributable to Reagan policies	−5.0	−2.4	−1.2	0.4	2.1	−0.3

Female-headed (nonelderly)						
1980 average disposable income	12,223	25,032	14,618	10,158	7,378	3,946
Percentage change in disposable income, 1980–1984						
Actual	−3.3	−0.2	−1.9	−4.8	−9.3	−12.0
Alternative policy scenario	−0.5	0.7	0.3	−0.7	−3.6	−7.6
Attributable to Reagan policies	−2.8	−0.9	−2.2	−4.1	−5.7	−4.4
Black (all)						
1980 average disposable income	14,723	29,708	18,302	12,441	8,602	4,610
Percentage change in disposable income, 1980–1984						
Actual	−2.1	−0.1	−0.6	−3.7	−8.2	−7.0
Alternative policy scenario	0.5	0.5	1.7	1.0	−1.9	−1.8
Attributable to Reagan policies	−2.6	−0.6	−2.3	−4.7	−6.3	−5.2
UNRELATED INDIVIDUALS						
Elderly						
1980 average disposable income	7,382	16,323	8,103	5,514	4,178	2,817
Percentage change in disposable income, 1980–1984						
Actual	14.9	19.6	13.5	11.2	9.2	5.9
Alternative policy scenario	12.8	16.5	12.0	9.6	8.4	5.8
Attributable to Reagan policies	2.1	3.1	1.5	1.6	0.8	0.1
Nonelderly						
1980 average disposable income	10,414	21,145	13,179	9,336	6,142	2,220
Percentage change in disposable income, 1980–1984						
Actual	8.7	12.3	7.9	6.6	4.2	0.7
Alternative policy scenario	9.5	11.2	8.8	8.7	7.8	6.1
Attributable to Reagan policies	−0.8	1.1	−0.9	−2.1	−3.6	−5.4

SOURCE: Urban Institute household income model.

two-earner couples fared better (see the figures for the third quintile in table 10.6).

Husband-wife families were not helped by Reagan policies. For these families the state of the economy is the most important component of economic well-being, and the losses from the higher unemployment under Reagan policies were greater than the benefits of the tax cuts. As shown in table 10.6, this was particularly true for the lowest income quintiles and for one-earner families. Higher-income, two-earner families benefited from Reagan policies, in part because of the tax deduction for two-earner couples that was introduced in 1982.

In contrast to families, nonaged individuals living alone experienced healthy income growth (8.7 percent) from 1980 to 1984, most of which was caused by trends operating independently of Reagan administration policies. Young individuals (under 25) did less well than older ones, and Reagan policies were partly responsible for widening this gap.*

Elderly Families and Individuals

Perhaps the most striking finding concerning the different demographic groups is how well elderly Americans have fared both absolutely and relative to others. Over the 1980–1984 period, the disposable incomes of families headed by someone 65 or older rose by 9.5 percent—nearly three times the increase reported earlier for all families. Older individuals living alone had even greater gains—their incomes rose by about 15 percent. Furthermore, despite some increase in income inequality among the aged, strong gains occurred for all quintiles. Even the bottom quintile enjoyed income increases of about 6 percent. Figure 10.2 highlights the contrast in the degree, and distribution, of income growth of elderly families and nonelderly two-earner families.

One major explanation for the relatively large income increases for the aged can be found in the performance of major economic variables over this period. On the one hand, the elderly were harmed little by the extraordinarily high unemployment rates; on the other hand, they reaped the benefits of rapidly falling inflation and abnormally high real interest rates. Another factor that increased the incomes of the elderly was a rise in real Social Security benefits of over 7 percent from 1980 to 1984, which reflected generally higher benefits to each new set of retirees and the lagged adjustment of benefits for earlier increases in the cost-of-living.

---

*See appendix A, table A.6.

FIGURE 10.2

PERCENTAGE CHANGE IN REAL DISPOSABLE INCOME OF ELDERLY FAMILIES AND
NONELDERLY HUSBAND-WIFE TWO-EARNER FAMILIES, 1980–1984

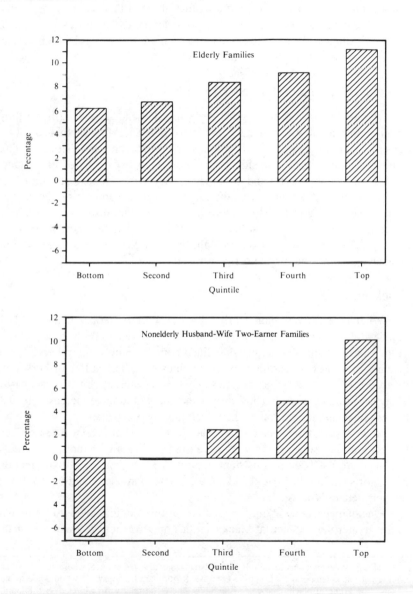

SOURCE: Urban Institute household income model.

Reagan policies were partly responsible for the elderly's good fortune. The benefits that resulted from the lower rate of inflation and lower taxes under Reagan more than offset the negative effects of greater unemployment and the small cuts in federal programs that affected this group. Indeed, the elderly comprise the only group that consistently did better as a result of Reagan's policies. (Recall, however, that we do not consider the 1983 Social Security amendments a Reagan initiative.)

Nonelderly Female-Headed Families

The income of a typical, nonelderly female-headed family (in the third quintile) shrunk by 4.8 percent from 1980 to 1984. Most of this loss (4.1 percentage points) is due to the policies of the Reagan administration. This is not surprising if one considers that more than two-fifths of all female-headed families are poor—and are thus dependent to some extent on government benefits. The Reagan program cuts had a greater impact on the second than on the first quintile. This pattern reflects the administration's policy of targeting benefits on the most needy and reducing benefits most sharply for those with some earnings, even though most families in the second quintile also have incomes below the official poverty line.

Black Families

Whether elderly or nonelderly, husband-wife or female-headed, black families fared relatively poorly over the past four years. With the exception of the elderly, their real incomes declined both absolutely and relative to the incomes of whites. In addition, black families were helped less or hurt more than were whites by Reagan policies. Under our alternative policy scenario, the typical middle-class black family's income would have increased by 1.0 percent over this period rather than declining by 3.7 percent.

In large part, the experience of black families from 1980 to 1984 reflects the fact that their average incomes were lower to begin with; and, as we have shown, there has been a consistent pattern of losses, or lower than average gains, for such families. But blacks fared worse than one would expect based on their generally lower income status.*

One can speculate about the reasons for this finding. It could be related to the greater dependence of black families on government assistance or the

---

*This is evident not only in table 10.6 but also in appendix A, table A.6, where the experience of different black demographic groups is contrasted with that of comparable white demographic groups. One group of blacks that gained both absolutely and relative to whites over this period was young, unrelated individuals.

smaller proportion of their income that represents interest, dividends, and rent even among those with similar incomes. In addition, a change in the degree of commitment to equal opportunity policies under the Reagan administration may have signaled to employers a lower likelihood of penalties for discrimination, making it harder for minorities to make gains in the job market. However, we have no direct evidence for any of these possible reasons.*

General Patterns

The two most general patterns that emerge from a close examination of the data for all demographic groups in table 10.6 mirror those reported in the last section. First, Reagan policies have contributed substantially to growing income inequality within each demographic group. The distributional consequences of the tax and budget cuts as well as the impact of slower economic growth on working families all contribute to this trend. Second, Reagan policies offer only a partial explanation for the average income changes of the various demographic groups (black and female-headed families excepted). Rather, changes in income are dominated by economic events that are common to both Reagan policies and our alternative policy scenario—high unemployment, high real interest rates, and rapidly falling inflation.

A Look Ahead: 1984–1988

The policies pursued by President Reagan not only have affected people's economic well-being to date, but also will play an important role in determining their future welfare. On the one hand, most families will be better off in 1988 than they were in 1984 if the economic recovery and the lower inflation that are the legacy of recent macroeconomic policies continue on their present course. The average family could also begin to benefit from the supply-side effects of the tax and transfer program changes enacted in the early 1980s, if these effects are significant enough to increase total income more than what it would have been under a different set of policies. On the other hand, the huge budget deficits projected for the late 1980s greatly complicate the picture. If they are not reduced, they will undermine the economy's long-run growth prospects by keeping interest rates high and discouraging investment. But if deficits are reduced, tax increases and further spending reductions will be required, and, other things being equal, these changes will reduce family disposable income in the near term. These budget

---

*But see chapter 6 for a review of the administration's equal opportunity policies.

actions will also have potentially important consequences for the distribution of family incomes that depend on the specific mix of policies chosen to resolve the deficit dilemma.

Projected Changes in Average Income per Family, 1984–1988

With the recession ended and the administration's supply-side policies in place, many expect real income gains for the rest of the decade to be substantial. The prospects for growth depend on the extent to which monetary and fiscal policy increase total demand and the extent to which the economy's capacity to produce goods and services expands to meet this demand. The administration is reasonably optimistic that demand will be strong for the next four years and that capacity will expand as well, as a result of its supply-side policies.* Thus, it has projected an annual growth rate for real GNP of about 4 percent a year for the remainder of the decade or slightly more than 17 percent over the 1984–1988 period.[7]

Macroeconomic forecasts are still an art rather than a science, however, and there are several reasons why the administration's projections about future economic growth could prove overly optimistic. First, greater concern about inflation may affect the Federal Reserve's willingness to permit a continued rapid expansion of demand. Second, although the administration's tax policies have encouraged investment, if large deficits are allowed to continue, keeping interest rates high, eventually the net effect will be to curtail the growth of industrial capacity and adversely affect living standards.

Nevertheless, under certain assumptions, the administration's projections seem quite plausible. These assumptions are that deficits will be reduced substantially between 1984 and 1988 and that monetary policy will offset the negative impact of a more restrictive fiscal policy—if this should prove necessary to keep the economy on a reasonable growth path. However, reductions in the deficit will necessitate some tax increases or benefit reductions, which will have adverse impacts on family disposable incomes analogous to the favorable impacts produced by the tax cuts of the last few years.

Based on the administration's economic projections—and the two assumptions that make them most plausible—we estimate that average real

---

*See chapter 3, figure 3.6, and accompanying text for a discussion of these supply-side effects.

disposable income per family should increase by only 4 percent during the period 1984–1988.*

The reason this growth is so modest is because reducing the deficit will require considerable sacrifices over the next few years in order to set the stage for healthy long-run growth. These sacrifices, in turn, will mean that gains in disposable incomes are likely to be small even if pretax and pretransfer incomes should grow at a healthy clip. In short, the next four years could turn out to be the mirror image of the last four. Although the economy performed poorly from 1980 to 1984, families were helped by the boost that lower federal taxes gave to their disposable incomes. And although the economy is expected to perform reasonably well from 1984 to 1988, families will be hurt by the tax and transfer changes needed to lower the deficit.

The Distribution of Family Incomes

The favorable implications of predicted economic growth and the unfavorable implications of reducing the deficit for real disposable incomes are, thus, reasonably clear. The implications of events over the next four years for the distribution of income are not.

The uncertainty derives from uncertainty about both the distributional consequences of growth itself and the policies that will be followed to reduce the deficit. Consider first the economy. On the one hand, economic growth widens income disparities between families with earners and those without, unless a portion of the gains from growth is taxed and used to increase the generosity of benefits provided to the nonworking poor. On the other hand, growth reduces the relative size of the population dependent on income transfers and makes the distribution of *earned* income more equal.† For these and other reasons, it is difficult to predict the precise pattern of effects across

---

*Note that this is far less than the assumed real GNP growth of 17.1 percent. About 6 percentage points of the difference are due to expected growth in the number of families. About 4 percentage points are due to the effects of the deficit reduction measures described later in this section. The remaining difference is due primarily to projected growth of both payroll taxes and retained earnings as a percentge of GNP. In the absence of any deficit reduction measures, disposable incomes would grow by 8 percent instead of 4 percent but only if a GNP growth rate of 17 percent were sustainable in the face of currently projected deficits.

†It should be noted, however, that the equalizing effect of tighter labor markets on earned income could be partly offset by a delayed response in the late 1980s to the administration's supply-side policies. As noted in chapter 3, a large part of any such response is likely to take the form of increased labor force participation (rather than increased savings or investment) and to be concentrated among nonemployed women facing high marginal tax rates. Since most of these women are married to high-earning men, economic growth may have a less equalizing impact on family incomes than it has in the past.

families of a given rate of growth of the economy, and we do not attempt to do so here.

In contrast, once a particular deficit reduction strategy is chosen, it is possible to predict its distributional consequences, which, as we will show, can be quite dramatic. The problem lies in specifying the particular mix of tax increases and spending cuts that might be adopted. Rather than speculate about the wide variety of particular plans that might be implemented, we have chosen to illustrate a possible range of outcomes by examining two alternatives designed to capture the flavor of what might be considered prototypical "liberal" and "conservative" approaches.

In keeping with the discussion of deficit reduction needs and strategies in chapter 4, we assume that both of our illustrative plans entail sufficient action to lower the large structural deficit now projected under current policies for 1988 to under $100 billion, or 2 percent of GNP. This requires tax increases and spending reductions with a total annual impact of $130 billion by 1988. Since these are to be phased in starting in 1985, they will result in additional 1988 savings of $30 billion in interest outlays because less debt will accumulate in the interim (see table 10.7). Since both plans involve the same amount of deficit reduction, differences in their distributional impacts are due to their composition, not their size.*

The Liberal Plan. Under this plan, about two-thirds of the required budget savings are achieved by raising taxes. These tax increases involve an increase in business taxes, in payroll taxes (to protect the solvency of the Medicare trust fund), and in excise taxes (on such items as alcohol and tobacco). However, higher revenues from the personal income tax dominate the package, and it is assumed that they will be raised in one of two ways: through a straight surtax on current-law tax liability or through a more thoroughgoing reform.

Recent tax reform proposals put forward by both liberals and conservatives have emphasized both broadening the tax base and lowering marginal tax rates. Our liberal tax reform plan produces roughly the same degree of progressivity as the current tax system does and exempts families below the poverty level from personal income taxation.† The latter is achieved under our plan by raising personal exemptions and zero-bracket amounts sufficiently to eliminate the inflation-caused erosion in their real value since 1979 (the effective date of their last increase). This particular provision is motivated

---

*We are indebted to Joseph Minarik for helping to specify and analyze the tax portions of different deficit reduction plans.

†This plan generally conforms to the most often discussed Democratic tax reform proposal sponsored by Senator Bill Bradley (D-N.J.) and Representative Richard A. Gephardt (D-Mo.).

TABLE 10.7

TWO DEFICIT REDUCTION PLANS AND THEIR IMPACT ON FEDERAL REVENUES,
OUTLAYS, AND THE DEFICIT IN 1988

	Projections for 1988 Based on Current Policies	Projections for 1988 Based on Deficit Reduction Plans		Changes in Revenues, Outlays, and the Deficit under Different Reduction Plans	
		Liberal	Conservative	Liberal	Conservative
		Billions of Dollars			
Revenues					
Individual income tax	438	495	469	57	31
Corporate income tax	85	109	95	24	10
Social insurance taxes	354	366	366	12	12
Excise and other taxes	68	80	80	12	12
Total	945	1,050	1,010	105	65
Outlays					
National defense	372	352	372	− 20	—
Social Security	227	227	212	—	− 15
Medicare	106	101	96	− 5	− 10
Means-tested entitlements	77	82	72	5	− 5
Other mandatory spending	120	115	110	− 5	− 10
Nondefense discretionary	189	189	164	—	− 25
Net interest	194	164	164	− 30	− 30
Total[a]	1,240	1,185	1,145	− 55	− 95
Actual deficit[b]	295	135	135	− 160	− 160
Structural deficit[b]	(260)	(100)	(100)	(− 160)	(− 160)
		Percentage of GNP			
Revenues	19.0	21.1	20.3	2.1	1.4
Outlays	24.9	23.8	23.0	1.1	− 1.8
Actual deficit[b]	5.9	2.7	2.7	3.2	− 3.2
Structural deficit[b]	(5.1)	(2.0)	(2.0)	(− 3.1)	(− 3.1)

SOURCE: Congressional Budget Office, *Baseline Budget Projections for Fiscal Years 1985–1989*, February 1984, and authors' calculations.

a. The totals include $13 billion of off-budget outlays and $59.6 billion of offsetting receipts that are not itemized in the table. They are not affected by either deficit reduction plan.

b. The structural deficit is a measure of what the deficit would be if the economy were at a 6 percent level of unemployment. The actual deficit is projected to be somewhat larger in 1988, since the unemployment rate is still expected to be above 6 percent. See chapters 3 and 4 for discussions of the concept and importance of the structural deficit.

by our earlier observation that the personal income tax burden on lower-income families has been rising since 1980 because of inflation, whereas that of higher-income families has fallen because of the Reagan tax cuts. (Both liberal tax schemes retain the general indexing feature of current law that goes into effect in 1985.)

On the expenditure side of the budget, the liberal plan includes a slow-down in the defense build-up to a 3 percent rather than a 5 percent real growth rate starting in 1985. Additional small savings are provided through reductions in Medicare, agricultural price supports, and federal employee pension programs. In addition, it is assumed that means-tested entitlement programs will be increased modestly to partly offset the effects of the recent program cuts on the poor. (The details are presented in table 10.7.)

The Conservative Plan. In contrast to the liberal plan, the conservative alternative puts more emphasis on reducing expenditures and less on raising taxes. However, because there are limits on the extent to which expenditures can be pared back (see chapter 4), tax increases still account for two-fifths of the total 1988 deficit reductions under this plan. We assume the same reliance on payroll and excise tax increases as in the liberal plan, but substantially less reliance on both corporate and personal income tax increases— although the latter still carries the major revenue-raising burden. Again we specify two ways of raising these revenues: a straight surtax on personal income tax liabilities and a reform option. Here the reform option involves moving to a broad-based, flat-rate tax with no itemized deductions.* (Personal exemptions and zero-bracket amounts are continued at current-law levels and are indexed to inflation beginning in 1985.) This results in a less progressive personal income tax structure than either the existing one or the liberal reform option, but it produces a lower marginal tax rate (less than 20 percent) for all but the lowest income taxpayers.

The more ambitious spending reductions under the conservative plan— totaling $65 billion (excluding interest)—are essentially across the board, except for the defense build-up, which is assumed to continue as currently planned. There is a freeze on all domestic discretionary spending, a reduction in cost-of-living adjustments by 2 percent a year in federal pension programs (including Social Security), further cuts in means-tested entitlement programs along the lines proposed by President Reagan, and substantial cuts in both Medicare and agricultural price supports.

---

*Such plans have generally been supported by conservative members of Congress—Senator Jesse Helms (R-N.C.) and Representative Philip M. Crane (R-Ill.) have both introduced similar proposals—and the Reagan administration has expressed a strong interest in them.

Impacts

Our estimates of the impacts of these prototypical liberal and conservative deficit reduction plans illustrate the sensitivity of the income distribution to the particular mix of tax increases and spending reductions chosen. Table 10.8 shows how much each quintile's disposable income would grow from 1984 to 1988 under the different plans. Everyone's disposable income growth is constrained by the need to reduce the deficit, as explained in the last section, but the distribution of sacrifices varies, depending on the particular plan chosen.

Looking first at the reform version of each plan, it is not surprising that the liberal plan implies a much smaller increase in the incomes of the most affluent families than in the incomes of the least affluent families. In contrast, the conservative plan implies the reverse. Although the typical middle class family is better off under the liberal plan, the conservative plan would yield lower marginal tax rates.

TABLE 10.8

PERCENTAGE CHANGE IN REAL DISPOSABLE FAMILY INCOME UNDER ALTERNATIVE
DEFICIT REDUCTION PLANS, 1984–1988
(In 1982 dollars)

	Quintile					
	Bottom	*Second*	*Third*	*Fourth*	*Top*	*All Families*
1984 real disposable income	6,391	13,163	19,034	25,724	40,880	21,038
Liberal plan						
With surtax[a]	9.1	6.0	5.3	4.4	2.7	4.2[b]
With tax reform[a]	9.8	8.0	6.5	4.5	1.3	4.2[b]
Conservative plan						
With surtax[a]	−0.3	3.7	4.7	4.7	4.1	3.9[b]
With tax reform[a]	−1.6	2.9	2.8	3.2	8.7	3.9[b]

SOURCE: Urban Institute household income model and authors' calculations.

a. Based on projections for real GNP growth contained in President's Reagan's FY 1985 budget. The 8.3 percentage point increase in real disposable family incomes resulting from this overall economic growth is assumed to be distributed equally across quintiles. Therefore, all of the differences in income growth across the quintiles are due to the distributional effects of the various deficit reduction plans.

b. Not all the tax increases and spending cuts in the deficit reduction plans can be allocated to families. Thus, there are slight differences between the liberal plan and the conservative plan in the total impact on real family disposable incomes, even though they entail the same amount of deficit reduction, because of the differences in the composition of the spending cuts and tax increases.

The surtax versions of the two plans fall between the two reform versions in terms of their distributional implications. Nonetheless, the liberal plan has a significantly more equalizing effect because of the conservative plan's greater emphasis on benefit reductions (which fall disproportionately on lower-income families) relative to surtax increases (which mimic the structure of the existing tax system and thus tend to raise revenues in a progressive fashion).*

Conclusion

When candidate Reagan was campaigning in the fall of 1980, the majority of Americans were pessimistic about their future financial prospects and those of their children. Four years later that pessimism has all but disappeared. Whatever else President Reagan may or may not have achieved, he has been able to rid the country of what his predecessor perceived as a "national malaise."

This achievement is all the more significant in light of what has happened to family incomes over the last four years. Average disposable family incomes adjusted for inflation rose from 1980 to 1984 by 3.5 percent—a modest increase by historical standards. For the "typical middle-class family" the increase was less than 1 percent.

Would another set of policies have worked better, or was there something more fundamental about the early 1980s that prevented faster income growth? Our analysis indicates that some degree of recession in 1981 and 1982 was inevitable, given the underlying economic situation that President Reagan inherited. Incomes had to go down before they could go up. Perhaps Americans understand that, hence their current optimism about the future. However, a plausible alternative set of macroeconomic policies that paid relatively more attention to unemployment than to inflation would have brought with it a somewhat milder recession and substantially stronger pretax family income growth even after adjustment for the somewhat higher inflation that these alternative policies would have implied. But the consequences for after-tax incomes would have differed little from what occurred because under these alternative policies there would have been a much smaller personal income tax cut. (Of course, the gains in disposable income attributable to the Reagan tax cut will prove very temporary to the extent that future tax increases and benefit reductions are utilized to reduce the deficit.)

---

*The full dynamic impacts of these tax and transfer changes on individual behavior and on the economy have not been captured here, but we doubt that a more complete analysis would change the general conclusions.

Along with this slow growth in incomes from 1980 to 1984, there was a major (by historical standards) redistribution of income away from lower-income families and individuals—particularly the poorest—and toward the most affluent. (The elderly are a partial exception to this.) Some widening of the income distribution would have taken place from 1980 to 1984 irrespective of who had been president. But the particular policy mix of tax and benefit reductions that President Reagan chose exacerbated the trend. His policies helped the affluent but not the poor or the middle class.

People's views about this trend will vary. There was nothing sacrosanct about the prevailing distribution of income when Ronald Reagan became president. Rising tax burdens and growing government benefits had reduced the degree of inequality over the prior two decades. The strong initial support President Reagan received for his tax and spending policies may reflect in part a view among the public that the equalizing process had gone too far by 1980, although there have been subsequent indications that people are growing concerned about the hardships suffered by families at the bottom of the income distribution and the contrasting treatment of the rich, the poor, and the middle class.

And what of the future? Will the longer-term effects of Reagan policies on family incomes match the optimism currently expressed in the polls?

The analysis of long-term growth presented in chapter 3 suggested that there is about an even chance that growth will be stronger in the future as a result of the impact of Reagan policies on saving, investment, work effort, and productivity. Thus, the growth of real GNP could be quite strong. Using the administration's own GNP projections for 1988, which assume that its policies will be successful—but adjusting them for the impact of deficit reduction measures on disposable incomes—we estimate that average real disposable income per family will grow by about 4 percent from 1984 to 1988, only a little more rapidly than it did from 1980 to 1984. If we are right, standards of living will increase more slowly in the 1980s than in the 1960s or 1970s.* The major reason for this pessimistic conclusion is the sacrifices we assume families will need to make in the future to lower the deficit.

The way in which these sacrifices are distributed will have major implications for who is better off by the end of the decade. Realistically, any deficit reduction plan must involve both tax increases and spending reductions.

---

*Using the administration's economic projections, we estimate that real family disposable income will rise by 8.7 percent, on average, in the 1980s. This compares with average family disposable income growth of 11.8 percent in the 1970s and 27.0 percent in the 1960s.

There is a wide range of combinations that would yield equivalent budgetary savings. Depending on the specific measures adopted, the recent trend toward greater income inequality could be accelerated, left unchanged, or reversed.

APPENDIX A

SUPPLEMENTARY STATISTICAL TABLES

TABLE A.1

FEDERAL LAND ACREAGE, BY AGENCY, BY STATE
(Thousands of acres)

State	Bureau of Land Management	Forest Service	National Park Service	Fish and Wildlife Service	Total Federal Acreage	Federal Percentage of Total State
Alabama	3.3	643.8	6.6	48.5	1,122.3	3.4
Alaska	73,600.0[b]	22,894.7[b]	51,015.2[b]	76,058.9[a]	226,200.0[b]	60.3[a]
Arizona	12,588.9	11,270.7	2,696.0	1,588.4	32,014.3	44.0
Arkansas	1.6	2,476.2	93.0	193.9	3,358.3	10.1
California	16,609.4	20,369.7	4,500.0	234.6	46,702.1	46.6
Colorado	7,993.9	14,414.2	600.0	56.9	23,607.9	35.5
Connecticut	—	—	1.1	0.2	9.3	0.3
Delaware	—	—	—	24.6	40.9	3.2
Dist. of Columbia	—	—	6.9	—	12.8	32.9
Florida	1.2	1,097.9	2,062.0	452.9	4,040.9	11.6
Georgia	—	862.9	36.7	469.3	2,277.4	6.1
Hawaii	—	—	245.0	255.8	660.6	16.1
Idaho	11,945.9	20,422.8	86.9	85.2	33,759.6	63.8
Illinois	—	260.7	—	117.0	606.6	1.7
Indiana	—	186.2	8.0	7.8	496.6	2.1
Iowa	—	—	1.7	73.6	227.4	0.6
Kansas	0.7	—	0.7	51.4	773.0	1.4
Kentucky	—	667.3	79.3	2.2	1,414.4	5.5
Louisiana	7.2	597.7	1.2	276.2	1,098.6	3.8
Maine	—	51.2	38.4	30.3	134.8	0.7
Maryland	—	—	37.7	26.1	203.0	3.2
Massachusetts	—	—	29.2	12.0	79.9	1.6
Michigan	0.9	2,728.3	618.4	107.1	3,467.4	9.5
Minnesota	43.6	2,796.1	134.4	442.8	3,423.0	6.7
Mississippi	0.6	1,140.6	106.7	107.3	1,730.6	5.7

Missouri	0.2	1,463.1	62.7	55.6	2,195.6	5.0
Montana	8,141.6	16,752.7	1,220.5	1,135.7	27,740.6	29.7
Nebraska	9.4	351.7	5.8	156.9	712.2	1.4
Nevada	43,844.8	5,146.0	697.6	2,362.7	60,506.1	86.1
New Hampshire	—	700.2	4.1	2.2	721.9	12.5
New Jersey		—	34.7	37.9	151.5	3.1
New Mexico	12,840.5	9,244.4	248.5	383.0	25,873.7	33.3
New York		13.2	33.7	23.5	245.9	0.8
North Carolina		1,162.7	374.2	136.1	2,050.9	6.5
North Dakota	68.1	1,105.5	71.3	1,272.6	2,386.4	5.4
Ohio	0.1	175.3	11.5	8.7	345.3	1.3
Oklahoma	7.0	293.2	9.2	141.0	1,590.0	3.6
Oregon	15,745.1	15,615.8	171.3	507.4	32,313.7	52.5
Pennsylvania		508.8	31.9	9.2	732.6	2.5
Rhode Island		—	—	1.0	8.0	1.2
South Carolina		609.4	20.9	189.5	1,176.4	6.1
South Dakota	276.4	1,995.3	183.3	458.4	3,492.3	7.1
Tennessee		622.0	263.2	82.4	1,853.9	6.9
Texas		782.6	1,087.4	255.5	3,408.7	2.0
Utah	22,052.6	8,045.9	2,009.2	101.7	33,530.0	63.6
Vermont		279.9	1.2	5.8	295.6	5.0
Virginia		1,617.4	299.3	103.7	2,409.7	9.4
Washington	311.2	9,052.6	1,909.9	181.1	12,472.7	29.2
West Virginia		967.1	2.4	0.3	1,097.1	7.1
Wisconsin	0.3	1,498.7	63.0	220.8	1,867.7	5.3
Wyoming	17,793.1	9,253.3	2,391.1	74.2	30,329.6	48.7
U.S. TOTAL	248,887.7	187,327.8	73,626.2	88,774.7	636,929.6	28.1

SOURCES: Robert H. Nelson, "The Public Lands," in Paul R. Portney, ed., *Current Issues in Natural Resource Policy* (Washington, D.C.: Resources for the Future, Inc., 1982), pp. 16–17.

NOTE: Most recent acreages available: Bureau of Land Management (BLM) and total federal for 1979; Forest Service, National Park Service, and Fish and Wildlife Service for 1980. Includes federal acreage only, thus excluding private holdings within national park and forest boundaries.

a Lands expected to remain federal after state of Alaska and native selections are completed—BLM estimates as of March 1982.
b Lands after enactment of Alaska National Interest Lands Conservation Act of 1980—agency estimates as of March 1982.

TABLE A.2

AVERAGE ANNUAL REAL GROWTH RATES IN FEDERAL SOCIAL PROGRAM OUTLAYS
(Percentage)

	Kennedy-Johnson FY 1961–1969	Nixon-Ford FY 1969–FY 1977	Carter FY 1977–FY 1981	Reagan FY 1981–FY 1985[a]	Projection Based on 1984 Policies FY 1985–FY 1989
Payments to individuals					
Social insurance and other[b]	6.7	9.2	4.0	2.5	3.0
Low-income assistance[b]	8.7	12.0	4.7	0.1	1.5
Other grants[b]	37.6	9.9	0.7	-7.4	0.1
TOTAL	7.9	9.7	3.9	1.5	2.5

SOURCES: Office of Management and Budget; Congressional Budget Office, unpublished tabulations; and author's calculations.
a. Calculated on the basis of Congressional Budget Office estimates of 1984 outlays and projections of 1985 outlays based on 1984 policies.
b. See figure 6.2 for definitions.

TABLE A.3

COMPONENTS OF DISPOSABLE INCOME FOR ALL FAMILIES, 1980 AND 1984

(In 1982 dollars)

	1980			1984		
	Families Receiving (%)	Average per Recipient ($)	Average for All Families ($)	Families Receiving (%)	Average per Recipient ($)	Average for All Families ($)
Labor income	86.0	26,162	22,508	85.2	27,431	23,366
Interest, rent, and dividends	68.6	2,289	1,570	65.3	2,673	1,745
Social Security	22.8	6,197	1,412	21.8	6,628	1,446
Means-tested						
SSI	3.5	2,504	87	3.2	2,638	84
AFDC	4.6	3,775	175	5.1	3,420	173
Food Stamps	11.9	1,110	132	10.9	1,129	123
All other income	37.9	4,138	1,564	39.2	4,088	1,602
TOTAL INCOME	99.6	27,570	27,447	99.4	28,702	28,539
Federal income taxes	79.1	4,834	3,821	81.5	4,683	3,818
Payroll taxes	85.9	1,519	1,305	85.0	1,785	1,518
State and local taxes	99.8	1,991	1,987	99.2	2,182	2,165
Disposable Income	99.4	20,451	20,333	99.3	21,193	21,038

SOURCE: Urban Institute household income model (TRIM-2).

TABLE A.4

THE DISTRIBUTION OF FAMILY INCOME, 1960, 1970, 1979, AND 1984

Income Divisions	1960		1970		1979		1984
	Share of Total Family Income (%)	Income Level at Upper End of Quintile ($)	Share of Total Family Income (%)	Income Level at Upper End of Quintile ($)	Share of Total Family Income (%)	Income Level at Upper End of Quintile ($)	Share of Total Family Income[a] (%)
1st quintile	4.8	6,823	5.4	9,533	5.3	9,830	5.1
2d quintile	12.2	11,765	12.2	15,553	11.6	16,220	11.2
3d quintile	17.8	15,598	17.6	21,121	17.5	22,985	17.2
4th quintile	24.0	21,568	23.8	29,032	24.1	31,590	24.3
5th quintile	41.3	—	40.9	—	41.6	—	42.2

SOURCE: Urban Institute household income model (TRIM-2).

NOTE: These figures are based on pretax income and thus are not strictly comparable to the shares in table 10.1 in the text.

a. The 1984 figure shown here is also pretax income and is extrapolated from the disposable income measures. It is likely to overstate the share to the bottom quintile and understate the share to the top.

TABLE A.5

<small>SHARE OF DIFFERENT FAMILY TYPES IN THE BOTTOM AND TOP INCOME QUINTILES
AND OF ALL FAMILIES, 1980 AND 1984</small>

	Percentage of All Families in the Bottom Quintile		Percentage of All Families in the Top Quintile		Percentage of All Families	
	1980	*1984*	*1980*	*1984*	*1980*	*1984*
Elderly[a]	25.4	20.6	8.4	9.1	15.0	14.6
Husband-wife families (nonelderly)[a]						
One earner	13.7	14.1	23.3	21.1	21.1	20.3
Two earners	15.8	18.3	62.3	64.4	44.9	45.5
Female-headed families (nonelderly)[a]	35.1	36.6	2.9	2.5	13.4	13.8
Black[b]	21.8	25.1	4.5	3.7	10.5	10.6

SOURCE: Urban Institute household income model.

NOTE: The income measure is real disposable income.

a. These family types do not account for all families. Another 10 percent or so consist of single-parent, male-headed families, and various collections of unmarried relatives.

b. Black families are also included in all of the other categories.

TABLE A.6

PERCENTAGE CHANGE IN REAL DISPOSABLE INCOME FOR FAMILIES AND UNRELATED
INDIVIDUALS BY SELECTED CHARACTERISTICS, 1980–1984
(In 1982 dollars)

		Percentage Change, 1980–1984		
	1980	*Actual*	*Alternative Policy Scenario*	*Owing to Reagan Policies*
Elderly families	16,363	+9.5	+8.3	+1.2
Blacks	10.965	+3.1	+3.7	+0.6
Whites	16,855	+9.9	+8.6	+1.3
Age 75 or above	14,394	+8.7	+7.2	+1.5
Elderly individuals	7,382	+14.9	+12.8	+2.1
Blacks	5,013	+6.1	+5.8	+1.3
Whites	7,539	+15.2	+13.0	+2.2
Age 75 or above	6,916	+15.0	+12.7	+2.3
Nonelderly husband-wife				
families	23,262	+3.7	+4.2	−0.5
One earner, black	17,243	−12.0	−8.7	−3.3
One earner, white	21,959	+2.5	+3.4	−0.9
One earner, with children	20,831	+1.9	+3.6	−2.7
Two earners, black	21,358	+0.6	+2.1	−1.5
Two earners, white	24,219	+4.6	+4.8	−0.2
Two earners, with children	23,727	+2.7	+3.6	−0.9
Nonelderly female-headed				
families	12,223	−3.3	−0.5	−2.8
Black	9,976	−3.6	+0.8	−4.4
White	13,202	−3.0	+1.3	−2.3
With children	10,895	−3.6	−0.5	−4.1
Nonelderly unrelated individuals	10,414	+8.7	+9.5	−0.8
Age 24 or under	7,481	+2.3	+4.5	−2.2
Age 25–34	11,749	+7.4	+8.3	−0.9
Black	7,807	+13.0	+15.1	−2.1
White	10,582	+8.2	+8.0	−0.7

SOURCE: Urban Institute household income model.

APPENDIX B

ALTERNATIVE POLICY SIMULATIONS

This appendix contains a description of the alternatives to Reagan policies that might have been pursued by a different administration. We have used simulations of the effects of these alternative policies to evaluate the impact of Reagan policies on economic performance (chapter 3), business profitability (chapter 9), and the level and distribution of family income (chapter 10).* We have made our alternative fiscal policy more restrictive than actual policy has been in order to eliminate large structural deficits. Our alternative monetary policy is less restrictive, not only to offset the additional fiscal restraint, but also to provide greater overall stimulus in order to avoid a recession as severe as the one we experienced.

Fiscal Policy

Our alternative fiscal policy assumes an overall budget stance that keeps the high employment federal government deficit in approximate balance throughout the simulation period (1981–1988).† Relative to Reagan policies, we assume slower real growth in defense spending, fewer cuts in nondefense expenditures, and smaller tax cuts.

Defense Spending. Although there was bipartisan support for the increase in defense spending begun in the Carter years, we assume that a different administration would not have supported a defense buildup as large as the Reagan buildup. In particular, we assume real defense spending growth of 5 percent in 1982, 4 percent in 1983, and 3 percent in 1984 and thereafter. Actual growth in defense spending was 7 percent in 1982 and 1983, and is

---

*Simulations of economic policy were done using the Data Resources Incorporated (DRI) quarterly econometric forecasting model. Simulations of the effects on families and individuals were done using The Urban Institute household income model (TRIM-2).

†At high employment, the deficit or surplus never exceeds 1 percent of GNP.

estimated to be 6 percent in 1984 and 5 percent thereafter in our simulation of Reagan policies.

Nondefense Spending. The real levels of three broad federal government nondefense spending categories—nondefense purchases of goods and services, transfers to persons, and grants-in-aid to state and local governments—were specified so that given our real defense spending growth path and our alternative tax policy (discussed later), the high-employment deficit is kept in near balance. These levels are broadly consistent with Congressional Budget Office (CBO) baseline projections made in 1981, hence they assume no substantial cuts from pre-Reagan policy levels. Real spending in these categories is higher than spending under Reagan policies.*

Transfers to Persons. With the exception of Social Security and Supplemental Security Income (which changed as part of the Social Security Amendments of 1983 and which we assume would have been enacted no matter who was president), we assume that transfer programs would have provided benefits based on 1980 law. These benefits are higher than those under Reagan policies, which lowered individual benefits and reduced eligibility. However, the higher unemployment resulting from Reagan policies worked in the other direction, raising total payments for these programs compared with what they would have been with the Reagan program changes but the same economic performance as was achieved with our alternative policies. Still, the net effect of Reagan policies was to lower overall spending for these programs.

Grants-in-Aid. Although government activity at the state and local levels is not under the control of any administration, the effects of economic and budget policies at the federal level are likely to induce responsive policy decisions. For example, the decisions since 1981 by eighteen states to raise their personal income taxes were undoubtedly influenced by the decline in grants-in-aid under Reagan policies and by the 1981–1982 recession. Since our alternative fiscal policy assumes fewer cuts in grants-in-aid and since a milder recession in 1981–1982 is one result of our alternative policies, we assume that state and local governments do not raise their taxes to such a degree.

---

*We did not make specific assumptions regarding the remaining nondefense spending categories—transfer to foreigners, net interest paid, and subsidies less current surplus of government enterprises—but interest outlays turn out to be lower because the federal deficit and interest rates are lower.

Tax Policy. General concern about the effects of inflation in increasing taxes as a share of income would probably have produced some kind of tax cut in 1981 no matter who was president. Our alternative tax policy assumes that personal income tax rates are indexed for inflation beginning in the fourth quarter of 1981. We assume no business tax cut. Given our concern with limiting the size of the budget deficit, any cut in business taxes would have required a smaller personal income tax cut or a reduction in spending else-where. However, if we had assumed a business tax cut, the differential stimulus to business investment that we now ascribe to Reagan policies would be correspondingly smaller. We assume that the changes in payroll taxes enacted as part of the Social Security reforms and the gas tax increase enacted as a part of the public works jobs program would have occurred no matter who was president.

Monetary Policy

We assume that growth of the money supply (M-1) would have been faster if this fiscal package had been accepted. In part this reflects our belief that the Fed would have been more willing to ease policy if there were fiscal restraint; in part it reflects our belief that a different administration would have been less committed to monetarism and more concerned about unemployment and would therefore have urged the Fed to ease the money supply earlier.

Results

Tables B.1 and B.2 show some of the important performance and policy variables for a number of simulations. The first block in each table shows these data for our simulation of Reagan policies* and the second for the alternative monetary and fiscal policies described in this appendix. We also show the results of two other simulations discussed in chapter 3: a policy combining Reagan fiscal policies with the easier monetary policy discussed here; and a policy combining the tighter fiscal policy discussed here with actual Reagan-Volcker monetary policy.

---

*Assumes no policy change in the 1984–1988 period.

TABLE B.1

ECONOMIC PERFORMANCE INDICATORS UNDER FOUR POLICY ALTERNATIVES

	1981	1982	1983	1984	1985	1986	1987	1988
I. Actual Policies								
Real GNP (billions of 1982 $)	3,132.0	3,073.2	3,176.4	3,352.3	3,465.7	3,566.8	3,677.5	3,806.0
Change (%)	2.6	−1.9	3.4	5.5	3.4	2.9	3.1	3.5
Inflation rate (CPI)	10.3	6.2	3.2	4.9	4.8	5.2	5.6	5.9
Unemployment rate (civilian)	7.6	9.7	9.6	7.6	7.2	7.3	7.3	7.1
Three-month Treasury bill rate	14.0	10.6	8.6	8.8	9.5	9.7	9.4	9.2
II. Easier Monetary, Tighter Fiscal Policies								
Real GNP (billions of 1982 $)	3,218.0	3,262.4	3,412.8	3,520.5	3,641.6	3,770.2	3,883.3	4,019.3
Change (%)	4.1	1.4	4.6	3.2	3.4	3.5	3.0	3.5
Inflation rate (CPI)	10.6	7.2	4.7	6.4	6.4	7.2	7.5	7.8
Unemployment rate (civilian)	7.2	8.0	7.3	6.2	6.1	6.1	6.1	6.0
Three-month Treasury bill rate	7.0	4.8	5.4	5.4	4.1	4.8	4.6	5.6
III. Easier Monetary, Actual Fiscal Policies								
Real GNP (billions of 1982 $)	3,247.9	3,355.7	3,486.0	3,576.8	3,691.1	3,809.2	3,950.9	4,086.5
Change (%)	4.6	3.3	3.9	2.6	3.2	3.2	3.7	3.4
Inflation rate (CPI)	10.7	7.6	5.3	6.6	6.4	7.1	7.7	7.8
Unemployment rate (civilian)	7.1	7.2	6.6	6.1	6.0	6.1	6.0	6.0
Three-month Treasury bill rate	5.9	3.4	7.7	5.9	6.7	6.2	6.8	6.3
IV. Actual Monetary, Tighter Fiscal Policies								
Real GNP (billions of 1982 $)	3,128.7	3,070.4	3,155.6	3,316.0	3,431.4	3,530.7	3,646.0	3,782.7
Change (%)	2.5	−1.9	2.8	5.1	3.5	2.9	3.3	3.8
Inflation rate (CPI)	10.3	6.2	3.2	4.7	4.7	5.2	5.6	6.1
Unemployment rate (civilian)	7.6	9.7	9.8	7.9	7.5	7.4	7.3	6.9
Three-month Treasury bill rate	14.0	10.4	7.4	6.6	6.8	6.3	5.4	5.4

SOURCE: Authors' simulations based on DRI model.

TABLE B.2

Monetary and Fiscal Policy Alternatives

	1981	1982	1983	1984	1985	1986	1987	1988
I. Actual Policies								
(Percentage)								
M-1 growth	5.1	8.9	10.0	6.4	6.4	5.8	5.6	5.6
Receipts/GNP	21.2	20.1	19.5	19.5	19.6	19.7	19.8	20.2
Expenditures/GNP	23.3	24.9	25.0	24.4	24.7	25.0	25.1	25.1
Deficit/GNP	2.1	4.8	5.5	4.9	5.1	5.3	5.4	4.9
... at high employment[a]	0.6	1.8	2.7	3.1	3.5	3.7	3.6	3.3
(Billions of current dollars)								
Receipts	627.0	617.4	644.3	712.4	775.7	842.0	920.1	1,027.9
Personal	298.6	304.7	296.0	314.5	344.5	375.9	414.1	460.0
Corporate profits	67.5	46.4	59.9	71.1	75.0	79.1	86.5	92.8
Other[b]	260.9	266.3	288.4	326.8	356.2	387.0	419.5	475.1
Expenditures	689.1	764.4	826.2	890.7	976.2	1,070.0	1,169.4	1,278.1
Defense purchases	154.0	179.4	200.1	222.5	248.8	275.5	305.9	340.1
Nondefense purchases	75.2	79.3	75.0	77.4	93.7	101.0	107.5	114.5
Transfers to persons	280.9	314.8	338.8	353.8	376.2	411.0	442.9	478.9
Grants-in-aid to state and local governments	87.9	83.9	86.5	93.0	101.3	108.0	116.5	126.0
Net interest paid	73.1	84.9	96.4	114.9	132.6	153.1	175.1	195.8
Other[c]	18.0	22.1	29.4	29.1	23.6	21.4	21.5	22.8
Deficit	62.1	147.0	181.9	178.3	200.5	228.0	249.2	250.3
... at high employment[a]	19.1	61.4	95.8	120.8	145.8	165.1	177.9	176.3
II. Easier Monetary, Tighter Fiscal Policies								
(Percentage)								
M-1 growth	10.0	10.1	9.9	6.1	8.1	7.1	6.9	6.6
Receipts/GNP	21.4	21.4	21.9	22.2	22.3	22.1	21.9	22.1
Expenditures/GNP	22.6	22.9	22.4	22.5	22.4	22.1	21.9	21.8
Deficit/GNP	1.2	1.5	0.5	0.3	0.1	0.0	0.0	-0.3[d]
... at high employment[a]	0.1	0.1	-0.4[d]	-0.3[d]	-0.5[d]	-0.5[d]	-0.6[d]	-1.0[d]

TABLE B.2 (continued)

MONETARY AND FISCAL POLICY ALTERNATIVES

	1981	1982	1983	1984	1985	1986	1987	1988
	(Billions of current dollars)							
Receipts	643.3	696.8	790.5	873.3	964.0	1,061.0	1,163.5	1,310.2
Personal	300.5	326.7	356.0	385.1	420.2	461.6	509.5	570.0
Corporate profits	78.2	90.3	124.1	136.6	154.1	166.3	176.2	188.3
Other[b]	264.6	279.8	310.4	351.6	389.7	433.1	477.8	551.9
Expenditures	679.3	747.6	810.3	886.3	969.0	1,062.4	1,165.6	1,290.3
Defense purchases	154.4	178.1	195.7	214.2	237.9	263.6	292.0	325.1
Nondefense purchases	75.3	80.8	83.0	91.0	110.2	120.7	131.0	142.6
Transfers to persons	279.9	316.0	344.2	379.2	411.3	457.2	503.5	557.8
Grants-in-aid to state and local governments	89.5	93.6	99.3	108.1	120.6	132.4	148.3	167.2
Net interest paid	62.1	56.9	58.6	64.8	65.5	67.1	69.4	74.8
Other[c]	18.1	23.1	29.5	29.0	23.5	21.4	21.4	22.8
Deficit	36.0	50.8	19.8	13.1	5.0	1.4	2.0	−19.9[d]
. . . at high employment[a]	4.4	2.9	−13.7[d]	−13.8[d]	−22.1[d]	−26.1[d]	−35.3[d]	−59.1[d]
III. Easier Monetary, Actual Fiscal Policies								
	(Percentage)							
M-1 growth	11.2	11.4	8.5	6.4	7.4	7.7	7.1	7.6
Receipts/GNP	21.3	20.8	20.3	19.9	19.9	19.9	20.0	20.3
Expenditures/GNP	22.4	21.8	21.6	21.7	21.9	21.9	21.6	21.5
Deficit/GNP	1.1	1.0	1.3	1.8	2.0	2.0	1.6	1.2
. . . at high employment[a]	0.1	0.2	0.9	1.3	1.5	1.4	1.0	0.6
	(Billions of current dollars)							
Receipts	643.9	699.0	750.5	804.0	880.1	970.8	1,089.9	1,234.8
Personal	301.6	330.1	334.4	349.8	390.5	438.3	501.2	571.1
Corporate profits	76.5	82.5	97.7	92.8	88.9	88.6	96.1	95.4

TABLE B.2 (continued)

MONETARY AND FISCAL POLICY ALTERNATIVES

	1981	1982	1983	1984	1985	1986	1987	1988
Other[b]	265.8	286.4	318.4	361.4	400.7	443.9	492.6	567.7
Expenditures	676.3	731.0	799.1	874.9	968.0	1,068.9	1,180.1	1,308.5
Defense purchases	154.5	182.3	206.7	232.6	262.9	294.8	332.6	376.6
Nondefense purchases	75.4	80.8	77.7	81.5	99.9	109.3	118.6	129.0
Transfers to persons	279.5	309.3	337.8	366.2	396.3	441.2	484.5	534.7
Grants-in-aid to state and local governments	88.1	85.1	89.2	97.2	107.2	115.8	126.8	139.2
Net interest paid	60.7	51.5	58.2	68.2	78.2	86.4	96.2	106.1
Other[c]	18.1	22.0	29.5	29.2	23.5	21.4	21.4	22.9
Deficit	32.4	32.0	48.7	70.8	87.8	98.1	90.3	73.7
. . . at high employment[a]	4.7	7.8	35.7	55.3	68.1	69.6	58.2	36.2
IV. Actual Monetary, Tighter Fiscal Policies								
				(Percentage)				
M-1 growth	5.1	8.9	10.0	6.5	6.3	5.8	5.7	5.7
Receipts/GNP	21.4	21.1	21.5	22.0	22.3	22.2	22.0	22.3
Expenditures/GNP	23.4	25.2	25.4	24.9	24.8	24.8	24.5	24.2
Deficit/GNP	2.0	4.1	3.9	2.9	2.5	2.6	2.5	1.9
. . . at high employment[a]	0.4	1.0	0.7	0.7	0.7	0.8	0.7	0.4
			(Billions of current dollars)					
Receipts	632.8	647.3	709.0	793.5	869.5	934.5	1,012.6	1,125.6
Personal	300.1	316.2	332.0	358.7	386.2	414.2	448.0	489.6
Corporate profits	72.1	65.0	90.2	111.7	131.5	138.4	149.5	162.9
Other[b]	260.6	266.1	286.8	323.1	351.8	381.9	415.1	473.1
Expenditures	690.4	773.7	835.2	897.6	967.4	1,043.5	1,125.1	1,220.3
Defense purchases	154.0	175.9	190.9	206.3	226.4	247.5	270.4	296.5
Nondefense purchases	75.1	79.7	80.8	87.1	104.0	112.2	119.7	127.9

TABLE B.2 (continued)

MONETARY AND FISCAL POLICY ALTERNATIVES

	1981	1982	1983	1984	1985	1986	1987	1988
Transfers to persons	281.1	319.5	346.0	370.8	393.9	429.3	463.9	504.3
Grants-in-aid to state and local governments	89.3	92.6	97.1	104.2	114.7	124.1	137.1	152.7
Net interest paid	72.8	83.8	91.1	100.0	104.9	109.1	112.6	116.0
Other[c]	18.1	22.2	29.3	29.2	23.5	21.3	21.4	22.9
Deficit	57.7	126.4	126.2	104.1	97.9	109.0	112.5	94.7
. . . at high employment[a]	13.1	34.5	24.9	28.3	27.6	33.6	33.8	21.1

SOURCE: Authors' simulations based on DRI model.

a. Assumes high-employment unemployment rate of 6.0 percent in 1981–1982, 5.9 percent in 1983–1986, and 5.8 percent in 1987–1988.

b. Includes indirect business tax and nontax accruals and contributions for social insurance.

c. Includes net transfer payments to foreigners and subsidies less current surplus of government enterprises.

d. Surplus.

APPENDIX C

SUMMARIES OF MAJOR SOCIAL PROGRAMS

The following pages summarize the major federal social programs and explain the most significant changes that have occurred in them under the Reagan administration. The consequences of those changes are also explored. The programs include the following: Aid to Families with Dependent Children; Elementary and Secondary Education; Employment and Training; and Food Stamps. Medicare, Medicaid, and Health Services Grants are listed under "Health." In addition, Housing Assistance Programs, Nutrition Programs, Postsecondary Student Aid, Social Services, Social Security, Supplemental Security Income (SSI), and Unemployment Compensation are described.

Aid to Families with Dependent Children (AFDC)

AFDC is a state-administered, means-tested, cash assistance program financed jointly by the federal and state governments for families with dependent children and a parent who is absent, incapacitated or, in some states, unemployed. States determine benefit levels and eligibility criteria under broad federal guidelines. Maximum benefit levels, which are received by nearly 90 percent of all recipients, range from a low of about $120 per month to a high of about $600 per month for a family of four. Federal outlays in FY 1984 are $8 billion. The average monthly caseload is 3.8 million families, or 10.9 million persons.

The administration achieved major reductions in benefits and eligibility in FY 1981. A gross income ceiling was set at 150 percent of state need standards, states were required to count a stepparent's income, and eligibility for certain family members was reduced by other measures. Benefit levels were effectively reduced for recipients with earnings by a change in the method used to deduct earnings in determining countable income, which is the basis for computing benefits. The most significant of those changes was placing a limit on the child-care expense deduction and restricting to four months in any twelve-month period the previously unlimited deduction of the first thirty dollars and one-third of all subsequent earnings. States were also given an option to reduce benefits further by counting food stamps and housing subsidies as income. Congress did not, however, accept the administration's proposals to prorate shelter costs for people in shared housing and to include energy assistance as countable income. The administration did adopt several measures to tighten program administration, but continued attempts by the administration to develop a national recipient information data base failed.

The administration made a major push in 1981 and 1982 to require states to install "workfare" projects for certain AFDC family members. Such projects require work by recipients; the wages paid are in lieu of the AFDC benefits that would have otherwise been received. Congress gave states the option to establish these projects but refused to make them mandatory (see the Employment and Training Program Summary in this appendix for further discussion of workfare). Although the administration had proposed further major reductions, Congress enacted only minor benefit reductions in subsequent years.

The effect of program changes has been to reduce AFDC outlays by 14 percent below the spending projected for 1985 under pre-Reagan policy. Estimates of the reductions in the caseload attributable to these changes range from 400,000 to 500,000 families. Another 300,000 have retained their eligibility but have found their benefit levels reduced on average between $150 and $200 per month.

The actual effect of the AFDC changes on work behavior has proved more difficult to quantify. Preliminary results from several studies suggest that any such effect has been very minor.

Elementary and Secondary Education

The federal role in elementary and secondary education is small, since federal spending is less than 10 percent of total public expenditures for this purpose. The major federal program, constituting nearly half of the $7 billion in FY 1984 federal outlays for elementary and secondary education, is chapter 1 of the Education Consolidation and Improvement Act (ECIA) of 1981. It supports compensatory education for disadvantaged students in nearly all school districts, but most of the funds are concentrated in districts with a higher percentage of poor children. The three other major programs are education for the handicapped, vocational and adult education, and impact aid (to contribute to the education of children whose parents live and work on federal installations and therefore do not pay property taxes). Funds for all three programs are distributed to states or localities according to various formulas based on need. These four programs represent nearly 80 percent of all federal outlays for elementary and secondary education. Other significant federal programs are for Indian education and a block grant to states (chapter 2 of the ECIA), to serve a variety of purposes, including improving the performance of schools and to help defray the costs of court-ordered or voluntary desegregation.

In 1981 President Reagan proposed to consolidate more than forty-five federal education programs into two block grants—one to help states and localities meet special needs and one to improve the resources and performance of schools—with a 25 percent reduction in overall funding.

Congress agreed to only part of the changes. Chapter 1 of ECIA modified Title I (aid to the disadvantaged) by reducing the regulation and reporting requirements. Almost thirty small programs were consolidated under chapter 2 of ECIA. The largest of these programs was the Emergency School Assistance Act (ESAA), which provided funds to districts undergoing court-ordered or voluntary desegregation. All other major education programs (aid to the handicapped, bilingual education, vocational education) remained categorical.

The policy changes in education have been much more modest than those the Reagan administration had originally proposed. However, education funding is still below the level that would be consistent with FY 1981 policies. Outlays in FY 1985 for compensatory education programs (chapter 1) will be almost 20 percent (in real terms) below what they would have been under pre-Reagan policies. The existing evidence indicates that these funds are not being replaced by states and localities; about 1 million (20 percent) fewer children will be served in school year 1983/84 than in 1979/80.

Distribution of funds under chapter 2 is based on the number of school-age children and differs from the distribution under prior programs, which was based on need. Thus, states that are undergoing desegregation or have a larger disadvantaged population requiring more enrollments in Follow-Through (the Head Start continuation program) receive no more funds per pupil than any other district. This represents a significant change in policy with regard to federal support for desegregation and compensatory activities.

Employment and Training

The major federal employment and training programs are conducted under the Job Training Partnership Act (JTPA). Most of the $3.6 billion expenditures in FY 1984 will go to training economically disadvantaged adults and youths, with a small amount set aside for retraining dislocated workers—those unemployed because of plant closings or mass layoffs. Other training programs are Job Corps ($580 million) for disadvantaged youths and the Work Incentive (WIN) program ($270 million) for welfare recipients. Since JTPA is a new program, no estimate of the number of people to be trained in FY 1984 is available. Youths in Job Corps will number about 100,000 and WIN will provide counseling, training, or job placement services to perhaps 225,000 AFDC recipients. In FY 1984 virtually all of the federal "employment and training" programs will be limited to training only. In addition, states may require some welfare recipients to "work off" the amount of their grants in unpaid public jobs (workfare), but few federal funds are involved.

At its peak in 1978 and 1979, the Comprehensive Employment and Training Act (CETA), the precursor to JTPA, distributed nearly $10 billion per year to local governments to create public service employment (PSE) and provide training. At the administration's request, Congress eliminated the PSE component of CETA early in 1981. Nearly 400,000 PSE jobs were terminated, two-thirds of which were with nonprofit organizations, at savings of $3.1 billion.

The CETA legislation expired in 1982 and was replaced by the (JTPA), which resulted from a compromise between the administration and Congress. The administration proposed eliminating income support (training allowances) and other services, such as child care, for people in training; Congress limited such costs to 15 percent of all funding. The administration proposed that responsibility for the entire program be shifted to the private sector (through private industry counsels, called PICs); Congress specified that the private sector and local government are to be "equal partners" in administering the new program. The administration proposed that funds for JTPA be in the form of unrestricted block grants to states; Congress concurred in the block grant, but placed restrictions on how states allocate funds to local jurisdictions. Finally, the administration proposed federal funding of under $3 billion; Congress funded the program at a level of about 15 percent above that requested.

In 1981 the administration also proposed to reduce funding for Job Corps by 40 percent, but Congress rejected the request and has maintained funding at approximately pre-Reagan policy levels.

Each year the administration has also proposed eliminating the federal WIN program and requiring mandatory state workfare programs instead. Congress, however, has continued to fund WIN at about two-thirds of its prior policy level, and has given states the option of running workfare programs. By 1983 less than half of the states had some AFDC workfare, and in all but four states workfare is limited to a few counties, often on a demonstration basis. (Only one of the statewide programs includes more than half of the eligible recipients.) Based on a recent U.S. General Accounting Office study, these programs do not appear to be effective either in saving states AFDC monies or in promoting private sector employment of AFDC recipients.

It will be several years before the employment and training system stabilizes because of the new roles of different levels of government and the shared role of the public and private sectors. The reduction in federal expenditures for training of 39 percent in real terms from FY 1981 to FY 1984 will not result in a drop of 39 percent in the number of people being trained because most of the reduction will be in training stipends and support services. But the restriction of the majority of the funds for training expenses will mean that the most disadvantaged portion of the JTPA-eligible population will receive less priority because those people will often be unable to take training without some income or service support. Adults not on welfare and troubled youths in need of counseling and other intensive services will be hardest hit.

Food Stamps

The Food Stamp program is federally financed and state administered, providing aid based on need without regard to other family or individual characteristics. Food coupons are dispensed by state agencies and redeemed by recipients at retail stores. The maximum monthly food stamp allotment in the continental United States is now $76 for a single person and $253 for a family of four. It is automatically adjusted each year for increases in food costs. Actual benefits are determined by subtracting 30 percent of a household's "countable" income (gross income minus certain allowable deductions) from this maximum. Outlays will total about $11 billion in FY 1984 and will help an average of 20.9 million recipients each month.

Changes made at the administration's request reduced real benefit levels for nearly all recipients and eliminated aid for more than a million people. Benefits were reduced across the board through delay in inflation adjustments and a 1 percent cut in benefit levels. Allowable income deductions used in determining countable income were also curbed. However, the administration failed in its efforts to count energy assistance payments and subsidized school lunches as income, to eliminate the minimum monthly benefit of ten dollars, and to increase the proportion of income that beneficiaries are expected to contribute toward the purchase of food from 30 to 35 percent.

The administration did persuade Congress to pass legislation tightening eligibility and participation requirements. People with gross incomes above 130 percent of the poverty level and net (after deductions) incomes above 100 percent of poverty were excluded, but the aged, blind, and disabled were exempt from these ceilings. Several administrative measures aimed at discouraging participation by able-bodied eligible persons, tightening program management, and reducing payment errors.

The reductions in food stamp benefits and eligibility will lower program outlays by 14 percent by FY 1985, compared with a projection of spending under pre-Reagan policy. The caseload, which is quite sensitive to unemployment and would normally have risen by well over 1 million recipients as a result of the recent recession, rose only about 300,000 because of the cutbacks. Given the nature of the cuts, recipients with the greatest income from other sources experienced the largest reductions in benefits.

Health

The Reagan administration had two major health policy objectives upon taking office: reducing the growth of federal health care spending and reforming private as well as public health insurance to promote efficiency through competition. With respect to the first goal, the administration has had only limited success, reducing expected FY 1985 spending by about 6 percent from their pre-Reagan policy levels. Reductions in Medicare accounted for three-fourths of those savings, but the largest proportionate cuts were in the much smaller health services grants programs. With respect to its second goal of promoting competition, the administration has taken minor action and made no progress. It did not introduce its promised "procompetition" legislation until its FY 1984 budget, and then in a form (limits on tax subsidies for the purchase of private insurance) that was far less comprehensive than its initially stated intent. The proposal, which has attracted little political support and considerable opposition, has made little headway in Congress.

Medicare. Medicare is a federally financed and administered health insurance program which insures 26 million elderly and 3 million disabled citizens against hospital, physician, and related medical expenses. In FY 1984, Medicare will cost the federal government about $64 billion, three-quarters of total federal spending on health care. The hospital insurance (HI) component is financed through a joint employer-employee payroll tax; the supplemental medical insurance (SMI) component is financed through a combination of general revenues and participant premiums.

Despite Medicare's fiscal prominence and rapid growth (17 percent annually since 1974), the administration's first two budgets proposed no major reforms in the program. Budgetary pressures forced Congress to initiate much needed reform of Medicare's method of hospital payment. Ironically, that reform bore a greater resemblance to Carter administration proposals for cost containment, generally perceived as "regulatory," than to the procompetition initiatives advocated by the administration.

Medicare will now fix rates in advance rather than reimburse hospitals whatever they spend. The previous payment system gave almost no incentives for efficiency, whereas the new method rewards efficiency and penalizes waste. But despite the improved incentives, efficiency is not guaranteed. Hospitals may avoid constraints by manipulating the system or shifting costs to other payers. Or hospitals may respond to the constraints by lowering the amount or style of care they give to Medicare patients (or, more immediately, to uninsured patients receiving charity care). The actual impact of the system remains to be seen.

After action was taken to contain payments to hospitals under Medicare, physician payments became the next target for budgetary restraint. In its FY 1984 budget the administration proposed a simple freeze in payment, rather than payment reform. Congress has rejected this proposal so far but is still debating possible reforms.

Budgetary pressure produced not only payment reforms but also marginal increases in the cost sharing Medicare requires of its beneficiaries and proposals from the administration for large additional increases. The marginal increases boost costs for the near-poor elderly who are too well-off for Medicaid but have difficulty buying supplementary private insurance. Marginal increases also do little to further structural changes that could enhance Medicare's efficiency and protection against catastrophic expenses. (Medicare now offers relatively extensive "first-dollar" protection, while leaving beneficiaries exposed to the risk of catastrophic expenditures should they become very ill.) In its FY 1984 budget, the administration proposed a partial solution to this problem, increasing cost sharing on the first days of a hospital stay, while adding coverage that is lacking for very long stays. Eager to avoid any reduction in benefits, Congress did not seriously consider this proposal and the administration subsequently dropped it.

Despite the actions taken, growth of the Medicare program continues to pose a major fiscal problem. Even under the new hospital payment system, Medicare (HI) spending is expected to grow almost 60 percent faster than payroll tax revenues over the next decade, as a result burgeoning deficits are expected in the hospital insurance trust fund in the 1990s. Physician benefits also are commanding a growing share of general revenues. Resolving these financing problems may require dramatic changes in Medicare structure that go well beyond any measures yet proposed by the administration or considered by Congress.

Medicaid. Medicaid is a state-administered entitlement program, jointly financed by the federal and state governments, which insures persons actually or potentially eligible for welfare (AFDC or Supplemental Security Income) benefits against the costs of medical and long-term care. It covers about half of the poverty population. In FY 1984, the federal share is expected to be about $21 billion, with states paying a roughly equal amount. The program will serve about 20 million persons—of whom about 70 percent are AFDC-related eligibles and the remainder aged or disabled. (States may use resource standards for Medicaid eligibility that exceed eligibility standards for welfare, covering the so-called medically needy.)

To contain rapidly rising federal Medicaid spending, the Reagan administration initially proposed to limit federal spending in FY 1982 to a 5 percent increase over FY 1981, with future rates of increase tied to growth in the gross national product (GNP). In addition, the administration would have given states nearly free rein to redesign their Medicaid programs. Under strong pressure from the governors, Congress rejected the cap but passed an alternative that retained the open-ended federal match at slightly reduced rates. Congress also gave the states considerably greater ability—although less than that which the administration sought—to target benefits and control costs through eligibility, benefits, and payment rules. Finally, congressional actions limiting AFDC eligibility indirectly cut Medicaid because eligibility for the two programs is linked. Since 1981, the administration has proposed more cuts in Medicaid, including an extension of reduced matching payments and a requirement that states charge beneficiaries at least a nominal amount for services received. Congress has rejected most of these proposed cuts because they would shift costs to the states or reduce service to the poor.

In 1982, Medicaid spending increases slowed to about half the average annual growth rate between 1979 and 1981, which was 18 percent. The recession, which put substantial pressure on state budgets, was a major factor in efforts by the states to control their Medicaid spending. But since the slowdown occurred in almost all states, even where the recession was mild, the federal actions also apparently either prompted state restraint or helped legitimize cuts the states wanted to make. (Some of the widespread reduction was attributable to the drop in inflation; some may reflect state reporting and accounting adjustments made to maximize federal reimbursements.)

The reported reductions in the growth of Medicaid spending indicate a substantial cut in service to the poor. Despite the recession, which otherwise would have resulted in an increase in the number of Medicaid recipients of a million or more, the number of Medicaid recipients actually fell because of eligibility restrictions. The most marked decline (12 percent) occurred among medically needy recipients who were elderly and disabled. The number of AFDC recipients increased slightly, but by several hundred thousand less than would have occurred in the absence of the elimination of the working poor from AFDC eligibility (see the AFDC Program Summary in this appendix).

Several states took advantage of the 1981 legislative change that gave them greater flexibility to pay hospitals less than costs, and more states may follow. This policy shift may buy for the poor equivalent access to care at lower costs. Other changes are more likely to reduce access to care for the poor, especially since local governments offset only a portion of Medicaid cuts with aid to public hospitals on whom an increased burden of providing medical care to the poor is falling. Reported cuts include reduced coverage of prescription drugs, dental care, various therapies, and other Medicaid optional services and arbitrary limits on hospital inpatient stays and a wide range of other services.

Health Services Grants. For FY 1984, the federal government has appropriated some $1.3 billion for health services "block grants" to states supporting a multitude of public health services (e.g., rodent control), medical care services for specific populations (e.g., persons living in underserved areas and victims of hypertension), and developmental programs (e.g., for home health care and emergency medical services).

The creation of block grants with greatly reduced federal funding was the Reagan administration's main goal for health services grants. Congress granted the administration much of what it proposed in 1981, as most prior categorical grants were consolidated into three "blocks" that gave states more flexibility to spend about 20 percent fewer federal dollars. However, several narrowly focused "categorical" programs, such as black-lung clinics and immunization, remain. Since 1981, Congress has rejected further administration efforts to consolidate programs and reduce funds.

States responded to the block grants by concentrating the more limited federal dollars on programs that they had traditionally favored (i.e., supported heavily with state money), even adding their own funds to such popular programs as crippled childrens' services and hypertension programs. The "losers" under block grants are previously categorical programs lacking a solid state-level constituency—notably programs that were new, served specialized groups, or were formerly funded mainly with direct federal grants, without state involvement in administration funding. Chief among these were lead-based paint prevention and rodent control.

States also have allocated the money more in accord with population than with the categorical needs formerly stipulated in federal law. Thus, big-city populations have fared relatively less well than nonmetropolitan ones. Research, long-range public health efforts, and nonacute care have also been deemphasized relative to immediate medical services.

Despite some state replacement of lost federal dollars, many providers are living with less. Block-grant-related funding reductions are only one of the causes, however; state and local government support is also often under pressure, and Medicare and other insurers have cut back. When local service providers (like community mental health centers or local public health clinics) have to tighten their belts, rather than restricting their eligibility standards or reducing the range of services offered, they have tended to extend waiting lists, reduce clinic hours or staff time per visit, or make service locations less numerous or convenient.

Housing Assistance Programs

The housing assistance programs are designed to improve the quality of housing occupied by low-income families, reduce the share of income they spend on housing to an acceptable level, and augment the overall supply of low-income housing. Programs have used rent supplements to help families occupy good-quality housing of their choice, as well as using subsidies for the development and operation of new projects to house families who are income eligible. Assistance is *not* available on an entitlement basis, since available funds can serve only about one-fourth of the eligible population. At present about 4.6 million households are participating in U.S. Housing and Urban Development (HUD) and Farmers Home Administration programs at a cost to the federal government of about $10 billion.

The administration's desired approach to housing assistance was most clearly revealed in its FY 1983 budget proposals. These would have (a) halted the increase in the number of households receiving assistance; (b) more tightly targeted assistance on poorer households; (c) increased the share of income all participants are required to spend on housing (i.e., reduced benefits); and (d) radically shifted toward the use of rent supplements for existing units versus building new projects to obtain good housing for participants.

Congress gave the administration much but not all of what it wanted. The number of newly assisted households fell from an annual average of about 300,000 for the 1976–1980 period to 100,000 for the 1981–1984 period. As a result, there will be about 1 million fewer recipient households and about 300,000 more families living in substandard housing at the end of 1985 than there would have been under a continuation of pre-Reagan policies. Targeting was tightened and benefits were cut by about 15 percent for the average recipient by increasing tenants' required housing contribution from 25 to 30 percent of income. However, Congress rejected the administration's proposal to count food stamps as income, a measure that would have meant a large benefit reduction for the poorest tenants. Renting existing dwellings has been emphasized over building new ones. Congress eliminated one costly new construction program and cut back appropriations for the others, but in 1983 created a new, relatively small-scale program that should cost less per unit but serve comparatively few poor households.

Overall, the administration clearly succeeded in getting a grip on future HUD funding levels by cutting budget authority appropriated from $27 billion in FY 1980 to $13 billion by FY 1984. The decline in actual outlays, however, is far less because of the long-term nature of the federal funding commitments in housing.

The administration accomplished much less change in the smaller Farmers Home Administration programs. Budgets have remained essentially constant. And Congress rejected a proposal, originated in the Senate and endorsed by the administration, for a wholesale transformation of all programs into a state-administered block grant.

Nutrition Programs

Federal child nutrition activities include free and reduced-price lunches for lower-income children in participating schools, a general subsidy for all meals served in those schools, a program of special food supplements for pregnant and lactating women, infants, and children (WIC), and several smaller programs. Altogether, these programs will spend $5 billion in FY 1984. School lunches served will reach an average of 23.1 million children per day (11.8 million free or reduced price), and school breakfasts will average 3.6 million daily (3.2 million free or reduced price).

Significant changes were made in the child nutrition programs in 1981 in response to administration proposals. Meal subsidies were cut for nonneedy students in both the full- and reduced-price lunch programs, the special milk program was removed from a large number of schools, and the summer feeding program was limited to high-poverty areas.

The president's subsequent proposals have been unsuccessful. Congress did not accept a proposed child feeding block grant that would have combined the school breakfast and child care feeding subsidies at a 12 percent lower funding level, or similar block grant proposals for the WIC and commodity supplemental food programs.

Child nutrition outlays as a whole will be 28 percent below the pre-Reagan baseline for FY 1985 because of the cutbacks. Participation in the school lunch program will be reduced by about 3 million children, including 1 million eligible for free or reduced-price meals. However, because of the popularity and effectiveness of the WIC program, Congress raised WIC spending by 4 percent above the baseline, despite administration proposals to combine it in a large block grant at reduced funding levels.

Postsecondary Education

Federal spending on postsecondary schooling is largely in the form of student aid—Pell grants to help low income students attend college, subsidized guaranteed student loans (GSL) for other low- and middle-income students, and grants to colleges, which are primarily used to aid low-income students.* FY 1984 expenditures for all three programs totals about $7 billion. The two largest programs—Pell grants and the GSLs—will aid about 2.5 and 3.0 million students, respectively. The maximum annual grant is $1,800 and the maximum annual loan is $2,500; however, both are scaled to school costs and family income.

The Reagan administration sought to scale back federal funds for student aid by tailoring aid more closely to student need. Between FY 1978 and FY 1981 outlays in these programs had increased by 114 percent, partially as a result of the extension of Pell grants to middle-income students, the removal of any income restriction on eligibility for subsidized loans, and the rise in the implicit GSL subsidy when market interest rates soared in the early 1980s, making the loans more attractive. By FY 1981 federal spending on student aid (excluding the GI bill and Social Security) was $6 billion and accounted for nearly 80 percent of the tuition and fee income of all colleges and universities in the U.S. (compared with 39 percent in FY 1976). Consequently, the administration included proposals in its FY 1982 budget to curb program growth by restoring income restrictions and reducing the interest subsidy in the GSL program (a Carter proposal) and by tightening the income limits on Pell grants, which were largely enacted by Congress. Although middle- and upper-income students bore most of the cuts, some cuts, such as the $80 reduction in Pell grant benefits, affected low-income students.

The administration's FY 1983 budget called for more stringent cutbacks in student aid. Had they been enacted, FY 1985 outlays would be $4 billion below their pre-Reagan policy level—a cut of 47 percent—but Congress did not grant the request. The administration's FY 1984 budget abandoned these deep cuts and outlined a proposal for student self-help that would better rationalize the student aid programs and result in modest savings. The maximum basic grant would be substantially increased, but grants would be restricted to lower-income students. Congress again rejected the proposal. Consequently, spending for FY 1985 is anticipated to be about 23 percent below its pre-Reagan policy levels but about the same in real terms as it was

---

*The GI bill and Social Security payments to enrolled dependents between the ages of 18 and 21 also provide financing to college students. The Social Security benefit is being phased out as part of the Social Security legislation, and the post-Vietnam era GI program is less generous than it was before 1977.

in FY 1981. Thus, spending for higher education has been curbed, but at an historically high level.*

Between academic years 1980/81 and 1982/83, the number of basic grant recipients declined by 100,000, a reduction of about 4 percent; and the number of new loans awarded in the GSL program dropped by 460,000, a decline of 13 percent. However, the number of beneficiaries remains considerably higher than the number before 1980. In the GSL program the number of beneficiaries declined in part because lower market interest rates made the subsidy less attractive, and in part because family incomes were above the new cutoff point (which, depending on family size and other factors, could be as high as $65,000). There is no evidence that fewer youths are able to attend college because of the GSL cutbacks. However, the small reduction in Pell grant recipients probably reflects the decline in the income eligibility standards and may be affecting the ability of some low-income youths to attend postsecondary educational institutions.

Social Services

Slightly more than half of the cost of public social service programs are federally funded, mainly through three programs: the Social Services Block Grant program to states (with federal funding of $2.8 billion in FY 1984), which can be used at the states' discretion but which has traditionally provided in-home support for the frail elderly and day care for the children of working welfare mothers; the Older Americans Act ($0.7 billion in FY 1984), which provides food and social and other services to older Americans regardless of income; and the child welfare service program ($0.6 billion in FY 1984), which pays for casework services to prevent children from having to be taken from their families and placed in foster care, and for foster care in the event those efforts are not successful. In general, funding for social services has been targeted toward abused, neglected, or dependent children and adults, the frail elderly, and mentally or emotionally disturbed adults.

In 1981, at the Reagan administration's urging, Congress converted the Title XX Social Services program into the Social Services Block Grant, eliminating the requirement of state matching of federal funds and targeting funds on the low-income population, and reducing reporting requirements and the level of federal funding by 20 percent for FY 1982 (the administration

---

*If Social Security student benefits and the GI bill were included, FY 1985 would show considerably lower levels of spending in real terms than at any time since the mid-1970s.

requested a 27 percent cut). In both FY 1983 and FY 1984 the administration asked for further budget cuts, but Congress did not grant them.

Elimination of the state matching requirement had little effect on state spending for social services because most states were already contributing more to social services than the federal government required. In fact, many states have responded to the reduced federal assistance by increasing their own expenditures for social services. They also have responded to reduced regulations by reordering their priorities toward more emergency services to children and adults in life-threatening situations.

Funding and services under the Older Americans Act have remained about the same under the Reagan administration as under the previous administration; however, child welfare services have taken a peculiar twist because of the administration's actions. During the last year of the Carter administration, Congress enacted a law designed to discourage foster care placements and to encourage preventive, reunification, and family support planning services through a complex relationship between funding for the two purposes. The Reagan administration, however, has consistently asked for less money for preventive services, while funding for foster care has remained essentially open-ended. Nowhere does the Reagan administration argue for foster care and against in-home support, but the net effect of its actions has been to slow down or reverse the trends in the states toward more preventive and ameliorative efforts, and to increase the likelihood that children will spend more time in foster care.

Social Security

The Social Security system is a federal program that protects most workers and their families against income loss due to retirement, disability, or the death of a breadwinner. It is financed mainly by a payroll tax on employees and employers. Benefits are based on each covered worker's earnings history and are automatically adjusted annually for inflation. Benefits range from a low of about 24 percent of a worker's last year of covered earnings for high-wage workers to a high of 63 percent for low-wage workers. The average monthly benefit for retired and disabled workers is currently about $450. Program outlays will total about $176 billion in FY 1984, with beneficiaries numbering 36 million.

In 1981 Congress enacted several small cuts that the Reagan administration had included in its initial budget proposals. Their primary purpose was to reduce costs by eliminating benefits believed to be least essential to the program's central objectives. Dependents' benefits for college students are being phased out, the minimum floor on benefits was ended for persons retiring after December 31, 1981 (the administration favored dropping the minimum completely), and a previously enacted liberalization of the retirement test was delayed.

In May 1981 the president followed up on this success with a package of reforms—intended to avert imminent insolvency in the Social Security trust funds—which would have sharply reduced early retirement benefits and eligibility for disabled persons, and restrained benefit levels from rising as rapidly as wage levels over the long term. Congress unanimously rejected these proposals as too harsh. Congress did, however, take the necessary actions later in March 1983 to avert imminent insolvency in the trust funds. In doing so it followed the guidance of a bipartisan commission which the president had recommended in the wake of congressional rejection of his earlier reform package. To solve the short-run (FY 1983–FY 1989) funding problem, Congress enacted measures to add $128 billion in trust fund revenues, including imposition of higher payroll tax rates, income taxation of half of Social Security benefits of beneficiaries with total incomes above certain levels, extension of coverage under Social Security (and, therefore, payroll taxation) of new federal workers and all nonprofit organization employees, and a transfer of general revenues to the trust funds to compensate for past military service credits that increase benefits. Some savings in outlays also were achieved primarily through a six-month delay in the 1983 cost-of-living adjustment, which effected an across-the-board 3 percent real benefit reduction.

Congress also voted to close an anticipated long-term funding deficit, placing more emphasis on benefit reductions than on revenue increases. The major provision was a gradual increase in the age (from 65 to 67) at which full benefits can be collected to be phased in beginning early next century.

The immediate result of all the Social Security changes is a modest reduction in outlays (4.6 percent by 1985) compared with what prior policy would have yielded. The benefit reductions affect all recipients, although low-income beneficiaries who also receive SSI will actually gain in total income because of an increase in SSI benefit levels which Congress passed, along with the delay in the Social Security cost-of-living increase, in order to protect the poor. The long-term effects of the changes are much more substantial and mean much greater losses in disposable income for recipients (up to 11 percent by 2030) relative to prior law. The percentage losses generally rise with the beneficiary's income, mainly because of the partial taxation of Social Security benefits. Also, a significant number of older people can be expected to delay retirement and continue to work once the higher age for full benefits is in effect next century.

Supplemental Security Income

Supplemental Security Income (SSI) is a federally funded and administered means-tested program providing cash assistance to low-income aged, blind, and disabled persons. Benefits are automatically adjusted for inflation each year. Maximum benefit levels are currently $314 per month for a single person and $472 for a couple. About half of the states also supplement the federal payments at their own expense by an average of about 12 percent. In FY 1984, federal SSI outlays will total $8 billion and assist an average monthly caseload of 3.4 million recipients.

In 1981 the administration proposed significant changes in benefits to achieve cost savings, but none was enacted. Congress did, however, pass a measure to reduce payment errors through changing the method of accounting for recipients' income.

In 1982 the administration again launched major proposals to reduce program benefits. Under these proposals the benefits of most recipients would have been cut, and eligibility based on disability would have been tightened. Congress responded by enacting only minor cost-saving measures, such as prorating the first month's benefits and rounding down benefit amounts.

The most important change to SSI occurred as a result of the 1983 Social Security Amendments, which included a six-month delay in Social Security cost-of-living increases. To reduce the impact of this delay on SSI recipients, Congress also passed a monthly benefit increase of $20 for individuals and $30 for couples, the first increase in excess of cost-of-living adjustments since the program's establishment.

This one-time increase amounted to a 6.6 percent real benefit increase for all SSI recipients. In addition, some SSI recipients realized automatic upward adjustments in their payments as a result of declines in benefits they were receiving from the cash programs (Social Security and AFDC) which were cut. As a result, SSI outlays will increase by nearly 9 percent by 1985 relative to pre-Reagan policies.

Unemployment Compensation

The federal-state Unemployment Insurance (UI) program pays benefits to most unemployed workers who meet a test of recent work experience. Benefits are paid from state accounts in a federal trust fund financed by a payroll tax on each state's employers. States have sole authority to set taxes (above a federally required minimum), eligibility criteria, and benefit levels. Most states pay compensation for up to twenty-six weeks of unemployment, with benefits ranging from 50 to 60 percent of previous wages up to a maximum. In addition, a jointly financed federal-state Extended Benefit (EB) program "triggers" on in states with high unemployment levels to provide up to thirteen additional weeks of compensation. Federal outlays are estimated at $26 billion for FY 1984, with the number of weekly claimants expected to average 4.7 million, while weekly benefits will range from about $90 to $160. In addition, the Trade Adjustment Assistance (TAA) program may provide compensation after UI benefits are exhausted for workers unemployed because of trade competition. Expenditures for the TAA program are less than $1 billion.

In 1981 Congress agreed to an administration proposal to eliminate the national "trigger" for the EB program, making the state triggers more restrictive, curtailing UI benefits for persons voluntarily leaving military service, and charging interest on loans to states whose trust funds were in debt (thus placing pressure on the states to cut back on basic UI benefits). The net result of these changes was to reduce federal outlays for UI by 17 percent. Also, major changes in Trade Adjustment Assistance sharply reduced this aid for the long-term unemployed in industries affected by trade policies.

In 1982 over the initial opposition of the administration, Congress passed a Federal Supplemental Compensation Program to provide six to ten weeks of additional UI benefits during the recession. To help finance these changes, Congress reduced the income limits for taxing UI benefits from $20,000 to $12,000 for individuals (and from $25,000 to $18,000 for couples). These supplemental benefits were less generous than those that had been provided in the two previous recessions (thirteen weeks in the 1972–1973 and twenty-six weeks in the 1975–1977 recessions). Although supplemental benefits were later extended for up to twenty-six weeks for certain unemployed workers, the less-generous supplemental benefits, combined with the cutbacks in EB benefits and the severity of the 1981–1982 recession, meant that an average of only 45 percent of the unemployed received UI benefits each month in 1982, compared with more than 75 percent at the peak of the 1975–1976 recession. In addition, the imposition of interest charges on loans to states has resulted in a tightening of eligibility, reduced benefits, or increased payroll taxes in many states.

Although the administration achieved many of its original goals, some proposals were rejected. One was that after receipt of benefits for thirteen weeks, claimants would be required to accept any offer of work paying at least the minimum wage or the equivalent of the claimant's weekly benefit amount. Efforts to repeal Trade Adjustment Assistance were also denied.

NOTES

NOTES TO CHAPTER 1

1. See Everett Carll Ladd, "Public Attitudes Toward Policy and Governance: Searching for the Sources and Meaning of 'The Reagan Revolution'," in Lester M. Salamon and Michael Lund, eds., *The Reagan Presidency and the Governing of America* (Washington, D.C.: The Urban Institute Press, 1984); and John L. Goodman, Jr., *Public Opinion during the Reagan Administration: National Issues, Private Concerns* (Washington, D.C.: The Urban Institute Press, 1983); chapter 2.

2. Text of President Reagan's inaugural address on January 20, 1981, as reprinted in *Congressional Quarterly*, vol. 39, no. 3 (January 29, 1981).

3. John L. Palmer and Isabel V. Sawhill, "Perspectives on the Reagan Experiment," in John L. Palmer and Isabel V. Sawhill, eds., *The Reagan Experiment: An Examination of Economic and Social Policies under the Reagan Administration* (Washington, D.C.: The Urban Institute Press, 1982), pp. 24–25.

4. See Richard A. Stubbing, "The Defense Budget," in Gregory B. Mills and John L. Palmer, eds., *Federal Budget Policy in the 1980s* (Washington, D.C.: The Urban Institute Press, 1984); Steven R. Weisman, "Reaganomics and the President's Men," *The New York Times Magazine* (October 24, 1982); William Greider, "The Education of David Stockman," *The Atlantic Monthly*, vol. 248, no. 12 (December 1981); Peter W. Bernstein, "David Stockman: No More Big Budget Cuts," *Fortune* (February 6, 1984); and William W. Kaufman, *Spending for a Sound Defense: Alternatives to the Reagan Military Budget* (Washington, D.C.: The Committee for National Security, 1984).

5. Richard Reeves, "The Ideological Election," *The New York Times Magazine* (February 19, 1984).

6. Greider, "The Education of David Stockman," p. 30.

7. Ibid.

NOTES TO CHAPTER 2

Acknowledgments: We are grateful to Lauren Saunders and Beth Lobel for research assistance and to Marla Taylor and Connie Blango for typing assistance. We also thank Hugh Heclo and James Sundquist for their helpful comments on an earlier draft of this paper, and participants in an Urban Institute conference on Governance in the Reagan Era for many useful insights.

1. Gerald R. Ford, "Imperiled, Not Imperial," *Time*, vol. 116, no. 19 (November 10, 1980), p. 30; Mondale as quoted in Joseph Kraft, "The Post-Imperial Presidency," *New York Times Magazine* (November 23, 1980), p. 31; James L. Sundquist, "The Crisis of Competence in Government," in Joseph A. Pechman, ed., *Setting National Priorities: Agenda for the 1980s* (Washington, D.C.: The Brookings Institution, 1980), p. 531; National Academy of Public Administration, *A Presidency for the 1980s* (Washington, D.C.: National Academy of Public Administration, 1980), p. 1; Lloyd N. Cutler, "To Form a Government," *Foreign Affairs*, vol. 59 (Fall 1980), pp. 126–143. For additional contributions to the conventional wisdom that by

1980 the prospects for presidential leadership looked exceptionally dim, see Godfrey Hodgson, *All Things to All Men: The False Promise of the Modern American Presidency* (New York: Simon and Schuster, 1980); Samuel P. Huntington, *American Politics: The Promise of Disharmony* (Cambridge, Mass.: Belknap Press, 1981); various chapters in Anthony King, ed., *The New American Political System* (Washington, D.C.: American Enterprise Institute, 1978); Paul Charles Light, *The President's Agenda: Domestic Policy Choice from Kennedy to Carter (With Notes on Ronald Reagan)* (Baltimore: The Johns Hopkins University Press, 1982), pp. 204–217; and Richard E. Neustadt, *Presidential Power: The Politics of Leadership from FDR to Carter* (New York: John Wiley, rev. ed. 1980, first published 1960), pp. 212–214. (Note that Neudstadt sees opportunities for presidents as well as obstacles in the recent trends, see p. 214.)

2. Sundquist, "The Crisis of Competence," in Pechman, *Setting National Priorities: Agenda for the 1980s*, p. 538.

3. Neustadt, *Presidential Power*, p. 10.

4. The quotation is from Anthony King, "The American Polity," in King, p. 391. Data on PACs are from U.S. Federal Election Commission, press release (January 10, 1984).

5. On the weakening of, and other changes in, the political parties, see Norman Nie, Sidney Verba, and John R. Petrocik, *The Changing American Voter* (Cambridge, Mass.: Harvard University Press, 1976) and Jeane Kirkpatrick, *The New Presidential Elite* (New York: Russell Sage Foundation and Twentieth Century Fund, 1976).

6. On turnover in Congress, see Christopher Buchanan, "House: Modest Gains for the Minority," *Congressional Quarterly*, vol. 36, no. 45 (November 11, 1978), pp. 3251, and in the same issue Charles W. Hucker, "Senate: Slightly More Conservative." The quote is from Hodgson, *All Things to All Men*, p. 138.

7. The War Powers Act limited unilateral presidential commitment of troops; the Congressional Budget Act restricted presidential impoundment of funds. Other presidency-curbing measures include new oversight investigations of executive branch activities, including intelligence activities; the requirement that the president's choice of director and deputy director of the Office of Management and Budget (OMB) be congressionally approved; and the passage of numerous laws containing provisions for a legislative veto. On presidency-curbing legislation, see Fred I. Greenstein, "Change and Continuity in the Modern Presidency," in King. The presidential success rates, as computed by the *Congressional Quarterly*, record the percentage of times that Congress supports the president on measures on which he has taken a clear-cut position. See Diane Granat, "Congress' Backing for Reagan Continues to Decline Steadily," *Congressional Quarterly*, vol. 41, no. 52 (December 31, 1983), p. 2782.

8. Increasingly, the courts have become an independent source of policy direction and administrative control. Traditional remedies have been expanded, restrictions on what constitutes a "case in controversy" have been relaxed, and a greater willingness has been shown to enter disputes once considered outside the judicial realm. See Donald L. Horowitz, *The Courts and Social Policy* (Washington, D.C.: The Brookings Institution, 1977).

9. By 1980 more than 70 percent of the federal budget—the principal vehicle for presidential control of the government—had become "uncontrollable," that is, outside the regular annual budget and appropriations process. Included here are the so-called entitlement programs—Social Security, civil service and military retirement, Medicare, and student assistance—all of which by law provide benefits to every eligible person, and spending for which is thus determined by demographic and economic circumstances; payment of interest on the public debt; and outlays resulting from liquidation of prior-year contracts and obligations, in both defense and domestic programs. Also, a massive "hidden budget" had taken shape, consisting of more than $100 billion in new loan and loan guarantee commitments each year, about $150 billion in "tax subsidies," and the more difficult-to-estimate costs of federal regulatory activity. Taken together, these developments left important decisions about government resources much less amenable to presidential influence. On uncontrollable spending, see Office of Management and Budget, *Budget of the United States Government, FY 1985* (Washington, D.C.: Government Printing Office, 1984), p. 9–45. On new loan and loan guarantee commitments, see Congressional Budget Office, *An Analysis of the President's Credit Budget for Fiscal Year 1985* (Washington, D.C.:

Congressional Budget Office, 1984), p. 5. On tax expenditures, see U.S. Congress, Congressional Budget Office, *Tax Expenditures: Budget Control Options and Five-Year Budget Projections for Fiscal Years 1983–1987* (Washington, D.C.: Congressional Budget Office, 1982), p. 13. On the resistance of the budget to presidential influence generally, see Lester M. Salamon, "The Budget: A Weak Reed," *Wall Street Journal* (December 8, 1980), p. 28.

10. Lester M. Salamon, "Rethinking Public Management: Third Party Government and the Changing Forms of Government Action," *Public Policy*, vol. 29, no. 3 (Summer 1981), pp. 255–275.

11. James MacGregor Burns, *The Deadlock of Democracy: Four-Party Politics in America* (Englewood Cliffs, N.J.: Prentice-Hall, 1963).

12. The quotation is from James Q. Wilson, "The Dilemmas of Conservatism II," *The American Spectator*, vol. 15 (March 1982), p. 13.

13. The headline is from the *New York Times* (November 6, 1980), p. A-1. Data on rejection of Carter are from Paul R. Abramson, John H. Aldrich, and David W. Rhode, *Change and Continuity in the 1980 Elections* (Washington, D.C.: Congressional Quarterly Press, rev. ed. 1983), p. 153. As further evidence of the ambiguity of the 1980 election results, academics themselves did not completely agree on how to interpret the election. Many emphasized dissatisfaction with Carter as an explanation for Reagan's victory. See, for example, Abramson et al., *Change and Continuity*; William Schneider, "The November 4 Vote for President: What Did It Mean?," in Austin Ranney, ed., *The American Elections of 1980* (Washington, D.C.: American Enterprise Institute, 1981); the chapters by Gerald M. Pomper, "The Presidential Election," and Kathleen Frankovic, "Public Opinion Trends," in Gerald M. Pomper et al., eds., *The Elections of 1980* (Chatham, N.J.: Chatham House, 1981); and Gregory B. Markus, "Political Attitudes During an Election Year: A Report on the 1980 NES Panel Study," *American Political Science Review*, vol. 76, no. 3 (September 1982), pp. 538–560. A second explanation points to the conservative preferences of the electorate as the reason for Reagan's victory. See, for example, Warren E. Miller and J. Merrill Shanks, "Policy Directions and Presidential Leadership: Alternative Interpretations of the 1980 Presidential Election," *British Journal of Political Science*, vol. 12 (July 1982), pp. 299–356. A third interpretation suggests not so much rejection of Carter or embrace of Reagan conservatism as the principal reason for Reagan's win, but rather the willingness of the electorate to vote for someone with a different approach to solving the country's economic problems. See Everett Carll Ladd, "Public Attitudes Toward Policy and Governance: Searching for the Sources and Meaning of 'the Reagan Revolution'," in Lester M. Salamon and Michael Lund, eds., *The Reagan Presidency and the Governing of America* (Washington, D.C.: The Urban Institute Press, 1984).

14. The data on the importance of economic issues and Reagan's advantage over Carter in this area is from Schneider, "The November 4 Vote," in Ranney, pp. 227,229. The quote is from Pomper, "The Presidential Election," in Pomper et al., p. 88.

15. The quote is from Schneider, "The November 4 Vote," in Ranney, pp. 247–248. The point that seniority and visibility hurt members of Congress is made in Thomas E. Mann and Norman J. Ornstein, "The Republican Surge in Congress," in Ranney, p. 295.

16. *New York Times* (November 4, 1980), p. B-7. Data on congressional races are from Charles O. Jones, "A New President, A Different Congress, A Maturing Agenda," in Salamon and Lund. On the importance of the Republican takeover of the Senate, see Norman J. Ornstein, "Assessing Reagan's First Year," in Norman J. Ornstein, ed., *President and Congress: Assessing Reagan's First Year* (Washington, D.C.: American Enterprise Institute, 1982), p. 91. The quote by polling expert Everett Carll Ladd is from his chapter "Public Attitudes," in Salamon and Lund.

17. For a useful discussion of the Reagan political beliefs, see A. James Reichley, "A Change in Direction," in Joseph A. Pechman, ed., *Setting National Priorities: The 1982 Budget* (Washington, D.C.: The Brookings Institution, 1981).

18. Hugh Heclo and Rudolph Penner, "Fiscal and Political Strategy," in Fred I. Greenstein, ed., *The Reagan Presidency* (Baltimore: Johns Hopkins University Press, 1983), p. 28.

19. David Stockman, "Avoiding a GOP Economic Dunkirk" (mimeographed, November 1980). For a statement of the need for such a "strategic approach" to the presidency by two former Carter appointees, see Benjamin W. Heineman, Jr. and Curtis A. Hessler, *Memorandum for the President: A Strategic Approach to Domestic Affairs in the 1980s* (New York: Random House, 1980).

20. Stockman.

21. On Meese's original designs and their subsequent undoing, see Laurence I. Barrett, *Gambling with History: Reagan in the White House* (New York: Doubleday, 1983), pp. 72–73. The Reagan quote is from Sara Fritz, "Cabinet Government Fades Away Once More," *U.S. News and World Report*, vol. 92, no. 12 (March 29, 1982), p. 28.

22. For descriptions of the executive budget process under Reagan, see Hugh Heclo, "Executive Budget Making," in Gregory B. Mills and John L. Palmer, eds., *Federal Budget Policy in the 1980s* (Washington, D.C.: The Urban Institute Press, 1984), and Frederick C. Mosher and Max O. Stephenson, Jr., "The Office of Management and Budget in a Changing Scene," *Public Budgeting and Finance*, vol. 2, no. 4 (Winter 1982), pp. 23–41.

23. For descriptions of the congressional budget process during Reagan's term, see Robert D. Reischauer, "The Congressional Budget Process," in Mills and Palmer, eds., *Federal Budget Policy in the 1980s* and Allen Schick, "The Budget As an Instrument of Presidential Policy," in Salamon and Lund, eds., *The Reagan Presidency and the Governing of America*.

24. Dick Kirschten, "Decision Making in the White House: How Well Does It Serve the President?," *National Journal*, vol. 14, no. 14 (April 3, 1982), pp. 584–589.

25. Kirschten, p. 588.

26. For an analysis of the pressures leading toward presidential involvement in the regulatory arena and of the early mechanisms for regulatory review, see Lester M. Salamon, "Federal Regulation: A New Arena for Presidential Power?," in Hugh Heclo and Lester M. Salamon, eds., *The Illusion of Presidential Government* (Boulder, Colo.: Westview Press, 1981), pp. 147–174.

27. For an account of centralized management of the regulatory process under Reagan, see chapter 6, "Regulatory Oversight in the Reagan White House," in George C. Eads and Michael Fix, *Relief or Reform? Reagan's Regulatory Dilemma* (Washington, D.C.: The Urban Institute Press, 1984).

28. On Reagan's preinaugural courting of Congress, see Irwin B. Arieff, "Reagan Courts Legislators in Visit to Hill," *Congressional Quarterly*, vol. 38, no. 47 (November 22, 1980), pp. 3393–3394, and Elizabeth Wehr, "Numerous Factors Favoring Good Relations Between Reagan and New Congress," *Congressional Quarterly*, vol. 39, no. 4 (January 24, 1981), pp. 172–175.

29. For an account of the early experiences of Reagan's legislative liaison operation, see Stephen J. Wayne, "Congressional Liaison in the Reagan White House: A Preliminary Assessment of the First Year," in Norman J. Ornstein. The quotation is from Bill Keller, "Budget Challenge Looms: Duberstein Starts at Fast Pace as Top White House Lobbyist," *Congressional Quarterly*, vol. 40, no. 18 (May 1, 1982), p. 971.

30. Dom Bonafede, "As Pollster to the President, Wirthlin Is Where the Action Is," *National Journal*, vol. 13, no. 50 (December 12, 1981), p. 2184.

31. On the administrative presidency generally and as it was practiced by Presidents Nixon and Reagan, see Richard P. Nathan, *The Administrative Presidency* (New York: John Wiley and Sons, 1983). The account of Reagan's appointment process is from G. Calvin MacKenzie, "Personnel Selection for a Conservative Administration: The Reagan Exercise, 1980–1981" (mimeographed, Colby College, April 1982); the quotation is from p. 4 of MacKenzie's paper.

32. The quotation on subcabinet appointees is from MacKenzie's paper, p. 12. The data and quotation on the extent of political appointments below the subcabinet level are from Edie N. Goldenberg, "The Permanent Government in an Era of Retrenchment and Redirection," in Salamon and Lund, eds., *The Reagan Presidency and the Governing of America*. As Goldenberg also notes, the percentage of noncareer employees grew most substantially in certain domestic agencies between September 1980 and September 1982—from 7 percent to 18 percent in the

Consumer Product Safety Commission, from 35 percent to 40 percent in the Department of Education, from 33 percent to 50 percent in the Federal Home Loan Bank Board, from 5 percent to 19 percent in the General Services Administration, and from 5 percent to 23 percent in the Federal Trade Commission.

33. The data on the overall drop in civilian employment are from U.S. Office of Personnel Management, *Monthly Release: Employment and Trends as of September 1983* (Washington, D.C.: Office of Personnel Management, 1983), p. 6. The same source indicates that, including civilians associated with Department of Defense military functions, total employment was down by only 33,000, or 1.2 percent, from 2,165,000 to 2,132,000, from January 1981 to September 1983. Data on RIFs and relocations are in Goldenberg. The note on RIFs in the Employment and Training Administration is from Nathan, p. 77.

34. On the drop in enforcement activity, see Joann S. Lublin and Christopher Conte, "The Rule Slashers: Federal Deregulation Runs into a Backlash, Even from Businesses," *Wall Street Journal* (December 14, 1983), p. 22; Caroline E. Mayer, "U.S. Relaxing Enforcement of Regulations," *Washington Post* (November 15, 1981) p. F-1; Michael deCourcy Hinds, "Reagan's Drive to Cut Rules: Impact Depends on Industry," *New York Times* (January 23, 1982), p. 9; and Michael Wines, "Reagan's Anti-Trust Line: Common Sense or an Invitation to Corporate Abuse?" *National Journal*, vol. 14, no. 28 (July 10, 1982), p. 1204. On the spirit of cooperation, see Richard Corrigan, "Industry Pleased, Mine Unions Fuming Over Mine Safety Enforcement Shift," *National Journal*, vol. 15, no. 36 (September 3, 1983), p. 1773; Michael Wines, "Auchter's Record at OSHA Leaves Labor Outraged, Business Satisfied," *National Journal*, vol. 15, no. 40 (October 1, 1983), p. 2009; Laurence E. Lynn, Jr. "The Reagan Administration and the Renitent Bureaucracy: A Study of Public Management in Five Federal Agencies," in Salamon and Lund; and Mayer, "U.S. Relaxing Enforcement," p. F-2. On the regulatory process in the agencies generally during the Reagan administration, see chapter 7, "Bringing the Agencies to Heel: Management Strategies at the Agency Level," in Eads and Fix.

35. Dale Tate, "Senate Committee Approves Budget as GOP Members Join Democrats to Break Impasse," *Congressional Quarterly*, vol. 41, no. 16 (April 23, 1983), p. 767.

36. The Friedersdorf quotation is from Hedrick Smith, "Taking Charge of Congress," *New York Times Magazine* (August 9, 1981), p. 20. On Republican fundraising, see Richard E. Cohen, "Democrats Take a Leaf from GOP Book with Early Campaign Financing Start," *National Journal*, vol. 13, no. 21 (May 23, 1981), p. 921.

37. On the Gypsy Moths, see Irwin B. Arieff, " 'Gypsy Moths' Poised to Fly Against Reagan's New Cuts; Charge Pledges Were Broken," *Congressional Quarterly*, vol. 39, no. 41 (October 10, 1981), p. 1951.

38. Bill Keller, "Voting Record of '81 Shows the Romance and Fidelity of Reagan Honeymoon on Hill," *Congressional Quarterly*, vol. 40, no. 1 (January 2, 1982), p. 19.

39. Irwin B. Arieff, "Conservatives Hit New High in Showdown Vote Victories," *Congressional Quarterly*, vol. 40, no. 2 (January 9, 1982), p. 50.

40. On House Republicans' hopes for a House majority, see Irwin B. Arieff, "Conservative Southerners Are Enjoying Their Wooing as Key to Tax Bill Success," *Congressional Quarterly*, vol. 39, no. 24 (June 13, 1981), p. 1025. On Reagan's deals with the Boll Weevils, see Arieff, " 'Gypsy Moths,' " p. 1950.

41. O'Donnell quoted in Barrett, *Gambling*, p. 174. House whip quoted in Dale Tate and Gail Gregg, "Congress Set for Showdown on First Budget Resolutions," *Congressional Quarterly*, vol. 39, no. 18 (May 2, 1981).

42. Diane Granat, "Makeshift Hill Bipartisanship Is Unlikely to Survive Recess; Election-Year Politics Ahead," *Congressional Quarterly*, vol. 41, no. 32 (August 13, 1983), p. 1648.

43. Increased federal regulation occurred in the Social Security Disability program, where the Social Security Administration instructed state agencies to speed up and toughen up their reviews of eligibility; Medicare, with reimbursements to hospitals according to federally determined diagnosis-related groups (DRGs); AFDC, with detailed federal standards for eligibility and income counting and optional workfare requirements; and unemployment insurance, with

increased federal involvement in setting eligibility standards, benefit levels, and financing procedures for state programs. On increased regulation by states, see chapter 10 in Eads and Fix; Clemens P. Work, "Deregulation Drive Runs Into Roadblocks," *U.S. News and World Report*, vol. 95, no. 24 (December 12, 1983), pp. 81–82; and "State Regulators Rush In Where Washington No Longer Treads," *Business Week*, no. 2808 (September 19, 1983), pp. 124–131. On the backlash, see chapter 5 in this volume and "A Bipartisan Swing Back to More Regulation," *Business Week*, no. 2792 (May 30, 1983), pp. 74–75.

44. On passive restraints, see Eads and Fix; on segregated schools, see Elder Witt, "Court Upholds Power of IRS to Deny Tax-Exempt Status to Schools That Discriminate, "*Congressional Quarterly*, vol. 41, no. 21 (May 28, 1983), pp. 1077–1078; on the federal workplace charity drive, see Al Kamen, "Parenthood Unit Included in Fund Drive," *Washington Post* (September 16, 1983), p. A-13; on minors seeking contraception, see *U.S. Law Week* (July 19, 1983), p. 52LW2028; on standards of tire wear see Irvin Molotsky, "U.S. Appeals Court Rejects Suspension of Tire Standards," *New York Times* (April 25, 1984), p. A-1.

45. On restricting EDB and sharing toxic waste cleanup costs, see Work, p. 81; on worker exposure to asbestos, see Lublin and Conte, p. 1; on air safety inspections, see Richard Witkin, "FAA Set to Hire More Inspectors," *New York Times* (February 14, 1984), p. A-1; on recall of autos, see Albert R. Karr, "Auto-Safety Agency Stalls in Deregulating After Setting Fast Pace," *Wall Street Journal* (December 9, 1983), p. 21; on agreements with oil companies, see "A Bipartisan Swing," p. 75; on preemption of state regulations, see "State Regulators," p. 131.

46. We are grateful to Hugh Heclo for emphasizing this point in comments on an earlier draft of this chapter.

47. The journalist is Richard Reeves, "The Ideological Election," *The New York Times Magazine* (February 19, 1984), p. 29. The poll is reported in Hedrick Smith, "One Campaign Issue Dominates: The Leadership of Ronald Reagan," *New York Times* (January 30, 1984), p. A-1.

48. Diane Granat, "House Partisanship Increases; Democrats Exhibit New Unity," *Congressional Quarterly*, vol. 41, no. 52 (December 31, 1983), p. 2790.

49. Elizabeth Drew, *Politics and Money: The New Road to Corruption* (New York: MacMillan, 1983), p. 23.

50. On the use of commissions and task forces by presidents before Reagan, see Daniel Bell, "Government by Commission," *The Public Interest*, no. 3 (Spring 1966), pp. 3–9, and Norman C. Thomas and Harold L. Wolman, "Policy Formulation in the Institutionalized Presidency: The Johnson Task Forces," in Thomas E. Cronin and Sanford D. Greenberg, eds., *The Presidential Advisory System* (New York: Harper and Row, 1969), pp. 124–143.

51. On the banding together of interest groups, see Harold L. Wolman and Fred Teitelbaum, "Interest Groups and the Reagan Presidency: Assessing Changes in Interest Group Behavior and Impact," in Salamon and Lund. On the efforts of the U.S. Chamber of Commerce, see Elizabeth Wehr, "Public Liaison Chief Dole Reaches to Outside Groups to Sell Reagan's Programs," *Congressional Quarterly*, vol. 39, no. 23 (June 6, 1981), p. 1981.

52. Richard E. Cohen, "Senate Republicans Control May Be Put to Test by Tough Issues This Fall," *National Journal*, vol. 15, no. 37 (September 10, 1983), p. 1824.

53. Pamela Fessler, "Conable's Retirement to Leave House Gap," *Congressional Quarterly*, vol. 42, no. 6 (February 11, 1984), p. 243.

54. Ronald Brownstein and Nina Easton, *Reagan's Ruling Class: Portraits of the President's Top 100 Officials* (Washington, D.C.: Presidential Accountability Group, 1982).

55. Richard Reeves, "The Ideological Election," *New York Times Magazine* (February 19, 1984), p. 26.

56. Ladd, "Public Attitudes," in Salamon and Lund, eds., *The Reagan Presidency and the Governing of America*. For a generally negative assessment of the prospects for party realignment as a consequence of the Reagan years, see Phillips, *Post-Conservative America*, pp. 220–233.

57. On the prospects for continued economic recovery in the face of growing deficits, see chapter 3 in this volume.

58. On Republican identifiers see "Opinion Roundup: Party Identifications," *Public Opinion*, vol. 7, no. 1 (February/March 1984), p. 31 and James L. Sundquist, "Whither the American Party System?-Revisited," *Political Science Quarterly*, vol. 98, no. 4 (Winter 1983–1984), p. 585. The Harris survey data are from "Country Becoming Less Conservative, More Moderate," *The Harris Survey* (June 6, 1983), p. 2.

59. On Stockman's use of OMB see Heclo, in Mills and Palmer, eds., *Federal Budget Policy in the 1980s*.

60. On the failure to institutionalize top-down budgeting, see Allen Schick, "The Budget As an Instrument of Presidential Policy," in Salamon and Lund.

61. According to the Office of Management and Budget, outlays which are relatively uncontrollable under present law—which includes spending for entitlements, interest on the debt, and the liquidation of prior-year contracts and obligations—have increased from 72.9 percent of total outlays in FY 1981 to 74.1 percent in FY 1984. Under a more restrictive definition of uncontrollables, which includes just spending for interest and prior-year contracts and obligations, uncontrollable outlays have increased from 27 percent of total outlays in FY 1981 to 30.7 percent in FY 1984. See U.S. Office of Management and Budget, *Budget, FY 1985*, pp. 9-44, 9-45.

Between FY 1981 and FY 1984 (projected), the value of federal "tax expenditures," as computed by the Joint Committee on Taxation of the U.S. Congress, grew from $228.6 billion to $327.5. Thus, tax expenditures were increasing at a rate of 43 percent at the same time outlays were increasing at a 30 percent rate. It should be noted, however, that measuring the value of individual tax expenditures is an inexact science, and that the sum of tax expenditures reported here is a rough estimate which does not take into account interaction effects among individual tax expenditure provisions. For data on tax expenditures, see U.S. Congress, Joint Committee on Taxation, *Estimates of Federal Tax Expenditures for Fiscal Years 1981–1986* (Washington, D.C.: Government Printing Office, March 16, 1981), p. 15 and *Estimates of Federal Tax Expenditures for Fiscal Years 1983–1988* (Washington, D.C.: Government Printing Office, March 7, 1983), p. 18.

62. Schick, in Salamon and Lund, eds., *The Reagan Presidency and the Governing of America*.

63. For a fuller discussion of many of these and other points, see Goldenberg, in Salamon and Lund, eds., *The Reagan Presidency and the Governing of America*.

64. On the size of the deficit, see OMB, *Budget, FY 1985*, p. 9-62. On "fiscalization," see chapter 4 in this volume; Reischauer, in Mills and Palmer, eds., *Federal Budget Policy in the 1980s*; and Allen Schick, *Reconciliation and the Congressional Budget Process* (Washington, D.C.: American Enterprise Institute, 1981).

65. On the ambivalent public attitude toward government, see Ladd, in Salamon and Lund, eds., *The Reagan Presidency and the Governing of America*.

NOTES TO CHAPTER 3

Acknowledgments: The authors would like to acknowledge the critical research support provided by Cathy Cromer, the assistance with the DRI model simulations provided by Eric Dressler, and the comments provided on an earlier draft by Herbert Stein, James Tobin, Robert Haveman, Gary Jefferson, Richard Muth, Frank Schiff, and Courtenay Slater—without holding any of them responsible for the final result.

1. For an expanded version of the material included in this chapter, see Isabel V. Sawhill and Charles F. Stone, *Economic Policy in the Reagan Years* (Washington, D.C.: The Urban Institute Press, 1984).

2. For further discussion of the rationale for, and internal consistency of, the Reagan program, see Isabel V. Sawhill, "Economic Policy," in John L. Palmer and Isabel V. Sawhill, eds., *The Reagan Experiment: An Examination of Economic and Social Policies under the Reagan Administration* (Washington, D.C.: The Urban Institute Press, 1982).

3. There has been one attempt to embody numerical goals for inflation and unemployment in national legislation—the Full Employment and Balanced Growth Act of 1978. For further

discussion, see Isabel V. Sawhill and Laurie J. Bassi, "The Challenge of Full Employment," in Eli Ginzberg, ed., *Employing the Unemployed* (New York, N.Y.: Basic Books, Inc., 1980).

4. For more discussion of the problems inherited by President Reagan see Sawhill, "Economic Policy," in Palmer and Sawhill, eds., *The Reagan Experiment*, pp. 32–36.

5. *America's New Beginning: A Program for Economic Recovery* (Washington, D.C.: Government Printing Office, February 18, 1981), p. 4.

6. This estimate is based on the U.S. Department of Labor, Bureau of Labor Statistics, *Trends in Multifactor Productivity* (Washington, D.C.: Government Printing Office, 1983); but see also John W. Kendrick, "The Implications of Growth Accounting Models," in Charles R. Hulten and Isabel V. Sawhill, eds., *The Legacy of Reaganomics: Prospects for Long-term Growth* (Washington, D.C.: The Urban Institute Press, 1984).

7. See, for example, Congress of the United States, Congressional Budget Office, *Balancing the Federal Budget and Limiting Federal Spending: Constitutional and Statutory Approaches* (Washington, D.C.: Government Printing Office, September 1982), pp. 16–22; and Mancur Olson, "Ideology and Economic Growth," in Hulten and Sawhill, eds., *The Legacy of Reaganomics*.

8. Charles R. Hulten and James W. Robertson, "The Taxation of High Technology Industries," Changing Domestic Priorities Discussion Paper (Washington, D.C.: The Urban Institute, September 1983), pp. 3–17; Don Fullerton and Yolanda K. Henderson, "Incentive Effects of Taxes on Income from Capital," in Hulten and Sawhill, eds., *The Legacy of Reaganomics*.

9. Barry P. Bosworth, "Capital Formation, Technology, and Economic Policy," Brookings Discussion Paper (Washington, D.C.: The Brookings Institution, 1983).

10. Martin Neil Baily, "Productivity and the Services of Capital and Labor," *Brookings Papers on Economic Activity*, 1981:1, pp. 1–50; Ernst R. Berndt and David O. Wood, "Engineering and Econometric Interpretations of Energy Capital Complementarity," *American Economic Review*, vol. 69, no. 3 (June 1979), pp. 342–354.

11. For a review of the literature, see Gregory B. Christainsen and Robert H. Haveman, "The Reagan Administration's Regulatory Relief Effort and Productivity," in George C. Eads and Michael Fix, eds., *The Reagan Regulatory Strategy: An Assessment* (Washington, D.C.: The Urban Institute Press, 1984).

12. A. S. Blinder and W. J. Newton, "The 1971–74 Control Program and the Price Level: An Econometric Post-Mortem," *Journal of Monetary Economics*, vol. 8, no. 1 (July 1981), pp. 1–23.

13. Otto Eckstein, "Disinflation," in William Nordhaus, ed., *Inflation: Prospects and Remedies* (Washington, D.C.: Center for National Policy, 1983).

14. Arthur Okun, "Efficient Disinflationary Policies," *American Economic Review*, vol. 68, no. 3 (May 1978), pp. 348–352; Robert J. Gordon and Stephen R. King, "The Output Cost of Disinflation in Traditional and Vector Autoregressive Models," *Brookings Papers on Economic Activity*, 1982:1, pp. 205–242; Lawrence H. Summers, "The Legacy of Current Macroeconomic Policies," in Hulten and Sawhill, eds., *The Legacy of Reaganomics*; Charles L. Schultze, "Some Macro Foundations for Micro Theory," *Brookings Papers on Economic Activity*, 1981:2, pp. 531–576; George L. Perry, "Inflation in Theory and Practice," *Brookings Papers on Economic Activity*, 1980:1, pp. 207–241.

15. Other studies, using different approaches, have reached conclusions that are similar to ours. See, for example, Eckstein, "Disinflation;" and George L. Perry, "What Have We Learned About Disinflation," *Brookings Papers on Economic Activity*, 1983:2, pp. 587–602.

16. Much of the discussion in this section is based on Courtenay Slater, "Income Loss Due to the Recession," Changing Domestic Priorities Discussion Paper (Washington, D.C.: The Urban Institute, January 1984).

17. Slater, "Income Loss Due to the Recession."

18. Wayne Vroman, "The Reagan Administration and Unemployment Insurance," Changing Domestic Priorities Discussion Paper (Washington, D.C.: The Urban Institute, September 1983).

19. Edward M. Gramlich and Deborah S. Laren, "How Widespread Are Income Losses in a Recession," in D. Lee Bawden, ed., *The Social Contract Revisited: Aims and Outcomes of President Reagan's Social Welfare Policy* (Washington, D.C.: The Urban Institute Press, 1984), table 3.

20. For a similar analysis and further elaboration, see Herbert Stein, "Focus on Money," *AEI Economist*, August/September 1983, pp. 1–12.

21. For a review of the evidence on the effectiveness of incomes policies, see Isabel V. Sawhill, "Incomes Policies," Urban Institute Discussion Paper (Washington, D.C.: The Urban Institute, 1981).

22. See, for example, James Tobin, "Inflation and Unemployment," *American Economic Review*, vol. 62, no. 1 (March 1972), pp. 1–18; and Arthur M. Okun, *Prices and Quantities: A Macroeconomic Analysis* (Washington, D.C.: The Brookings Institution, 1981).

23. The estimate is from Gordon and King, "The Output Cost of Disinflation," and is based on Stanley Fischer, "Towards an Understanding of the Costs of Inflation: II," *Carnegie-Rochester Conference Series on Public Policy*, vol. 15 (1981), pp. 5–42.

24. Sawhill and Stone, *Economic Policy in the Reagan Years*; and Alan S. Blinder, "The Message in the Models," in Hulten and Sawhill, eds., *The Legacy of Reaganomics*.

25. Harvey Galper and Eugene Steurle, "The Design of Tax Incentives to Encourage Saving," Brookings Discussion Papers in Economics (Washington, D.C.: The Brookings Institution, 1983).

26. See Robin C. DeMagistris and Carl J. Palash, "Impact of IRAs on Saving," *Federal Reserve Bank of New York Quarterly Review*, vol. 7, no. 4 (Winter 1982–83), pp. 24–32.

27. Detailed methods and sources for these calculations can be found in Sawhill and Stone, *Economic Policy in the Reagan Years*.

28. Assumes the cost of capital falls by about 3 percent as the result of the 1981/1982 tax legislation and that this increases the stock of capital by an equivalent amount. See Fullerton and Henderson, "Incentive Effects of Taxes on Income from Capital," in Hulten and Sawhill, eds., *The Legacy of Reaganomics*; Stephen Oliner, Robert Haveman, and Martin David, "Investment in Equipment, Structures, and Research Capital Under the Reagan Tax Acts," unpublished manuscript, University of Wisconsin-Madison, March 1983. Note that this is an estimate for all types of capital. The increased demand for business capital, especially structures, is predicted to be greater than this.

29. Based on a comparison of the ratio of residential and nonresidential investment to GNP under simulations II and III in appendix B table B.1 with some adjustments for impact of recession on depreciation of the capital stock. Results of this exercise suggest that the ratio of net investment to GNP is reduced by 1.0 to 1.5 percent for 3 to 5 years as the result of the excessive slack engendered by the recession relative to a more reasonable alternative. Impacts on stock of capital and GNP estimated using a simulation model described in Sawhill and Stone, *Economic Policy in the Reagan Years*.

30. Assumes a net tax decrease of 10 percent attributable to Reagan, increasing the after-tax rate of return to saving by 7 percent and savings itself by 0 to 4 percent for every 10 percent increase in rate of return. See Michael J. Boskin, "Taxation, Saving, and the Rate of Interest," *Journal of Political Economy*, vol. 86, no. 2, pt. 2 (April 1978), pp. S3–S27; E. Philip Howrey and Saul H. Hymans, "The Measurement and Determination of Loanable-Funds Saving," *Brookings Papers on Economic Activity*, 1978:3, pp. 655–685; and Herbert Stein and Murray Foss, "Taxes and Saving," *AEI Economist*, July 1981.

31. Summers, "The Legacy of Current Macroeconomic Policies," in Hulten and Sawhill, eds., *The Legacy of Reaganomics*.

32. See, for example, Benjamin M. Friedman, "Implications of the Government Deficit for U.S. Capital Formation," in Federal Reserve Bank of Boston, Proceedings of a Conference held in October 1983 at Melvin Village, New Hampshire, *The Conference Series* No. 27 (October 1983).

33. Lower bound assumes deficits reduce net savings as a percent of GNP by 2 percentage points. Upper bound assumes a reduction of 1 percentage point. See Sawhill and Stone, *Economic Policy in the Reagan Years*, for a description of the model used to generate these results.

34. Donald A. Nichols, "Federal Spending Priorities and Long-term Economic Growth," in Hulten and Sawhill, eds., *The Legacy of Reaganomics*; Kiran Bhatt, Ronald Kirby, and Michael Beesly, "The Federal Role in Infrastructure Renewal," Changing Domestic Priorities Discussion Paper (Washington, D.C.: The Urban Institute, December 1983); Charles L. Schultze, "A Note on Federal Spending Priorities," in Hulten and Sawhill, eds., *The Legacy of Reaganomics*. According to Schultze, real federal spending on physical investment (both direct and grants-in-aid) declined from 14.0 billion in 1981 to 12.1 billion (estimated) in 1984 or by 13.5 percent. Including just "growth-oriented" expenditures, there was an increase from 7.3 to 7.7 billion or 5.5 percent. The stock of government-owned fixed capital represents about 25 percent of the total stock, so the estimated percentage changes in the total stock are between minus 3 percent and plus 1 percent. Since these figures exclude direct spending by state and local governments and since the prior trend in spending for public capital had been positive, if anything, these estimates probably understate the impact of Reagan policies.

35. We add up the numbers from table 3.5 and apply a coefficient of 0.3 to translate them into changes in output. If anything, the results are too optimistic since the positive effects of the tax cuts on investment depend to some extent on the assumption that the required savings will be available.

36. Robert H. Haveman, "How Much Have Reagan Tax and Spending Policies Increased Work Effort," in Hulten and Sawhill, eds., *The Legacy of Reaganomics*.

37. We start with Haveman's results which indicate an increase in the labor supply of between 0.8 and 2.5 percent (table 3.5). This translates into a 0.6 to 1.8 percent increase in GNP via a Cobb-Douglas production function in which labor's share of GNP is assumed to be 0.7 percent.

38. We assume an increase of between 0 and 0.2 percent a year in multifactor productivity for a period of about five years, leading to a 0 to 1 percent increase in GNP at the end of the period. See Christainsen and Haveman, "Reagan Administration's Regulatory Relief Effort and Productivity"; and Kendrick, "The Implications of Growth Accounting Models" in Hulten and Sawhill, eds., *The Legacy of Reaganomics*. These estimates are very sensitive to what one assumes the growth of social regulations would have been under a different administration.

39. Congress of the United States, Congressional Budget Office, Human Resources and Community Development Division, and Human Resources Cost Estimates Unit of the Budget Analysis Division, "Major Legislative Changes in Human Resources Programs Since January 1981," Staff Memorandum, August 1983. Daniel H. Saks, "Human Resource Consequences of Reagan's Social Policy," Changing Domestic Priorities Discussion Paper (Washington, D.C.: The Urban Institute, 1983).

40. We assume outlays on education and training as a proportion of GNP are reduced by 0.3 percentage point. In the upper bound estimate, we assume a 75 percent replacement rate and a 5 percent rate of return to these investments. In the lower bound estimate we assume a 25 percent replacement rate and a 10 percent rate of return. The returns are assumed to cumulate (at a compound rate) over a ten-year period. See Saks, "Human Resource Consequences of Reagan's Social Policy"; and Schultze, "A Note on Federal Spending Priorities."

41. Bosworth, "Capital Formation, Technology, and Economic Policy."

42. We assume outlays on R&D as a proportion of GNP are increased by 0.05 percentage point (mainly by R&D tax credit) in upper bound estimate and that it is decreased by 0.1 percentage point in lower bound estimate (mainly due to reductions in nondefense R&D budget outlays). The rate of return in both cases is assumed to be 25 percent (compounded over ten years). See Oliner, Haveman, and David, "Investment in Equipment, Structures and Research Capital"; Schultze, "A Note on Federal Spending Priorities"; Zvi Griliches, "Returns to Research and Development Expenditures in the Private Sector," in John W. Kendrick and Beatrice N. Vaccara, eds., *New Developments in Productivity Measurement and Analysis* (Chicago: University of Chicago Press for the National Bureau of Economic Research, 1980); Edwin Mansfield, et al.,

"Social and Private Rates of Return from Industrial Innovations," *The Quarterly Journal of Economics*, vol. 91, no. 2 (May 1977), pp. 221–240; Bosworth, "Capital Formation, Technology, and Economic Policy"; Eileen L. Collins, "An Early Assessment of Three R&D Tax Incentives Provided by the Economic Recovery Tax Act of 1981," PRA Report 83-87 (Washington, D.C.: National Science Foundation, 1983).

43. For a similar set of observations, see William Nordhaus, "Reaganomics and Economic Growth: A Summing Up," in Hulten and Sawhill, eds., *The Legacy of Reaganomics.*

44. Blinder, "The Message in the Models," in Hulten and Sawhill, eds., *The Legacy of Reaganomics.*

NOTES TO CHAPTER 4

Acknowledgments: The author wishes to acknowledge the valuable research assistance of Mary Kate Smith and the helpful comments of Van Ooms, John Ellwood, and Robert Hartman.

1. See Congressional Budget Office, *Baseline Budget Projections for Fiscal Years 1985–1989* (Washington, D.C.: Government Printing Office, 1984), Appendix D.

2. Charles R. Hulten and June A. O'Neill, "Tax Policy," in Palmer and Sawhill, eds., *The Reagan Experiment: An Examination of Economic and Social Policies under the Reagan Administration* (Washington, D.C.: The Urban Institute Press, 1982), p. 105; and author's calculations of the Social Security payroll tax.

3. Congressional Budget Office, *Baseline Budget Projections*, p. 115.

4. The major provisions of ERTA were three successive reductions in individual income tax rates (5 percent in October 1981 and 10 percent in July 1982 and 1983), amounting to a cumulative, across-the-board reduction of 23 percent; a reduction in the "marriage penalty" by allowing two-earner couples to deduct a portion of the earned income of the lesser-earning spouse; a reduction from 70 to 50 percent in the maximum rate for unearned income and estate and gift taxes; the upward adjustment (starting in 1985) of tax brackets, the zero bracket amount, and the personal exemption in the individual income tax, to correct for inflation (a provision referred to as "indexing"); and accelerated depreciation rules, allowing a faster corporate write-off of capital expenditures. The major tax provisions of TEFRA were a tightening of the investment tax credit; a partial repeal of ERTA's accelerated depreciation and "safe harbor leasing" rules (where the latter allowed the transfer of unused investment tax credits and depreciation deductions from unprofitable to profitable companies); tax withholding on interest and dividend income (repealed in the summer of 1983); and further strengthened enforcement of existing tax rules.

5. Office of Management and Budget, "Federal Government Finances," February 1984, pp. 82–86.

6. Congressional Budget Office, *Baseline Budget Projections*, p. 115.

7. Congressional Budget Office, *Baseline Budget Projections*, p. 117. The published CBO savings estimate, $58 billion in 1985, includes an illusory $2 billion in spending reductions due to the shift from on-budget to off-budget status of the strategic petroleum reserve.

8. Congressional Budget Office, *Baseline Budget Projections*.

9. See Frank de Leeuw and Thomas M. Holloway, "Cyclical Adjustment of the Federal Budget and Federal Debt," *Survey of Current Business*, vol. 63, no. 12 (December 1983), pp. 25–46.

10. See Edward M. Gramlich, "How Bad Are Large Deficits?" in Gregory B. Mills and John L. Palmer, eds., *Federal Budget Policy in the 1980s* (Washington, D.C.: The Urban Institute Press, 1984).

11. The individual income tax has itself become a less progressive form of taxation because of ERTA's across-the-board rate reduction, the lowering of the marginal tax rate on unearned income, and the eroded value of tax advantages for the low-income population. See Hulten and O'Neill, "Tax Policy," in Palmer and Sawhill, eds., *The Reagan Experiment*," esp. pp. 115–120.

12. Those who have registered concern over the Reagan administration's emphasis on sophisticated military hardware include former Defense Secretaries James Schlesinger (Ford administration) and Harold Brown (Carter administration), Retired Admiral Noel Gayler (former commander-in-chief of U.S. forces in the Pacific and former director of the National Security Agency), Senator Sam Nunn (Democrat of Georgia, member of the Senate Armed Services Committee, and acknowledged as a defense expert by members of both parties), and Professor William Kaufman (Massachusetts Institute of Technology, advisor on defense matters to both Democratic and Republican administrations).

13. For further discussion of these developments, see Robert D. Reischauer, "The Congressional Budget Process," in Mills and Palmer, eds., *Federal Budget Policy in the 1980s*; and Allen Schick, "The Budget as an Instrument of Presidential Policy," in Lester M. Salamon and Michael Lund, eds., *The Reagan Presidency and the Governing of America* (Washington, D.C.: The Urban Institute Press, 1984).

14. The following observations are derived from survey data collected by ABC News/ Washington Post, CBS News/New York Times, Time Magazine, The Gallup Poll, and the Advisory Commission on Intergovernmental Relations.

15. Further detail on the prospects for policy action to restrain spending and raise revenues is contained in Mills and Palmer, eds., *Federal Budget Policy in the 1980s*.

16. See Richard A. Stubbing, "The Defense Budget," in Mills and Palmer, eds., *Federal Budget Policy in the 1980s*. For many years Stubbing was head of the OMB staff overseeing the defense budget. See also Committee for National Security, *Spending for a Sound Defense: Alternatives to the Reagan Military Budget*, 1984. This report, prepared in consultation with William Kaufman, describes a five-year "prudent defense" plan averaging less than 4 percent annual real growth in budget authority during 1985–1989.

17. Stubbing, "The Defense Budget," in Mills and Palmer, eds., *Federal Budget Policy in the 1980s*."

18. Congressional Budget Office, *Reducing the Deficit: Spending and Revenue Options* (Washington, D.C.: Government Printing Office, 1984), pp. 25–37.

19. Congressional Budget Office, *Baseline Budget Projections*, p. 117.

20. See John L. Palmer and Barbara Boyle Torrey, "Health Care Financing and Pension Programs," in Mills and Palmer, eds., *Federal Budget Policy in the 1980s*.

21. See, for example, William Greider, "The Education of David Stockman," *The Atlantic Monthly*, vol. 248, no. 12 (December 1981), p. 27ff; and Steven R. Weisman, "Reaganomics and the President's Men," *The New York Times Magazine* (October 24, 1982), p. 26ff.

22. Peter Bernstein, "David Stockman: No More Big Budget Cuts," *Fortune* (February 6, 1984), p. 53ff.

NOTES TO CHAPTER 5

Acknowledgments: For helpful discussions or comments on earlier versions of this chapter, the author is grateful to John Ahearne, Joan Bernstein, Sarah Chasis, Edwin Clark, Robert Crandall, Joel Darmstadter, J. Clarence Davies Everett Ehrlich, Peter Emerson, Kenneth Farrell, Katherine Gillman, Deanne Kloepfer, Allen Kneese, John Leshy, Molly Macauley, Robert Nelson, Steven Quarles, Isabel Sawhill, and James Vertrees. Neither they nor Resources for the Future bears any responsibility for the conclusions.

1. Robert Mitchell, "Public Opinion and Environmental Politics," in Norman Vig and Michael Kraft, eds., *Environmental Policy in the 1980s: The Impact of the Reagan Administration* (Washington, D.C.: Congressional Quarterly Press, 1984), pp. 51–74.

2. For further detail, see Robert Crandall and Paul R. Portney, "Environmental Policy," in Paul R. Portney, ed., *Natural Resources and the Environment: The Reagan Approach* (Washington D.C.: The Urban Institute Press, 1984).

3. National Commission on Air Quality, *To Breathe Clean Air* (Washington, D.C., 1981), pp. 3.4–4 through 3.4–9. General Accounting Office, "Air Quality: Do We Really Know What It Is?" CED-79-84, May 31, 1979, p. 5.

4. General Accounting Office, "Improvements Needed in Controlling Major Air Pollution Sources," CED-78-165, January 2, 1979.

5. General Accounting Office, "Air Quality," p. 16.

6. Robert Litan and William Nordhaus, *Reforming Federal Regulation* (New Haven: Yale University Press, 1983), pp. 192–194.

7. Lawrence White, *Reforming Regulation: Process and Problems* (Englewood Cliffs, N.J.: Prentice-Hall, 1981), pp. 47–70.

8. Congressional Budget Office, "The Clean Air Act, The Electric Utilities and the Coal Market," April 1982, p. 62.

9. Jane Stein, "Warning from Health Experts: Anti-Lead Drive is Running Out of Gas," *National Journal*, vol. 14, no. 23 (June 5, 1982), p. 1007.

10. Congressional Budget Office, "The Environmental Protection Agency: Overview of the Proposed 1984 Budget," Staff Working Paper, April 1983, p. 5.

11. Congressional Budget Office, "Overview," p. 6.

12. Testimony of Kenneth Hagg on behalf of the State and Territorial Air Pollution Program Administrators before the Senate Appropriations Subcommittee on HUD-Independent Agencies, May 23, 1983.

13. P. D. Reed, "NRDC v. Gorsuch: D.C. Circuit Bursts EPA's Nonattainment Area Bubble," *Environmental Law Reporter*, vol. 12 (October 1982), pp. 10089–96.

14. See John Leshy, "Natural Resource Policy," in Portney, ed., *Natural Resources and the Environment*.

15. See Marion Clawson, *Rethinking the Public Lands* (Washington, D.C.: Resources for the Future, 1983).

16. Bill Gilbert, "Alone in the Wilderness," *Sports Illustrated*, vol. 59 (October 3, 1983), p. 111.

17. See Robert Nelson, "Public Lands," in Paul R. Portney, ed., *Current Issues in Natural Resource Policy* (Washington, D.C.: Resources for the Future, 1982), pp. 46–48.

18. U.S. Department of Interior, *A Year of Progress: Preparing for the 21st Century*, 1983, pp. 6–7.

19. General Accounting Office, *Analysis of the Powder River Basin Federal Coal Lease Sale*, GAO/RCED-83-119, May 11, 1983, p. 44.

20. Report of the Commission on Fair Market Value for Federal Coal Leasing (Washington, D.C.: Government Printing Office, February 1984), p. 533.

21. Report of the Commission on Fair Market Value, p. 536.

22. The Wilderness Society, *The Watt Record: Wilderness* (Washington, D.C.: The Wilderness Society, 1983), pp. 9–12.

23. U.S. Geological Survey, *Petroleum Potential of Wilderness Lands in the Western United States*, Geological Survey Circular no. 902-A-P, 1983, p. 4.

24. Office of Technology Assessment (OTA), *Management of Fuel and Nonfuel Minerals on Federal Land: Current Status and Issues* (Washington, D.C.: OTA, 1979).

25. U.S. Department of Interior, *A Year of Progress*, p. 21.

26. The Wilderness Society, *The Watt Record: The National Park System* (Washington, D.C.: The Wilderness Society, 1983), pp. 6–13.

27. Congressional Budget Office, *Reducing the Federal Budget: Strategies and Examples, Fiscal Years 1982–1986* (Washington, D.C.: Government Printing Office, 1981), p. 55.

28. Gilbert, "Alone in the Wilderness," p. 111.

29. Harry Broadman and W. David Montgomery, *Natural Gas Markets After Deregulation* (Washington, D.C.: Resources for the Future, 1983).

30. See Hans Landsberg and Joseph Dukert, *High Energy Costs: Uneven, Unfair, Unavoidable?* (Washington, D.C.: Resources for the Future, 1981).

31. See U.S. Department of Energy, *The National Energy Policy Plan*, DOE/S-0014/1 (Washington, D.C.: Government Printing Office, October 1983).

32. See U.S. Department of Energy, *Reducing U.S. Oil Vulnerability. Energy Policy for the 1980s*, November 10, 1980.

33. Congressional Budget Office, *Comparative Analysis of Alternative Financing Plans for the Clinch River Breeder Reactor Project*, September 1983.

34. J. B. Penn, "Economic Developments in U.S. Agriculture During the 1970s," in D. Gale Johnson, ed., *Food and Agriculture Policy for the 1980s* (Washington, D.C.: American Enterprise Institute for Public Policy Research, 1981), pp. 3–47; also Bruce Gardner, "Agriculture Policy," in Portney, ed., *Natural Resources and the Environment*.

35. Fred Sanderson, "U.S. Farm Policy in Perspective," *Food Policy*, vol. 8, no. 1 (July 1983), p. 4.

36. Fred Sanderson, "Retrospective on PIK," *Food Policy* (forthcoming 1984).

37. Fred Sanderson, "Retrospective on PIK."

38. See "11% of Farmers Paid by Program Did Not Follow Rules, U.S. Finds," *New York Times*, January 9, 1984.

39. George C. Eads and Michael Fix, *Relief or Reform? Reagan's Regulatory Dilemma* (Washington, D.C.: The Urban Institute Press, 1984).

40. Environmental Protection Agency, *National Air Quality and Emissions Trends Report, 1981*, EPA-450/4-83-011, April 1983.

41. Congressional Budget Office, *Crop Price-Support Programs: Policy Options for Contemporary Agriculture*, Washington, D.C., February 1984.

42. John Donahue, "The Political Economy of Milk," *The Atlantic Monthly*, vol. 252, no. 4 (October 1983), pp. 59–68.

NOTES TO CHAPTER 6

Acknowledgments: We wish to acknowledge the very able research assistance of Mary Kate Smith in the preparation of this chapter.

1. For more extensive discussions of the extent to which President Reagan's philosophy and proposals entail a rejection of the Great Society in general, and social engineering in particular, see Samuel Beer's foreword to John Ellwood, ed., *The Reductions in U.S. Domestic Spending* (New Brunswick, N.J.: Transaction Books, 1982), and Nathan Glazer, "The Social Policy of the Reagan Administration," in D. Lee Bawden, ed., *The Social Contract Revisited: Aims and Outcomes of President Reagan's Social Welfare Policy* (Washington, D.C.: The Urban Institute Press, 1984).

2. Ronald Reagan, "State of the Union, 1982," *Vital Speeches of the Day*, vol. 48, no. 9 (February 15, 1982), p. 261.

3. Richard B. Morris and William Greenleaf, *U.S.A. The History of a Nation*, vol. 2 (Chicago, Ill.: Rand McNally and Company, 1969), p. 830.

4. Timothy M. Smeeding, "Is the Safety Net Still Intact?" in Bawden, ed., *The Social Contract Revisited*.

5. U.S. Congress, House, Committee on Ways and Means, *Background Material and Data on Programs Within the Jurisdiction of the Committee on Ways and Means*. Committee Print. 98th Congress, 2d Session, February 1984, p. 324; and U.S. General Accounting Office, "An Evaluation of the 1981 AFDC Changes: Initial Analyses," April 2, 1984.

6. *Background Material and Data on Programs*, p. 367.

7. *Background Material and Data on Programs*, p. 324.

8. David A. Stockman, "Statement Before the House Ways and Means Subcommittee on Oversight, and Public Assistance and Unemployment" (mimeographed), November 3, 1983, table 15, p. 21.

9. See, for example, Kenneth W. Clarkson (an assistant director of the Office of Management and Budget in the Reagan administration), "The Safety Net After Three Years: Reagan Administration Perspective" (mimeographed) (Washington, D.C.: American Enterprise Institute, December 1983).

10. The remainder of this discussion on the lower tier of the social safety net is based on Smeeding, "Is the Safety Net Still Intact?" in Bawden, ed., *The Social Contract Revisited*.

11. Some argue that in-kind benefits should not be counted because the poverty threshold was originally established on the basis of cash income only; if in-kind income had been considered,

the threshold would have been set higher. There are also difficulties in measuring the value of in-kind benefits since they are often of less value to the recipient than their cost to the government. For a discussion of these issues and estimates of alternative methods of evaluating in-kind benefits, see Timothy M. Smeeding, Bureau of the Census, *Alternative Methods for Valuing Selected In-Kind Transfer Benefits and Measuring Their Effects on Poverty*, Technical Paper 50 (Washington, D.C.: Government Printing Office, 1982).

12. U.S. Department of Commerce, Bureau of the Census, *Estimates of Poverty Including the Value of Noncash Benefits: 1979 to 1982*, Technical Paper 51 (Washington, D.C.: Government Printing Office, 1984), p. xvii.

13. Peter Gottschalk and Sheldon Danziger, "Macroeconomic Conditions, Income Transfers, and the Trend in Poverty," in Bawden, ed., *The Social Contract Revisited*, pp. 196–197.

14. According to analysis by Sheldon Danziger, Peter Gottschalk, and Eugene Smolesky, 1.2 percentage points of the increase can be attributed to the specific tax and spending changes under President Reagan, 1.4 to macroeconomic conditions, and the remaining 0.7 to continuing secular trends such as the demographic shifts discussed earlier. See their "Reagan, Recession, and Poverty in the United States" (Institute for Research on Poverty, University of Wisconsin: processed February 1984).

15. Gottschalk and Danziger, "Macroeconomic Conditions, in Bawden, ed., *The Social Contract Revisited*" p. 204.

16. Blanche Bernstein, "Welfare Dependency," in Bawden, ed., *The Social Contract Revisited*.

17. U.S. General Accounting Office, "CWEP's Implementation Results to Date Raise Serious Questions About the Administration's Proposed Mandatory Workfare Program," April 2, 1984.

18. Mary Jo Bane and David T. Ellwood, "The Dynamics of Dependence: The Routes to Self-Sufficiency" (Cambridge, Mass.: Urban Systems Research and Engineering, Inc., June 1983).

19. Kristin A. Moore and Martha R. Burt, *Private Crisis, Public Cost: Policy Perspectives on Teenage Childbearing* (Washington, D.C.: The Urban Institute Press, 1982).

20. See Charles Muller et al., *The Lasting Impacts of Job Corps Participation*, Youth Knowledge Development Report 3.4, U.S. Department of Labor, May 1980; J.C. Edozien, B.R. Switzer, and R.B. Bryan, *Medical Evaluation of the Special Supplemental Food Program for Women, Infants and Children (WIC)*, Department of Nutrition, University of North Carolina, July 1976; U.S. Department of Health, Education and Welfare, *Annual Evaluation Report on Programs Administered by the U.S. Office of Education: FY 1979* (Washington, D.C.: Government Printing Office, 1980); and Laurie J. Bassi, "CETA—Did it Work?" *Policy Studies Journal*, vol. 12, no. 1 (September 1983).

21. This entire section draws heavily on two papers: Norman C. Amaker, "The Reagan Administration's Civil Rights Policies" (Washington, D.C.: The Urban Institute, forthcoming); and Lynn C. Burbridge, "The Impact of Changes in Policy on the Federal Equal Employment Opportunity Effort" (Washington, D.C.: The Urban Institute, November 1983).

22. Administrative Office of the United States Courts, *Annual Report of the Director*, p. 367 in 1981, p. 216 in 1982, and p. A-20 of Appendix I in 1983.

23. Burbridge, table 2, p. 40.

24. James Nathan Miller, "Ronald Reagan and the Techniques of Deception," *The Atlantic Monthly* (February 1984), p. 67.

25. Donna St. George, "Administration May Have to Shelve Its Relaxed Minority Hiring Rules," *National Journal*, vol. 15, no. 43 (October 22, 1983), p. 2172.

26. Dan Fagin, "In Winning His Battle for Rights Commission, Did Reagan Lose the War?" *National Journal*, vol. 15, no. 51–52 (December 17, 1983), p. 2624.

27. St. George, "Administration May Have to Shelve Its Relaxed Minority Hiring Rules," p. 2172.

28. U.S. Commission on Civil Rights, *Equal Opportunity in Presidential Appointments* (Washington, D.C.: Government Printing Office, June 1983), p. 11.

29. Rochelle L. Stanfield, "Reagan Courting Women, Minorities, But It May Be Too Late to Win Them," *National Journal*, vol. 15, no. 22 (May 28, 1983), p. 1118.

30. Michael Wines, "Administration Says It Merely Seeks a 'Better Way' to Enforce Civil Rights," *National Journal*, vol. 14, no. 13 (March 27, 1982), pp. 536-537.

31. In the preparation of this section of the chapter we have benefited considerably from work done by Raymond J. Struyk. See his "Administering Social Welfare: The Reagan Record," Changing Domestic Priorities Discussion Paper (Washington, D.C.: The Urban Institute, April 1984).

32. For more details on these proposals and the issues they raise, see Rochelle L. Stanfield, "If Vouchers Work for Food, Why Not for Housing, Schools, Health and Jobs?" *National Journal*, vol. 15, no. 17 (April 23, 1983).

33. Morton Isler, "Policy Implications: Moving from Research to Programs," in Raymond J. Struyk and Marc Bendick, Jr., eds., *Housing Vouchers for the Poor* (Washington, D.C.: The Urban Institute Press, 1981).

34. See Struyk, "Administering Social Welfare: The Reagan Record," p. 35.

35. This is the interpretation emphasized by Richard P. Nathan, in his "The Reagan Presidency in Domestic Affairs," in Fred I. Greenstein, ed., *The Reagan Presidency: An Early Assessment* (Baltimore, Md: The Johns Hopkins University Press, 1983).

NOTES TO CHAPTER 7

1. David Stockman, director of the Office of Management and Budget, testimony before the Subcommittee on Manpower and Housing, Government Operations Committee, U.S. House of Representatives, April 28, 1981. On other perceptions of "overload," see Samuel Beer, "Political Overload and Federalism," *Polity*, vol. 10, no. 1 (Fall 1977).

2. Jeffrey L. Pressman and Aaron B. Wildavsky, *Implementation* (Berkeley: University of California Press, 1973); Walter Williams, *The Implementation Perspective* (Berkeley: University of California Press, 1980).

3. President Ronald Reagan, Inaugural Address, January 20, 1981.

4. Edward M. Gramlich, "An Econometric Examination of the New Federalism," *Brookings Papers on Economic Activity, 1982:2* (Washington, D.C.: Brookings Institution, 1983), pp. 327–360.

5. Advisory Commission on Intergovernmental Relations, *Changing Public Attitudes on Governments and Taxes, 1981* (Washington, D.C.: Government Printing Office, 1981); Everett Carll Ladd, Jr., and Seymour Martin Lipset, "Anatomy of a Decade," *Public Opinion*, vol. 3, no. 1 (December/January 1980).

6. Executive Order No. 12,291 (1982).

7. C. Boyden Gray, "Regulation and Federalism," *Yale Journal of Regulation*, vol. 1, no. 1 (1983), pp. 93–110.

8. See Michael Fix, "Transferring Regulatory Authority to the States," in George C. Eads and Michael Fix, eds., *The Reagan Regulatory Strategy: An Assessment* (Washington, D.C.: The Urban Institute Press, 1984).

9. John L. Palmer and Gregory B. Mills, "Budget Policy," in John L. Palmer and Isabel V. Sawhill, eds., *The Reagan Experiment* (Washington, D.C.: The Urban Institute Press, 1982).

10. Office of Management and Budget, *Budget of the United States Government, Fiscal Year 1985: Special Analyses* (Washington, D.C.: Government Printing Office, 1984), p. H-18.

11. George E. Peterson, "The State and Local Sector," in Palmer and Sawhill, eds., *The Reagan Experiment*.

12. This is based on a price elasticity of −0.4 to −0.5. For reviews of the empirical literature on the price elasticity of state-local expenditures, see Edward M. Gramlich, "Intergovernmental Grants: A Review of the Empirical Literature," in Wallace Oates, ed., *The Political Economy of Fiscal Federalism* (Lexington, Mass.: Lexington Books, 1977), and Robert Inman, "Fiscal Performance of Local Governments," in Peter Mieszkowski and Mahlon Straszheim,

eds., *Current Issues in Urban Economies* (Baltimore, Md.: The Johns Hopkins University Press, 1979).

13. Similar results have been reported for a fourteen-state sample by Richard P. Nathan and Fred C. Doolittle, *The Consequences of Cuts: The Effects of the Reagan Domestic Program on State and Local Governments* (Princeton, N.J.: Princeton Urban and Regional Center, 1983), chapter 3. The twenty-five states in the Urban Institute sample are Alabama, Arizona, California, Colorado, Florida, Idaho, Illinois, Kansas, Kentucky, Massachusetts, Michigan, Minnesota, Mississippi, Missouri, Nevada, New Jersey, New Mexico, New York, Ohio, Oregon, Pennsylvania, Texas, Vermont, Virginia, Wisconsin.

14. John Holahan, research in progress, The Urban Institute.

15. E. Richard Brown, Ruth Roemen, Michael Cousineau, and Walter Price, "Medi-Cal Selective Hospital Contracting," in *Medi-Cal Legislation Report* (Berkeley: Institute of Government Studies, University of California, 1983).

16. This section draws on findings reported more fully in George E. Peterson, Randall Bovbjerg, Barbara Davis, Eugene Durman, Albert Fries, and Neil Mayer, *Block Grants* (Washington, D.C.: The Urban Institute Press, 1984, forthcoming).

17. Nathan, Doolittle, and Associates; and George F. Peterson, "The State and Local Sector," in Palmer and Sawhill, eds., *The Reagan Experiment*.

18. Many economists predicted that the block grants would reduce state-local spending from own resources. See, for example, Wallace E. Oates, "Strengths and Weaknesses of the New Federalism," in William Craig Stubblebine and Thomas D. Willett, eds., *Reaganomics: A Midterm Report* (San Francisco: ICS Press, 1983): "[A] movement to broad block grants will certainly provide less stimulus to state and local spending than will the categorical grants that they are displacing. These are fungible funds. State and local governments can use dollars under block grants simply to replace funds that they would have spent otherwise."

19. Richard P. Nathan, Philip M. Dearborn, Clifford A. Goldman, and Associates, "Initial Effects of the Fiscal Year 1982 Reductions in Federal Domestic Spending," in John Ellwood, ed., *Reductions in U.S. Domestic Spending: How They Affect State and Local Governments* (New Brunswick, N.J.: Transaction Books, 1982), p. 320.

20. David R. Beam, "New Federalism, Old Realities: The Reagan Administration and Intergovernmental Reform," in Lester M. Salamon and Michael S. Lund, eds., *The Reagan Presidency and the Governing of America* (Washington, D.C.: The Urban Institute Press, 1984).

21. Michael D. Reagan and John G. Sanzone, *The New Federalism*, 2d ed. (New York: Oxford University Press, 1981), pp. 164–168.

NOTES TO CHAPTER 8

Acknowledgments: This chapter draws heavily on the results of The Urban Institute's Nonprofit Sector Project, a national effort to examine the scope and structure of the private, nonprofit sector in this country and the impact on this set of organizations of recent changes in public policy. The Nonprofit Sector Project is supported by more than thirty corporations, community foundations, and national foundations from all parts of the country. The author wishes to express his gratitude to all these supporters, as well as to the other members of the Nonprofit Sector Project staff who made important contributions to developing the data reported here: Alan Abramson, Leah Goldman, Michael Gutowski, Paul Lippert, Anita MacIntosh, James Musselwhite, Harriett Page, and Lauren Saunders.

1. Alexis de Tocqueville, *Democracy in America*.

2. See for example, Robert A. Nisbet, *Community and Power*, 2d edition (New York: Oxford University Press, 1962), pp. 98, 109, 268.

3. This line of thought is developed most clearly in Burton Weisbrod, *The Voluntary Nonprofit Sector* (Lexington, Mass.: Lexington Books, 1978), pp. 1–15.

4. Henry Hansmann, "The Role of Nonprofit Enterprise," *Yale Law Journal*, vol. 89, no. 5 (April 1980), pp. 835–901.

5. This view of government is articulated in the Commission on Private Philanthropy and Public Needs, *Giving in America* (Washington, D.C.: Government Printing Office, 1975) See also Nisbet, *Community and Power*; and Brian O'Connell, ed., *America's Voluntary Spirit: A Book of Readings* (New York: The Foundation Center, 1983).

6. This alternative-to-government view has been developed most forcefully in the writings of Robert Nisbet, who views "the momentous conflicts of jurisdiction between the political state and the social associations lying intermediate to it and the individual" as "the most fateful...of all the conflicts in history." See his *Community and Power*, p. 268.

7. For a fuller explanation of this concept of third-party government, see Lester M. Salamon, "Rethinking Public Management: Third-Party Government and the Changing Forms of Government Action," *Public Policy*, vol. 29, no. 3 (Summer 1981), pp. 255–257; Lester M. Salamon, "Block Grants and the Rise of Third-Party Government: The Challenge to Public Management," Testimony before the Joint Economic Committee, U.S. Congress, July 15, 1981.

8. Estimates from *Giving, U.S.A., 1982 Annual Report* (New York: American Association of Fund Raising Counsel, Inc., 1981), p. 32.

9. *Giving in America: Toward a Stronger Voluntary Sector*, Report of the Commission on Private Philanthropy and Public Needs (Washington, D.C.: Government Printing Office, 1975).

10. Peter L. Berger and Richard John Neuhaus, *To Empower People: The Role of Mediating Structures in Public Policy* (Washington, D.C.: American Enterprise Institute for Public Policy Research, 1977), p. 1. See also Robert Woodson, *A Summons to Life* (Washington, D.C.: American Enterprise Institute for Public Policy Research, 1981); John Egan, John Carr, Andrew Mott, and John Roos, *Housing and Public Policy: A Role for Mediating Structures* (Cambridge, Mass.: Ballinger Publishing Company, 1981).

11. Stuart Butler, *Philanthropy in America: The Need for Action* (Washington, D.C.: The Heritage Foundation and the Institute for Research on the Economics of Taxation, 1980).

12. Lester M. Salamon and Alan J. Abramson, *The Federal Budget and the Nonprofit Sector* (Washington, D.C.: The Urban Institute Press, 1982), p. 26.

13. Ibid., p. 51

14. See, for example, Michael K. Taussig, "Economic Aspects of the Personal Income Tax Treatment of Charitable Contributions," *National Tax Journal*, vol. 20, no. 1 (March 1967), pp. 1–19; Robert A. Schwartz, "Personal Philanthropic Contributions," *Journal of Political Economy*, vol. 78, no. 6 (November-December 1970), pp. 1264–1291; Martin Feldstein, "The Income and Charitable Contributions: Part I—Aggregate and Distribution Effects," *National Tax Journal*, vol. 28, no. 1 (March 1975), pp. 81–100; James N. Morgan, Richard F. Dye, and Judith H. Hybels, "Results from Two National Surveys of Philanthropic Activity," in Commission on Private Philanthropy and Public Needs, *Research Papers*, vol. 1 (Washington, D.C.: Department of the Treasury, 1977), pp. 157–323; and Charles T. Clotfelter and C. Eugene Steuerle, "Charitable Contributions," in Henry Aaron and Joseph Pechman, eds., *How Taxes Affect Economic Behavior* (Washington, D.C.: The Brookings Institution, 1981), pp. 403–466.

15. For a more detailed analysis of the likely impact of the 1981 Tax Act on private individual giving, see Charles Clotfelter and Lester M. Salamon, "The Impact of the 1981 Tax Act on Individual Charitable Giving," *National Tax Journal*, vol. 35, no. 2 (June 1982), pp. 171–187.

16. "Remarks of President Ronald Reagan at the Annual Meeting of the National Alliance of Business," *Public Papers of the President of the United States: Ronald Reagan, 1981* (Washington, D.C.: Government Printing Office, 1982), p. 885.

17. For further details on this task force and its operations, see Renee Berger, "Private Sector Initiatives in the Reagan Era: New Actors Rework an Old Theme," in Lester M. Salamon and Michael Lund, eds., *The Reagan Presidency and the Governing of America* (Washington, D.C.: The Urban Institute Press, 1984).

18. "The Hard-Luck Christmas of '82: With 12 Million Unemployed and 2 Million Homeless, Private Charity Cannot Make Up for Federal Cutbacks," *Newsweek*, December 27, 1982.

19. Testimony of Brian O'Connell before the Subcommittee on Legislation and National Security of the Government Operations Committee of the United States House of Representatives, March 1, 1983.

20. In particular, one large metropolitan area, one medium-size metropolitan area, one small metropolitan area, and one rural county were selected in each of the four major Census regions. In most of these sites, the full population of nonprofit service organizations other than hospitals and higher education institutions was identified and surveyed by mail. In the larger communities (New York, Chicago, San Francisco, Pittsburgh, and the Twin Cities) random samples of organizations were used. Altogether, 6,868 valid organizations were surveyed, of which 3,411—or 49.7 percent—responded. For a fuller discussion of the results of this survey and of the methodology employed, see Michael Gutowski and Lester M. Salamon, *The Invisible Sector* (forthcoming).

21. This conclusion finds support as well in the data on national patterns of private giving as of 1983, which were recently released by the American Association of Fund-Raising Counsel. According to these data, nonreligious private giving increased from $26 billion to $33.9 billion between 1980 and 1983. After adjusting for inflation, this represents a real increase of $2.05 billion, or 8 percent. Of this total, almost half represents contributions to hospitals and other health providers, leaving an increase of $1.07 billion for all other nonreligious organizations. By comparison, between FY 1980 and FY 1983 we estimate that federal government support for these same types of nonprofits declined by $4.2 billion. In other words, with these data, it appears that private giving made up for about one-fourth of the projected government cuts experienced by nonprofit service organizations outside of hospitals. Although some portion of the increased religious giving that occurred during this period may also have found its way to these organizations, the overall picture from the national giving estimates still seems highly consistent with our more detailed survey results. See, *Giving USA: 1983* (New York: American Association of Fund-Raising Counsel, 1984).

NOTES TO CHAPTER 9

Acknowledgments: I would like to acknowledge the most welcomed help of Marc Bendick, James Capra, Geoffrey Carliner, Robert Crandall, Les Denend, Larry Dildine, George Eads, William Finan, Michael Fix, Abbott Lipsky, Kenneth McClennan, Robert Shapiro, and Sheldon Weinig. Joseph Minarik made major contributions to the section on corporate taxes; he also made many helpful comments pertaining to the entire chapter.

1. Paul Krugman, "International Competition and U.S. Economic Growth," in Charles R. Hulten and Isabel V. Sawhill, eds., *The Legacy of Reaganomics: Prospects for Long-term Growth* (Washington, D.C.: The Urban Institute Press, 1984).

2. Congressional Budget Office, *The Industrial Policy Debate* (Washington, D.C.: Government Printing Office, December 1983).

3. *Economic Report of the President* (Washington, D.C.: Government Printing Office, 1984), p. 88.

4. *Economic Report of the President*, 1982, pp. 134–143.

5. U.S. Congress, Senate, Committee on Small Business, *The State of Small Business: A Report of the President*. Hearings. 97th Congress, 2d session, March 31, 1982; Dun & Bradstreet, Inc., "Report of Business Failures," Annual.

6. *Economic Report of the President*, 1984, pp. 50–55.

7. U.S. Department of Commerce, Bureau of Economic Analysis, *Survey of Current Business*, vol. 64, no. 2 (February 1984), pp. S16–S17.

8. "Deregulating America," *Business Week*, November 28, 1983, pp. 80–96.

9. Stephen S. Roach, "The 'New' Capital Spending Cycle," in Morgan Stanley & Co. Incorporated, *Economic Perspectives*, July 13, 1983.

10. "Executives See Some Benefits in Recession," *Wall Street Journal*, January 13, 1984.

11. Joseph A. Schumpeter, *Capitalism, Socialism and Democracy*, 3d ed. (New York: Harper and Row, 1950), pp. 81–86.

12. John W. Kendrick, "The Implications of Growth Accounting Models," in Hulten and Sawhill, eds., *The Legacy of Reaganomics.*

13. Wayne Vroman, "The Wage Deceleration of 1982–1983," Changing Domestic Priorities Discussion Paper (Washington, D.C.: The Urban Institute, January 1984).

14. Robert S. Gay and Jeffrey D. Hedlund, "The Labor Market in Recession and Recovery," *Federal Reserve Bulletin*, vol. 69, no. 7 (July 1983), pp. 477–488.

15. See A. Steven Englander and Marie Chandoha, "Will Wage Givebacks Be Revised?" *Federal Reserve Bank of New York Quarterly Review*, vol. 8, no. 3 (Autumn 1983), pp. 24–25.

16. See, for example, Audrey Freeman, "A Fundamental Change in Wage Bargaining," *Challenge*, July/August 1982, pp. 14–17.

17. Vroman, "The Wage Deceleration."

18. Marc Bendick, Jr., and Phyllis M. Levinson, "How's Business in the Reagan Era? The Perceived Impact of Federal Policies," Changing Domestic Priorities Discussion Paper (Washington, D.C.: The Urban Institute, December 1983), pp. 18–21.

19. Stephen S. Roach, "Cost Cutting and Profitability: The 'Leaning' of Corporate America," in Morgan Stanley & Co. Incorporated, *Economic Perspectives*, March 9, 1983.

20. Michael Porter, *Competitive Strategies* (New York: The Free Press, 1980), pp. 175–199.

21. See *Economic Report of the President*, 1982, pp. 122–125.

22. Board of Governors of the Federal Reserve System, "Flow of Funds Accounts, Fourth Quarter, 1983," February 1984.

23. See Charles R. Hulten, "Tax Policy and the Investment Decision," *American Economic Review*, forthcoming, May 1984; Lawrence H. Summers, "The Effects of Economic Policy on Investment," in Laurence H. Meyer, ed., *The Supply-Side Effects of Economic Policy* (Boston: Kluwer-Nijoff, 1981), pp. 115–148; Martin S. Feldstein, "Inflation, Tax Rules and Investment: Some Econometric Evidence," *Econometrica*, vol. 50, no. 4 (July 1982), pp. 825–862; Robert S. Chirenko and Robert Eisner, "Tax Policy and Investment in Major U.S. Macroeconomic Models," *Journal of Public Economics*, vol. 20, no. 2 (March 1983), pp. 139–166; Peter K. Clark, "Investment in the 1970s: Theory, Performance, and Prediction," *Brookings Papers on Economic Activity*, 1979:1, pp. 73–113.

24. U.S. Congress, Joint Committee on Taxation, *Proposals Relating to Tax Shelters and Other Tax-Motivated Transactions* (Washington, D.C.: Government Printing Office, 1984).

25. Eileen L. Collins, "An Early Assessment of Three R&D Tax Incentives Provided by the Economic Recovery Tax Act of 1981," PRA Report 83-7 (Washington, D.C.: National Science Foundation, 1983).

26. Edwin Mansfield, "Public Policy Toward Industrial Innovation: An International Study of R&D Tax Credits," presented at the Harvard Business School's 75th Anniversary Colloquium on Productivity and Technology (Cambridge, Mass.: Harvard University Press, forthcoming).

27. Charles R. Hulten and James W. Robertson, "The Taxation of High-Technology Industries," Changing Domestic Priorities Discussion Paper (Washington, D.C.: The Urban Institute, September 1983).

28. David Stockman, "Avoiding A GOP Economic Dunkirk," December 1980, U.S. Office of Management and Budget, p. 15.

29. Murray L. Weidenbaum, "Regulatory Reform under the Reagan Administration," in George C. Eads and Michael Fix, eds., *The Reagan Regulatory Strategy: An Assessment* (Washington, D.C.: The Urban Institute Press, 1984).

30. Harvey J. Goldschmid, H. Michael Mann, J. Fred Weston, eds., *Industrial Concentration: The New Learning* (Boston: Little, Brown and Company, 1974); R. Posner and F. Easterbrook, *Cases and Economic Notes on Antitrust*, 2d ed. (St. Paul, Minn.: The West Publishing Company, 1980).

31. Gregory B. Christainsen and Robert H. Haveman, "The Reagan Administration's Regulatory Relief Effort and Productivity," in Eads and Fix, eds., *The Reagan Regulatory Strategy.*

32. George C. Eads and Michael Fix, *Relief or Reform? Reagan's Regulatory Dilemma* (Washington, D.C.: The Urban Institute Press, 1984).

33. Christainsen and Haveman, "The Reagan Administration's Regulatory Relief Effort and Productivity."

34. Eads and Fix, *Relief or Reform? Reagan's Regulatory Dilemma..*

35. See, for example, William E. Brock, opening statement before a joint oversight hearing of the Senate Committee on Finance and the Senate Committee on Banking, Housing, and Urban Affairs on U.S. Trade Policy, 1981.

36. Robert E. Baldwin, "Trade Policies under the Reagan Administration," paper presented at the Conference on Recent Issues and Initiatives in U.S. Trade Policy, National Bureau of Economic Research, Inc., August 8, 1983, and Stephen O. Cohen and Ronald I. Meltzer, *United States International Economic Policy in Action* (New York: Praeger, 1981).

37. Robert A. Leone, "Ronald Reagan and the Automobile Industry," The Urban Institute, mimeographed, June 1983.

38. *America's New Beginning: A Program for Economic Recovery* (Washington, D.C.: Government Printing Office, February 18, 1981), p. 3.

39. "Executives Want Reagan to Run Again," *Business Week*, August 22, 1983.

NOTES TO CHAPTER 10

Acknowledgments: We wish to express our particular thanks to Frank Levy and Richard C. Michel for their help with this chapter. Much of our thinking in this area was shaped by their findings and discussion in "The Way We'll Be in 1984: Recent Changes in the Level and Distribution of Income," Changing Domestic Priorities Discussion Paper (Washington, D.C.: The Urban Institute, 1983). They also provided helpful comments on various drafts of the chapter itself. In addition, Joseph Minarik provided general comments and calculated the specific tax distributions for 1988. Randy Webb and Douglas Murray provided programming assistance for the household income model.

1. Ronald Reagan, closing statement, presidential campaign debate sponsored by the League of Women Voters, Cleveland Convention Center, October 28, 1980.

2. John L. Goodman, Jr., *Public Opinion during the Reagan Administration: National Issues, Private Concerns* (Washington, D.C.: The Urban Institute Press, 1984); William Schneider, "The Divided Electorate," *National Journal*, vol. 15, no. 44 (October 29, 1983), pp. 2200–2210.

3. ABC News Poll, press release, December 1983.

4. For a discussion of the historical context of these income changes, see Levy and Michel, "The Way We'll Be in 1984."

5. This figure is based on analysis contained in the Congressional Budget Office, "Major Legislative Changes in Human Resources Programs since January 1981" (staff memorandum), August 1983. Some of the programs included in that memorandum and not now incorporated in our analysis will be included in Marilyn Moon, "The Impact of the Reagan Years on the Economic Well-Being of Families and Individuals," Changing Domestic Priorities Discussion Paper, forthcoming.

6. Arthur M. Okun, "Upward Mobility in a High-Pressure Economy," *Brookings Papers on Economic Activity*, 1973:1, pp. 207–252; Edward M. Gramlich and Deborah S. Laren, "How Widespread Are Income Losses in a Recession?" in D. Lee Bawden, ed., *The Social Contract Revisited: Aims and Outcomes of President Reagan's Social Welfare Policy* (Washington, D.C.: The Urban Institute Press, 1984); Peter Gottschalk, Testimony for Committee on Ways and Means, U.S. House of Representatives, October 18, 1983.

7. Office of Management and Budget, *Budget of the United States Government, Fiscal Year 1985* (Washington, D.C.: Government Printing Office, 1984), pp. 2-10–2-11.

INDEX

403

ABOUT THE AUTHORS

Alan J. Abramson is a research associate in the Governance and Management Center of The Urban Institute and a graduate student in political science at Yale University. Mr. Abramson is currently working on studies of the U.S. nonprofit sector and of federal budgeting. He has been on the staff of the National Academy of Public Administration where he examined management problems of the American presidency and is coauthor of *The Federal Budget and the Nonprofit Sector* and of "The Nonprofit Sector," in *The Reagan Experiment*.

D. Lee Bawden is director of the Human Resources Policy Center at The Urban Institute. Dr. Bawden has conducted research on welfare policy, poverty, and employment and training policy for nearly twenty years, the last ten at the Institute. Before that he was professor of economics and agricultural economics at the University of Wisconsin—Madison, and a fellow at the Institute for Research on Poverty. Dr. Bawden is coauthor of the chapter on "The Well-Being of Families and Individuals" in *The Reagan Experiment*.

Gregory B. Mills is a research associate on the staff of The Urban Institute's Changing Domestic Priorities project. His prior research has focused on federal policies to improve welfare administration, especially in the Aid to Families with Dependent Children program. Before joining the Institute, Dr. Mills served as an economist in the U.S. Department of Health and Human Services. He is a contributing author of *The Reagan Experiment*, a coauthor of *The Deficit Dilemma*, and coeditor of *Federal Budget Policy in the 1980s*.

Marilyn Moon is a senior research associate at The Urban Institute, working on the Changing Domestic Priorities project of which this volume is a part. Her research interests include the distribution of income, and welfare and health policy. Dr. Moon has been an associate professor of economics at the University of Wisconsin—Milwaukee, and a senior analyst at the Congressional Budget Office. Her publications include *Economic Transfers in the United States*, *The Measurement of Economic Welfare*, and "Changing the Structure of Medicare Benefits."

John L. Palmer is codirector of The Urban Institute's Changing Domestic Priorities project of which this volume is part. His current research interests include economic, social, and budget policy. Dr. Palmer has been an assistant professor of economics at Stanford University, a senior fellow in the Economic Studies Program of the Brookings Institution, and an assistant secretary for the U.S. Department of Health and Human Services. His publications include *The Deficit Dilemma*, *The Reagan Experiment*, *Inflation, Unemployment and Poverty*, *Creating Jobs*, *Toward an Effective Income Support System*, and several chapters in the Brookings Institution's annual *Setting National Priorities* volumes.

George E. Peterson is director of The Urban Institute's Public Finance Center. His research has dealt with the financing of state and local governments and includes recently completed studies of state and local pension systems, public capital financing, and the grants-in-aid system. Dr. Peterson is a member of the National Urban Policy Committee of the National Academy of Sciences. He is the senior author of the series of volumes, *America's Urban Capital Stock*, and of The Urban Institute's forthcoming books *Block Grants* and *Pragmatic Federalism*. He is also general editor of the series *Papers on Public Economics* published in conjunction with the Committee on Urban Public Economics.

Paul R. Portney is a senior fellow at Resources for the Future. Dr. Portney has served as senior staff economist at the Council on Environmental Quality in the Executive Office of the President and has been a visiting professor at the Graduate School of Public Policy, University of California—Berkeley, and a research fellow at the Brookings Institution. He is the author of a number of journal articles and books, the most recent of which is *Current Issues in Natural Resource Policy*, and is currently investigating the adverse health effects associated with air pollution and other environmental pollutants.

Perry D. Quick is a private economic consultant in Washington, D.C. Dr. Quick is a former senior staff economist at both the Federal Reserve Board and the Council of Economic Advisers.

Lester M. Salamon is director of the Center for Governance and Management Research at The Urban Institute. His current research interests are alternative instruments of government action, the processes of policy formulation and implementation, and the structure and role of private, nonprofit organizations. He has been deputy associate director of the Office of Management and Budget and associate professor of policy sciences at Duke University. Dr. Salamon's most recent publications are *The Illusion of Presidential Government*, "The Federal Government and the Nonprofit Sector: Implications of the Reagan Budget Proposals," and "Voluntary Organizations and the Crisis of the Welfare State."

Isabel V. Sawhill is codirector of The Urban Institute's Changing Domestic Priorities project, of which this volume is part. Dr. Sawhill's areas of research include human resources and economic policy. She has directed several of the Institute's research programs and held a number of government positions, including that of director of the National Commission for Employment Policy. Her publications include *Youth Employment and Public Policy*; *Time of Transition: The Growth of Families Headed by Women*; *The Reagan Experiment*; *The Legacy of Reaganomics: Prospects for Long-term Growth*; and *Economic Policy in the Reagan Years*.

Charles F. Stone is a research associate at The Urban Institute, working on Changing Domestic Priorities project of which this volume is a part. His current research interests include macroeconomic and budget policy. He is coauthor of *Economic Policy in the Reagan Years*. Dr. Stone has worked as an economist at the Federal Trade Commission and at the Office of Economic Policy of the Office of Management and Budget, and was a member of the Review Panel on New Drug Regulation in the U.S. Department of Health, Education and Welfare. He has also taught extensively, most recently at Swarthmore College.